"Written by distinguished journ~~..... ....~~ ~. Mehta and his wife Julie B. Mehta, this book reveals interesting stories, some of them perhaps for the first time, about the long conflict. What makes the book so interesting is that it is not a hagiography but a critical biography of Hun Sen. It is a must-read for Cambodian observers, especially students of Southeast Asian studies, and will be interesting to the public in general." —*Jakarta Post*

"Utilising extensive interviews with Hun Sen, the book succeeds in shedding light on several gray areas of history, including Hun Sen's flight to Vietnam from Pol Pot's internal purges and his role in Vietnam's 1979 invasion of Cambodia." —Philippe Agret, Agence France-Presse

"*Strongman* contains interesting material on Hun Sen's youth and probably the most detailed account yet on his defection to Vietnam in mid-1977... One of the more affecting passages describes the death of Hun Sen's first son, who was dropped at birth by a midwife. The incident sums up tidily the Khmer Rouge's capacity for intrusiveness, inhumanity and downright incompetence." —Dominic Faulder, *AsiaWeek*

"Felicities of style abound: waterways are 'pregnant', Phnom Penh is a city of 'silk and open drains'; time, we are told, 'hung as still as fishing nets put out to dry'. The book is fascinating as the first insight we have had into the early and private life of Hun Sen, whose democratic credentials have not been recommended by a tight cloak of personal secrecy. For this reason alone it is required reading." —Simon Johnstone, *The Nation* (Bangkok)

"The book movingly describes how the Khmer Rouge tried to block their marriage, how Bun Rany lost her first child in a Khmer Rouge hospital, and how they were forced to perform hard labour in punishment for her husband's defection from the Khmer Rouge." —Toh Han Shih, *The Business Times* (Singapore)

STRONGMAN

THE

EXTRAORDINARY LIFE

OF

HUN SEN

From Pagoda Boy

to Prime Minister of Cambodia

HARISH C. MEHTA & JULIE B. MEHTA

 **Marshall Cavendish**
Editions

To Maha Kali,
Whom we discovered
In golden spires piercing Khmer skies,
In dried blood at Tuol Sleng,
In overripe fruit and birdsong,
Within wildgrass
Covering old killing fields.

Published in 2013 by Marshall Cavendish Editions
An imprint of Marshall Cavendish International
1 New Industrial Road, Singapore 536196

First published in 1999 by Graham Brash as *Hun Sen: Strongman of Cambodia*

Other Marshall Cavendish Offices:
Marshall Cavendish Corporation. 99 White Plains Road, Tarrytown NY 10591-9001, USA •
Marshall Cavendish International (Thailand) Co Ltd. 253 Asoke, 12th Flr, Sukhumvit 21 Road,
Klongtoey Nua, Wattana, Bangkok 10110, Thailand • Marshall Cavendish (Malaysia) Sdn Bhd,
Times Subang, Lot 46, Subang Hi-Tech Industrial Park, Batu Tiga, 40000 Shah Alam, Selangor
Darul Ehsan, Malaysia

Marshall Cavendish is a trademark of Times Publishing Limited

National Library Board Singapore Cataloguing-in-Publication Data:
Mehta, Harish C.
Strongman : the extraordinary life of Hun Sen : from pagoda boy to Prime Minister of
Cambodia / Harish C. Mehta & Julie B. Mehta. – Singapore : Marshall Cavendish Eds., 2013.
p. cm.
ISBN 978-9814-36-129-3 (pbk.)
1. H'un Saen. 2. Prime ministers – Cambodia – Biography. 3. Cambodia – Politics and
government – 20th century. 4. Cambodia – Politics and government – 21st century.
I. Title. II. Mehta, Julie B.
DS554.83
959.604092 – dc23   OCN828884009

Cover: The strongman at a military ceremony in Phnom Penh in 1998 (photograph courtesy of
Hun Sen); Angkor Wat temple complex, symbol of Cambodia (photograph by Bjørn Christian
Tørrissen, from Wikimedia Commons). Back cover: Nineteen-year-old Hun Sen in 1971, a year
after joining the Khmer Rouge (courtesy of Hun Sen).

Printed in Singapore by Markono Print Media Pte Ltd

CONTENTS

Acknowledgments   9

Introduction   11

Hun Sen's Life and Times   26
The Players and their Relationship to Hun Sen   34
List of Abbreviations Used in the Book   40
Map of Cambodia and Its Neighbours   44
Map of Hun Sen's Secret Journeys   45

Prologue: A Short History of Cambodia   47

I   Days in the Kompong and the Pagoda: 1952–70   60

II   Deep Inside the Maquis: 1970–77   72

III   Escape to Vietnam: 1977–79   100

IV   Liberation War Against the Khmer Rouge: 1977–89   116

V   Ascent of a Peasant to Power: 1978–97   139

VI   U.S. Cold War Policy toward Phnom Penh
      and Hun Sen: 1982–90   163

VII   At Crossroads in the Post-Cold War: 1990–93   180

VIII   The Peasant and the Princes: 1991–97   209

IX   The Coalition: 1993–97   247

X   The Huns: 1975–98   262

XI   Taking Charge: 1995–99   281

XII   Planning the Royal Succession: 2001–2003   299

XIII   Embracing Democracy: 2002   310

XIV   The Widening Clan: 1999–2003   315

XV   The Grooming of the Manet Generation: 2003   338

XVI   An Eventual Validation: 1990–2013   347

       Notes   361
       Bibliography   383
       List of Interviews   386
       Index   389

       About the Authors   400

ACKNOWLEDGMENTS

THERE ARE MANY Cambodians to whom we owe a debt of gratitude—Prime Minister Hun Sen, his wife Bun Rany, their son Hun Manet, and Hun Sen's elder brother Hun Neng. We are grateful to the late King Norodom Sihanouk, his sons Norodom Ranariddh and Norodom Chakrapong, Sihanouk's half-brother Norodom Sirivudh, and long-time supporter of the royal family Son Sann—for being generous with their time.

Among others who helped us, Indian Army Colonel A.N. Bahuguna arranged a prized interview with Hun Neng, while Hun Sen's senior advisor, Prak Sokhonn, responded to our endless queries and arranged for us to travel by military helicopter with the prime minister to the provinces. The final touches to the elaborate portrait of Hun Sen were given by his brother-in-law, Nim Chandara, who provided rare insights into the Hun family. At the last minute, when we still had a few unanswered questions, Ros Kosal, a prime ministerial aide, made a request to Hun Sen to give us written answers. We also acknowledge the guidance provided by Nouth Narang, a former minister of culture, who enlightened us on the nuances of Khmer politics and culture.

In 1990, we met a young Cambodian woman, Phalla, who had survived the Khmer Rouge genocide, living through the trauma of witnessing a Khmer Rouge soldier bayonet one of her young family members. Now, as we write, we can almost see her tear-filled eyes, her words still resonating in our ears, and we want her to know that it was her story that inspired us to explore recent Khmer history.

Stephen Troth, publisher and long-time resident of Southeast Asia, made valuable suggestions on an early draft of the manuscript.

We also recognise the contribution of the people at Graham Brash Publishing, Chuan Campbell and Evelyn Lee, who brought out the first edition in 1999, and the wonderful people at Marshall Cavendish—publisher Chris Newson and managing editor Lee Mei Lin—who believed it was time to release an updated second edition in 2013. We were fortunate in having Tara Dhar Hasnain and Justin Lau as our editors, who offered thoughtful comments and valuable suggestions. We acknowledge the assistance of Dr. Mary Curry of the National Security Archive in Washington D.C., for her guidance in locating important U.S. historical documents on Hun Sen, which appear in this new edition. When the manuscript was finally coming together, Drs. Anima and Tarun Banerjee offered us hospitality at their home in Calcutta, a haven of calmness where we read the proofs. We thank them all.

INTRODUCTION

THIS IS THE FIRST full-length biography of Hun Sen, a man of complexity and contradiction, and one whose life, or lives, have been extraordinary in range and diversity—*kompong* child, pagoda boy, Khmer Rouge soldier, romantic hero, liberator, diplomat, kingmaker, strongman, and patriarch of a new generation of Huns. In the course of this formidable project, the authors had complete editorial independence: Hun Sen cooperated enthusiastically in the interviews, but maintained an arm's length from the writing process. Neither he nor his staff required the authors to show them draft chapters or the manuscript before it was sent to press. They never raised the issue. They cooperated with the authors in a spirit of collegiality to see the project to its conclusion.

When we decided to write a biography of Prime Minister Hun Sen in the early 1990s, there was the obvious hurdle of getting Hun Sen to agree to grant lengthy interviews: this was a crucial matter because he rarely gave interviews. Harish casually broached the subject with an assistant of Hun Sen's, Uch Kiman, who liked the idea. Some five years later, in mid-1997, Harish made a formal request in writing to a senior prime ministerial advisor, Prak Sokhonn: would he kindly arrange several hours of interviews with Hun Sen to enable us to write his biography? Within a week or so Sokhonn got back to us. He had shown our letter of request to Hun Sen, and Hun Sen had agreed.

IN DECEMBER 1997, we arrived at the strongman's sprawling mansion on Boulevard Suramarit, facing the Independence Monument in Phnom Penh. We were to meet Prak Sokhonn there. After being screened by a young guard who seemed reluctant to admit us, we were allowed inside. The garden was ablaze with red hibiscus bushes, and flowers such as *champei* (frangipani), *kolab* (rose), and *rumdul*. Shrubs sculpted in the shape of deer and dogs framed a lush, sharply cut lawn.

Prak Sokhonn was waiting for us. A tall, beaming man, he was the former editor of an army newspaper. "When I started telling the prime minister about both of you," Prak Sokhonn said, "he raised his hand to interrupt me. He said, 'It's okay. I know them well. You can call them.'" Prak Sokhonn informed us that we were to interview Hun Sen on December 3 in the northwestern city of Siem Reap, where the third Angkor Ramayana festival of dance was to take place under the night skies at the ruins of the Angkor temples. Prak Sokhonn invited us to fly with him to Siem Reap. "We will fly by a Russian Antonov-24," he said, and, noticing our discomfiture, quickly added, "It's very safe." We were not convinced. An Antonov had crashed earlier that year on the fringes of Phnom Penh's Pochentong Airport. So we declined, and chose the Royal Cambodian Airlines' European-built ATR-70, and arrived in Siem Reap—overflying the great Tonle Sap lake—ahead of the arrival of Hun Sen's aides on the Antonov flight. From the air the Tonle Sap looked like a giant bowl of soup steaming in the sun, fringed by overhanging coconut trees, wild herbs, and endless rice fields, and crested with hummocky mountains in the north. It was in this rich cradle that many Cambodian empires had flourished and then gone into terminal decline. Egrets, startled by the noise of the aircraft, took to the air in flurries as we touched down.

"It's winter. The temperature's a cool thirty degrees Celsius," said our taxi-driver in fluent English, apparently relishing a bit of sarcasm. Pink lotuses bloomed on pools of stagnant rainwater, and a post-monsoon carpet of grass and waist-high paddy cloaked the poverty of the land that sped past our taxi.

We checked into the Nokor Kok Thlok Hotel. The hotel manager explained the impact on tourism that had been caused by Hun Sen's military takeover of the government in July, when he wrested power from his co-premier, Norodom Ranariddh. "There were 150 tourists stranded here, and Hun Sen sent a special plane to evacuate them," he said. "But Siem Reap remained calm even at that time. They know how to control things around here." The hotel had lain empty for two months after that.

In the morning, army commandos began arriving, carrying assault rifles. They took up positions in a large vacant plot fronting the hotel. In the middle of the expanse was a helipad. As the sun rose, a few commandos waited in the sparse shade of a single palm tree. Beyond the helipad acres of palm fronds brushed the skyline, and, further on, the spire-like *gopuram* of Angkor Wat was visible in the clear air.

Hun Sen's arrival was delayed by two hours. At 5 p.m. a pair of olive-green helicopters drifted into view above the tree-line. As they approached, the beaming faces of Hun Sen and his wife Bun Rany were visible through the glass window of a new Franco-Italian helicopter. The couple touched down and walked into the hotel, while their escort helicopter continued to patrol the evening skies. That night they were treated to Cambodian, Indian, Vietnamese, and Laotian classical dance at the gaunt, brooding ruins of Angkor. Afterwards, Hun Sen led a dance around the swimming pool at the hotel.

The next morning Hun Sen was ready for the interview soon after breakfast. Beside him sat interpreter Bun Sam Bo, advisor Prak Sokhonn, and a note-taker. Wearing a dark suit over an open-necked blue shirt, Hun Sen smoked steadily, his fingers deeply discoloured with nicotine. He spoke for two-and-a-half hours about his childhood and his years in the Khmer Rouge, dragging hard on his cigarettes in a huge effort to pull memories out of the past. He covered a lot of ground. It was a promising beginning to the oral-history biography. Soon afterwards he flew out in his helicopter. We followed him to Phnom Penh.

Two days later we were scheduled to interview him at his country house, *Roun Khlar* ("Tiger's Den"), on the edge of Takhmau city in Kandal province, twelve kilometres south of Phnom Penh. From Takhmau we took an unpaved rural road that forked off the highway and led us to a roadblock. We were stopped by guards in military uniform. Beyond the roadblock a red and white radio antenna spiked the horizon. An artillery gun peeped out from under the flap of a blue tent on the outer flanks of the camp. This was Hun Sen's rural residence: an impregnable military fortress manned by a battalion of troops, ringed by watchtowers armed with machine guns, and dotted with artillery guns. It was unapproachable as it was protected by marshes. We drove along the dirt road, and halted under a bougainvillea-draped wrought-iron gate. The residence was hidden behind high walls mounted with surveillance cameras.

The gate swung open onto a fashionably paved driveway that climbed up to a wheat-coloured villa with a red-tiled roof. Arched windows, mock balconies, terrace washing lines swaying with white sheets, satellite dishes, and a profusion of antennae lent the house a lived-in look. A porch supported by Corinthian columns overlooked a lake on which pelicans glided silently, and a mini golf course where Hun Sen perfected his swing. The three-storey house, built in November 1997, was surrounded by coconut trees, a swimming pool, a lakehouse, and waterfalls. The interior of the house showed a decidedly period-European touch, with chandeliers and faux seventeenth-century French furniture. Pillars made of local *beng* wood were rooted on marble floors. Hun Sen's tastes were not always so extravagant. Before this he had lived in a simple two-storey home that was built in 1989, and which still stood—right next door to the new residence. It was a large but plain structure, with an ordinary reception area furnished with a Vietnamese-style carpet and traditional carved chairs. The plainness had been replaced by new opulence.

Hun Sen walked into the room wearing a dark-blue suit over a blue shirt. He had just wound up a meeting with a group of Muslim students. Between sips of Chinese tea he spoke into a microphone about his escape from Cambodia, the months spent in Vietnamese jails, the years consumed by his desire to liberate his country, his anger at its past rulers, and his rage against genocide. The interview was proceeding smoothly until we asked him a question in which we referred to the Vietnamese military action to overthrow the Khmer Rouge as an "invasion." This brought forth a long, impassioned, and indignant response from Hun Sen, who was quick to correct our interpretation of history, asserting that it was never an invasion but an act of liberation from a genocidal regime. "How could I, a Cambodian, invade my own country?" he asked in carefully modulated English, a foreign language he found difficult and had never felt the need to master. By this time his equanimity had been disturbed, and we felt that it was time to end the interview. It had been a productive session, with Hun Sen speaking on tape for more than two hours. We were to travel with him the next day to Prey Veng province, east of Phnom Penh. "You are coming with me, aren't you?" he said warmly. "Come tomorrow before 8 a.m. I am going to harvest rice." He had forgiven us our "error" of history, and was soon seeing us off at the front porch.

The next morning we drove into his fortress through another point of entry further down the road, past another roadblock, past piglets tethered to a banana tree, rows of banana trees known as *chek pong moan* (or "chicken-egg banana"), barking dogs, and a watchtower manned by a smiling soldier. Four Russian-made helicopters stood on a concrete strip ringed by lotus ponds and water hyacinths. We were invited to take our seats in a helicopter that would accompany Hun Sen's. One by one the helicopters lifted off, and flew low over the marsh towards our steaming rural destination. After thirty minutes of cruising over lush terrain and pregnant waterways we touched down in a vast yellowing rice field in the midst of a thousand villagers, their heads covered in colourful *kramas*. As soon as he hit the ground Hun Sen was hugging grandmothers and grandchildren. He then started cutting rice stalks with a *kandeav* (a kind of sickle) at a rapid pace, and within minutes he had harvested about twenty-five metres of the field with the expertise of a rice farmer. Afterwards, sitting under a makeshift tent he delivered a speech over a loudspeaker that had been screwed onto the handlebars of a bicycle. All around him the village folk squatted and listened. Sweating profusely through his stonewashed shirt he told us, "I am a farmer. I am very poor. I am not like a prince." His *krama* fell to the ground. A bodyguard picked it up and threw it over his own shoulder. A poignant act. Prime minister and bodyguard were one.

The biography would be incomplete without speaking to Hun Sen's wife. We raised the possibility of an extended session with Bun Sam Hieng, better known as Bun Rany, and Hun Sen agreed without hesitation. The next day we met her, a farmer's daughter who had come, literally, through slaughter. Dressed in a chocolate-and-ochre silk *ikkat sampot,* Bun Rany held herself straight as a ramrod. At forty-four she boasted a slim-enough waistline, and was generously endowed in the Cambodian way. She sat with her hands folded in her lap. With her black platforms and Dior bag, the wife of Cambodia's most powerful man exuded a quiet charm that was quite disarming. Her porcelain skin was the perfect foil for the wiry jet-black hair that, she told us, had been cropped short on the orders of the Khmer Rouge during their rule. Now, decades later her long hair hung loose on her shoulders. Khmer sapphires adorned her long, burgundy-painted fingernails. As the soft afternoon rays caught the gilded edges of the ornately carved faux Louis XIV sofas on the second floor of her new home in Takhmau, her gentle drone almost sounded like a lullaby. Our chat turned out to be a four-hour saga about her life and losses, her hopes and disappointments, her loves and lessons learnt, as she dredged up painful memories through a monsoon of tears.

The interviews for the biography were half-done. Hun Sen agreed to answer a further set of questions in writing. Sure enough, his written answers were delivered right on schedule. He said he would grant us one more interview a couple of months later. In the meantime we put together all our interviews with the other Cambodian leaders—Ranariddh and Son Sann being among the many we had spoken to. Some of the most insightful comments came from Hun Sen's childhood friends who had lived with him in the pagoda during the mid-1960s, and from his teachers at high school. One of our most prized interviews was with his elder brother, Hun Neng, whom we had met in 1993. The brothers Hun were military allies. Their combined forces had helped overthrow the Khmer Rouge in 1979.

THE INTERVIEW CAME THROUGH with the suddenness of the Cambodian rain. Prak Sokhonn informed us that the prime minister had only "one window" to meet us in early June 1998. Once again we drove to his home in Takhmau for a two-hour session. Hun Sen talked about his days as a pagoda boy, and the challenges he confronted when he became prime minister. He inquired gently how his biography was progressing. He did not ask to see the manuscript. It seemed that he would rather not see the manuscript, and would have us write it the way we pleased.

It was clear that his staff adored, and admired, this man who had risen out of crushing poverty to become the most powerful leader Cambodia had known in the twentieth century—more powerful even than Prince Sihanouk, who was easily toppled, and more resilient than Pol Pot. Prak Sokhonn, who had at that time been with Hun Sen for more than four years, said that his boss was unlike most ministers. "They sign documents without reading them," he said. "But Hun Sen reads every word. None of his aides dare make a mistake, which is met with a stern rebuke. But once he's had his say, it's back to normal." It was with the same care and concern that Hun Sen built schools and irrigation canals across the country. He accepted donations, and pumped the money right back into the development projects. A strongman he was, but with a strong conscience and a sense of duty. And there was always a hint of another motive: to shower the people with largesse so as to win their support in the elections.

AFTER SEVERAL JOURNEYS to Cambodia between 1990 and 2000, when we returned to set foot on the flaky red earth of Phnom Penh in May 2001, it was to see Hun Sen revel in the role of strongman. King Sihanouk would teasingly call him *le strongman* in Franglais, and diplomats would use the same title.

In the post-Cold War years, he had become synonymous with the party, the government, the national assembly, and the armed forces. "Not even fish could spawn in the river without his approval," a human rights worker joked in reference to his control over Khmer society and state: he set high moral standards for young women, he ordered karaoke bars shut if they promoted prostitution, and he personally selected bright young men to serve in his government.

Beyond that, he had a hand in the selection of the king. People in Phnom Penh spoke about his new role in whispers at first, and then with growing boldness in cafes and curbside newsstands. As he came to exercise complete power over the country's political institutions, he solidified his hold over the Council of the Throne, which would choose a new king on the death of the ailing Sihanouk. Not surprisingly, two-thirds of the council's members owed allegiance to the strongman. Not content with being just *le strongman*, he laid claim to the title of kingmaker.

At this time, some members of the Cambodian elite were looking towards France's bitter experiences with its kings and queens in order to find some answers to their own conundrum: should Cambodia have a monarchy at all? Voltaire had posed the searching question to all of France: "Which is better? A monarchy or a republic?" And he had answered it himself: "For 4,000 years this question has been tossed about. Ask the rich for an answer—they all want aristocracy. Ask the people—they want democracy. Only the monarchs want the monarchy." The Cambodian people loved and revered King Sihanouk, but they were not enamoured of any of his possible successors. Indeed, the monarchy would lose some of its popularity after Sihanouk abdicated in favour of his son Norodom Sihamoni in 2004. And after Sihanouk's death in 2012, the royal Norodom family would lose the one person who could watch over the government and publicly criticise it, and yet maintain a cordial relationship with Hun Sen and the Cambodian People's Party (CPP). It was a role that Sihamoni could not play because he lacked both an interest in politics and his father's political acumen. Hun Sen ensured the preservation of the monarchy because it was a historically relevant and widely popular institution that served as a link to the ancient Khmer Empire, and because it did not pose a political threat to the government. A former communist, Hun Sen reluctantly became a democrat. The farmer's son was not inimical to stacking his government with aristocrats or with royalty, though peasant-class fires still burned within him.

To these many political roles, Hun Sen added those of the maverick philosopher, part-time songwriter and storyteller. In modern-day Cambodia's barren fields of creative writing and the arts, Hun Sen stood out as a successful artist, with hundreds of songs to his name. Many of his songs were hopelessly tragic, others dripped with romance. He took on the role of custodian of the arts: he set about restoring at least some of the creative energy that had been slashed and burned by Pol Pot. He often spoke about his rustic philosophy. But where did he find his muse? He had mastered the Cambodian classics, but unlike his rivals in the royal family who savoured the French literary classics, Hun Sen stayed rooted to the familiar literature of his own soil. He had read Marx and Lenin in translation, and the works of Ho Chi Minh, whom he admired. He had also read the ideas of Pol Pot, whose views he would vehemently denounce. As self-appointed guardian of his country's cultural aesthetics, he frowned upon the craze to build houses cloned from those in Thailand. And when he commented upon the profusion of foreign restaurants and the singular lack of restaurants serving Cambodian food, he did appear to be a nationalist.

He reached the hearts of the poorest people—wading knee-deep in muddy water and covered in leeches to get to remote villages—and then their minds. He touched them deeply with his impulsiveness, to take them by the hand and smoke a cigarette or two with them. He showed he really was one of them, happy to sit down in the middle of a rice field to a simple meal of rice and dried *pra hok* fish, a diet that most Cambodian princes and the Francophone aristocracy would rather avoid. People spoke of him endearingly as a "benign dictator."

With Hun Sen fronting it, the CPP improved its standing in every election, taking a progressively bigger share of the vote. After narrowly losing the general election in 1993, he led his party to victory in the general election of 1998, and then prepared it for its biggest challenge, the commune election in February 2002. It was no surprise that his party swept most of the seats in the communes. It was a Hun Sen landslide, with his party winning 1,598 out of the 1,621 communes, leaving the Sam Rainsy Party with thirteen, and the royalist Funcinpec Party with ten. His triumph was reminiscent of the huge margins by which Sihanouk had, in his heyday, trounced his opponents. He had done the impossible for his CPP. The party with dismal electoral prospects had triumphed on the rising popularity of Hun Sen.

HAVING BEEN IN AND OUT of this tiger's den at Takhmau several times, we were now returning to his city residence at 41 Boulevard Suramarit. The young commando duo standing guard at the gate had the benefit of advance notice of our arrival. We walked past the same sculpted garden towards the reception area, and then waited in a holding room at the bottom of a mosaic staircase leading up to Hun Sen's office. Through glass double-doors, we watched the kingmaker's team at work—Sry Thamarong, Darryl Eang, and Bun Sam Bo—his trusted and handpicked aides. Soon we were ushered upstairs by his chief of protocol, Madame Bora.

Hun Sen's office was a spacious rectangular room dominated by a large polished dark-wood conference table. The table bristled with two rows of built-in microphones. This was where the strongman met dignitaries, where iron met velvet. During the four hours we spent with him, sipping chilled Coke and breathing in his side-stream smoke, he confessed to his failure to quit smoking. A couple of days later we would interview Bun Rany again, but in another part of the house—a place more homely, a sanctuary of flowers and family albums. The four-hour interview with her would be an epic of emotions, swinging from confidence to concern, family matters to fundraisers. We would also interview, back in Bangkok, their bright young son, Manet, a graduate student at New York University, who shared a meal with us at our home, and looked set for a career as an economist. His parents, having endured the Khmer Rouge genocide, did not want him to enter politics. Manet was doing just that: he was about to register for a PhD in the United States (he eventually completed doctoral studies in England), and had done an internship at the World Bank in preparation for his eventual homecoming with expertise in rural development. At this time, the parents did not want any of their children to seek a career in politics. But they dropped their opposition after the children completed their higher education. Some of the children began working for the government, and their youngest son, Hun Mani, was nominated as a candidate of the CPP in the general election in 2013. Manet, however, kept himself out of politics: he joined the army as an officer and rose up the ranks to become a major-general—a role that he preferred, as it enabled him to work for national stability and development.

For now, in the strongman's office, the mood was light-hearted. Hun Sen joked and laughed easily. Behind him stood an imposing presence: a writing table with three grey phones that were hotlines to his military commanders and trusted ministers; more power was evident in a black phone, and a data port with a computer. But the table was also stacked with proof of his "other" life: his prolific outpourings as a songwriter. He let his muse take over around midnight, working on a poem or storyline with the devotion of a Buddhist monk, while the family slept. A state-of-the-art sound system displayed on one of the many wall units was switched on only to listen to music, his own. Many of the compact discs of his songs lined a cabinet. Up against the wall to the far left of the writing table was evidence of the strongman's entry into cyberspace: a long table with a bank of three laptop computers, three fax machines, and a data port. Cold authority was offset by a white porcelain vase painted with blue irises, a motif that seemed to appear out of another planet, its tranquillity so far removed from the dry red earth just outside on Boulevard Suramarit. More personal touches helped soften the long-calcified image: family photos, a beautifully wrought dark-blue globe, a cache of awards he had received over the years from various international institutions, a couple of honorary PhDs among them, and the ubiquitous stonehead of the twelfth-century Khmer emperor, Jayavarman VII, the master-builder of the Bayon temple in the heart of Angkor Thom.

Like his ancestors, Hun Sen was intent on leaving his mark as the architect of a new Cambodia.

SINCE THE PUBLICATION of the first edition of this biography in 1999, no other book or monograph has appeared on Hun Sen, who has now been in power for almost three decades.[1] With thirteen years having elapsed, the authors believed it was time to update the work with substantial new material—new interviews with Hun Sen and his family, and new U.S. historical documents about the prime minister. This completely revised and updated edition spans the period from the early 1950s to 2013, and draws on interviews with the principal characters in the twentieth- and early-twenty-first-century history of Cambodia, as well as on the documentary resources of Cambodia and various archives in the United States, such as the National Security Archive in Washington, D.C., the George H.W. Bush Presidential Library at College Station, Texas, and recently declassified documents of the Central Intelligence Agency. These official U.S. papers reveal, for the first time, how Hun Sen was viewed by the United States and its allies in Europe and Southeast Asia, and how their perceptions changed through the course of the Cold War. For instance, in one revealing U.S. document from 1989, French President Francois Mitterrand tells U.S. President George H.W. Bush that Hun Sen is "the strong point of his government," that he is "governing well," and that he "really needs to be taken into account by us."[2] Based on historical evidence, this book argues that Hun Sen had gained the support of important Western countries early in his career.

Chapter One explores the early life of Hun Sen and Bun Rany, both of whom grew up in rural Cambodia and were deeply affected by the events that followed the deposal of Sihanouk in 1970. Chapter Two examines the reasons they left home to join the resistance forces led by the Khmer Rouge, and explains the traumas they faced under the Khmer Rouge regime. Chapter Three argues that

Hun Sen decided to defect to Vietnam in 1977 because he refused to carry out Khmer Rouge orders to kill innocent Muslim Cambodians and launch attacks on Vietnam. In Vietnam he spent several months trying to convince the reluctant Vietnamese to help him overthrow the Khmer Rouge. Chapter Four provides a detailed account of the process by which Hun Sen and his compatriots Heng Samrin and Chea Sim were able to liberate their country, and establish normalcy and stability.

Chapter Five examines Hun Sen's early days as foreign minister and his rapid rise to become prime minister while Cambodia remained in virtual isolation from the outside world, facing as it was a U.S.-imposed economic embargo. Chapter Six presents new archival materials that demonstrate how Cambodia, and Hun Sen, became embroiled in global Cold War politics, and the slow process by which the United States dropped its initial opposition toward Hun Sen, and came to recognise his party as a guarantor of stability in the region. Chapter Seven consists of snapshots of Cambodia during both the Cold War and the Cambodian civil war, when Hun Sen's only allies were the communist countries and India. Once the Soviet Union disintegrated in 1991, the country eagerly opened its markets to foreign investment.

Chapter Eight discusses the vexed relationship between Hun Sen and Cambodia's royal family, who were both rivals and allies. Chapter Nine explores the impact of Hun Sen's defeat in the elections of 1993 to his rival Ranariddh and the political exigencies that forced the two to forge a coalition government. It then provides a blow-by-blow account of the military confrontation that broke out between the co-premiers' factions, a confrontation that both men claimed was a coup against them, and which ended with Hun Sen imposing his authority.

Chapter Ten provides a rare window into the Hun family, and uncovers common factors that linked all their lives through the genocide. Chapter Eleven demonstrates that Hun Sen tightened control by winning the 1998 general election against the background of allegations of voter intimidation. As he took charge, he made an effort for his country to join the Association of Southeast Asian Nations (ASEAN).

Chapter Twelve examines Hun Sen's efforts to ensure political stability in the event of the death of King Sihanouk. Chapter Thirteen turns the focus back on Hun Sen's efforts to rebuild the newly installed democracy, as his party triumphed in the election to the rural communes, even though the poll was marred by allegations of violence. Chapter Fourteen presents a rare glimpse into the personal side of Hun Sen and his young family: his belief in folklore and the spirit world, and his habits and home life.

Chapter Fifteen focuses on the early life of Hun Manet, the culture shock he experienced on being immersed in an American lifestyle as a cadet at the West Point Military Academy and as a graduate student at New York University. It encapsulates the worldview of the young student, and his desire to develop his country on his return from New York.

The concluding chapter offers an overall assessment of Hun Sen's policies, his contributions to Cambodian diplomacy and national development, and the steps he has taken to groom a new generation of Huns.

HUN SEN'S LIFE AND TIMES

1952   Born August 5, in Peam Koh Sna village, Stung Trang district, Kompong Cham province. Later amends his date of birth in his personal resume to April 4, 1951, in order to appear older and thus more credible when given the job of foreign minister in 1979.

1953   Cambodia gains independence from France. Under King Sihanouk, it becomes the Kingdom of Cambodia.

1954   Vietnam is partitioned into North and South.

1955   Sihanouk abdicates in favour of his father, Suramarit, and becomes prime minister.

1959   Hun Sen commences studies at Peam Koh Sna Primary School.

1960   King Suramarit dies; Sihanouk becomes head of state.

1965   Hun Sen enrols at the Lycée Indra Dhevi in Phnom Penh, and lives in the Neakavoan Pagoda.

        Sihanouk allows North Vietnamese guerrillas to set up bases in Cambodia to fight the U.S.-backed government of South Vietnam.

1969   The U.S. Air Force begins covertly carpet-bombing Cambodia in an effort to destroy North Vietnamese bases and supply routes.

1970   Prime Minister Lon Nol overthrows Sihanouk in a coup; proclaims himself president of the new Khmer Republic.

Civil war ensues, with the government forces, supported by the United States and South Vietnam, fighting the North Vietnamese, the Viet Cong and the Khmer Rouge (Communist Party of Kampuchea).

Hun Sen joins the underground movement known as the maquis—led by the Khmer Rouge—to oppose the Republican government of Lon Nol. Wounded five times in heavy fighting.

Sihanouk, in exile in Beijing, offers support to the Khmer Rouge.

1975   Hun Sen appointed Chief of Special Regimental Staff of the Khmer Rouge in the Eastern Region. Loses left eye in battle.

Led by Pol Pot, the Khmer Rouge take over Phnom Penh, toppling Lon Nol. The country is renamed Democratic Kampuchea.

Under the Khmer Rouge's genocidal four-year regime, more than 1.7 million are killed—through execution, torture, forced labour and starvation.

Communist North Vietnam uses military power to over-throw the South Vietnamese regime, and unifies the two halves of Vietnam under communist rule.

1976 Marries Bun Sam Hieng, better known as Bun Rany, on January 5, 1976. (Children: Komsot, male, born November 10, 1976, died at birth after being dropped by Khmer Rouge nurses; Manet, male, born October 20, 1977; Mana, female, born September 15, 1980; Manith, male, born October 17, 1981; Mani, male, born November 27, 1982; Maly, female, born December 30, 1983; Maline, female, adopted.)

1977 Fighting escalates between Khmer Rouge troops and Vietnamese forces.

Hun Sen appointed Deputy Regimental Commander of a Special Regiment of the Khmer Rouge in the Eastern Region.

Escapes to Song Be province in South Vietnam to avoid being purged by Pol Pot.

1978 Joins Heng Samrin in organising the Kampuchean United Front for National Salvation, a 20,000-strong force of Cambodian nationalists, and prepares to overthrow the Khmer Rouge.

Vietnamese armed forces, with the participation of the United Front, launch full-scale invasion of Cambodia.

1979 Vietnamese forces take Phnom Penh. Khmer Rouge retreats into the jungle on the Thai border.

Hun Sen flies back to Phnom Penh after the Khmer Rouge regime is toppled.

The People's Republic of Kampuchea (PRK) is established under the aegis of the Vietnamese military, bringing an end to the Khmer Rouge's reign of terror.

Hun Sen appointed foreign minister in the PRK government.

Reunites with Bun Rany.

1981   The pro-Vietnamese Kampuchean People's Revolutionary Party (KPRP) holds its First Party Congress, tracing its historic links to the original anti-colonial KPRP, which had been founded in 1951 during French rule and had maintained close fraternal links to Ho Chi Minh's communist Vietnam Workers' Party and the communist party in Laos.

Hun Sen appointed deputy prime minister.

1982   In opposition to the newly created state, a government-in-exile is formed—a coalition of the Khmer Rouge, Sihanouk's royalist Funcinpec party, and the Khmer People's National Liberation Front (KPNLF).

Guerrilla warfare throughout the country persists, waged primarily by the former Khmer Rouge militia. Hundreds of thousands of Cambodians are displaced.

1984   Hun Sen denounces UN decision to allow the Khmer Rouge to occupy Cambodia's seat in the UN General Assembly.

1985   Appointed prime minister—becoming one of the youngest prime ministers in Southeast Asia.

1986   Relinquishes post of foreign minister to concentrate on job as premier.

1987   Takes back foreign ministerial post in order to build his stature ahead of peace talks.

Meets Sihanouk in France for the first in a series of peace talks aimed at reconciliation between Phnom Penh and the government-in-exile.

1989   Plans and executes the final withdrawal of Vietnamese military forces from Cambodia.

The country is renamed the State of Cambodia.

1991   Signs a peace accord in Paris with Sihanouk and the other Cambodian factions, bringing the civil war to an end. A UN-sponsored transitional government is installed, with Sihanouk as head of state.

1993   General election held. A coalition government is formed, with the royalist Funcinpec party's Prince Norodom Ranariddh as First Prime Minister and Hun Sen as Second Prime Minister.

The Kingdom of Cambodia is restored; Sihanouk returns to the throne.

1994   Khmer Rouge guerrillas numbering in the thousands surrender in a government amnesty.

1996   Relationship with Ranariddh deteriorates.

1997   Armed clashes erupt in Phnom Penh between the forces of Ranariddh and Hun Sen. Overthrown by Hun Sen, Ranariddh goes into self-imposed exile. The world's press acknowledges the emergence of Hun Sen as a strongman.

Hun Sen requests UN assistance in setting up tribunal to try Khmer Rouge leaders for war crimes.

1998   Ranariddh, granted amnesty by Sihanouk, returns to contest elections in July but loses to Hun Sen.

1999   Cambodia becomes the tenth member of ASEAN (Association of Southeast Asian Nations).

2000   Members of the U.S.-based Cambodian Freedom Fighters (CFF) attack government buildings in Phnom Penh in an attempt to overthrow Hun Sen.

2001   Senate approves a law creating a tribunal to frame genocide charges against Khmer Rouge leaders.

International donors pledge $560 million in economic aid to Cambodia.

2002   The first multi-party local elections are held in the country, with the ruling CPP winning in all but 23 out of 1,621 communes.

2003   Hun Sen's CPP wins general election, but fails to gain sufficient majority to govern alone.

2004 Re-elected prime minister after CPP strikes a deal with Funcinpec, ending a year of political deadlock.

National Assembly ratifies Cambodia's entry into the World Trade Organisation.

King Sihanouk abdicates the throne; succeeded by his son Norodom Sihamoni.

2005 Opposition leader Sam Rainsy sentenced in absentia to nine months in prison for defaming Hun Sen; later pardoned by the king.

2006 Ranariddh removed as leader of Funcinpec.

2007 UN-backed court tribunal begins interrogating suspects about allegations of genocide by the Khmer Rouge.

2008 CPP wins general election—hailed by diplomats from several countries as the freest and fairest the country has seen.

2009 National Assembly again denies immunity to Sam Rainsy, who fails to appear in court.

2010 Khang Khek Ieu ("Comrade Duch," chief of Tuol Sleng prison camp), convicted of crimes against humanity during the Khmer Rouge regime; sentenced to thirty-five years; later extended to life imprisonment. Four other top-tier Khmer Rouge leaders await trial: Nuon Chea, Ieng Sary, Khieu Samphan, and Ieng Thirith. Pol Pot died in 1998.

2011 Border conflict with Thailand escalates over disputed territory adjoining the Preah Vihear Temple.

2012 Cambodia and Thailand withdraw troops from border at Preah Vihear Temple.

Sihanouk dies.

U.S. President Barack Obama visits Cambodia.

2013 Hun Sen enters his twenty-ninth year as prime minister.

THE PLAYERS AND THEIR
RELATIONSHIP TO HUN SEN

NORODOM SIHANOUK

Born in 1922, he dominated Cambodian politics on becoming king in 1941, embarking on a reign that would encompass the French Indochina War, the U.S. War in Vietnam, the U.S. bombing and invasion of Cambodia, and the Cold War. He abdicated in 1955, and became the chief of state in 1960. His political career ended when he was ousted in a coup in 1970. He was reappointed king in 1993 after two decades in exile. Sihanouk was Hun Sen's adversary during the peace talks that began in France in the 1980s. He gradually and tentatively began to consider Hun Sen as his "son," and even respected his authority, realising that the strongman provided the stability his country needed. Sihanouk abdicated voluntarily in October 2004 in favour of his son Norodom Sihamoni. He died at the age of eighty-nine, after a heart attack in Beijing on October 15, 2012.

VAN TIEN DUNG, TRAN VAN TRA,
& LE DUC ANH

The three Vietnamese Army generals who helped Hun Sen and the Cambodian rebels raise a military force to overthrow the Khmer Rouge. They planned and launched the Vietnamese military attack on the Khmer Rouge in 1978–79. Le Duc Anh later became the president of Vietnam, and remained close to Hun Sen, who in turn owed the diplomatic support he enjoyed in Vietnam to his links with the generals.

HENG SAMRIN

Born in 1934, he joined the Khmer Rouge and served as a commander of the Khmer Rouge 4th Infantry Division from 1976 to 1978. He led an abortive coup against Pol Pot, and defected to Vietnam in 1978. He became the president of the People's Revolutionary Council, which governed the country after the Vietnamese overthrew the Pol Pot regime in 1979, and served for several years as head of state. Heng Samrin was one of Hun Sen's earliest mentors.

CHEA SIM

Born in 1932 into a peasant family in the Ponhea Krek district of Kompong Cham province, Chea Sim was recruited by the Vietnamese communists during the war against the French in the 1950s. He joined the Khmer Rouge, and became a committee secretary for Ponhea Krek. After the Pol Pot regime was toppled, he rose to become minister of the interior, and later chairman of the National Assembly of the State of Cambodia. He retained the post of chairman of the assembly that was formed after the elections of May 1993, and became the head of the senate in 1999. Like Heng Samrin, Chea Sim groomed Hun Sen in the 1980s to play a major role in government.

PEN SOVANN

Born in 1935, he entered the Issarak independence movement when he was just thirteen, and later joined the Communist Party of Indochina in 1951. Sovann served as bodyguard to Ta Mok, who went on to become a Khmer Rouge general responsible for genocide. Sovann split with Ta Mok after independence in 1953, and attended communist training camps in Vietnam. He tried to mobilise Cambodians living along the Lao border to topple Pol Pot. After overthrowing the Khmer Rouge, the Vietnamese installed Sovann as secretary-general of the People's Revolutionary Party.

He was elected prime minister in July 1981, but was sacked soon afterwards following policy differences with Heng Samrin. He was flown to Hanoi where he was jailed for seven years. Sovann blamed Hun Sen for his imprisonment.

HUN NENG

Born in 1949 in Kompong Cham, Hun Neng is an elder brother of Hun Sen's. His rise coincided with the latter's meteoric ascent. Jailed by the Khmer Rouge in the mid-1970s, Hun Neng was exiled to the hills of Kompong Thom for nine months. He played an important role in mobilising rebel military forces in Kompong Cham to overthrow Pol Pot. Later, Hun Neng studied economics in Phnom Penh, and served as an economic advisor to the local government of Kompong Cham. He rose to become the chief of a district, and was appointed the governor of Kompong Cham province in 1985, the year that Hun Sen became the prime minister.

POL POT

Mystery surrounds Pol Pot's date of birth. Some historians believe he was born in 1925, but French records date his birth to 1928. Given the name Saloth Sar, he grew up in a wealthy farming family in Kompong Thom province. He won a scholarship to study radio electronics in Paris in 1949, but was more interested in communism than science, and did not complete his studies. He returned home in 1953 to join the Cambodian Communist Party and became its secretary-general in 1962. As the supreme leader of the Khmer Rouge guerrillas, he presided over the killing of some 1.7 million innocent Cambodians between 1975 and 1979. Eventually, Hun Sen was able to overthrow Pol Pot with the help of the Vietnamese army in 1979. Consigned to the margins of Cambodian politics, Pol Pot lived a fugitive's life in the jungles bordering Thailand. He died in April 1998 after being held in captivity by his own cadres, who charged him with the murder of a colleague.

The Players

KHIEU SAMPHAN

Born in 1932 in Svay Rieng province, he was educated at the University of Paris. On returning to Phnom Penh, he founded the French-language journal, *L'Observateur*. He was a member of the national assembly as a member of Sihanouk's Sangkum Reastr Niyum party, and served as secretary of state for commerce. He joined the Khmer Rouge in 1967, and at various times served as head of state and prime minister of Democratic Kampuchea, battling the Vietnamese forces from 1979 to 1991. Samphan was one of Hun Sen's most vociferous critics, and locked horns with him during the peace talks through the early 1990s.

SON SANN

Born in 1911 in Phnom Penh, he was educated in Paris, and later served as the governor of the National Bank of Cambodia from 1954 to 1968, and minister of state for finance and national economy from 1961 to 1962. After the collapse of the Pol Pot regime, he created the Khmer People's National Liberation Front. He served as prime minister of the Coalition Government of Democratic Kampuchea, the regime in exile, from 1982 to 1991. He remained a bitter critic of Hun Sen, blaming the CPP for the misfortunes that visited his country. He died in 2000 of heart failure.

NORODOM RANARIDDH

Born in 1944, this son of Sihanouk was educated in Paris and Aix-en-Provence in France, and returned to Cambodia with a PhD in law. Following the elections of May 1993, he was appointed First Prime Minister, with Hun Sen as Second Prime Minister. The two men worked in close cooperation initially but quickly fell apart, and Ranariddh was overthrown in a military takeover by Hun Sen in 1997. After the elections in 1998, the two men resumed their cooperation to form a coalition government, and were again on cordial terms. He was removed as chairman of his Funcinpec party by a party vote in 2006. He then launched his own Norodom Ranariddh Party.

NORODOM CHAKRAPONG

Born in 1945, this feisty son of Sihanouk rose and fell like a shooting star. He and half-brother Ranariddh were bitter political rivals. Chakrapong defected from his father's party to join Hun Sen's government in the early 1990s. He quickly became close to Hun Sen, who wanted to use his royal appeal to win votes in the general election. But they were irreconcilably divided after Chakrapong attempted to form a rebel autonomous zone following the 1993 election. Ranariddh and Hun Sen, seeing a common foe in Chakrapong, conspired to exile him. Chakrapong believed he was betrayed by the CPP.

NORODOM SIRIVUDH

Born in 1951, a half-brother of Sihanouk, Sirivudh earned a master's degree in macroeconomics from the University of Paris. A member of the Funcinpec party, he was appointed foreign minister in 1993. He resigned in October 1994, claiming he had serious differences with Second Prime Minister Hun Sen. Sirivudh was exiled to France in December 1995 following allegations that he had plotted to kill Hun Sen. Bitterly opposed to Hun Sen, Sirivudh turned into a relentless critic of Hun Sen and his style of government. He was allowed back to Cambodia in 1999. Elected a member of parliament in 2003, he was appointed a deputy prime minister and privy counsellor to the king in 2006. In 2010, he was appointed a member of the Constitutional Council.

SAM RAINSY

Born in 1949, this son of former Deputy Prime Minister Sam Sary went to study in France, where he earned a master's degree in economics in 1973, and an MBA from INSEAD University in 1980. He returned to Cambodia in 1991 to make his debut in politics by joining the Funcinpec party. He was appointed finance minister, but was sacked from the government in 1994, and then removed from the party and the national assembly the following year. He became a fierce critic of Hun Sen and his government, and formed his own party, the Khmer Nation Party, later renamed the Sam Rainsy Party. In 2005, a Cambodian court found him guilty of defaming the CPP and Funcinpec, but he received a royal pardon.

YASUSHI AKASHI

A senior Japanese diplomat, Akashi was appointed the chief of the United Nations Transitional Authority in Cambodia (UNTAC), the international body mandated to organise and supervise the general election in 1993. Akashi's formal title was Special Representative of the Secretary-General. After the completion of his Cambodian mission, he was appointed the head of the UN mission in Yugoslavia. He maintained a neutral position toward Hun Sen and other political leaders.

JOHN SANDERSON

The Australian army general who served as commander of UNTAC forces in Cambodia, Lieutenant-General Sanderson also maintained a neutral position toward the Cambodian politicians.

ABBREVIATIONS USED

IN THE BOOK

ANKI   *Armée nationale pour un Kampuchea independent*, or
        National Army for an Independent Kampuchea;
        formerly known as ANS.

ANS   *Armée nationale Sihanoukienne*, or the National Army
        of Sihanouk; ANS changed its name to ANKI in 1990.

ASEAN   Association of Southeast Asian Nations; formed in
        1967, and to which Cambodia was admitted in 1999.

BLDP   Buddhist Liberal Democratic Party; ahead of the 1993
        election, Son Sann renamed the KPNLF as the BLDP
        in order to revive Buddhism among the people.

CGDK   Coalition Government of Democratic Kampuchea; the
        tripartite coalition government formed by Sihanouk,
        Son Sann and the Khmer Rouge in 1982.

CPK   Communist Party of Kampuchea (1951–81); its mem-
        bers originally consisted of communists and national-
        ists who opposed French colonial rule, but under Pol
        Pot the party's core leadership adopted an extreme
        form of Maoist ideology.

CPP   Cambodian People's Party; the political party headed by Chea Sim, Heng Samrin and Hun Sen. The CPP evolved from the KPRP and the SOC. The leaders changed the name of the party in order to refurbish its tainted authoritarian image ahead of the elections in 1993, and also to cast off its communist ideology and adopt a more conciliatory democratic style.

DK   Democratic Kampuchea; the formal name of the government of the Khmer Rouge, 1975–79.

Funcinpec *Front uni national pour un Cambodge independant, neutre, pacifique, et cooperatif,* or National United Front for an Independent, Neutral, Peaceful, and Cooperative Cambodia; the royalist political party created by Sihanouk in 1981 to fight the Phnom Penh regime of Heng Samrin and their patrons, the Vietnamese. After the peace accord was signed in 1991, Sihanouk handed over the party's leadership to Ranariddh.

FUNK *Front uni national du Kampuchea,* or National United Front of Kampuchea; the militant movement that sought to restore Sihanouk to power following his deposal by Lon Nol in 1970; also referred to as the maquis.

FUNSK *Front uni national de salut du Kampuchea,* or Kampuchean United Front for National Salvation; the politico-military organisation, founded in 1978 by Cambodians under the leadership of Heng Samrin, that fought along with Vietnamese forces to liberate Cambodia from the Khmer Rouge regime.

KPNLF   Khmer People's National Liberation Front; set up by Son Sann in 1979 to fight the Vietnamese forces based in Cambodia and the forces of the PRK/SOC.

KPNLAF   Khmer People's National Liberation Armed Forces; the military arm of the KPNLF.

KPRP   Kampuchean People's Revolutionary Party; an off-shoot of the Indochinese Communist Party (ICP), which played a vital role against French colonial rule and the Japanese occupation of Cambodia. Formed in 1951 after the ICP was dissolved and reorganised into three communist parties for Vietnam, Laos, and Cambodia. The party in Cambodia split in 1962 into pro-China and pro-Soviet Union factions. Pol Pot led the pro-Chinese group that was vehemently anti-Soviet. In January 1979, the division became permanent when the pro-Soviet and pro-Vietnamese faction under Pen Sovann replaced Pol Pot as the leader in Phnom Penh.

NCR   Non-Communist Resistance; an entity consisting of Sihanouk's ANKI, and the KPNLAF. These two non-communist fighting forces were allied to the Khmer Rouge military forces. But Western and Southeast Asian powers referred to ANKI/KPNLAF as the NCR in order to separate them from the communist Khmer Rouge, thereby enabling them to funnel aid to the NCR.

NGC   National Government of Cambodia; the interim government headed by Sihanouk formed after the general election of 1993.

PRK   People's Republic of Kampuchea; founded in 1979 by Cambodians under the Kampuchean United Front for National Salvation, which overthrew the Khmer Rouge regime with the support of Vietnamese military forces. The PRK failed to win UN membership because of opposition from the United States, Britain, China, and ASEAN. The PRK changed its name to the State of Cambodia in 1989 in order to win international sympathy and support.

SNC   Supreme National Council; created under the Paris peace accord of 1991 to represent the sovereignty of Cambodia through the transitional period until the elections. It represented the country externally and occupied its seat at the United Nations.

SOC   State of Cambodia; the government that ran the country from 1989 till the elections of May 1993. The SOC had its origins in the KPRP, as most of its politburo members were KPRP veterans.

SPK   Sarapordamean Kampuchea; the Cambodian news agency.

UNTAC   United Nations Transitional Authority in Cambodia; created under the Paris peace accord of 1991 to organise and supervise elections, and to demobilise and disarm the Cambodian military factions. Its mandate ran from late 1991 through late 1993. Elements of the UN remained in Cambodia till 1994–95.

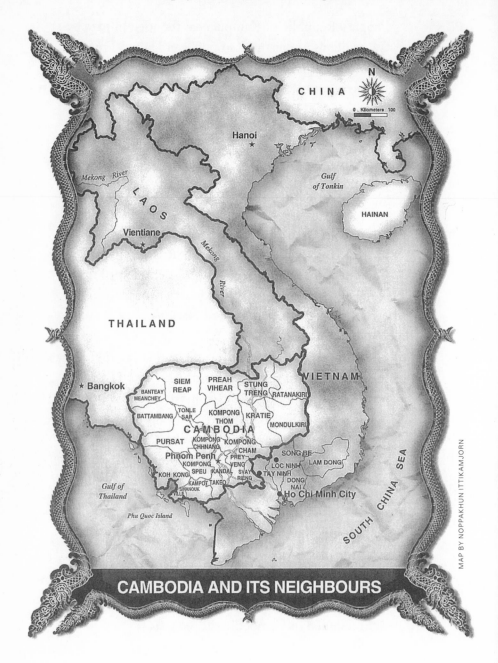

CAMBODIA AND ITS NEIGHBOURS

MAP BY NOPPAKHUN ITTIKAMJORN

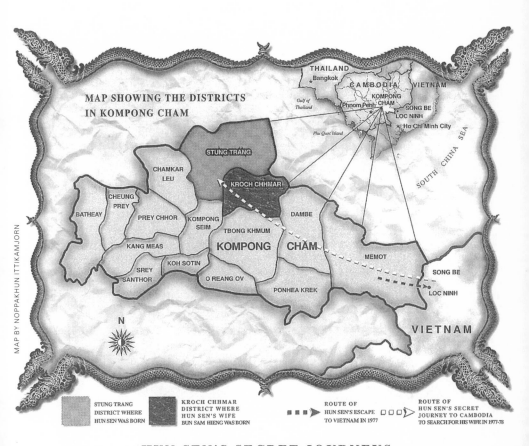

HUN SEN'S SECRET JOURNEYS

A SHORT HISTORY OF

CAMBODIA

OF ALL THE Cambodian leaders to have headed governments in Phnom Penh since independence from France on November 9, 1953, Hun Sen has been the longest-serving and the most resilient, with a record twenty-eight years in power by 2013. In good health and firm control of government, he appears set for an even longer innings as prime minister. With his extraordinary staying power, he has carved for himself a political stature equal to former chief of state Norodom Sihanouk by at least one yardstick—their tenure in active politics. Sihanouk's political career as the head of government lasted fifteen years—he abdicated the throne in favour of his father in 1955, paving the way for his election as chief of state in June 1960, and ran the country till he was toppled in a coup in March 1970. Sihanouk's previous role as king had lasted fourteen years till his abdication. Other Cambodian leaders had much shorter stints— Lon Nol's government survived just five years, while Pol Pot and Norodom Ranariddh were in power less than four years each.

During these twenty-eight years in power, Hun Sen has tightened his control over the government in four distinct phases, starting with his appointment as prime minister in early 1985. In the second phase, from the general election in 1993 to 1997, he served as the Second Prime Minister, but wielded more power than First Prime Minister Ranariddh, a son of Sihanouk. In the third phase, 1997 to 1998, Hun Sen consolidated power after overthrowing

Ranariddh. The fourth phase began with the victory of Hun Sen's CPP in the general election of 1998, and his reappointment as prime minister. In a carefully choreographed ascent to power, his party won the next general election in 2003 but failed to secure a majority in the national assembly. Hun Sen and his party eventually triumphed in the general election of 2008, winning a clear majority on a popular wave of support for the economic policies of his government that had spread prosperity across cities and villages.

The story of Hun Sen and his country is inextricably woven into the fabric of a 2,000-year saga. In order to understand the controversial man who has ruled Cambodia with an adamantine grip, as well as his troubled nation, it is necessary to travel down that patterned past and picture him in the cross-currents of Khmer history. It is a history riddled with fiery civil strife within the shifting boundaries of a Khmer kingdom ruled by chieftains in the first eight centuries of the first millennium C.E., followed by about a thousand years of bloody wars with the Cham kingdoms in the east (present-day Vietnam) and the Siamese (Thais) in the west. While these wars were being waged, the unparalleled edifices of Angkor (an adaptation of the Sanskrit word *nagara*, meaning city) and a whole civilisation of temples were being built by thousands of men toiling incessantly.

THE SPIRIT OF ADVENTURE among Indian seafarers—the desire to discover Suvarnabhumi, land of gold—brought a continuous flow of Indian immigrants through the many trading posts in Southeast Asia from the first century C.E. onwards. They arrived at the lower Mekong Delta in the southeastern corner of Cambodia and the southernmost point of Vietnam, known as Funan.[1] Sometimes the Indian traders' stops at the new ports of call were unscheduled: they were forced by the onslaught of the monsoons—a not very well understood phenomenon—to anchor for months before sailing home. The temptation then, as it is now among long-distance business travellers, was to sink roots in a new land.

In the process of settling beside fertile riverine deltas that yielded enough fish and rice for a comfortable existence, many of the merchants married local women and imperceptibly passed on their social, religious, and cultural products, processes, and performances over hundreds of years. The new religions—Hinduism and Buddhism—were transmitted in the new languages of Pali and Sanskrit. There is evidence of Indian influences such as Sanskrit literature, temple rituals, a legal system, astronomy, and a whole new written script being willingly adopted by the Khmers, who imprinted it onto the weave of the complex nation we now know as Cambodia.[2]

Funan soon surpassed every other state in the area. The capital was at Vyadhapura, near the present-day capital city of Phnom Penh, and its borders were extended under its powerful ruler Fan Shih-man in the early third century C.E. to south Vietnam, Cambodia, central Thailand, northern Malaya, and southern Myanmar.[3] Owing to its powerful trading fleet and navy, Funan exercised firm control over Southeast Asian sea-lanes. A glowing account of Funan is written in the Chinese historical text, the *Book of Tsin*: "The kingdom of Funan is more than 3,000 *li* to the west of Lin-yi [Vietnam], in a great bay of the ocean... There are many walled towns, palaces, and houses. [The people] mostly take their food on silver utensils. The taxes are paid in gold, silver, pearls, and perfumes. They have many books and there are libraries and archives. In writing they use an alphabet derived from India. Their funeral and marriage ceremonies are like those of Champa."[4]

From Chinese records it appears that the wealth and pomp of Funan lasted until the sixth century C.E. The territorial ambitions of the adjoining state of Chenla, and other principalities jostling for power in the region, changed the fortunes of Funan. There was civil strife and Chenla became the dominant base from where different dynasties wielded power between the seventh and eighth centuries.[5]

The Khmers, who supplanted the supremacy of the Funanese, were ethnically close to the Mon people of Lower Myanmar. They styled themselves as Khmers descended from the hermit Kambu and goddess Mera, and their kingdom was Kambuja. The Khmers had arrived from their earlier abode in southwest China or north-east India, moving eastward along the Mekong River into southern Laos and Thailand's Korat plateau. It was here that the Khmers set up the state of Chenla, which came under the political domination of Funan. However, their new mountainous homeland made it difficult for agriculture to flourish, so a southward move by the Khmers toward the Mekong Delta became necessary. By the mid-seventh century, the expansionist Khmers had overthrown the dominance of Funan. The Khmers did not, however, undergo any cultural changes, having already absorbed Hindu culture from the Mon in the west and their former Funanese overlords in the south.

The consensus among scholars regarding post-Funan Khmer rule is that Chenla was possibly a loose confederation of states. The names of King Bhavavarman, Chitrasena-Mahendravarman, Isanavarman, and Jayavarman I feature prominently in inscriptions and records of the seventh and eighth centuries.

THE SOMETIMES TEMPESTUOUS and mostly towering destiny of the Angkor Empire came in the form of King Jayavarman II.[6] He established an empire that would stretch from the Gulf of Tonkin (present-day Vietnam) in the east to Kanchanaburi (present-day Thailand) in the west. Ian Mabbett and David Chandler in *The Khmers* pay measured tribute to his reign: "the very fact that it was later looked back upon as the beginning of a pan-Khmer regime indicates that there was, however gradually it was consolidated, a real discontinuity between the jostling principalities of Chenla and the empire that came into being during the ninth and tenth centuries."[7] In other words, the expanding Khmer Empire was distinctly different from the earlier kingdoms that had exercised power and hegemony over the region.

During the reign of Jayavarman II, the cult of the *devaraja*, or god-king, flourished as a highly ritualistic form of belief and worship where *linga*—the phallic icon of the Lord Shiva—were installed in temples and consecrated by Brahmin priests. The *linga* were believed to hold the power of the king, seen to be god on earth. The power, bestowed on the families of royal priests by Jayavarman II, became a permanent feature of court life for later monarchs to emulate. Towering temples built in the shape of mountains functioned as the locus of the cult of the *devaraja,* through which the king's sacred personality was enshrined in *linga* and worshipped. Upon his death the temple became the god-king's mausoleum, not unlike practices of the pharaohs of Ancient Egypt.

In the twelfth century the cult of the god-king was honed to perfection when Khmer emperor Suryavarman II, a staunch follower of Lord Vishnu, built a sanctum in Angkor Wat and installed an image of Vishnu that was believed to hold the very essence of his godly power.[8] The kings of Angkor believed with unquestioning faith that to perpetuate their power they needed to build more temples. So desperate did Jayavarman VII become in his bid to propagate his image through the cult of the god-king that in less than forty years he built no fewer than twelve mammoth structures—the best known being the Angkor Thom and Ta Prohm.

So, between 802 and 1431, a line of great Khmer kings dominated the vast political stage of ancient Cambodia—beginning with Jayavarman II, and including such stalwarts as Rajendravarman II (944–68), Suryavarman I (1020–50), Udayadityavarman II (1050–66), Suryavarman II (1113–50), Jayavarman VII (1181–1219), and ending with the weaker ones such as Thommo Soccorach and Ponha Yat in the fifteenth century. These kings ruled over a lush and fertile land, sometimes blessed with up to four rice crops a year, and the fish from the huge Tonle Sap lake in the heart of the country that fed the thousands whose blood and sweat built the magnificent temples, and still others who fought the constant wars with the Cham and Siamese armies. Vivid scenes of these battles are chiselled on the walls of the Bayon and Angkor Wat, bearing witness to the valiant and brave who died to protect the Khmer motherland.

The Thais captured Angkor in 1431, but the Khmers regained it for a brief period of time. In 1434, the defeated Khmer Empire abandoned Angkor and shifted its capital city to the region of Phnom Penh.[9] In the fifteenth and sixteenth centuries, Cambodia was a state ruled by the Thais. Then came the tussle to take over Cambodia—a constant struggle between Thailand and Vietnam lasting nearly 150 years.

THE ACCESSION OF Ang Duong to the Cambodian throne in 1848 ushered in a twelve-year period of peace, sometimes described as the golden years. Duong, who had suffered several years of captivity in Thailand, continued paying obeisance to the Thai king even after his release, while his country remained under Thai protection. At the same time, he was frightened of Vietnam's motives. Trapped between two powerful neighbours, Thailand and Vietnam, Duong perhaps had no choice but to seek the protection of the French. An insecure Duong sent gifts to the French Emperor, Napoleon III, via the French consulate in Singapore, hoping to defend his country against Vietnam, and to avoid the humiliation of remaining under the protection of the Thais. The French grasped the opportunity, demanding teak and trading privileges from Duong in return for protection. Little did Duong realise that France also had territorial designs on Cambodia.

When Duong died in 1860, to be succeeded by Norodom I, French military forces were fighting Vietnamese forces in Cochin China (Southern Vietnam). Till then, France had recognised Thai hegemonic control of Cambodia, but that policy changed in 1862.

As the French now saw it, the Cambodian king had asked for protection, which the Emperor of France would willingly provide. Some historians argue that Cambodia willingly became a protectorate of the French; others believe that Norodom I did not want a formal treaty setting up the protectorate. At any rate, in 1863 Cambodia became a French protectorate, and France gradually tightened its grip over Cambodia, establishing a Resident-Superior in Phnom Penh in 1884, the year the true French protectorate was set up.[10] In 1904, Norodom died and was succeeded by his half-brother Sisowath.

In the early stages of colonial rule, the Cambodians were grateful to France for pressuring Thailand to return to Cambodia in 1907 its provinces of Battambang and Siem Reap after a century of occupation. But discontent was simmering in the villages. While the Khmer court appreciated the French presence, the overtaxed villagers suffered under the colonialists. A flashpoint was the murder of a senior French official, Felix Louis Bardez, and his local staff. In the early 1920s, Bardez, who was the Resident of Prey Veng province, had dramatically increased the tax collections, and had been promoted as the Resident of Kompong Chhnang province. In April 1925, Bardez visited a village in Kompong Chhnang that chronically reported low tax yields. He summoned tax evaders, handcuffed them, and threatened to imprison them. He then ate lunch while refusing to let the prisoners eat. A crowd of bystanders, incited by Bardez's arrogance, attacked Bardez, killing him, his interpreter, and a Cambodian militiaman.[11]

These injustices gnawed at the hearts of the Cambodian intelligentsia, in whom anti-colonial feelings readily took root. Nationalists such as Pach Chhoeun, Sim Var, and Son Ngoc Thanh succeeded in starting the first newspaper in Cambodia, *Nagara Vatta,* in 1936.[12] It was no mean achievement for them to have convinced the French to grant them a licence—a process that normally took several years and usually ended in rejection. Rather than run the risk of opposing the French, the editors patiently bided their time. A perfect opportunity to challenge French authority presented itself when Japanese troops landed in Cambodia in May 1941. The paper took an increasingly pro-Japanese and anti-French colonial line, leading to a dozen editorials being censored. The paper cleverly exploited two developments: it took full advantage of French military weakness and Japanese sympathy for anti-colonial movements.

In April 1941, an eighteen-year-old Sihanouk was crowned king, following the death of his maternal grandfather, King Sisowath Monivong. The French colonialists saw in the debonair young Sihanouk an urbane, Westernised playboy who could be counted on to preserve French interests, which he did till the early-1950s. The inexperienced king witnessed his country being buffeted by the politics of the Second World War, as Cambodia was occupied by Japanese military forces that had also invaded southern China and Indochina. In August 1941, some 8,000 Japanese troops set up a garrison in the French protectorate of Cambodia. After Germany defeated and occupied France in 1940, France's hold over its Indochinese colonies grew tenuous. Yet, Japan allowed France to continue administering Cambodia. Towards the end of the war, in March 1945, Japan seized control of all French command posts, disarming French troops in an attempt to gain the support of Cambodians for Japan's effort in the war. Japan also encouraged Sihanouk to proclaim independence from France. In March 1945, Sihanouk duly proclaimed an independent Kingdom of Kampuchea. The Japan-installed puppet state lasted for five months, from March to August 1945. Confronted by the politics of the world war, Sihanouk has revealed that he had resigned himself to "acting the role of playboy." The young prince remarked that he spent his time on "horse riding, the cinema, the theatre, water skiing, basketball, without speaking of my amorous adventures."[13]

The surrender of Japanese forces on August 16, 1945 saw a

resurgence of French influence in Cambodia. At this time, a communist movement was gathering steam in the countryside. It was led by Saloth Sar, a French-educated intellectual who later adopted the name Pol Pot. He had won a scholarship to study radio electronics in Paris, but he neglected his course work, and is believed to have joined the Communist Party of France. Soon, he and other young Khmer communists in Paris began to perceive Sihanouk's absolute monarchy as authoritarian. Saloth Sar wrote a polemical article calling for the elimination of the monarchy. Sihanouk was furious, and cut off scholarship funds. Saloth Sar returned to Phnom Penh in 1953 to join the Indochinese Communist Party and take charge of the newly emerging Kampuchean People's Revolutionary Party. The focus of his anger was French colonial presence and Sihanouk's authoritarianism in the 1950s, and he would oppose U.S. intervention in Vietnam, Cambodia and Laos in the 1960s and 1970s.

The prince, previously labelled "comical" and "exotic," suddenly turned independence-minded. On a visit to France in February 1953, Sihanouk told French President Vincent Auriol that many Cambodians did not feel any loyalty towards the French flag, adding that he himself had been faithful to France. From there, Sihanouk travelled to Canada, the United States and Japan, raising the question of his country's future, and complaining about French reluctance to loosen its grip. On returning home, Sihanouk openly demanded independence. Sihanouk later recollected in his memoirs that French President Charles de Gaulle was "one of the few Frenchmen who understood that my affection for France was deep and sincere and in no way contradicted by my fierce determination to gain Cambodia's independence from France."[14] In a display of annoyance, Sihanouk went into exile in Thailand, and refused to communicate with French officials. In June, he announced a royal crusade for independence. The French, fighting a bitter war in Vietnam, did not wish to risk another conflict in Cambodia, and ultimately relented, granting independence to Cambodia in

November 1953. Sihanouk's non-violent campaign had triumphed. From then on he saw himself as another Mohandas Gandhi, who only a few years earlier had won India its independence from the British in a non-violent manner.

Sihanouk then plunged headlong into politics. He abdicated the throne in favour of his father, Norodom Suramarit, in March 1955 to pursue an ambitious political agenda. The very next month he created his political party, the Sangkum Reastr Niyum, marking the beginning of the Sangkum era, a period of plenty, with farmers reporting bumper harvests, and Sihanouk personally laying the foundations of industry.

On the political front, Sihanouk's police launched a campaign of terror against Pol Pot's communists, whom the French-speaking Sihanouk derisively labelled the *"Khmers rouges,"* or Red Khmers. Pol Pot would later find inspiration in Mao Zedong's brand of communism, and would seek to recreate the Maoist model in Cambodia through class struggle, and agrarian reforms.

Sihanouk saw himself as a proud nationalist, and put his country on a collision course with the United States. He openly provided support to Ho Chi Minh's Viet Minh forces, which were battling U.S. troops in South Vietnam. In 1965, he allowed the Viet Minh to travel across Cambodia over what came to be known as the Sihanouk Trail, a system of roads and tracks that—together with the larger Ho Chi Minh Trail—was used by North Vietnam and the Vietcong to transport supplies to their guerrilla fighters battling U.S. and Saigon regime troops in South Vietnam. U.S. officials frowned upon this strategy that sabotaged the U.S. war effort in Vietnam. Sihanouk's support for the Vietnamese revolutionaries also alienated an influential group of Cambodian politicians that was growing increasingly close to Washington. Sihanouk explained his fraternising with the Viet Minh and the Vietcong: "My own militant support for the Vietcong was, on the contrary, no mere gesture. I granted them safeholds on the Cambodia–South Vietnam border and ordered my army to transport Chinese and Soviet arms from Sihanoukville [port in southern Cambodia] to the Vietcong bases."[15]

Sihanouk's anti-Western proclivity had become evident when he cut off diplomatic relations with two of Washington's strongest Asian allies—Thailand and South Vietnam—in 1961 and 1963, respectively. Three months after breaking with Saigon, Sihanouk rejected U.S. aid in November, and went on to write scathing anti-U.S. editorials in his journal, *Kambuja Monthly Illustrated Review*, arguing eloquently in favour of his country's neutrality. By 1964, U.S. and South Vietnamese forces launched attacks on Cambodian villages, with the result that Cambodia's diplomatic relations with the United States were ruptured in May 1965, and its neutrality lay in tatters. By 1969, the United States had begun secret bombings of suspected North Vietnamese sanctuaries inside Cambodia. New evidence released by President Bill Clinton has shown that the United States bombed Cambodia more heavily between 1964 and 1975 than previously believed.[16]

Against the backdrop of thousands of Cambodians dying in U.S. bombing raids, Sihanouk left for France for his annual holiday in January 1970. By this time, his political adversaries within Cambodia, such as Sisowath Sirik Matak and others within the military, had begun plotting against him. In Sihanouk's absence, Matak and a few army officers visited the house of Prime Minister Lon Nol and, at pistol point, ordered him to support a vote in parliament to overthrow Sihanouk the next day. The coup was launched like clockwork on March 18. The national assembly voted 86–3 to remove Sihanouk, agreeing unanimously that it lacked confidence in his governance. Lon Nol stayed on as prime minister, with Matak as deputy. The new Republican government instantly won recognition and financial aid from Washington.[17]

The new Khmer Republic resumed diplomatic relations with Thailand and South Vietnam in May 1970. Out in the jungles,

the Khmer Rouge aimed to use the global stature of Sihanouk—
in exile in Beijing—to overthrow the Lon Nol regime and rein-
state Sihanouk as the rightful ruler. In April 1973, Sihanouk visited
zones controlled by the Khmer Rouge, who were fighting the forces
of Lon Nol on many fronts. The Khmer Rouge revolution was
spreading across the country, with more and more areas coming
under their control. In anticipation of the advance of the Khmer
Rouge into Phnom Penh, the U.S. embassy was hastily shut down
on April 12, 1975. The Khmer Rouge entered Phnom Penh on April
17. Massacres began on the first day and continued for almost four
years. At the end, the death toll was estimated at 1.7 million to
two million innocent Cambodians. The Khmer Rouge permitted
Sihanouk to return to Phnom Penh in December 1975, where he
remained virtually under palace arrest, and unaware that his Khmer
Rouge friends had evacuated cities, banned money, and turned the
country into a concentration camp.

It was in this vitiated atmosphere, with Cambodians killing one
another, that Hun Sen grew up. Unable to pay for his education,
his parents sent him to school in Phnom Penh. The child was an
ardent admirer of Sihanouk, and was deeply pained when he was
removed in a coup. When Sihanouk called upon his countrymen in
1970 to rise up and join the movement to overthrow Lon Nol, Hun
Sen responded. He gave up his studies, and went into the jungle to
enlist in the Khmer Rouge, unaware of its murderous intent. Hun
Sen eventually broke ranks with the Khmer Rouge in 1977, and
defected to Vietnam, where he was initially kept prisoner. Later,
he sought Vietnamese help to fight Pol Pot, whose inhuman regime
was toppled at last in 1979.

This book contains the untold story of Hun Sen. It is also
the story of a country that fell victim to Cold War politics that
conspired to create the conditions, first, for the Khmer Rouge to
come to power, and then for a strongman like Hun Sen to rise
from obscurity, overthrow the genocidal regime, and take control

of his war-ravaged country. With Hun Sen tightening his grip, the country became stable by degrees, with investors reporting that never before had business confidence been so high. When the old cancers of corruption and crime proved difficult to remove, Hun Sen warned his own partymen to change their ways, or risk being sacked. Clearly, Hun Sen aimed to build a transparent and economically prosperous Cambodia. Ironically, the most formidable stumbling blocks to his vision were the influential politicians and powerful civil servants within his own government. Hun Sen had succeeded in preventing the return of the Khmer Rouge and had ensured stability, but he would be criticised by many Cambodians for failing to stem the growth of corruption within the government, and for adopting an authoritarian form of governance.

I

DAYS IN THE KOMPONG

AND THE PAGODA

1952–70

TUOL KROSANG VILLAGE would never be quite the same again. The little-known hamlet near Takhmau city, home to rice farmers and swarms of egrets, was aflutter with the arrival of birds of a different kind. When Hun Sen moved into his country home right next door in 1989, the tiny settlement was alarmed by roaring helicopter engines and the sound of soldiers setting up camp. Through gaps in the rows of flowering *krosang* trees and the groves of mango, banana, and palm, the villagers watched the ungainly aircraft lift off and touch down at helipads far beyond the marshes. They knew that neighbour Hun Sen had come to stay.

They were bewildered at the rapid rise of this poor *kompong* boy. Regarding him with a curious mixture of fear and reverence, they knew he was now stronger than ever, and were grateful to him for liberating them from the genocidal Khmer Rouge, who had starved, tortured, and killed about 1.7 million Cambodians during their four-year rule in the mid-1970s.

How did Hun Sen see his role in Cambodia? "Among strong students I was strong," Hun Sen told the authors in mid-1998, a year after he overthrew his co-premier First Prime Minister Norodom Ranariddh, a son of King Norodom Sihanouk. "Among strong soldiers I was strong. Now, among strongmen I am strong." Picking up a copy of *Time* magazine with a cover picture of President Suharto of Indonesia, another Southeast Asian strongman with whom he was often compared, he affirmed with a grin: "He's gone. I am still here." Long before Suharto was toppled from power, Hun Sen had voiced his innermost desire: "I want to develop my country like the other Southeast Asian strongmen did."

The Cambodian strongman, sixty-one years old in 2013, was born neither into great wealth, nor into power. After his family lost its modest wealth he was no different from a poor village child. His parents did not plan for his future and would have been happy to see him become a rice farmer.

CHILD OF THE FULL MOON

It was at midnight under a full moon on Tuesday, August 5, 1952, that Hun Sen was born.[1] His mother gave birth in their home in Peam Koh Sna village in the district of Stung Trang in Kompong Cham province, along the Mekong River—his maternal grandmother was a midwife who had delivered all the children in the family. "We should correct my birth date," Hun Sen said during an interview with the authors. "It has been wrongly mentioned in the media as April 4, 1951." He revealed that he had concealed his true age when he was in his twenties, in order to pass for older.[2]

"According to Cambodian belief children born in the year of the dragon, especially on Tuesday, are very stubborn." In later life his stubbornness and, equally, his resilience confirmed the accuracy of ancient Khmer beliefs.

Blessed with the mighty river, the province of Kompong Cham was the rice bowl of a very poor and very wet country. People there made their living off the river, or by farming. He waded through country roads during the rainy season when the village was flooded. His family lived in a typical open-plan Khmer-style home: a wooden structure built on stilts and divided into three areas—two living spaces, and an area for cooking.

His parents named him Bunall, or Nal for short. "They tried

61

to find a name for me that bore a close rhythm to the name of my father," he explained. "My father's name was Hun Neang so they named me Hun Nal. Also, when I was born I was rather fat, and according to rural custom when a boy is fat he is called Nal." Four decades later, people in the village would still call him by his childhood name.

When the teenager left home to study in Phnom Penh, his name was changed a second time. He was variously called Sen and Ritthi Sen. In an ancient Khmer story, Ritthi Sen was a boy who suffered at the hands of eleven stepmothers.

He changed his name a third time when he became a guerrilla in 1970. "When I took to the jungle I did not use the name Sen or Bunall," he clarified. "Instead, I used the name Hun Samrach. 'Samrach' means one who completes all his life's work. But for me this name was inauspicious. I was wounded many times while bearing this name."

After completing an intelligence mission in Kompong Cham in 1972, he abandoned his old names and decided to adopt the name Hun Sen. The habit of changing names ran in the family. His two older brothers, Hun Long San and Hun Long Neng, had both dropped their middle names. Besides them, Hun Sen had three younger sisters—Sengny, Sinath and Thoeun—all of whom lived through terrible times. "One older brother died even before I was born," he said. A hint of long-suppressed grief now clouded his face.

Hun Sen's father, Hun Neang, had entered the monkhood as a young man, a rite of passage for many Cambodians. In 1945, when the Japanese took over all the military command positions in Cambodia, temporarily eliminating French control following their invasion of Indochina in 1941, he had lived as a Buddhist monk in the pagoda of Unalong in Kompong Cham and had been a disciple of a holy man named Samdech Chunnat. After leaving the monkhood, he joined the Khmer Issarak, a revolutionary movement launched by two former Khmer monks that sought to create an independent Khmer state after expelling France from Cambodia with diplomatic assistance of Thailand.

The family suffered a blow when a group of Issarak members kidnapped Hun Sen's grandmother for ransom, knowing that Hun Sen's grandfather was rich. The family was forced to sell its property to pay off the kidnappers. Hun Sen's grandmother was released without being harmed, but life became more difficult as the family had lost most of its land. Desperately in need of money to support the family, Hun Neang now quit the Issarak—he had felt betrayed and angered by the kidnapping—and joined the government as a militiaman. He was trained by the French, and led his troops to attack the Issarak. After Cambodia became independent in 1953, he became the chief of a self-defence force in his commune. "He had the blood of a soldier," Hun Sen said of his father, with pride in his eyes.

Hun Sen's mother, Dee Yon, was a housewife. All she could write was her own name and the names of her husband and their six children, but she had a good head for mathematics. Her mother, Hun Sen's grandmother, exerted tremendous influence over the family, and having acquired working knowledge of local laws was able to advise the local people on their legal problems. His maternal grandparents were relatively poor, but they had good standing in rural society. In contrast, his paternal grandparents owned substantial tracts of land, but they too had become poorer.

Living amid poverty and sickness, the child Hun Sen learned the art of survival. He spent six years studying at the Peam Koh Sna Primary School in the village. The lack of a high school in the village left his parents with no choice but to send him to Phnom Penh to study at the Lycée Indra Dhevi from 1965 to 1969. "I did not finish my high school studies, but later I did complete my study programmes by learning while continuing to work part-time," he explained. "I enjoyed studies very much."

He excelled in mathematics after being coached by his mother, and developed a fondness for Khmer literature. At school, he immersed himself in Cambodian poetry—especially verse by Preah Bat Ang Duong—the teachings of Krom Ngoy, and books on education written by Tiv Ol. He was moved by the sheer power of sentimental stories such as *Kolap Pailin* (Pailin Rose), *Phkar Srapoan* (A Faded Flower), Tum Teav's *Romeo and Juliet*, and ancient works such as the Hindu epic, *Ramayana*, translated into Khmer as the *Reamker*. He read with pleasure the works of Preah Chinavong, Preah Thinnavong, Luong Preah Sdech Kan, and the Cambodian *sastras*, which were ancient stories written on palm leaves. He did not have a taste for popular movies, with the exception of film adaptations of ancient Khmer stories. A keen sportsman, he liked athletics and volleyball, and continued playing when he became prime minister.

Even as a teenager Hun Sen had a sharp political mind, an instinct that developed prematurely, even precociously, owing to the widening social and economic inequalities in Cambodian society. As a child, he respected and admired the chief of state Prince Sihanouk, but he hated the corrupt officials and members of parliament. "These people never went to the villages to get in touch with the people, nor did they keep the promises they made during the election campaigns," he said disapprovingly. As a boy, he deeply mistrusted the rich and the powerful. "I hated the impudent children who came from families that had authority and wealth, and who despised the poor. They did not read their textbooks, and were not good at studies, yet they always passed the examinations," he said.

NOT TOO FAR AWAY, yet worlds apart from Hun Sen's village, a little girl was growing up in Rokarkhnau village in the Kroch Chhmar district of Kompong Cham. As sunbeams caught the treetops covering the little hillock bordering picturesque Rokarkhnau, making the frail tributary of the Rokarkhnau River gleam like a narrow sheet of silver, a seven-year-old girl could be spotted skipping over the stones on the riverbed. Like most children, whenever she got the opportunity, the fair-skinned Khmer girl kicked up her heels in the shallow waters of the little stream.

"My school was a half-hour walk from the house," Bun Rany told the authors. "During the dry season we would wade in ankle-deep water, or walk across the river bed." In the rainy season, she would have to wait to be ferried to school in a flimsy dinghy.

It was the summer of 1961. As she neared the door of her father's farmhouse, little Bun Rany could hear the *trey kahor* fish sizzle in the family pot, with the spicy aroma of *pra hok* filling the house. She could almost see the reassuring smile on her grandmother's face as she ladled out the rice and fried fish. The anticipation of drinking the cool water of the family well made Bun Rany walk a little faster. She was glad she was nearly home. It had been a long day at school, and an opponent had dug her elbow deep into little Bun Rany's ribs at basketball practice. "I liked all the subjects in school," she recalled. "But I liked to play basketball a lot."

The district of Kroch Chhmar was a fairly prosperous one, with most farmers, like Bun Rany's father Lynn Kry, living comfortably off the yields of the fertile land. Here she grew up along with her two brothers and three sisters. The Chinese-Khmer family traced its ancestry to Canton in China, and had integrated smoothly into Cambodian society.

Hun Sen would not meet Bun Rany for several years, but his world would change the day he saw her.

PAGODA BOY

Standing on the windblown jetty at Kompong Cham, Hun Sen, now thirteen and about to depart for the Lycée Indra Dhevi, hugged his mother desperately, and said goodbye with a sinking feeling. Tears flowed on both sides. She had hurriedly put twelve riels into his pocket—worth thirty-four U.S. cents—and given him a small packet of rice that was knotted into his *krama.* The only clothes he took with him were the ones he was wearing. Her heart cried out for the boy. There was little she could do for him. The family had lost its wealth, and its land. They could barely afford to pay his school entrance fees in Phnom Penh. They could not rent a small room for him, or pay for his meals. They were forced to entrust their bright little boy to the care of Buddhist monks at the Neakavoan Pagoda in Phnom Penh.

The boat slowly pulled away and headed downstream and out of sight of his waving mother, taking the boy to his new life in Phnom Penh—then, as always, a city of wealth and poverty, of silk and open drains.

All alone on the boat, with only his *krama* for comfort, the young Hun Sen could not help thinking about the lives of many of his schoolmates, who were well looked after by their parents. He felt terribly let down by Prince Sihanouk's government, which had not, as his parents explained to him, provided a high school in Kompong Cham, forcing him to be separated from his family, and sending him far downriver to a life of hardship and deprivation. At that time, unknown to the boy, Sihanouk's Royal Palace came alive every night with champagne parties, and the city's elite jived in the dancehalls, while the great mass of people led lives huddled around their bowls of rice and dried fish.

In darkness, the boat pulled into a jetty in Phnom Penh. It was 3 a.m. The passengers went home by cyclo, but Hun Sen walked from the riverside to the pagoda so he could save three riels.

It was fortunate that education was almost free at the Lycée Indra Dhevi. "We paid only for chalk and for sports. But when we enrolled at the school we had to pay 1,800 riels," Hun Sen said. "It was very difficult for poor children to enter school because 1,800 riels was equal to US$51, which was a lot of money." The Cambodian riel was fairly strong against the U.S. dollar during Sihanouk's rule. From 1958 to 1968, one U.S. dollar was worth thirty-five riels, according to the Statistical Yearbook for Asia/Far East, 1969.[3] During the Lon Nol regime, in November 1971, the National Bank of Cambodia devalued the riel by 150 per cent.

The boy's day at the Neakavoan Pagoda began at 5 a.m, except during examinations, when he and the other pagoda boys had to rise at 4 a.m. First, he cooked rice porridge for the monks, and then read his textbooks. He sometimes read his lessons while stirring the porridge, since time was precious. After that, he swept the compound of the pagoda where two huge trees constantly shed leaves and flowers. "Sometimes I was punished because of these two big trees," he said in a mildly complaining tone. "When I took the porridge to the monks they always looked across the compound to check if I had swept it or not. If a lot of leaves and flowers fell from the trees I would be punished."

He walked to school at 6.30 a.m., taking with him several empty rice bowls, and left school early on the days when it was his turn to collect food in the streets for the monks. The pagoda boys came under pressure to beg quickly for food from door to door because the monks insisted on eating before noon. "Some monks did not understand the suffering of the others," he gently complained. "Sometimes I was punished by the monks if I brought the food late. If I brought the food before noon they would eat and talk cheerfully, but I also felt very hungry." To keep the monks in good humour he tried to bring in the food as close to midday as possible, so that they could eat on time. After they had eaten their fill the boys were given the leftovers. Then they washed the bowls, and it was time to return to school.

In the afternoon the boys fetched water from Kampuchea Krom Street, carrying it in large jars all the way to the pagoda. They found it very difficult to lift the heavy jars. By the time they finished their work for the day it was as late as 7 p.m. Afterwards, they chanted Buddhist prayers. The ritual was performed twice a day, in the morning while cooking porridge, and at night before retiring.

The pagoda boys did not have the luxury of relaxing on Sundays. The monks ate every day, and the boys had to collect food seven days a week. On Sundays they had to collect food early. And it was on Sundays that Hun Sen learned to play chess when he stopped over at a barber's shop on his rounds. The barber, who donated food to the monks, provided a chessboard for his waiting customers. Hun Sen joined them in the queue. "I learnt chess by looking at other people playing," he said.

Back at the pagoda, the boys were mere pawns in a simple hierarchy. They were not given rooms. There were, in fact, no rooms in the pagoda, in accordance with Khmer tradition. "I slept in a mobile manner," Hun Sen recollected. "Where there was a vacant space, I took it. When it was cold I slept in the space under a monk's bed to keep warm. When there were mosquitoes we asked the monks to let their mosquito nets drape below the bed so we would be protected." The boys dreaded the monsoon nights when it rained long and hard. "We had to find a dry place to sleep, a place that did not leak," he said without regret. "When we were young we could sleep anywhere."

Life at the pagoda came as a shock to Hun Sen, whose paternal great-grandparents had been rich. They owned about fifteen hectares of land and property in Kompong Cham, but lost some of it in massive erosion along the Mekong River. The financial losses compelled them to leave their village, and move to a village close to where Hun Sen's family lived. The sudden change in the family's fortunes, combined with the lack of schools in Kompong Cham, made life very difficult for him. Widespread poverty had forced thousands of children to leave home, and lead isolated lives in the capital's pagodas. "I am now determined to build more schools— more than any other Cambodian—because I do not want our children to share the same fate as I," Hun Sen declared in 1998 as he looked back at his childhood. "I hated the regimes at that time, even the regime of Sihanouk. It was a regime of injustice that often cheated the people by buying their votes. At the time my father was a propagandist for a politician, but when the politician was elected as a member of parliament he did nothing for the people."

Hun Sen did not wear saffron robes, did not shave his head, and was not ordained. One of his close friends was Ea Samnang, who lived in the same pagoda. The two were friends even though Samnang was twenty and Hun Sen was fourteen. Samnang recalled that one day, just for fun, Hun Sen borrowed a cyclo and a hat from a cyclo driver, and rode the cyclo around the pagoda. But he lost the hat. When he was told to pay thirty riels to its owner, he fetched his clay piggybank, which was full of small coins. "He had to break his piggybank," Samnang laughed. Samnang studied at the Lycée Sangkum Reastr Niyum—a school named after Sihanouk's regime—and later became a teacher at the Bak Touk High School in Phnom Penh. He recounted that Hun Sen's mother visited him at the pagoda frequently. "She would tell us to study hard because we were poor." After Hun Sen became prime minister, Ea Samnang went to a public meeting at the Olympic Stadium in Phnom Penh where Hun Sen was attending a ceremony. He sent a note up to Hun Sen with his name on it. The prime minister saw the note, and invited his childhood friend to his residence. "I went to his house, and we talked about the old days," Ea Samnang said appreciatively. "He remembered how a friend of ours broke his leg playing football at the pagoda."

Another pagoda boy, Chhim You Teck, who shared the same holy residence with Hun Sen, remembered him as an "ordinary child, who worked very hard, walking from house to house to collect food." Hun Sen said that he knew Chhim You Teck and his family very well, and that they lived on the other side of the Mekong River. Hun Sen was one of eight boys given the task of collecting food. Their expeditions usually yielded simple goodies such as sour soup, fish, and bananas. Chhim You Teck said animatedly: "I was in charge of the boys, and I used to wait for them to return with the food. I would then collect it, and offer it to the monks." The boys did not like to bathe, Chhim You Teck said. "They were too small to draw water from the well," he added genially. "So I used to draw the water and force them to bathe." In their spare hours the pagoda boys happily played the game of *beth pouk*, a Cambodian version of hide-and-seek, oblivious to the terrible times that lay ahead.

At school, Hun Sen was considered a good student, and wrote letters of application, even love letters, for family and friends. Path Sam, a former teacher at the Lycée Indra Dhevi, said that he had heard one of Hun Sen's teachers commenting that he was a "clever boy, but very quiet." In 1969, however, Hun Sen quit school before completing his final high school examination. "I left because of the happenings in the pagoda," he said portentously. Sihanouk's secret agents had entered the pagoda between 1967 and 1969, and rounded up people suspected of harbouring anti-Sihanouk views, he revealed. "One of my cousins, Neu Kean, was arrested, and I was afraid I would have to leave the pagoda," Hun Sen added in a low tone suggestive of impending calamity. "Eventually I had to leave, but I always wanted to return to the pagoda."

"But the coup d'etat [in which Sihanouk was overthrown] happened on March 18, 1970, and I could not return." That singular event transformed the pagoda boy into a guerrilla. While at school he had wanted to be a teacher when he grew up. But after he joined the national liberation front led by Sihanouk in 1970 he changed his mind: he now wanted to be a pilot. "My aspirations and dreams had to be abandoned due to the war and the genocidal regime," he said without bitterness. "Political events altered my desires, compelling me to enter politics, which I did not want to do. I led a rough life, full of suffering and the pain of separation caused by living far from my parents since childhood." After witnessing the horrors of war as a teenager, he consciously adopted the life of a revolutionary. "I was shocked by the acts of aggression and the bombing of Cambodia carried out by the United States and South Vietnam," he said in quiet anger. His Buddhist upbringing and fondness for religion were set aside in the pursuit of a political cause. He wanted nothing more than to restore Sihanouk to power. "I took to the forest because I saw the clouds of civil war gathering on the horizon," he said with finality.

OVER IN KROCH CHHMAR, Bun Rany was living the carefree life of a child, happily unaware of the coming conflict, or the existence of Hun Sen.

"I had two brothers and three sisters, and I remember my childhood as a very happy one," Bun Rany said buoyantly as she delved back in time. "There was no fear, and we all seemed a pretty normal bunch. I did not see my grandparents on my father's side, but my grandparents on my mother's side were very much around. They died in 1970. They chatted a lot to me, and, without my even knowing it, very gently they taught me how to live in the Cambodian way, the traditional way. Their influence on me was substantial. Their advice was not to play too much and work hard on the lessons. And of course, they always encouraged us to help my parents with housework. Their advice saw me through much of the hardship I was to suffer later in life." It would turn out to be a troubled young life. "It seems to me now, the most precious lessons I put to use in my life were the ones taught to me by my grandparents," she said gratefully.

II

DEEP INSIDE THE MAQUIS

1970–77

HE STUFFED A SMALL BAG with a few shirts and a pair of old shoes, and reported at a jungle base to enlist in the maquis—the grand-sounding resistance movement started by Sihanouk after he was overthrown by General Lon Nol in the coup d'etat of March 1970. The movement, officially known as the National United Front for Kampuchea (*Front uni national du Kampuchea,* or FUNK), was joined by patriotic Cambodians, who lived in the jungle and waged war against the coup leaders in an attempt to restore Sihanouk to power. The maquis also teamed up with Vietnamese and Laotian communists to struggle against "U.S. imperialism" in Indochina. The Cambodian nationalists borrowed the word "*maquis*" from the French Resistance, who were named after the underbrush and thickets, or *maquis,* that grew in Europe and served as cover as they fought the German occupation forces in the Second World War. They transplanted an essentially French idea from thousands of miles away into an Asian country, where it took root among francophone Cambodians.

GUERRILLA

Penniless and angry, Hun Sen was ripe for the picking. He sensed the onrush of war clouds when Sihanouk was overthrown. He saw in their dark eddies a bleak future for himself. With hardly any incentive to attend school, he abandoned his studies and went into the jungle to become a guerrilla. He was eighteen. He entered the maquis for the same reasons that young men had joined standing armies in centuries past: to escape a life of poverty and unemployment, and to fight for a national cause. He wanted to overthrow the Lon Nol regime that had recently toppled Sihanouk—he had grown to admire Sihanouk's efforts to build an urban industry, in spite of his failure to provide education and healthcare in the rural areas, and his inability to orchestrate the agricultural green revolution the farmers pined for but were unable to achieve, owing to a lack of modern techniques. On April 14, 1970, less than a month after Sihanouk's removal, Hun Sen had become a member of the resistance. "I joined the maquis during the Cambodian New Year," he said, gathering his memories and his premonitions of life ahead. "I did not know what a soldier's life in the maquis would be like. So, I brought along a bag containing shoes and clothes like a person who lives in the city."[1] Before long, he had a new life in the jungle as a member of the maquis. What he did not know was that Pol Pot and his Communist Party of Kampuchea (CPK), or the "*Khmers rouges*," as Sihanouk called them, were the leaders of the maquis.

One of the first steps he took was to change his name to Hun Samrach in order to disguise his identity. Two years later the twenty-year-old, by then a crack commando, changed his name again, this time to Hun Sen.

As he faithfully served the organisation he began to realise that it was under the complete control of the Khmer Rouge. Unperturbed by the Khmer Rouge's bizarre regulations, their pathological mistrust of the Cambodian people, and their strictness, Hun Sen worked hard, trained hard, and rapidly climbed the ranks. "Not many people from the city or from places of high culture joined the maquis," Hun Sen explained. "So, in the maquis I was called *lo kru*," meaning teacher or guru, even though he was one of the youngest soldiers in his group. He quickly earned the respect of his colleagues in the area where he carried out his covert activities. He attracted the attention of his leaders, who noticed that he spent much of his time teaching the illiterate guerrillas, and making friends. "This is because besides being a soldier, I was, in a way, an author and an actor," he said. "I was like an author who writes the story, and also like an actor who acts out the story."

In the depths of the jungle, time hung heavily on him. He spent much of it contemplating the future of his family and his country. He was alarmed at the deep divisions in society. He viewed with dark humour the manner in which Sihanouk had conveniently colour-coded the Cambodians into five factions in the mid-1960s: (1) The Red Khmers were the communist Khmers (the Khmer Rouge); (2) the Blue Khmers were the members of the Free Khmer movement (Khmer Serei), who were anti-Sihanouk, anti-communist, and pro-United States; (3) the White Khmers contained elements of the Free Khmers, but were closer to South Vietnam and Thailand; (4) the Pink Khmers were the progressives who leaned slightly to the political left, but who did not take to the forest; and (5) the Khmers in power till 1970 were the members of Sihanouk's Sangkum Reastr Niyum (SRN) regime, whose flag colours were blue and red. After Sihanouk was overthrown, both the Blue Khmers and the White Khmers cooperated with Lon Nol. Responding to an appeal by Sihanouk to the people, Hun Sen initially joined the Pink Khmers during his years in Phnom Penh.

"Among all these groups I hated the Khmer Rouge the most," Hun Sen said in retrospect. "But Sihanouk supported the Khmer Rouge. In those days they [the leaders of the maquis] did not mention that the Sihanoukist forces were led by the Khmer Rouge. They only said that the entire movement was led by the Sihanoukist forces. At that time, we had no choice. We were hostage to the war. If I had not joined Sihanouk's side, I would have had to join Lon Nol." His early political instincts were correct. Later, when the bloodshed began, he realised that the Sihanoukist forces were, in fact, led by the Khmer Rouge.

JUST WHEN HUN SEN was preparing to join the Sihanoukist forces, a sixteen-year-old girl's life was about to undergo a sweeping change.

"It was my seventh year in high school, and it was a year I will not forget," Bun Rany recollected. "My grandparents died that year. It was a terrible blow to me. And then there was the coup d'etat, which interrupted my education. It was as if my entire life changed overnight. The ousting of Prince Sihanouk by Lon Nol made a deep impact on our young minds. We were all rebels with a cause and, for the sake of liberating Cambodia, I joined the maquis. In April 1970, I was answering Prince Sihanouk's call to join the movement to liberate Cambodia from the Lon Nol regime."

At first, she kept her plans to herself. She knew that if her parents guessed she was anywhere near the maquis they would have been very annoyed. "A lot of people joined the maquis from our village," she said. Her voice dropping to a whisper, she added: "In our neighbourhood there were two of us who did not tell our parents that we were joining the maquis. I was one of them."

A day later, Bun Rany's parents discovered that she may have joined the maquis. They followed her into the jungle. "But they could not reach the spot we were in because it was very deep in the jungle—about two or three kilometres," she said, reconstructing the past with precision. "There, for the first time, I met the local cadres who were under the command of the Angkar [the political bureau of the central committee of the CPK, led by Pol Pot]. The Angkar welcomed us."

After joining the maquis, the recruits were asked which part of the organisation they wished to contribute to. The leaders told them that they would be trained in the area they chose. Their attitude in the early days was gentle and very persuasive, Bun Rany said. She opted for medical training. She was trained by doctors who had come from Phnom Penh to lecture the fresh recruits. After six months, the recruits were sent back to the district of Kroch

Chhmar to look after the needy and the sick.

"The good thing was that while we were getting theoretical training, we were also encouraged to be hands-on, and we got to see the practical side of how to heal and care for the wounded," she explained. "Simultaneously, we were trained to be midwives. And after six months' training, we were given the title of public health officers."

When she joined the maquis, Bun Rany had made it a point to get acquainted with as many people as she could. "Slowly, as I began to realise that in order to survive I would need all the support I could muster, it became second nature for me to network," she said. It seemed to work for her in the beginning. The person in charge of the district appeared to care for her, and referred to her as "daughter."

Bun Rany worked at the hospital for five years before the Khmer Rouge management made her the director of that establishment. It was a formula that worked for the Angkar. Catching them young meant they could be brainwashed quickly and easily. It was the fourteen-to-twenty-four-year-old, fresh-faced, easily inspired youth that could be persuaded to kill, maim, and torture for a cause. The responsibility thrust on Bun Rany made her feel proud, but it challenged her a great deal as well. More than two decades later the overflow of self-confidence was visible as she gathered the memories of the years gone by. "I headed all the general fields of medicine," she said with pride. She had managed to attain a high rank without a formal degree, or even graduating from high school. As she rewound the twenty eventful years to her youth, her voice became tremulous. A quiver of a smile hovered around her mouth. It was another world.

Spurred by nationalistic idealism she was one of thousands of young people who gave up a normal life, a regular job, an education, a family, liberal thought, in fact all freedom, to join the mass movement so well orchestrated by the Angkar—who had successfully sold these starry-eyed youths an empty dream. Life in the maquis was getting to be more and more regimented. Slowly, the patriotic song was beginning to sound like a wake-up bugle in a prison cell. The Khmer Rouge considered women with long hair to be representatives of a bourgeois elite who looked down upon the peasants that formed the core of Pol Pot's revolution. "In 1970, when I first joined the maquis I had long hair. [But] during that time [the Khmer Rouge period] no girl was allowed to keep long hair," she said ruefully about the authoritarian system.

"At the time no one was given any wages," she said plainly and without regret. "Currency was never used in our area, and the maquis provided everything for us to live on. We did not realise from 1970 to 1975 that there was the Angkar ruling everything in our area. It was only in 1975, just after the liberation of Phnom Penh that we realised that the country was divided into regions. After the takeover of Phnom Penh in 1975, the people from other parts of the country were not allowed to come to Phnom Penh." As a result, Bun Rany was separated from her family. When she first joined the maquis she had often taken leave and returned to her family for a few days. But now, suddenly, all leave was cancelled.

It was as if the organisation had turned into a demonic cult. The recruits who had joined it voluntarily to restore Sihanouk to power were shocked and dismayed at the brutality. Some senior commanders refused to follow orders because they vehemently opposed the gratuitous cruelty. Others did what they were told. Bun Rany wanted to run away. But there was no place to hide from the Angkar. She stayed to see tragedy unfold before her eyes.

ROMANCING REBELS

It was a rough life deep in the canopy of the jungle, where danger lurked in dank trenches, time hung as still as fishing nets put out to dry along the waterways, and loneliness gnawed at the young guerrillas. Separated from his family, Hun Sen craved to be loved and cared for. Romance became the forte, even refuge, of the young man who had left home, and who now sought the affections of female guerrillas. But the Angkar frowned upon the pursuit of romance. Young guerrillas were prohibited from developing relationships with the opposite sex. "When I say that I was popular with any girl I do not mean that I had a love affair with her," Hun Sen said somewhat defensively. "It was just a normal friendship which I still cherish till today."

An old, faded photograph of a callow nineteen-year-old Hun Sen was discovered in 1997—the only photograph of him that survived the civil war. It had been preserved by a family in Kompong Cham. In it, the teenager looks lean and handsome. It is clear why young Khmer women were attracted to him. But he did not develop any serious relationships until he met Bun Rany. She was the director of a Khmer Rouge hospital, located about fifty kilometres from the line of fighting against the forces of Lon Nol. The wounded and sick soldiers under Hun Sen's command were sent there for treatment. They playfully addressed her as *sau*, or sister-in-law.

Bun Rany remembered the summer of 1974 as a particularly dry one, with the earth parched over like a jigsaw puzzle. Red dust, like crumbled vermilion, stained the clothes, blinded the eyes, and filled the nostrils. Drifting back to 1974, the year of romance, Bun Rany said exuberantly: "Hun Sen's band of followers played the matchmaking game to perfection. When they met Hun Sen they told him that the beautiful lady director of the hospital sends her regards, and when they met me they said that Hun Sen had sent his regards." Hun Sen and Bun Rany were left completely in the dark about what was going on. Hun Sen's soldiers wanted them to get married someday when the war ended. The unspoken, incipient romance soon became known to two of Hun Sen's "jungle sisters," female Khmer Rouge soldiers who lived nearby. Hun Sen added: "My sisters started addressing her as *sau* as well. It posed a problem for me to maintain discipline among the soldiers."

PHOTO COURTESY OF HUN SEN

Nineteen-year-old Hun Sen with a pistol at his hip and an ammunition pouch clipped to his belt. This 1971 photograph, taken one year after he joined the Khmer Rouge, survived miraculously: it was kept safe by a farmer in Kompong Cham who presented it to Hun Sen in 1997. "This is the only picture where I had my two eyes," Hun Sen told the authors. He lost his left eye in combat in 1975.

It was a year of living dangerously and of secret courtship for the pretty Khmer Rouge hospital director. "The first time I learnt about Hun Sen was in 1974. His 'jungle brothers' used to come and stay in the hospital and they seemed to like me. It was they who began to fancy being the liaison between him and me. In the hospital I was the director, but in the battlefield Hun Sen was a very famous soldier," she said with characteristic pragmatism. "He belonged to a prestigious special unit. So in a way, we were equally matched, and people had a tendency to pair us together." Whispers reached both parties' ears, and each wanted to get to the bottom of the mystery. The hide-and-seek game finally ended when Bun Rany got her chance to send a message directly to her unseen lover through a health officer from her hospital, who had been sent to the battlefield to take care of the soldiers under Hun Sen's command. "I asked this health official to request Hun Sen to come and see me personally, and solve the mystery of the messages being passed back and forth," Bun Rany explained. "But I must say I feared his anger because there was so much implied in these messages from other people."

Till then, Hun Sen had never seen Bun Rany. A silent and mysterious romance charged the air. He could no longer bear the suspense. Just before the Cambodian New Year in 1974, he asked his commander, a woman, to accompany him to meet Bun Rany. He reckoned that he would have easier access to her if he went with a woman. Hun Sen clarified: "I only knew that the chief of the hospital was named Rany, but I did not have enough time to see her." When they arrived at the hospital his commander went to visit a local leader, and Hun Sen was told to wait for her at the hospital. "At the time Rany did not know me and neither did I know her," Hun Sen said. "So I asked her, 'Who is Rany?' She did not tell me the truth, and said that Rany had gone to fetch water. She did not tell me that she was Rany, nor did she know who I was." For her part, Bun Rany said with a smile: "When he met me he wanted to know where Rany was. I told him that she was out somewhere. Afterwards, he came to my living quarters on the first storey of the building, and we sorted things out." That night he knew that he was falling in love. "I thought that if she was so beautiful I should not try to solve the mystery, but just love her. It was fortunate that after the meeting we continued staying there as it was a bit late, and we could not return to our unit." But they had no bedclothes. It was the month of March when the nights were chilly along the Mekong. They were relieved when the local girls brought pillows and blankets for them. With a giggle, Bun Rany said: "The two of them [Hun Sen and his commander] stayed in the hospital. At night we gave them the usual bedding—pillows and blankets—that we provided visitors with. We don't know who took whose blanket, though." It happened that Hun Sen used the blanket that belonged to Bun Rany.

What attracted Bun Rany to Hun Sen? "I've had a great liking for soldiers ever since I was a little girl, and later that feeling grew into a very large envelope of sympathy for the army," she explained. In her years as hospital director, the sight of the hundreds of wounded, tormented men in uniform, some as young as fourteen, left a deep impression on her. "They were so brave in the battle-field," she added admiringly. "And they suffered so many difficulties. I felt a tug in my heart for them."

After that first meeting, Hun Sen lost contact with Bun Rany for several months. He missed her, he said, and suffered in silence. Fortuitously, during the rainy season that year he saw her at Peam Chi Laang commune in Tbong Khmum district in Kompong Cham province. She had come to treat Hun Sen's soldiers who were suffering from malaria. "I met her by chance when I was travelling with three friends, all of whom died later," he recollected. "I was travelling by bicycle, and she was travelling in a car with a group of people from the hospital. In order to be close to her I collected money from my friends and invited her, and her girlfriends, to have breakfast with us. We really enjoyed that meal." Hun Sen was overjoyed to see his beloved. "Some of our friends still paired us off as husband and wife," he said of his romantic dilemma. "It was an old disease. I was concerned about maintaining discipline, and wanted to stop such talk. I wondered what I should do." Bun Rany added with a sigh of relief: "When we'd sorted out all the little glitches between Hun Sen and myself—the details about who was sending love messages to whom—he finally asked the Angkar for permission to marry me."

The Angkar controlled everything, even personal matters of love and marriage, and had turned down many applications. Hun Sen was twenty-two when he applied in 1974. His request stood a good chance of being approved, however, as he was liked by the commanders at all levels. But now that he had filed his application for marriage he had to work even harder to please many more commanders. At the time he headed a special commando force and was also an instructor. His commanders valued him for his abilities and, as expected, they did not turn down his request outright. But they laid down a condition. They asked him to wait until Phnom Penh had been liberated. "I knew that it was a rejection," he complained. "A young man was only allowed to marry at the age of thirty, except the disabled, who could marry before that. But I was not disabled yet. My commander was very clever. He did not reject my request, and only said that I should wait until Phnom Penh was liberated. The situation was not good for Bun Rany and me."

One day before the Khmer Rouge captured Phnom Penh, Hun Sen was struck in his left eye by shrapnel from an artillery shell in Kompong Cham on April 16, 1975, resulting in the loss of sight in that eye. Later, he had an artificial eye fitted at a hospital in Kompong Cham. "According to what he told me, flying shrapnel grazed his left eyebrow and lodged itself in his left eye," Bun Rany explained. Did it bother the attractive young woman that she was going to marry a disabled man who could see with only one eye? "He was in good condition at the time when we planned to marry," Bun Rany said with a laugh. "Ironically, he was wounded only after he made the formal request to marry me. Eventually, that eye had to be removed, but it wasn't at my hospital that we cut out his eye." Hun Sen was actually under the care of his future wife's colleague, who was training to be a health officer.

Bun Rany's commanders, on hearing the news of Hun Sen's plans, tried to block the marriage, and produced another suitor for her. The blatant interference by her commanders shattered Bun Rany, who was deeply in love. "Imagine my horror when, on my return from a short absence, there were arrangements made for me to marry another man," she said in a tone of annoyance. And when Hun Sen found out, he flew into a rage. "That really made him very angry, and he fired a few rounds of ammunition wildly," she added. "This is what he told me after we were married." The Angkar had arranged for the marriage to take place within three days. "As it turned out, he [the new suitor] was the director of a printing house. I went straight to the person in charge of the district, and I told him that he could arrange the marriage with anyone else but not me. I did not want to get married to this man." She encountered new resistance from the most unexpected quarters. "When I refused to get married to this man, the people in charge of the district—the very same people who I thought were my well-wishers, and whom I had known for some time—were extremely angry with me, and they stopped speaking to me," she said with a sigh.

Now Hun Sen approached the district leadership to formally ask for permission to marry Bun Rany. Once again, Bun Rany was wrong in believing that she had the support of those who were responsible for social action—the wing of the Khmer Rouge that was supposed to take care of relationship issues. It was not a decision for the lovers to make. It was a matter for the "teachers" in the Khmer Rouge to deliberate upon. One of them, she explained, was very annoyed: "The particular man who handled the request for our wedding was not happy because he had a 'jungle brother' whom he had nearly fixed me up with. It was as if a business deal had fallen through for him, and he sulked and turned really ugly

83

towards me." On his side, Hun Sen felt totally helpless. His marriage plans had been put on ice by his commanders, and there was nothing he could do about it. "I was very angry because my request had been accepted when I was healthy, but denied when I was disabled," he said, bemoaning the intrusiveness of the Khmer Rouge.

Soon afterwards, his commanders lied to him in order to make him forget Bun Rany. They told him that she was going to marry another man. Hun Sen reacted in anger, and decided to marry another woman. He realised in the nick of time that his commanders had played a trick on him. "Rany was always waiting for me," he explained. "But I was given the wrong information. I acted in haste. I was determined to take revenge and take a wife from the Kroch Chhmar area, which was my mistake. I made a request to marry this other girl who lived near Rany's unit because I could not accept being discredited in this way. But I was criticised by my friends. They told me that Rany was waiting for me. When I realised the truth, I withdrew the request to marry the other girl, and apologised to Bun Rany."

The lovers faced more heartbreak when the commanders pressured Bun Rany to marry yet another man who worked in the Kroch Chhmar district. She refused. Next, the commanders turned on Hun Sen. They asked him to take another woman as his wife, a woman who was twelve years older than him. "That woman was a professor, and she had been told to marry a man with the rank of commander," he said, constructing the terrible episode in fine detail. "She later became a member of the national assembly of the Pol Pot regime and used to speak on Khmer Rouge radio. It was very risky for me to reject that proposal, as it would appear that I did not listen to the Angkar. But I rejected it." Thereafter, he faced yet another matrimonial hurdle. "My commander, named Soeurng, encouraged, and even persuaded me, to marry his daughter," he revealed. "It was even more difficult because it was not normal for a commander to request his staff to marry his daughter. The only way I could reject the offer was by telling him that I considered him to be my father, and his daughter as my sister. By using this approach, he tolerated my reasoning, and I successfully avoided marrying his daughter."

For Bun Rany to have spurned one direct order of her leaders was a dangerous step. Her refusal to follow two consecutive orders to marry men of their choice was an act of extreme provocation. "And Hun Sen's persistence, coupled with my request to marry him, did not help our image with the leaders either," she said with a smile. Eventually, they were able to get married when he turned twenty-four, and she was twenty-two. They could only do so after he had wriggled out of two unwanted proposals, and she had rejected a couple of men she was being forced to marry. Such were the ways of the Angkar.

In typically collectivist style the Angkar organised a group wedding of thirteen disabled couples instead of going through the trouble of marrying them separately. "Finally, I could get married along with the disabled," Hun Sen said, smiling at the positive turn in their lives. The loss of one eye had helped him win his bride. Bun Rany said: "It was the first time that the Angkar had allowed such a marriage. And, ironically enough it was only the disabled that could have had this privilege—as if being wounded or disabled was like wearing a badge of honour of sorts. We would have liked to get married in the traditional way, and have our own exclusive ceremony, but those were very different circumstances. Just the fact that we were allowed to marry was a great blessing." Hun Sen's commander was so displeased at the rejection of his daughter that he refused to provide any assistance to Bun Rany for the marriage. She had to travel alone to the remote place where the wedding was to take place. Bun Rany explained: "At the time of the wedding, I was accompanied by one of the cabinet chiefs whom I did not know at all. No one else went with me." Hun Sen added: "We got married with the help of the soldiers. It was the first marriage of the disabled." Bun Rany and Hun Sen were registered as "the thirteenth couple."

Of the thirteen couples, eleven were matches arranged by the local Khmer Rouge leaders. "In the case of the twelfth couple it was the woman who made the request to the man," Bun Rany clarified. "For us, the thirteenth couple, it was Hun Sen who made the request." Many of the couples had relatives in attendance, but Hun Sen's and Bun Rany's families were not present as they lived very far away. Couple number thirteen, despite its unfortunate numerological connotation, was in the best physical shape compared to the other couples, many of whom had lost their hands or legs in landmine explosions, or in combat. "The thirteenth couple could be considered the best couple so far as their physical condition and rank were concerned," Hun Sen said with a low laugh. "I was the least disabled among them. I was also the highest-ranking commander among them."

The marriage ceremonies were conducted on January 5, 1976, in martial style, with the brides sitting in a tight row in front, and the grooms sitting right behind them. "That was the way Pol Pot arranged marriage ceremonies," he said dryly. Then, the chairman of the ceremonies began reading the resumes of the brides and the grooms. Hun Sen's commander had advised him to delete some points from his resume, especially his rank, so that the other disabled couples would not be envious. "According to Pol Pot's system, we were classified as being middle-wealthy persons, a class that was disliked by Cambodians at the time," he said.

Before the ceremonies began Hun Sen had been asked four questions, and Bun Rany three. The other couples had been asked only one or two questions. One of the questions put to Hun Sen was whether he could turn his wife, who came from a wealthy family, into a proletarian, the class that had no property. "Only those people who had dark skin were considered to be Cambodians," he said. "My wife had fair skin like the Chinese. So, they did not think that she could be turned into a proletarian, and they questioned me about it."[2] Was she ever the butt of ridicule, or envy, among the Pol Pot cadres and the guerrillas because of her porcelain skin? Bun Rany replied candidly: "In my district there was no such problem. People who lived along the Mekong River had light skin, not dark. But there was a problem after my marriage to Hun Sen when we moved to live in Memot, not close to the river. People there were not light-skinned like those of us who came from the river. So, I suppose there was some jealousy there."

The honeymoon that followed was nothing short of a disaster. "After the marriage ceremony, we rested at the village for one night," Bun Rany recalled, reconstructing a day-by-day account. "After that we took a cyclo-pousse. We knew it would take a long time to reach Hun Sen's home, so on the way we stopped and rested at a village called Ta Hil. Though we were allowed to stay in the village, we were separated at night as the villagers did not believe that we were husband and wife." Between giggles Bun Rany explained that the villagers thought that they were indulging in an illicit and clandestine relationship. The next morning the couple travelled to one of the headquarters of the Angkar, at a place known as Ta Nou. They travelled all of the next day and eventually reached Hun Sen's hometown. But they did not have a place to live. They had to pack their bags, and find a home to move to.

The Angkar now sent the newly wed Bun Rany to work as a health officer in the districts of Ponhea Krek and Tbong Khmum in Kompong Cham province, where irrigation work was being carried out; Hun Sen was posted to the district of Memot, bordering Vietnam. So just a week after she was married, Bun Rany was being made to work long hours by the local leaders. She and a woman cook were sent to level the rice fields—a long and arduous task. Soon afterwards, Hun Sen was transferred to a new headquarters, and was no longer engaged directly in the fighting. Later, the Angkar set up a hospital, to which Bun Rany was sent to work. Their life was a struggle.

The gloom was dispelled by Bun Rany's pregnancy in 1976. The overworked couple were overjoyed at the imminent arrival of their first child. Yet, distance compounded their troubles. The hospital where she worked was thirty kilometres away from where he was stationed. Although she did not get time off to visit him, he came to see her. "When I was seven months pregnant, he requested permission to take me with him so I could stay with him for two months," she said.

When the time came to deliver the baby she was sent to the hospital in Memot, but the authorities did not allow Hun Sen to return for his child's birth. Recalling the event, Bun Rany broke down. "I have not spoken about this incident for many years," she said, sobbing inconsolably. It took her a few minutes to compose herself. "I can see the day as clearly as if it were unfolding right now," she wept. "I really don't know how it could have happened because the midwife had trained with me. She dropped the little baby boy, and his head hit the edge of the bed. The infant bled profusely, and died. But the medical report was made up to present quite another story—it said that the baby had died in the womb, even before he was born!"

How did the twenty-two-year-old and her young husband cope with their baby's death? "We were hurt very deeply because in the Cambodian tradition the husband always stands by the wife, literally, when she is pregnant, to give her moral support," she said. "In my case, even when the child died they did not allow Hun Sen to come and visit me. Our first child and his father were separated, never to meet." Hun Sen described it as one of the greatest tragedies of his life. "It was one of the earliest tortures I faced," he said, making an effort to keep his grief in check. "When the baby was born, the nurse dropped it. The child hit the edge of the bed and broke its spine. It emitted just one wail." There was no place for emotions in the Angkar. "My commander did not allow me to bury the child, or to look after my wife," he said. "He forced me to travel further. Till now I do not know where my child was buried."[3]

The loss of her first child in such circumstances made Bun Rany realise that the Angkar was bereft of humanity. "Slowly, I saw for myself that all the talk about everyone being a part of the revolution was humbug," she declared. "There was no equality among us. The commander, or the big boss, as we called him, lived with his wife. But we were not allowed to have a normal family life." Did the incident sow the seeds of discontent and make her want to leave the Khmer Rouge? "At the time we did not really have any idea of leaving the organisation, but we began to worry about the future," she explained. "We also discovered that some of the good people— the commanders of a higher rank than my husband who were sent for training—did not return. But even then it took us a long time to take stock of what was really happening. It was only several months later, when more people were sent for training and did not return, and when this began to happen very regularly, that we realised our lives, too, might be in grave danger."

After her baby died, Bun Rany was denied post-natal care, and she developed oedema, which caused her body to retain water and swell. It was only after much pleading with the authorities that Hun Sen was able to take her to his place of residence for two months. But his leaders subjected him to constant criticism, accusing him of being soft and over-concerned about her. He could not stand the incessant barbs, and was forced to send her back.

An exhausted and ailing Bun Rany returned to the hospital where she worked. Fortunately, Hun Sen was allowed to visit her there. Three months later she was pregnant with their second child. "The men who worked in the hospital were being taken away, so it worried us very much," she said. "You know, one day they were there, the next day they were gone." The newlyweds pined for each other, but were kept apart. She was prohibited from visiting her husband. In early 1977, working conditions became really difficult. When the four midwives who worked at the hospital got pregnant at the same time, their duty roster had to be rotated. After their babies were delivered, there was no medicine for the mothers. They had no ante-natal or post-natal care.

In June 1977, Hun Sen had to leave Bun Rany to command the Khmer Rouge Eastern Zone forces. She was carrying their son Manet. But there was not enough food for either mother or son. They lived on maize. "We would cook the maize like porridge, pour a lot of water, boil it, and then eat it like gruel," she revealed. "For weeks on end this was all we got." Hun Sen began to view his personal troubles not just as a struggle to be reunited with his wife and children, but as a revolution to liberate the divided nation. "If I did not wage the struggle, neither my family nor the nation would have survived," he said categorically. "The difficulties we faced convinced us of the value of national liberation. Whenever I met my wife I was encouraged by her."

BREAKING AWAY

He felt the thousand eyes of the Angkar on him at all times. He felt violated. He accepted their strict, inhuman rules for several years until he could take no more. He would pay dearly for challenging their authority when he turned against the organisation. Then they placed his wife under custody. The thousand eyes, which to many Cambodians were like the eyes of a pineapple, were now on her as well. "I had become the enemy of the Angkar so my wife had to be in prison," Hun Sen said straightforwardly. "No one could be trusted any more when their husband joined the struggle." With extreme stealth, he began a secret rebellion against the Khmer Rouge.[4] But it was not effective. So, on June 20, 1977, he took the first steps towards an open struggle against their senseless brutality.

Even before the killings took on a broad genocidal overtone, as early as 1974 Hun Sen realised the mistakes committed by the Khmer Rouge. "At that time we did not know who Pol Pot was," he explained. "We only knew Sihanouk and Penn Nouth [a Sihanouk loyalist who had served as a minister in Sihanouk's former Sangkum Reastr Niyum government]." Hun Sen's seven years in the Khmer Rouge, from April 14, 1970, to June 20, 1977, were not a complete waste. The Khmer Rouge trained him to fight and to think like a guerrilla. They taught him communist-style military tactics that would later give him an edge over his opponents. His first rank in the Khmer Rouge military was that of a volunteer soldier. As thousands of young guerrillas such as Hun Sen saw it, the war they were fighting was a war against U.S. imperial aggression; it was the militant response of Cambodian patriots to President Richard Nixon's bombing of Cambodia—kept secret from the American public— and the invasion of their country by U.S. ground troops.

"We were soldiers without any salary," he said without emotion. "We lived under great difficulties." He stood out from the rest, and was noticed by the military high command. The boy who had joined the guerrillas together with 500 young people was voted a member of a leading group and, after being trained, led a section of forty-eight soldiers. It was baptism by fire. After just two weeks' training in 1970 the fresh volunteers were divided into units.

On May 1, 1970, having been a section leader for only two days, Hun Sen had his first experience of combat. He was sent to fight U.S. and South Vietnamese military forces that had entered Cambodia's Snoul district in Kratie province. In a sudden exposure to combat, he faced the world's most powerful army, that of the United States.[5] The result was predictable. "We were defeated by the U.S. forces because we were a new and small group that had to fight against large-scale forces consisting of tanks and airplanes," Hun Sen argued. "Out of forty-eight soldiers in my section, there remained only sixteen. Some were killed, some fled home, some ran away to the cities, and one is now living in America." With a low laugh he remembered the fragile state of his unit. "The fighting in Snoul depleted my troops so rapidly that from being a chief of a section I became the chief of a small group," he said. "Then we merged with another unit, and I became the chief of a section again."

The military high command then sent him to a commando school, where soldiers were prepared for higher posts. When he graduated after a year, he was appointed a company commander in charge of more than 130 men. He also served as an instructor, training soldiers to read maps and use compasses and binoculars. The Angkar reserved such jobs for high school graduates. "Among the seventy-eight trainees at the time, I was the only one who survived," he said. "Some were killed while fighting the U.S. forces, but most were killed during the years when Pol Pot ruled the country. Even I, a survivor, was a disabled person."

He was not required to develop connections with the ruling political cadres as his role was limited to military operations. As a result, an opportunity to meet Pol Pot, Nuon Chea, or Khieu Samphan never arose, although he had once met Ieng Sary, who worked as a special overseas envoy of Sihanouk, in a liberated zone in late 1972. At the time, Hun Sen was undergoing training at a higher command school where junior officers were groomed to become commanders of battalions and regiments. Throughout his career in the Khmer Rouge he was sent, time and again, to military schools. The Khmer Rouge, clearly, had major plans for him. "My expertise and profession is soldiering and intelligence-gathering. The basis of being trained as a commander is intelligence," he explained.

In 1974 he was promoted to the command of a 500-strong infantry battalion. After being wounded in several battles against Lon Nol's forces, he was later appointed a regimental commander supervising more than 2,000 soldiers. His official posts were Chief of Special Regimental Staff from 1975, and Deputy Regimental

Commander of the Special Regiment from 1977. "I used this force as an instrument for the struggle [first against Lon Nol, and then against the Khmer Rouge]," he disclosed.

Why did he—and thousands of young people—stay on to serve the Khmer Rouge even though they had come to dislike and distrust them? "Where could we go?" Hun Sen argued. "We were hostages to the war. We were convinced of the terrible things Pol Pot did, but even then we did not know where to move to. Those who fled to Vietnam were sent back by Vietnam to Pol Pot, only to be killed by him. I hated the Khmer Rouge. My anti-Khmer Rouge feelings surfaced when Sihanouk was in power. But I joined the maquis for two reasons. First, how could I stand it when the United States sent its troops into Cambodia, and bombed Cambodia? It was an invasion by a foreign country of a peaceful country." The second reason, he said, was the irresistible appeal of their charismatic young leader, Sihanouk. Teenagers flocked in large numbers to join the maquis to ensure that Sihanouk returned to power. Hun Sen had cast his lot with the Khmer Rouge unwittingly.

"I did not know that all these people belonged to the Khmer Rouge," he confessed, referring to Pol Pot, Nuon Chea, Ieng Sary, and Khieu Samphan. "I had simply responded to the appeal of Prince Sihanouk. I realised only in 1974 that it was not Sihanouk but the Khmer Rouge who ran the show." Hun Sen and his young compatriots were aware of the crimes that the Khmer Rouge were committing. With Sihanouk lending an aura of respectability to the maquis, most Cambodians did not believe that the top cadres could authorise mass murders, and they were quick to accuse the lower levels. They were wrong. The decisions flowed from the top. In the end, it made no difference which side a young Cambodian joined—be it a Pink Khmer, or a Blue one—because all Cambodians were hostage to the widening civil war.

As the Lon Nol regime bled from sustained Khmer Rouge attacks, it made an effort to recruit better people, and even attempted to woo Hun Sen over. "I had relatives on Lon Nol's side," Hun Sen revealed. "One of them was Nou Thol, a two-star general. They asked me to come to the city. They even promised to give me the rank of a colonel." The two-star general sent a team of officers to talk to Hun Sen and attract him to the city. But he did not go. "Even if I went to the city I would still have been a soldier," he said emphatically. "And if I stayed in the liberated zone I would still have been a soldier. So I had no choice. I, however, gained more knowledge about the Lon Nol regime through that encounter."

In such circumstances, he could no longer stay where he was. He developed a revulsion for the inhuman practices of the Khmer Rouge, and began devising ways to quit. When he began his struggle against the Khmer Rouge he was stationed by the eastern part of the Mekong River, close to where his parents lived. The Angkar classified his father as a person with "an old political tendency to hanker after monarchy, private wealth, and a rich lifestyle." He made up his mind to quit the Khmer Rouge when more than ten of his uncles and nephews were killed by the Khmer Rouge. A plan to set up a secret network accelerated when Hun Sen was admitted to a field hospital where he had more time to plot his moves. But the network collapsed when out of ten members, eight were arrested. "Then we decided to take another route," he said decisively. "We would no longer work secretly."

In April 1975, the Khmer Rouge military ring was tightening around Phnom Penh. On April 16, Hun Sen, as an officer of the 55th Company of Region 21's Special Forces regiment, lost his left eye in a battle against Lon Nol's forces. The next day, Phnom Penh fell to the Khmer Rouge.

Hun Sen was still recuperating in hospital when he was appointed Chief of Special Regimental Staff. He returned to his base in Memot, and within two days he was ordered by Region 21 Chief of Staff Kun Deth to mobilise his forces. "It happened during Phchum Bun, a day of mourning," Hun Sen recalled. His guess was that he would be asked to attack Vietnam, since his troops were stationed not far from the border with Vietnam. At the eleventh hour, however, he was told that he was being sent to suppress an uprising of Cham Muslims in Kroch Chhmar district. Pol Pot feared the Muslims, who were strong and united as a community, and he was aware that they disapproved of his extreme policies that had caused widespread starvation, disease, and death. "I was dismayed and disappointed that we would use such a big force against a small Muslim community that was unarmed," he said disapprovingly. "I rejected the order under the pretext that I had to return to the hospital the next day. I advised my assistant that I could not move my forces because more than seventy per cent of the soldiers were suffering from malaria. I returned to the hospital as my wounds had not healed, and my forces were not used against the Muslims." The violent suppression of the Chams was eventually carried out by other CPK military units from Kroch Chhmar. A few days after he left the hospital, he was seconded to an infantry and artillery battalion that consisted of about 600 and 100 soldiers, respectively.

Khmer Rouge radio now propagated the myth that the "Islamic Khmers" were "equals" and were free to perform their religious duties. Yet, CPK officials never mentioned the Chams—who had disappeared from their discourse. They only mentioned minorities and the Khmer people. In October and November 1975, Cham religious practice was abolished in Tbong Khmum district—to the immediate south of Kroch Chhmar—and Cham villagers were dispersed to other locations in the country in an effort to destroy their solidarity. The intention was to ethnically "cleanse" the country of the Cham race. The following year, Cham village chiefs were sacked from their positions, mosques destroyed, and killings of Chams occurred on a mass scale. In mid-1976, CPK officials announced that there were to be no Chams, or Chinese, or Vietnamese, and everybody would have the same Khmer nationality. Historian Ben Kiernan has shown that only 30 out of 1,000

Chams who had performed the Haj in Mecca survived and were still alive in 1979; and only 38 out of 300 Koranic school teachers, 25 out of 226 Muslim deputies, and 20 out of 113 Muslim community leaders survived the killings.[6]

Besides the atrocities against the minority communities, the Khmer Rouge regularly purged their military commanders. They executed at least two senior commanders from the Eastern Zone in 1978: Chen Sot, the CPK secretary in Region 21, who was also a commander, and Kun Deth.[7]

There were other times when Hun Sen found the orders of the CPK military high command impossible to carry out. While in hospital he had received an order to attack Vietnam on May 30, 1977, on three fronts along a thirty-kilometre stretch of the Cambodian–Vietnamese border. "We were to use one battalion commanded by me, and one battalion led by Heng Samrin," Hun Sen explained. "I delayed the fighting until I escaped. We used the pretext that we could not attack because we lacked field intelligence." But the CPK Military Commission and Armed Forces persisted in their design to move the border markers, or posts, and encroach on Vietnamese territory. In the end, he carried out a minor border incursion as a token gesture to satisfy the military high command. "I moved just one border marker, some 200 metres into Vietnam," he clarified. "This was the place where my forces, and those of Vietnam, were attacking each other."

Questions have lingered about the role played by Hun Sen and his associates. Did he ever launch a major attack on Vietnam? Did the forces of another Khmer Rouge commander, Heng Samrin, ever attack Vietnam? Hun Sen revealed that he was ordered by higher command to attack the Vietnamese village of Or Lu in Loc Ninh province in southern Vietnam in March 1977. "I left the area one year before Heng Samrin and Chea Sim [would leave]," Hun Sen told the authors. "It is a distortion of facts that I attacked the Vietnamese provinces of Tay Ninh and Song Be, because the forces in the eastern part of the country, including the forces of Heng Samrin, no longer enjoyed the confidence of the Angkar." As a result, troops commanded by a senior Khmer Rouge commander, Ta Mok, were sent to the eastern Cambodian provinces to suppress Heng Samrin's forces. They forced Heng Samrin to go on the offensive. From April to June 1977, CPK security launched purges of various regiments and killed 200 soldiers belonging to Region 21 forces under Hun Sen's command. Twenty soldiers who were very close to Hun Sen were also purged.[8] Eventually, when Hun Sen refused to launch a large-scale attack on Tay Ninh province, the attack was carried out in September 1977 by other military officials. Following the attack, Heng Samrin, a forty-three-year-old commander, was promoted in the Khmer Rouge chain of command, though it is not clear what role, if any, he played in the attack. At any rate, Heng Samrin would emerge as one of Vietnam's strongest allies, along with Bou Thang and Hun Sen.[9]

Those skirmishes presented Hun Sen a golden opportunity to flee to Vietnam. It was clear by then that if he stayed on in Cambodia he would be captured and killed by CPK military and security forces.

"It is true that Pol Pot sent soldiers to kill me," Hun Sen said. "The day I left for Vietnam in June 1977, my commander was arrested. A motorcycle rider picked me up at the regiment near Memot and took me to the battalion nearby. There, I saw my friends, about thirty of them who held the rank of commanders of regiments and battalions. I knew that they had all been arrested. I found it very difficult to make a decision. What should I do to free them? Then the solution came to me in a flash: the only option was to kill the commander who was talking to me."

Normally, Hun Sen carried two pistols. One was hidden in his bag. The other, a loaded weapon, was strapped to his back. "I attempted, three times, to remove the gun from my bag in order to kill the commander," Hun Sen said. "The commander was smaller than me, and he had hidden his pistol in his armpit, so I knew that he wouldn't be able to take it out quickly. The first time I reached for my bag I decided not to remove the gun, and instead I took out a book. The second time I hesitated again, and instead of pulling out the gun, I pulled out a pen. The third time I was still indecisive, and I took out a ruler." Why was he indecisive? "It was because if I had killed the commander, I would have had to order the force to carry out a general offensive," he said. "At that time, there was no clear understanding within the army. If I killed the commander I was not sure whether the soldiers would follow me, or whether some of them would try and kill me. Then, we would certainly have turned ourselves into killers. So, I tried to find a way to get out of that situation by reporting to him about the location of all the forces." Under pressure, Hun Sen told the commander that he still had 1,776 soldiers under his command. Even after he disclosed the information the commander stayed on. He confiscated the telephones and equipment, and moved out all the heavy weapons such as the DK-75 and 20-mm guns.

Then, Hun Sen was forced to write a letter authorising the arrest of all the local commanders who were his friends and colleagues. At the time, most commanders were afraid of signing their names on any document, and they wanted others to take the responsibility. This was because if anything went wrong, the CPK higher military command would hold them accountable. So, Hun Sen was told to write that the commanders, now under arrest, had been summoned by the Angkar for training, and were requested to proceed the same afternoon. But the commander did not pay attention to a sentence that Hun Sen had cleverly added to the letter: that Hun Sen had asked all the commanders to leave for Vietnam with him.

The idea of escaping to Vietnam was anathema to Hun Sen, in whom a deep mistrust of Vietnam was ingrained. Like most young Cambodians, he was proud of the monarchy and his country's independence, and he viewed Vietnam with suspicion. "Since I was a child I did not really have good relations with Vietnam," he said with a chuckle. "The young Cambodians and young Vietnamese at school in Phnom Penh were divided, and were not on good terms with each other." During school holidays he worked as a labourer at a construction site in Phnom Penh, where an institute of technology was being built. The Vietnamese and Cambodian workers quarrelled frequently and, as the sparks of nationalism ignited in him, he could not remain on good terms with the Vietnamese workers. He developed a love-hate relationship with them. Soon after joining the maquis, he briefly lived in the same camp with the North Vietnamese communist armed forces, who were cooperating with the Sihanoukists. "It was agreed that the Vietnamese would help us, but we also tried to strike against them," Hun Sen said candidly. "The Vietnamese also helped us in 1970 following an appeal made by Sihanouk. They were willing to provide the good quality rice to us, and keep the bad rice for themselves. At the time, I used to attack them, and also steal their weapons from their warehouses when they were away, because the Cambodians did not have enough. I also moved the border markers into Vietnam, provoking a lot of fighting between my forces and the Vietnamese army."

There was no premeditated plan for him and his guerrillas to escape to Vietnam. "We had been thinking the whole night about what we should do before we left for Vietnam," Hun Sen said, adding that he had a powerful sense of trepidation about the mission they were about to undertake. "It was at 2 a.m. [on June 20, 1977] that we decided to cross over into Vietnam."

III

ESCAPE TO VIETNAM

1977–79

THEY WAITED NERVOUSLY for the night. As darkness fell around them, four Khmer Rouge soldiers and their commander prepared to walk away from their small base near the border with Vietnam. They were escaping from the clutches of the Angkar. They were running from one enemy straight into the hands of another. It was a chance they were willing to take. Death by a Vietnamese bullet was preferable to a living death under the Khmer Rouge regime.

Hun Sen and four of his trusted soldiers—Nhek Huon, Nuch Than, San Sanh, and Paor Ean—muttered a brief prayer, and started their long trek to Vietnam at 9 p.m. on June 20, 1977. They moved one step at a time, picking their way carefully through landmines that had been planted both by the Vietnamese army and the Khmer Rouge military. All they carried in their knapsacks was a very small ration of uncooked rice, cigarettes, and matches. Flitting among the tall palm trees that grew sparsely in the flatlands, they came perilously close to Vietnam.

Their crossing point on the Cambodian side was the tiny village of Koh Thmar, which was a part of Tunloung commune in Memot district, in Kompong Cham province. Just ahead lay the forbidding Vietnamese district of Loc Ninh in the province of Song Be. When they crossed the Vietnamese border the time on Hun Sen's watch was 2 a.m. It was June 21.

PRISONER

They advanced in fear. The darkness made it difficult for them to see where the Vietnamese units were located. After walking some 200 metres into Vietnam, Hun Sen advised his men to rest. They cooked some rice porridge. They drank the watery gruel. There was never enough rice to go around as near-famine conditions prevailed under Pol Pot's rule. "During the small meal I found that all the people who were accompanying me were crying," Hun Sen said, and added candidly: "I also cried, but I had to go and cry in private as I could not allow myself to be seen by the others, otherwise they would not have any confidence in me."[1]

After the brief halt they walked four more kilometres, then rested again. Once more they cooked half a kilogramme of rice porridge. They ate nervously. Hun Sen had decided to take only four people with him. A bigger squad would have increased the risk of being attacked by the Vietnamese, and that would have muddied his plans. "After finishing the meal we abandoned our weapons, and continued our trip without weapons," Hun Sen said with a hint of trepidation. "As we walked, we did not encounter any Vietnamese troops. I felt that the Vietnamese were being a little negligent at a time when Pol Pot was planning to attack them. Pol Pot had said that the Vietnamese had deployed twenty divisions along the border, but when I was fleeing I did not see anyone."

When the sun rose in the clear sky, their fears increased. The five Cambodians walked in broad daylight through the day. Not once did they come across Vietnamese border guards. At about 2 p.m. they reached a Vietnamese village, some twenty kilometres from the border. None of them spoke Vietnamese, except for one who could speak a few broken sentences, but he could not make himself understood. They ran into a group of Vietnamese rubber plantation workers who were returning home. Hun Sen approached them and found that they could speak a little Khmer. The plantation workers led the five Cambodians to the village office. After several minutes, about twenty soldiers belonging to the Vietnamese self-defence forces arrived on the scene armed with rifles.[2] "It was the first time that guns were pointed at me," Hun Sen said as he drifted back into the distant past. "But I felt that it was normal for a stranger to be greeted in such a way."

The Vietnamese treated the five Cambodians with extreme suspicion, and detained them for interrogation. They laid out a mat on the floor for them to sit on, in an inferior position. They then arranged three tables in an obviously superior position. The chairman, who posed the questions, sat at the head table while two note-takers and the interpreters sat at the other two tables. The interrogation lasted about ninety minutes. "They considered me to be a spy who had entered Vietnam to get information," Hun Sen said of the ordeal he faced. "I told them that normally a commander would not undertake intelligence work himself. I said that I had many people to do this kind of work, and that there was no need for me to do it myself. I told them that if we wanted to attack the Vietnamese villages we could have done so easily, because we faced no soldiers on the way to Vietnam." Seemingly convinced by Hun Sen's replies, the Vietnamese officials removed the tables and sat down on the mat with the Cambodian escapees. The Cambodians were relieved by that gesture. No sooner did they sit together than Vietnamese hospitality flowed. The Vietnamese cooked rice in "pot number ten," a pot that was normally used to cook rice for ten to sixteen people. They also prepared a dish of vegetables and pork. "We finished all the food between the five of us because it was the first time in two years that we were given rice to eat. For two years all we got was porridge."

After the meal, at about 4 p.m., they were ordered to travel another four kilometres. Hun Sen was relieved that the Vietnamese no longer pointed their guns at him, but he remained apprehensive about the immediate future. They made their way slowly through rubber plantations and down country roads. "I began shivering, maybe because we had eaten too much, or maybe because of malaria," he said. He had most likely contracted malaria during their long march through rubber plantations and country roads. Seeing him shiver, the military chief of a commune who was accompanying them helped him carry his bags.

At the end of the march they arrived at Lang Xinh, literally "nice village," in the rubber plantation of Loc Ninh. There the five escapees became a curiosity. "We were considered to be a type of strange animal that many people wanted to see," Hun Sen said. "The village people gathered to look at us. If they had organised tickets to be sold they would have earned a lot of money."

They were subjected to another round of interrogation by the commander of a Vietnamese battalion. He asked Hun Sen questions through an interpreter, an old lady who had worked in a rubber plantation in Cambodia and could speak some Khmer. "They asked us to identify on a map where Pol Pot's forces were located," Hun Sen said, explaining that he now faced increasing hostility. "After I finished telling them, the commander of the battalion shouted at me, but I did not understand what he was saying as he was shouting in Vietnamese." Then the interpreter cut in. He explained that the Vietnamese commander had called Hun Sen a liar because he appeared to know more than what a person of his age should know. Hun Sen spoke knowledgeably and told the commander that he was twenty-five years old. The commander could not believe that a man so young could hold such a high rank. He thought that generally it was the senior Cambodians who led the struggle, and was unaware that Hun Sen was among a batch of young people, dubbed the Group of March 18, who had joined the movement following an appeal by Sihanouk after his removal in the coup of 1970.

The interrogation over, the five Cambodians were driven in a General Motors truck from Lang Xinh to the town of Loc Ninh. When they arrived, they were given another meal of rice cooked in pot number ten. But this time they were only offered morning-glory greens, and rice with fish sauce. The Vietnamese apologised for serving the frugal fare, explaining that it was the best they could do as it was past their meal time. "We finished all the rice," Hun Sen said, emphasising that they were malnourished under the Khmer Rouge regime. "We were eating with a vengeance. Within the space of four hours the five of us had finished two enormous quantities of rice cooked in pot number ten."

After the meal Hun Sen was separated from the other four and questioned again. The Vietnamese had come to accept, albeit sceptically, that he did indeed hold the high rank of a commander. "The others thought that I would be killed," he said, clarifying that he was now being interrogated for long periods of time. "The Vietnamese regimental commander who held the rank of a lieuten-ant-colonel questioned me alone from 7.30 a.m. to 12 p.m. He was acquainted with me, but he did not reveal that he knew me." It was a stroke of luck that he had met the commander in 1970. At the time, Hun Sen, a fresh recruit, had travelled to a forest in an area where the Vietnamese commander and his Viet Cong forces were based. "So, when I refreshed his memory, he realised that I had vis-ited a unit that was stationed close to his unit," he said, smiling for the first time during the interview. "Normally, in such a situation, both the sides know each other's commanders." The Vietnamese commander was still not convinced. The interrogation was long and exhausting. At 11.30 a.m., the commander threatened him with dire consequences. "I told him that I was the commander of a regiment, but the interpreter miscommunicated that I was the commander of a section," Hun Sen said, a shadow of anxiety clouding his face. "I told him that I had more than 2,000 forces under me, but due to battlefield casualties and imprisonment, there remained only 1,776 troops. Then, the commander shouted and accused me of lying. I then understood that I had been misinterpreted." He tried a differ-ent approach. He wondered if the ageing Vietnamese commander could speak French, as he had served the Vietnamese revolutionary army since French colonial rule. "I told him that I was responsible for a *régiment*, not a *section*," explained. "The commander then understood, and advised the interpreter to change his terminology from *trung doi* (section) to *trung doan* (regiment)."

When he returned from the interrogation Hun Sen found his four compatriots crying. He, the youngest among them, had turned out to be the toughest.

At 3 p.m. the next day they were put on board a General Motors truck stacked with firewood. They did not know where they were headed. They feared they were being driven back to Cambodia, to be killed by the Khmer Rouge military. "It was fortunate that I was not handcuffed from the time that I met the Vietnamese till the time that I was interrogated," Hun Sen said of those moments when their fates hung in the balance. "But after we sat down inside the truck, five soldiers pointed their guns at me. I was prepared to commit suicide by slashing my throat with a sewing needle if the Vietnamese sent me back to Pol Pot. As soldiers, we always carried sewing needles with us in case we needed to mend our clothes. So I watched the kilometre posts on the road to see whether we were headed towards Cambodia, or towards Song Be and Ho Chi Minh City." He was relieved to see from the kilometre posts that they were driving south into Song Be province, in the general direction of the provincial capital Thu Dau Mot and Ho Chi Minh City, and not towards Cambodia.

They arrived at their destination in Song Be province at about 5 p.m., and were taken to a sprawling army headquarters. On the way, they were asked to walk about one kilometre through a marketplace and, once again, they became "strange animals" that many people stared at. They were herded into a detention centre for undisciplined soldiers and locked in a cell that was ringed on the outside with barbed wire. A corrugated iron sheet was then erected around the cell to prevent them from looking out. Their jailor told them that they would be provided with 6,000 dongs a day for rations. Hun Sen thought that was a lot of money, and imagined that he would spend 3,000 dongs on food, and use the rest to buy cigarettes. But he did not realise that 6,000 dongs of the old South Vietnamese currency that he was familiar with was equivalent to less than a dollar in the new currency of communist Vietnam. Still, the allowance was fairly generous, considering that a Vietnamese soldier received only 7,000 dongs a day.

That first night, Hun Sen and his jittery friends were assaulted by an offensive stench. "They had kept a group of undisciplined women soldiers in a nearby cell," Hun Sen explained. "The smell of their urine was too strong." To add to their discomfort, they were told to sleep on the hard floor, without mats. At 10 p.m. the chief of the detention centre had a change of heart, and they were provided with beds, mosquito nets, and blankets. But they had to put up with the stench.

After twenty-two days in custody, having contracted malaria, Hun Sen was moved to a hospital. "It was fortunate that I suffered from malaria and grew thinner and thinner," he said, explaining that his sickness turned out to be a blessing. "So, I was sent to one of the military hospitals in the province of Song Be, while my four colleagues were still kept in the prison." There he was provided much better rations because the Vietnamese had now accepted that his rank was that of a lieutenant-colonel. He saved a portion of his daily allowance for his compatriots who were under detention.

After he was discharged from the hospital, a little more freedom was given to him and his friends. "But it was freedom within the military compound," he said. "We had won their confidence. We were allowed to walk around the camp and talk to the soldiers. Those disciplined and undisciplined Vietnamese soldiers were friendly towards me." Living conditions improved with the 6,000 dongs in daily allowance, and life became bearable as some of the Vietnamese soldiers shared with them the food their families sent. They even gave Hun Sen clothes to wear. But Hun Sen was plagued by a constant throbbing fear. Would they remain prisoners forever? Or would they be sent back to Pol Pot's Democratic Kampuchea to be butchered?

NEWS OF HIS DEFECTION soon reached the ears of the Angkar. When they realised that Hun Sen had fled to Vietnam they retaliated by forcing Bun Rany to perform hard labour. She was constantly spied on, and her movements were monitored. In a brutal coincidence, both husband and wife were prisoners under different circumstances.

"Although I wasn't restricted to a cell, I was guarded all the time," she said. "During the day I was sent to uproot the stems of the trees and big shrubs and bushes in order to clear the land. It was backbreaking work." The Khmer Rouge worked in very devious ways to erode the self-esteem and will of those whom they wanted to punish and torture. They separated the women into two groups of "widows": one group that had actually lost their husbands in the war, and a second group whose husbands were alive, but whom the Angkar wanted dead.[3] "The fact that our husbands had fled to Vietnam made us damned and punishable criminals in their eyes, and so they tortured us day and night by calling us 'widows'—to ensure we were brainwashed into believing, sooner or later, that our husbands had died," Bun Rany said, her voice breaking a little. "It was horrible, macabre." The Angkar called her a *kbal yuen khluen khmae*, a person who had a Vietnamese head, and Cambodian body.[4] And when the people around her found out why she was called a widow, they stopped speaking to her.

Bun Rany had to overcome all sorts of difficulties. Hun Sen had left for Vietnam when Bun Rany was five months pregnant with their second child in 1977. Hun Sen recalled: "Twelve days after she delivered the child she was put under custody." The Angkar tried to break Hun Sen's spirit by spreading the rumour that Bun Rany had died after the birth of the child as a result of malnutrition and overwork. The "widows" had to leave their children under the care of old ladies in an unfamiliar place when they were sent to clear the land. It broke her heart to leave her child with someone else. The "widows" generally ate a gruel made of maize, and it was only on rare occasions that they were given vegetables by some kind-hearted village folk. When she asked the Angkar for permission to visit her parents, the Angkar told her that she would only be allowed to see them if they were ill. Among Bun Rany's group of "widows" was a young woman who had been married on the same day as her, as one of the group of thirteen disabled couples. Accompanied by this woman, Bun Rany secretly went to visit her parents. She was briefly reunited with her family. But they were advised not to stay at her parents' home. They moved from one friend's house to another. "We were afraid that if we were discovered by the Angkar as being part of the village they might come after us and kill us," she said anxiously. "There were three of us women whom the Angkar suspected of disloyalty, and we lived together in the same area," she explained. But she was temporarily reprieved because the Angkar believed that Hun Sen was dead; they merely monitored her activities. "Later when they heard that Hun Sen was still alive they pretended to call us for a meeting, with the overt intention of moving us to another area. From what had happened time and again to our friends and acquaintances that had disappeared I knew that if we were taken in this way, we would certainly be slaughtered." Even farmers who ventured into the area in search of better living conditions were taken away to be killed. She was tormented by the thought of how the families of her two maternal aunts had been taken away and killed.

One night, Bun Rany overheard two Khmer Rouge chiefs saying that she would be taken away and killed the next morning. "We planned to flee into the forest that night," she confided. The same night she and a few "widows" made their getaway. The escapees were tired and thirsty. Although they were near the river they did not dare venture anywhere near the water because it was full of floating dead bodies. It was a terrible sight. The Angkar had a grotesque practice—if the starving people stole food, whatever they had stolen would be tied to their hands with a *krama*. "I shall never forget the sight of a dead child floating on the river, a stolen guava tied to its hand," Bun Rany said, her eyes widening in horror. People were starving but no one was allowed to touch any of the bananas on the trees that grew around the camp, she added. The Khmer Rouge even confiscated all the dishes, pots, and utensils, to prevent people from cooking and eating anything at home. Each person was allowed to keep one plate and one spoon. Like slaves, the people in the camp would be summoned by a bell to come and eat watery broth. "Even if we found a frog, or a tiny fish, we were not allowed to eat that extra ration."

POLITICAL ASYLUM

The interrogators were bad-tempered and aggressive. They questioned Hun Sen relentlessly. He was on the edge of a breakdown. The questions were always the same. What is your real name? Which regiment of the Khmer Rouge do you belong to? Where is it located? Why did you come to Vietnam? Were you spying for Pol Pot? But even after hours of probing they came up empty-handed. Gradually they began to believe that Hun Sen was no longer loyal to the Khmer Rouge, that his defection was final and irrevocable, that he had burnt all his Cambodian bridges, and that he would be killed if he was sent back.

After he had spent twenty-two harrowing days in jail in Song Be, his detention was extended by three months in the same province. It was then that he requested political asylum. The five Cambodians were relocated to another detention centre while the matter of political asylum was being considered. Until it was granted they were kept under custody. Even so, there were saving graces. Hun Sen was given living expenses worth 21,000 dongs per

109

day, equal to the rations of a Vietnamese government minister. The money, paid at the end of each month, was an indication that he was gradually winning the confidence of the Vietnamese, who were making a slow transition from being jailors and interrogators to hosts and, eventually, allies.

"Not only did I have enough to eat, and enough cigarettes to smoke, but I also had some money to spare," he said, his eyes lighting up.[5] A man of simple Cambodian tastes, Hun Sen did not have a palate for exotic foreign cuisines, and was happiest with a diet of rice and fish. His one passion was cigarettes. When he was denied this indulgence he grew agitated. Throughout his time in assorted Vietnamese prisons he smoked the popular Vietnamese Vam Co brand of cigarettes, and sometimes rolled his own. "It was hard for me to quit smoking," he explained. "In times of difficulty I even smoked papaya leaves. In custody, I saved cigarette ends, and used them to make a new cigarette. My theory was that I always tried to find something to smoke in times of scarcity, so why stop smoking when there was abundance?"

As he gained the confidence of the Vietnamese, he presented a five-point proposal to them, outlining the ways in which they could help him. First, he urged Vietnam to give the Cambodians who were flooding into Vietnam their rights as refugees and not send them back home. Second, he asked that Vietnam give political asylum to the Cambodian forces that were fleeing the purges of Pol Pot. Third, he requested that he be given sanctuary along the Cambodian–Vietnamese border to allow him to recruit his armed forces from among the Cambodian refugees, and that these forces be allowed to enter Vietnam when engaging Pol Pot's forces in battle. Fourth, he requested weapons, materials, and financial assistance to build his armed forces. Lastly, he asked the Vietnamese to let his people use Vietnamese territory as they were rebelling against Pol Pot.

After months of living nervously he finally made a breakthrough. As a result of his request for political asylum, he was given the rare opportunity to meet General Van Tien Dung, the chief of the Vietnamese general staff, and other senior army officers, in Ho Chi Minh City on September 30, 1977. The date was significant. On that very day Pol Pot visited China, after an earlier trip in 1966. As Pol Pot grew closer to the Chinese, Hun Sen was embraced by Hanoi. The Vietnamese needed a Cambodian ally in order to counterbalance the China–Khmer Rouge axis that threatened Vietnam. The discussions with General Dung, who later became minister of defence, were the first flash of the vision Hun Sen saw of liberating his country. They spoke frankly, and he openly sought Dung's assistance. But he was disheartened by the general's response. "When I requested their assistance I was rejected," he said. "The Vietnamese said that if they acceded to my request for assistance, they would be seen as interfering in the affairs of Democratic Kampuchea [the formal name of the government of the Khmer Rouge]. The Vietnamese were then trying to negotiate with Democratic Kampuchea to ease the military tensions on their common border." It was not easy for Hun Sen to convince the Vietnamese to help him liberate Cambodia from the genocidal Khmer Rouge regime that was bolstered by at least 50,000 fanatical fighters. After all, the Vietnamese had traditionally been the Khmer Rouge's staunchest allies. Hanoi had trained Pol Pot's forces in the early days of the CPK movement, and the two sides had conducted joint operations against the Republican forces of Lon Nol and the armed forces of the United States and South Vietnam. "Some Vietnamese generals and colonels requested that I should go to Thailand [to seek their assistance]. I told them I could not abandon my people. If they could not help me, I said, 'Just give me some weapons, and I will go back to Cambodia and die with my people.'"

He did not draw a complete blank, however. He was granted political asylum. Still, he had not come to Vietnam just to seek political asylum: he wanted their help to liberate his country. Hun

Sen explained why Hanoi did not wish to get too involved with his request for assistance: "Vietnam always respected the independence and sovereignty of Cambodia, and the Vietnamese leadership rejected my appeal for help, saying that it may harm the relationship between the two countries."

Events would very soon move in Hun Sen's favour. The halcyon days of the friendship between the Khmer Rouge and Vietnam were fast coming to an end as Pol Pot grew closer to China and hostile to his original friends, the Vietnamese. When Pol Pot relocated his forces from southwestern Cambodia to eastern Cambodia in readiness to attack Vietnam, he forced large numbers of Cambodians to flee to Vietnam, adding to the tens of thousands already seeking refuge there from his murderous regime.

Hun Sen's golden opportunity appeared when Pol Pot launched a series of large-scale attacks on the Vietnamese border in mid-1977, prompting Hanoi to abandon its stance of non-interference. Hanoi now began planning a military response, as around 60,000 Cambodian refugees from the killings carried out by Pol Pot's Democratic Kampuchea sought refuge in Vietnam, and four times more fled to safety in Thailand.

On September 24, 1977, soldiers from the Khmer Rouge 3rd Eastern Division crossed over into Tay Ninh province in Vietnam, killing almost 300 civilians, mostly ethnic Khmer and Vietnamese residents of Cambodia. About a week later, Vietnamese military forces reoccupied the area.[6] In October, the Vietnamese army retaliated and, feigning retreat, lured Khmer Rouge units into Vietnam, where another Vietnamese unit trapped them.[7] The fighting continued along the border over the remainder of 1977, and in December Vietnam launched a major cross-border attack using some 30,000–60,000 ground troops as well as air power, tanks, and artillery. On December 22, two Vietnamese tanks drove across the border into Kandol Chrum town in order to contact So Phim, their ally within Cambodia. They failed to make contact, but Hun Sen and Heng

Samrin made several incursions into Cambodia.[8]

"If Pol Pot had not attacked Vietnam I don't think we would have got the support of the Vietnamese to overthrow the Khmer Rouge," Hun Sen conjectured. "The mistake Pol Pot made was to kill his own people [including ethnic Vietnamese], and launch attacks on Vietnam. It was then that the Vietnamese decided to help Cambodia. By myself, I could not convince Vietnam. But when Pol Pot attacked, then Vietnam retaliated. They felt insulted and decided to help us. The Vietnamese began to believe my prediction that Pol Pot had been planning to attack Vietnam. When more and more people fled to Vietnam, the Vietnamese were convinced that there was a grave danger to their security. Then the Vietnamese called me to their headquarters and asked me to pinpoint the places [inside Cambodia] they should attack. That was the golden opportunity for me," Hun Sen told the authors. "It was an opportunity for us to recruit our armed forces from among the Cambodian refugees who had entered Vietnam."

Incensed by the savage attacks launched by Pol Pot, whose forces had burned Vietnamese village homes and occupied parts of Tay Ninh province in September, the Vietnamese struck back against Khmer Rouge forces in Svay Rieng, Prey Veng, Kompong Cham, Kratie and Kandal, in places thirty to seventy kilometres into Cambodian territory.

Hun Sen said intently: "That was the opportunity for me to return to Cambodia, and to try and seek out my wife, who had been evacuated to another place." Given the short duration of his incursion into Cambodia and the widening war, Hun Sen failed to locate his wife.

The Khmer Rouge grew bolder and launched further attacks deep inside Vietnam's Tay Ninh province in January and February 1978. The Vietnam News Agency reported that Democratic Kampuchea turned its 130-mm artillery on Tay Ninh—a provincial town teeming with Cambodian refugees, located ninety kilometres north of Saigon—killing or wounding thirty civilians. At the same time, Vietnamese divisions supported by tanks, artillery, and aircraft, penetrated thirty kilometres deep inside Cambodia along the 700-kilometre border, from Ratanakiri in the north to Svay Rieng in the south. Phnom Penh Radio quoted an appeal by head of state Khieu Samphan to troops and civilians to defend themselves against "all enemies" that invaded Cambodia to plunder the rice crop. Samphan accused the Vietnamese forces of destroying rubber plantations, burning down forests and houses, and strafing people.[9] Cambodia severed diplomatic relations with Vietnam, and snapped air links as well.

Hun Sen urged the Vietnamese to play a more decisive role, but he was disappointed. "I felt very angry with the Vietnamese because after attacking Cambodia they decided to withdraw their troops," he said in dismay. "They did not create a safe sanctuary for us in Cambodia where we could set up our forces. They withdrew after launching brief attacks for their self-defence. We did not have our own self-defence forces. But I was grateful to them for allowing the Cambodians to move out of their areas, which were being attacked, and to come and live in Vietnam. That provided me an opportunity to recruit soldiers for my forces. In this way we could build twenty-eight battalions. Many of the one- and two-star generals who are with me now were recruited by me in 1977." As he fashioned a fighting force out of the streaming refugees, he emerged as their top leader. "They called me the commander of the eastern part of the Mekong River," he said with pride. "There were many people who were older than me, but they gave the leadership role to me. The battalions that we raised to fight Pol Pot were mainly built around my forces."

While under political asylum, Hun Sen gradually developed an enduring relationship with Vietnam's top military commanders. After meeting with General Van Tien Dung, he was introduced to General Tran Van Tra, commander of Region 7 and the

Ho Chi Minh City area, as well as to the deputy commanders of the region. One of the most profitable friendships Hun Sen developed was with General Le Duc Anh, who would become president of Vietnam in the early 1990s. They met at a hospital reserved for medium- and high-ranking officials. "As I used to fall ill frequently I had to go to the hospital," he explained. "I was the youngest person to be admitted to the fourth storey of the hospital, which was reserved for generals. I had to disguise myself as a person from Laos." His Vietnamese friends gave him a new identity so that he would not attract attention, or give rise to suspicions. "They named me Mai Phuc, which means happiness forever, aged twenty-six, a high-ranking cadre from Region X," Hun Sen said. "Nobody knew where Region X was located. The people in the hospital suspected something, because normally in Vietnam only people aged sixty upwards could be considered high-ranking cadres. The people on the fourth storey were aware of my rank, but when I was sent to the X-ray room, the people there wondered, 'How could a high-ranking cadre be only twenty-six, and where is he from?'" General Anh was then the commander of Region 7. "He helped me a great deal from his Region 7 resources in building up our Cambodian armed forces," Hun Sen said appreciatively. "He also sent several generals and colonels to help me in my work. He was the main person who ensured that the overthrow of the Khmer Rouge was successful."

Up till then, the Vietnamese were cautious, even grudging, about how much assistance they would extend to Hun Sen and his band of revolutionaries. "The Vietnamese rejected giving us political assistance," he clarified. "But they helped us financially. They gave us weapons and training, and left the work of the political leadership and education to us. I, therefore, knew how to write official documents at the age of twenty-five. I wrote lessons for the [Cambodian] officers and gave lectures myself." By slow degrees he built up his forces from scratch.

IV

LIBERATION WAR AGAINST THE KHMER ROUGE

1977–89

A SECRET PLOT to overthrow the Pol Pot regime was gradually taking root in the fertile soil of southern Vietnam. Hun Sen's original plan was to liberate Cambodia in five years. He reckoned that it could not be achieved sooner even though the Vietnamese had found a reliable ally in him and had agreed to give him funds and weapons to unshackle his country.

"The idea was to liberate the eastern part of Cambodia, and use it as a springboard to free the western part," Hun Sen said. "The five-year plan involved infiltrating troops into western Cambodia through the Vietnamese town of Ha Tien, to carry out incursions and raids, whereas the main forces would attack from the east. The grand liberation would be launched from the Cambodian provinces of Kratie, Stung Treng, Ratanakiri, and Mondulkiri. We would disguise our plans by attacking Svay Rieng and Prey Veng provinces, and capturing a part of Kompong Cham. Then, we would send a force to strengthen our troops in the eastern part of the Mekong River. Later, we would enlarge our areas to engulf Svay Rieng and Prey Veng. This was the plan to liberate Cambodia in five years."[1]

UNITED FRONT

As an experienced guerrilla commander with a sharp military mind, Hun Sen's first step had been to set up a liberation army, and only then did he think of creating a political organisation. He suggested to his Cambodian compatriots that their political organisation be named the Kampuchean United Front for National Salvation, Solidarity, and Liberation. It was accepted by the two people closest to him—Sin Song (who was later involved in a failed coup d'etat in 1994), and Sar Not (who later became Hun Sen's advisor on religious affairs).

The slow-track five-year plan was speeded up, and national liberation took on a sudden urgency when Pol Pot ordered the 3rd, 5th, and 18th divisions to attack Vietnam in September 1977. According to Hun Sen, the Khmer Rouge employed elements from as many as eighteen divisions in this major incursion into southern Vietnam. The sheer magnitude of the military action forced the Vietnamese to counterattack with speed and firepower. "That was not only a golden opportunity, but a diamond opportunity for me, because the strongest units of Pol Pot were defeated by the Vietnamese," Hun Sen said. "The decision of the Vietnamese to help us gave us more confidence. The growth of my forces multiplied by three because Pol Pot's strongest forces were depleted."

On a clandestine visit to Cambodia in December 1977 and early 1978, Hun Sen invited some of the top Khmer Rouge Eastern Zone commanders to join the front. The need to bolster the liberation forces became even more pressing when he received intelligence information that Pol Pot was planning to send forces led by Ta Mok—a brutal commander—from the southwest to the Vietnamese border. Hun Sen had to make contact with his allies in Cambodia, but it was not easy to communicate with them. "I tried to get in touch with Heng Samrin, who commanded a battalion, and Chea Sim, who was the chief of a district but did not control a force," he said. Gradually, he built up his forces, made up of anti-Khmer Rouge nationalists, and infiltrated them into Cambodia.

By December 1977, with the fighting along the Cambodian–Vietnamese border having escalated and diplomatic relations between the two countries severed (Democratic Kampuchea clari-fying that its decision to break relations was "temporary"),[2] it was obvious that Cambodia and Vietnam had conflicting and over-lapping claims to their borders and territories. Vietnam accused Cambodia of using military force to settle the dispute in its favour.

In early January 1978, more than 100,000 Cambodians who lived near the border escaped into Vietnam under cover provided by Vietnamese military units that had briefly entered Cambodian territory. Among the escapees was Heng Samrin's brother Heng Samkai, who was a senior official of the Eastern Zone. Samkai had realised that it would be impossible to overthrow Pol Pot using only Cambodian rebel forces, and that the help of Vietnam would be needed. Samkai was flown from the border to Ho Chi Minh City on a Vietnamese helicopter for consultations with other Khmer Rouge escapees on the construction of a new government that would over-throw the Khmer Rouge.[3] The Vietnamese began training the defec-tors in order to organise them into a resistance movement.

"When we entered Cambodia there was a big uprising in the eastern part of the country," Hun Sen said. "Our forces made con-tact with the defectors [who were escaping from the Khmer Rouge regime]. By May 1978, we had set up liberated zones in Kompong Cham and Kratie provinces. Heng Samrin and Chea Sim were the leaders in these liberated areas. At the time we did not have direct contact with them, but we established indirect contact through their forces." In September, the Vietnamese sent tanks into Cambodia in order to escort Heng Samrin, Chea Sim, and their supporters back to safety in Vietnam. Le Duc Tho, the chief advisor to the Kampuchean United Front for National Salvation, flew in from Hanoi for a two-day conference with Heng Samrin, Chea Sim, Pen Sovann, and Chea Soth on September 21–22. They decided to launch a full-scale military assault to overthrow the Khmer Rouge regime in December.[4]

The trio of Heng Samrin, Chea Sim, and Hun Sen had known each other for years. They met face to face in Song Be province in southern Vietnam in November 1978. It was their first meeting on Vietnamese soil. It was not just a meeting between two sides; it involved five factions. "I was so happy not only to see them, but also to hear the news of the uprising in Cambodia," Hun Sen said of his encounter with Heng Samrin and Chea Sim, who were his friends although they were older than him. Heng Samrin had escaped from Khmer Rouge purges earlier that year and sought refuge in Vietnam. The uprising, carried out spontaneously by the liberation forces and the rural people, took place in the eastern regions of Cambodia. At a meeting, the leaders of the five rebel parties drafted the military and political policies of the United Front. One of the parties, led by Heng Samrin and Chea Sim, had staged an uprising inside Cambodia. The second party, under the leadership of Bou Thang, had revolted in 1975 in the northeast. The third party were the communists led by Hanoi-trained intellectual Pen Sovann, and others such as Chea Soth, and Chan Si; they had lived in Vietnam for many years since the Geneva conference in 1954. The fourth party were the new forces formed by Hun Sen, and the fifth party had led the anti-Khmer Rouge resistance in Thailand under the leadership of Say Phuthang and Tea Banh.

Was it difficult for the five parties to work together? "For Heng Samrin, Chea Sim and me, it was not difficult, as we used to be in the eastern region together," Hun Sen said. "Our final goal was to merge. But the high-ranking leaders did not have the time to meet each other. In November 1978, we were very busy setting up the United Front, creating the political programme, and the congress. We declared the formation of the front on December 2, 1978. At the time we had already prepared our forces, food supplies, and weapons for the attack. It was not that we formed the front first and then prepared the army." The fledgling group, led by Heng Samrin, began operating under the name of the Kampuchean United Front for National Salvation. By then, a portion of Hun Sen's forces had entered Cambodia to help the people stage an uprising.

For the first time he saw the possibility of overthrowing the Khmer Rouge within a year. "We were thinking that, at least, we could liberate Cambodia in the New Year in 1979," Hun Sen said. "Then, Heng Samrin and Chea Sim fled into my area with their forces. With our combined forces we set up the liberated zone. We estimated that we should liberate the country by April 1979. We did not expect that the Pol Pot regime would be so weak, and that the people were just waiting to rise up against it."

IN HANOI, a crisis-like atmosphere hung over the higher echelons of the People's Army of Vietnam (PAVN). In response to the troubled situation in Cambodia, Hanoi abolished the PAVN General Department of Economic Construction, and redeployed its military units along the Cambodian border. The department, an army wing that supervised the military's involvement in agriculture and industry, would not be re-established till 1986, long after the Cambodian civil war was over.[5]

In December 1978, the plot to overthrow the Khmer Rouge was carried through. Hanoi Radio announced on December 4 the formation of the Kampuchean United Front, and said that the front called on the people of Cambodia to "rise up and overthrow the Pol Pot and Ieng Sary clique."[6] Diplomats in Bangkok interpreted the announcement as a decisive step in Vietnam's war against Cambodia and predicted a full-scale Vietnamese military and political campaign to eject the Pol Pot regime and replace it with a pro-Hanoi government.

The attack came as expected. The Vietnamese launched a general offensive against the Khmer Rouge on December 25, 1978, backed by the troops of the United Front. A Vietnamese-led force crossed the Mekong River for the first time, and encircled the provincial capital of Kompong Cham, sixty-four kilometres from Phnom Penh, reports said on January 1, 1979.[7] Troops believed to be Vietnamese army regulars entered Kompong Cham on New Year's Day, with the attackers capturing "thousands of weapons" from Pol Pot's forces. As a military commander Hun Sen knew that the success of any military campaign depended on weapons and food supplies. His forces had been armed by the Vietnamese, and now they were given enough food supplies as well, with a little extra for the new recruits who were joining the front inside Cambodia. The task of raising a massive liberation force consisting of grassroots Cambodians was daunting. Eventually, some 20,000 Cambodians fought in the grand liberation. "Our forces were not vanguard units, but they could carry out attacks, occupy land, and motivate people to join us, and thus move our forces forward," Hun Sen clarified. "We carried on fighting [the Khmer Rouge], while at the same time recruiting new troops." At times, his forces had to await the arrival of the Vietnamese because, by his own admission, "nobody on our side knew how to drive a tank." In places where his forces encountered strong resistance, they waited for the Vietnamese forces to arrive and punch through Khmer Rouge defences with tanks and artillery. "After Pol Pot's border forces were defeated, his inland units could not withstand the attacks," he said. "We encountered resistance in Samlaut and Ta Sanh along Cambodia's border with Thailand."

Hun Sen and his cohorts were aware that they could never have overthrown the Khmer Rouge without the military support of Vietnam. "I do not know for sure how many troops the Vietnamese used, because the Vietnamese armed forces were very smart in keeping secrets," Hun Sen said. "The Vietnamese do not reveal their cards, even after they finish playing a hand. If they left their cards open, their opponents could estimate their next move. Even if you read the history books you will not come to know how the Vietnamese won the war against the French in Dien Bien Phu.

I think there were about 100,000 Vietnamese forces involved in the liberation of Cambodia. [The liberation forces included the Kampuchean United Front's 20,000 resistance fighters.] The plan was to launch a rapid offensive to liberate the country in a very short time. Therefore, a very large force was used." In comparison, Democratic Kampuchea's armed forces under the control of Pol Pot fielded about 70,000 troops.

"According to my understanding the Vietnamese used three key forces—their strongest force was the 4th Army of regular units that was used [later on, in 1979] in the border war against China," Hun Sen said. "Their second force was the 7th Army of General Le Duc Anh, and the third force was the 9th Army. They used a variety of tactics. The 4th Army attacked Svay Rieng province, and then moved to station itself in Siem Reap province. When they attacked Pol Pot's troops in Svay Rieng, they chased them all the way to Siem Reap." He asked rhetorically: "Why didn't the Vietnamese use another army in Siem Reap? This was because the 4th Army had studied Pol Pot's units carefully, and knew how to fight them." Throwing new light on the way the campaign was conducted, he said: "The Vietnamese didn't use many tanks and artillery. They used their experience of attacking from the jungles into the clear areas. They used no airplanes to bombard the enemy, and used them only for transport. They mainly deployed their infantry."

Hun Sen did not take part in the actual fighting as he had done in his early days as a guerrilla. He now played a bigger role. He planned, coordinated, and monitored the movements of his forces. Faced with the massive onslaught of the Cambodian and Vietnamese forces, the Khmer Rouge's defences disintegrated without resistance. The Cambodian and Vietnamese forces coordinated their movements closely, but they attacked separate targets in pursuit of specific objectives. They operated under separate commanders because they did not speak the same language. The Cambodian forces also worked the ground in Cambodia, awakening the people with their political activism. "Our common target was to oust the Pol Pot regime, yet there were many other military objectives that had to be carried out separately," Hun Sen said. "The Vietnamese could not speak Khmer, so the Cambodian forces had to conduct their own operations."

While the Cambodian forces took on the Khmer Rouge in areas where Pol Pot's divisions were relatively weak, the Vietnamese fought the Khmer Rouge in the provinces where they were strongest. After having ejected the Khmer Rouge from a particular area, the Vietnamese army would move on, leaving the Cambodian forces to take over and restore order among the people living in that area. As the Cambodian liberation army swarmed across the border, its numbers grew. "When we liberated the people they asked to join the armed forces too. The 20,000-strong force that we started with ended up as 40,000, as the Pol Pot regime collapsed before the people's forces. When Pol Pot's army fled they left their weapons behind, so we acquired new forces with new weapons. My elder brother Hun Neng collected 700 pieces of weapons from the fleeing Pol Pot soldiers." At the end of the war he was surprised to see that his Cambodian forces had grown enormously. "I asked myself whether we could recruit twenty-eight battalions in order to deploy at least one battalion per province, and we did," he said. "And if it was a big province we deployed two battalions there."

LIBERATION

The collapse came sooner than expected and surprised even Hun Sen. By January 8, 1979, Phnom Penh had been captured by the Vietnamese military and the Cambodian rebels. According to the first reports from the news agency of the rebels, Sarapordamean Kampuchea (SPK), Phnom Penh fell without a fight. The leaders of the Khmer Rouge were evacuated to Beijing in an emergency airlift, and the rebels, who called themselves the Revolutionary Armed Forces, occupied most of the important buildings. Kampot province, on the southern coast, also fell. "The dictatorial and militaristic Pol Pot–Ieng Sary clique has totally collapsed," SPK reported.

Once the country had been liberated, two U.S.-built Dakota aircraft operated by the Vietnam People's Air Force took off from Tan Son Nhat Airport in Ho Chi Minh City, bound for Pochentong Airport in Phnom Penh. One of them carried Hun Sen and Chea Sim, the other carried Heng Samrin and Pen Sovann. They were the four main players who had engineered the liberation and in February 1979 they were all coming home in triumph. Heng Samrin would soon be appointed president of the People's Revolutionary Council of the new state of the People's Republic of Kampuchea (PRK); Chea Sim would become interior minister; Pen Sovann would become vice-president and minister of national defence. And twenty-six-year-old Hun Sen, though he did not know it yet, would soon be foreign minister.

Since his defection from Pol Pot's Democratic Kampuchea, Hun Sen had stepped onto Cambodian soil only once before, on his clandestine visit in 1977–78. Now a victorious Hun Sen was returning, secure in the knowledge that the Khmer Rouge regime had collapsed, and that his army was in the process of occupying Pochentong Airport and the capital. "The liberation forces urgently needed their leaders, so I had to come by plane," he said.

At Pochentong Airport, a party of Cambodian officials and a few Vietnamese diplomats, who had travelled to Phnom Penh ahead of them, had gathered to welcome the revolutionary leaders. But all eyes were on the fresh-faced young man among them, Hun Sen. Soon after his arrival, Hun Sen was taken to the Royal Palace that was once the abode of Sihanouk and his ancestors. It was an honour given to the young leader. He stayed at the palace for two weeks before he was given an official residence.

He was crestfallen when he did not see Bun Rany among the welcoming party at the airport. He had been separated from her for almost two years since May 1977, and had scarcely seen her for the past nine years. "I thought she was dead because she didn't appear at the airport," he said. Bun Rany had lived through terrifying times in separation from her husband. "She did not dare reveal that she was my wife," he said. "She went and hid in the countryside. After the liberation, my wife, my son, and my relatives stayed in the village and harvested ears of rice for a living." The last time he had seen her she was five months pregnant and living at a hospital run by the Khmer Rouge. "Fortunately, the Khmer Rouge had announced twice that I had been killed along the Cambodia–Vietnam border, so they did not pay much attention to my wife," he said. "They declared, in June and December 1977 that I was dead. She faced a lot of suffering unlike the other 'widows.' Although the Khmer Rouge said that I had been killed, they knew very well that I was alive. When there was an uprising in the eastern region she went into the forest with my son and relatives." Hun Sen clarified that during the uprising the Khmer Rouge shifted his wife, son, and some of their relatives to a location in the forest. The first piece of disinformation about Hun Sen's death in June coincided with his departure to Vietnam. The second was broadcast in December when he appeared briefly in a Cambodian village at about the same time as a rapid attack by the Vietnamese along the Cambodian border. "They said that I was killed by a landmine explosion when I was assisting some Cambodians to seek safe passage to Vietnam. At the time, some Khmer Rouge commanders had also been killed, so the news of my death was connected with this news. My wife was given the news, and she was not killed."

After the liberation of Phnom Penh, Bun Rany's group of detainees was forced to evacuate. They had to walk through the forest for three days and two nights. When they arrived at the designated place they rested for a couple of days. Then she and four other "widows" were ordered to prepare the staple fish paste to feed the cadres. "We didn't have anything to eat when Phnom Penh was liberated," she said. "So we had to cut the rice from the field and eat it."

By this time, news from the war front filtered through to her, and she heard that her husband was still alive. Her heart leapt with joy. "But he had no clue that I was alive," said Bun Rany. Because the Khmer Rouge soldiers still maintained tight control in the provinces, there was no chance for her to escape. "Even after being liberated we did not dare to speak freely because we had no idea about who were the real soldiers of liberation, and who were the Pol Pot men," she said. "The atmosphere was full of intrigue and you could almost smell the danger all around."

Hun Sen, who had his hands full with the task of rebuilding the foreign ministry, went to the town of Chup in Kompong Cham for a meeting. There, he asked the authorities to locate his wife, who was believed to be living at the Chup rubber plantation, but they did not oblige. Buny Rany added: "So he sent my father-in-law and my sister-in-law to locate me. Even though they stayed for fifteen days in the area they could not find me. But it so happened that one of the soldiers accompanying them was eventually able to find me. They returned to pick me up." Bun Rany now smiled for the first time in the three hours that we had been talking. Bun Rany and her sister-in-law travelled by motorcycle to Phnom Penh. They took turns to carry the baby. They arrived after driving non-stop for a day and a night.

Hun Sen was delirious with joy when he saw her. "I was in the ministry of foreign affairs when she arrived in Phnom Penh, and somebody told me that she had come to see me," he said. "I didn't believe it. When I came home I saw her. I asked her who was the boy with her. She said, 'He is your son.' But the boy didn't call me Dad." With tears welling up in her eyes, Bun Rany added: "My son was seeing his father for the first time. He called him Uncle."

The happiness of reunion did not remain unclouded for long, however. A year later, Pol Pot's soldiers broke into the family's village home and killed Bun Rany's father. "It was the same day when my mother arrived in Phnom Penh," said Bun Rany, her voice breaking. Quickly controlling her tears, she added: "When Phnom Penh was liberated we adopted three girls who were orphans of the civil war. They are now all married." They also gave shelter to an orphan whom they trained as a cook. She remained with the family. They even invited some of their distant relatives into their fold, and lived as an extended family for several years. After almost nine years of separation she wanted nothing more than to see Hun Sen, and to lead a regular life as a family. "I thought I'd help him set up a farm," she said. "Politics was the last thing on my mind. I was completely fed up with my life between 1970 and 1979, when I hardly got to see him. But the winds changed, and he had to take care of the country because there was no one else to do it."

When she first arrived in the city there was not much food for the people, and no water. People starved, lived on leaves and roots, and rarely ate maize and rice. Bun Rany had participated in Pol Pot's failed experiment, and was deeply hurt by it. She had never met Pol Pot, but she had come across another Khmer Rouge leader, Hou Youn, who had passed through her hospital and whose meals she had provided. But in the end, she was left with nothing except deep pain. Her wounds healed as she settled down to a new life as the wife of the young foreign minister. Even then, they faced difficulties. Hun Sen was not paid a salary. "We had nothing," she said. "We had only maize and rice to eat, and the maize was not Cambodian-grown maize. It was food sent as aid by Vietnam. For those of us who have experienced the generosity of Vietnam, we know that it would have been very difficult to survive without their help. Those who did not know the reality doubted the real story." The young Hun family lived in the same house in Phnom Penh for ten years, until they moved into their new home in Takhmau. "And I still cook for the family," she said with a laugh. Her life remained simple even though her husband was in the limelight. "I hardly met any celebrities because I mostly stayed at home to look after the children," she said.

127

THE OPPRESSED PEOPLE welcomed the Vietnamese forces. They were grateful to them for putting an end to the Khmer Rouge massacres. They believed that the days of peace and plenty were about to return.

The initial euphoria evaporated about a year later when many Cambodians felt that the Vietnamese liberators had turned into occupiers. Many wondered whether the Heng Samrin government was created under Vietnam's guidance, or whether it was an independent Cambodian initiative. "Even though we had some assistance from foreign countries, the government was our idea," Hun Sen said. "We were more independent than the tripartite coalition government [the Coalition Government of Democratic Kampuchea, or CGDK, formed in 1982 by Sihanouk, Son Sann, and the Khmer Rouge]. When Sihanouk, Son Sann, and Khieu Samphan organised a meeting in Singapore [in September 1981], they had no agreement, and tremendous pressure was put on them by ASEAN and, as a result, they could form their government in Kuala Lumpur. We were much more independent than these people. We arranged that Heng Samrin would be the chairman of the front, as well as the party. Pen Sovann would be vice-president and minister of defence. Chea Sim would be minister of the interior, and I was the foreign minister. We made the arrangement in the manner of an integrated force."

Looking back, he said: "I underestimated the idea of the ASEAN leaders in forming the tripartite government. They told us that our Heng Samrin government, created by the Vietnamese, was meaningless. We knew well what they had been doing with Sihanouk, Son Sann, and Khieu Samphan, and what these people had been receiving from them [in terms of military and non-military aid]. We knew who was independent, and who was under commission. There were no foreigners close to me, whereas the rest were working with foreigners."

At this stage of the interview with Hun Sen in December 1997, we referred to the liberation of Cambodia as an "invasion." The faux pax instantly drew an outraged response. "May I correct the word you used. We were liberating the country, not invading," he said. "You can see whether there is any form of foreign invasion in Cambodia. The question of foreign troops coming to Cambodia is not new. There were the French and the Japanese. Then, there were forces from the United States, South Vietnam, the Philippines, Thailand, and Australia. In short, the ASEAN countries invaded Cambodia, and they helped the tripartite coalition and the Khmer Rouge to fight against us." The Vietnamese, he said, had played a liberating role in Cambodia in 1979, a role markedly different from the South Vietnamese forces that pillaged and destroyed Cambodia in the early 1970s. "Without the Vietnamese armed forces we would die."

Denouncing the United States and ASEAN for fuelling the fire of civil war in Cambodia, he said: "There is no way that ASEAN and America could teach Cambodia. They are the cause of the violation of human rights and destruction in Cambodia. We want to be polite to the new generation, and we don't want to use such words. Would you like us to motivate three million people to stage demonstrations seeking compensation for the war? We cannot accept the word invasion," he said. "Without Pol Pot there wouldn't be any Vietnamese armed forces in Cambodia. And without ASEAN and the American invasion of Cambodia there would be no Pol Pot. Today [December 6, 1997], I have rejected a meeting with an American delegation because I don't want to be advised. Or else, I will advise them in return. It is better not to use any strong words against each other. It is better not to meet each other." He added: "Why do they advise us about human rights? When we realised that there was no good word from Washington I just cancelled the meeting. I am the head of a nation. I cannot listen to everyone's advice.

I am not a tripartite coalition that seeks advice from ASEAN. I am young, but I am equal to those people who worked with us, like Le Duc Anh, Le Duc Tho, and Nguyen Van Linh. When I asked them [Vietnam] to withdraw their experts, they did. We do not owe any debt to these people."

VIETNAM'S ROLE

It was said that with his seven eyes Hun Sen could foresee every move his enemies were planning to make. "I have one Cambodian eye and six Japanese eyes," he said about the various glass eyes that were fitted by Japan and the Soviet Union after he was blinded in his left eye. When the combined forces of the resistance—Pol Pot, Sihanouk, and Son Sann—failed to overthrow the Heng Samrin government, they grew frustrated and resorted to petty name-calling, even abuse. Hun Sen and his government suffered the indignity of being called, among other things, "Vietnam's lackey," "stooge," "puppet," "quisling," and "one-eyed Hun Sen." The presence of Vietnamese soldiers in Cambodia was a "military occupation," his critics charged. Retold hundreds of times, these fighting words soon became an ideological narrative that clouded the real issues of the genocide and the civil war. These words were used to admonish the liberators of the country from the murderous Khmer Rouge and, in turn, to anoint the Khmer Rouge as the legitimate representative of Cambodia at the United Nations.[8]

The West, and most of non-communist Asia, supported the Khmer Rouge and the CGDK. They glossed over the genocide, and were deaf to the rising cries within Cambodia for justice and the need to punish the perpetrators. This fuelled Hun Sen's anger, but he contained his rage in the hope that some day the Khmer Rouge would be brought to justice. The Vietnamese, alarmed at the unreasonable and unconscionable international support for the Khmer Rouge, decided to stay on in Cambodia to prevent Pol Pot from recapturing power.

Yet fears persisted that Vietnam was turning Cambodia into its colony. A report in the *Bangkok Post* in June 1983 revealed that Hanoi had set up "development villages" in Cambodia where one out of every five families was Vietnamese. Quoting "highly reliable military documents," the newspaper reported that such villages had been created in provinces along Cambodia's border with Vietnam and even in the western Cambodian provinces of Battambang and Koh Kong. It claimed that Vietnam was trying to achieve a twenty-per-cent mix of Vietnamese at all levels. The central Cambodian administration was being strictly controlled by Vietnamese experts who had been inducted into the higher levels of the administration to oversee and guide the officials of the Phnom Penh government, it argued.[9] Three years later, in May 1986, the New China News Agency reported that the Cambodian government was backed by a committee of Vietnamese advisors and specialists, without whom it could not survive a single day. It alleged that Hanoi had set up a "Cambodia Working Committee," code-numbered 478, through which it was manipulating the Heng Samrin government and its army.[10] Several scholars have made the claim that the PRK— renamed the State of Cambodia (SOC) in 1989—was under the close and constant tutelage and surveillance of Vietnamese advisors.[11] Indeed there is no denying that Vietnamese officials guided the PRK in its early years, but the claim that Cambodia was a satellite of Vietnam, or that the Vietnamese lectured the PRK leaders, who had no choice but to follow orders, is erroneous because it strips the PRK of all political agency, and runs counter to the narratives of patriotism and nationalism that the PRK espoused. Words such as "satellite," and "puppet" were distortions created by diplomats and picked up by journalists, and were crafted to deny the PRK political legitimacy.

Hun Sen was realistic about the necessity of having Vietnamese troops based on Cambodian soil. They were not there as colonisers. They were there to fight and mop up the Khmer Rouge. "Without

Vietnam's help we would die," he emphasised. From the start, Hun Sen knew the answers to two existential questions: how long did the Vietnamese plan to stay in Cambodia? And, was "occupation" ever a part of the plan to liberate the country? "According to the discussions, we planned that the Vietnamese would attack, and then withdraw immediately in 1979," Hun Sen revealed. "It was I who then talked with Le Duc Tho and others. I told them that if they withdrew, and Pol Pot returned, more people would be killed," he said. "At the time, the Cambodian forces were not able to handle Pol Pot, and we needed time to strengthen our forces and our economy." Thus Vietnam ensured the very existence of the new state of the PRK.[12] Fortunately for Hun Sen, Hanoi never vacillated in its support. Vietnam's foreign minister, Nguyen Co Thach, gave an assurance in June 1983 that his country would only withdraw its forces from Cambodia after a political settlement was reached between his country and China. That pact would ensure that China stopped aiding and arming the Khmer Rouge, and that Vietnam withdrew its 140,000-strong force from Cambodia.[13] Hun Sen, then playing the crucial role of foreign minister, did not want to be left isolated in a situation where the Vietnamese withdrew their forces, but China continued arming Pol Pot.

"The Vietnamese did not want to stay," he clarified. "It was our side that made such a request. We then agreed that they would try to reduce their forces in 1982. The Vietnamese would decrease their numbers, and we would increase our forces. Even as foreign minister I was involved in such a strategy. I still remember the meeting of the foreign ministers of Cambodia, Laos, and Vietnam in Hanoi in 1985 where we agreed that the Vietnamese forces would be withdrawn in ten to fifteen years. But owing to the progress in developing the Cambodian armed forces, and the peace talks between Sihanouk and me, we withdrew the Vietnamese forces earlier."

For its part, Vietnam miscalculated the reaction of the world to its Cambodian adventure. It was counting on the support of the major powers for having overthrown a genocidal regime, but when the support did not come through, and the international community nursed the Khmer Rouge back to life and helped develop the resistance forces, Hanoi realised that it had been drawn into a long and costly conflict. Once it was committed, Vietnam raised its troop strength in Cambodia to as many as 180,000–200,000. In the early 1980s, General Le Duc Anh's "Cambodianisation Plan" was enforced, a strategy that aimed to strengthen the PRK forces so they could shoulder the burden of fighting the Cambodian resistance. According to Australian defence analyst Carlyle Thayer, the strategy involved attacks on the Cambodian resistance positions along the border under a five-phased plan code-named "K-5" (*ke hoach nam* in Vietnamese). In its totality, the plan included sealing the border with Thailand, destroying the resistance fighters, and building up the forces of Phnom Penh. It was an expensive adventure, and soon Hanoi admitted that its Cambodian intervention was bleeding its economy, and began devising ways to get out.

One of the earliest indications that the Vietnamese were serious about pulling out came from Hun Sen's friend and ally, Indian Prime Minister Rajiv Gandhi, who visited Vietnam in November 1985. Gandhi confirmed that Hanoi had agreed to withdraw its troops from Cambodia by 1990, and might do so even sooner.[14] At any rate, the withdrawals had started even earlier, in 1982, when Hanoi conducted a series of troop withdrawals, although some military observers dismissed these as troop rotations.

A full Vietnamese withdrawal seemed possible when Soviet Foreign Minister Eduard Shevardnadze declared in May 1987 that the Soviet model of withdrawal from Afghanistan in twenty-two months might become a model for solving the Cambodian conflict. The most definitive statement came from Hun Sen, who announced in Paris in 1989 that, whether or not the Cambodian problem was resolved, Vietnam would withdraw its troops from Cambodia in September that year. In the end, he said, "we withdrew the

[Vietnamese] forces even before the [Paris peace] accord was signed [in 1991]." Diplomats speculated that Hun Sen would not survive long, and that the Khmer Rouge would recapture power. They joked that "Hun Sen would last in power only for as long as it took a Khmer Rouge tank to drive from the Thai border to Phnom Penh." In January 1978, Pol Pot had told Sihanouk that the war against Vietnam was going well, and "within two months we will wipe out the Vietnamese."[15] But Hun Sen was confident that his country would be stable after the final withdrawal, as it had remained secure after six previous partial pullouts.[16]

The Vietnamese withdrawal in September 1989 turned into a major media event, with many reporters camping in open parks in Phnom Penh because the few hotels were full. As newspapers published pictures of smiling Vietnamese soldiers sitting atop departing battle tanks, it appeared that the Vietnamese had indeed gone home for good, a decade after they had arrived.

Did some Vietnamese experts stay back to advise the Cambodians? "That is a wrong impression," Hun Sen said. "We had prepared ourselves to become self-reliant. The military, economic, and political advisors of Vietnam were withdrawn in 1988— one year before the withdrawal of the Vietnamese armed forces. Why did we do it this way?" he asked rhetorically. "We could benefit from the Vietnamese units who helped us in fighting, but we could not rely on the Vietnamese thinking." In February 1988, a very worried Hun Sen visited Vietnam, where he expressed his concerns to Nguyen Van Linh, the General Secretary of the Vietnamese Communist Party, and they struck a deal to repatriate the advisors ahead of the pullout of the armed forces. Thus the Vietnamese advisors, who had arrived in 1979, were withdrawn in phases between June and August 1988. However, according to the Cambodian resistance, about 70,000 to 80,000 Vietnamese troops stayed behind, disguised as Cambodians, and Vietnamese civilian advisors continued their attachment with various ministries in Phnom Penh, while Cambodian officers received training in Vietnam for two more years. To this Hun Sen responded: "The role of the Vietnamese advisors was the same as that of the foreign advisors [in the embassies and in foreign organisations] who worked in Cambodia through the 1990s." He clarified: "I have the impression that these foreign advisors were interfering much more in the internal affairs of Cambodia than the Vietnamese advisors. They only agreed to advise us, and left it to us, the Cambodians, to make the decisions."

Like many Asian leaders, Hun Sen could not tolerate being lectured by Western governments and their Southeast Asia experts. "The foreign advisors to Cambodia—if we don't listen to them— threaten to cut assistance to us," he said. "The foreign advisors were doing what they accused the Vietnamese of doing. They were behaving like the masters of Cambodia. They said that Vietnam occupied Cambodia, but in reality Vietnam did a lot for us. Vietnam was good to us. The most important role the Vietnamese played was to prevent the Pol Pot regime from returning. On the political side, it was the Cambodians who made the decisions."

As Vietnam prepared to leave Cambodia, U.S. intelligence assessments believed that Hun Sen would dominate Cambodian politics. U.S. officials observed that Hun Sen was becoming a powerful political personality, and that he would enhance his standing after the Vietnamese withdrawal. For instance, in June 1989 the U.S. Central Intelligence Agency argued that Hun Sen "probably believes his chances for international recognition will improve substantially after Hanoi leaves." It further argued that if Hun Sen actually held elections within three months, as he had promised to do, it "would help his cause and enhance his standing if he is challenged politically."[17]

Before they left, the Vietnamese built up a large stockpile of weapons for the Phnom Penh military. The Soviet Union also contributed to the supplies. General Vu Xuan Vinh, the Chief of the

Vietnamese defence ministry's International Relations Department, revealed that Hanoi advised Cambodia not to launch any major offensive as that would drain the stock of weapons, and instead to pursue a policy of attacking the resistance forces only when attacked. United Nations military observers claimed that in spite of the ostensible withdrawal, Vietnamese special forces continued limited operations inside Cambodia, with elite Vietnamese troops still based in Siem Reap in early 1992. In addition, according to press reports, Vietnamese troops entered Kampot province in March 1991 to repulse a Khmer Rouge attack, and, as U.S. Assistant Secretary of State Richard Solomon told a senate hearing in April 1991, the Vietnamese had left in place thousands of military advisors, in the range of 5,000–10,000, and had sent their forces in and out of Cambodia to deal with specific engagements.

Apart from the military and political criticisms, Heng Samrin and Hun Sen were also accused of setting up a communist-style economic system by giving the state a disproportionately large share in the economy and, in doing so, blindly following Vietnam. "The economic systems of Vietnam and Cambodia are different," Hun Sen countered. "We had some Vietnamese economic advisors, but the economy of Cambodia is different from that of Vietnam. We listened to their opinions, but we made the decisions. But now, if we do not follow what they [the West] say, they will threaten to cut assistance, or raise an outcry in the newspapers." It was speculated that the Vietnamese had taken away millions of dollars of natural resources such as timber and rubber during their long stay in the country. Hun Sen rejected the allegation. "It is not true. The trade between our countries was a normal affair. Vietnam could buy timber and rubber from Cambodia at the same price as other countries bought these commodities from us."

Vietnam paid for its Cambodian adventure in blood. After withdrawing their forces in 1989, Vietnamese officials released conflicting reports on their human losses. According to one estimate,

40,000–50,000 Vietnamese troops were killed or wounded in Cambodia between 1978 and 1988. A Vietnamese study that was presented to the Vietnamese National Assembly in Hanoi claimed that some 67,000 Vietnamese were killed or wounded during the ten-year campaign in Cambodia. The highest numbers were claimed by Major-General Nguyen Van Thai, who believed that about 55,300 Vietnamese were killed, 110,000 seriously wounded, and 55,000 slightly injured, making a total of 220,300 war casualties.

The Phnom Penh government felt indebted to the Vietnamese. General Secretary Heng Samrin had said in his report to the Fifth Congress of the Kampuchean People's Revolutionary Party (KPRP) in October 1985 that Cambodia must strengthen its alliance with Vietnam, Laos, and the Soviet Union, because such an alliance was a "law" that would guarantee the success of the Cambodian revolution. He tried to change the mindset of the people, who were suspicious of the presence of the Vietnamese forces, urging them to give up their "narrow-minded chauvinism," which infringed on the friendship between Cambodia and Vietnam. But many Cambodians watched with dismay and disgust as Hanoi stamped its authority. Ministries and departments were headed by Cambodian and Vietnamese officials. Resentment mounted when, in 1985, people spoke out about being forcibly conscripted into the Cambodian Army by the Vietnamese. Many Cambodians did acknowledge that it was Hanoi's experts who had helped rejuvenate the education system that had been completely destroyed by the Khmer Rouge. Still, an anti-Vietnam feeling remained a dark shadow that deepened the mistrust between the two countries.

Despite the lingering perception of Cambodia's domination by Vietnam, U.S. officials believed that the Phnom Penh government was rapidly gaining international stature. An influential U.S. intelligence report revealed in December 1989 that Western Europe and ASEAN were deeply worried about a return to power of the Khmer Rouge, and were "shifting toward de facto recognition of, and outright support for, the Phnom Penh regime." The European Parliament was calling for the European Union "to recognise the Phnom Penh regime," and to "assist it in isolating the Khmer Rouge." The report noted with alarm that a "French foreign ministry official recently went to Phnom Penh to prepare for the opening of a quasi-governmental cultural centre." The PRK was, in fact, winning new friends abroad, despite its connections with Vietnam.[18]

V

ASCENT OF A PEASANT TO POWER

1978-97

THE HUN FAMILY and friends watched the rapid political rise of Hun Sen with a mixture of disbelief, amazement, and admiration. Elsewhere, the once-powerful Norodom family and the Khmer Rouge, still lusting for power, were shocked and confounded. A young peasant without formal higher education was emerging as the most powerful leader in post-independence Cambodia.

Hun Sen's political ascent had begun long before he became foreign minister at the age of twenty-seven. His first political post was that of a founding member of the United Front created on December 2, 1978. But even before that, he was already politically active. "Before the birth of the front I was already the leader of the resistance movement on the east side of the Mekong River ever since I broke away from the Pol Pot clique," he affirmed. "I was a military commander and a political leader with the task of building both the military and political forces."[1] But he was reluctant to step into active politics. When the top members of the communist Kampuchean People's Revolutionary Council asked him to become foreign minister he refused to take the job. He was aware of his shortcomings and realised that he had much to learn. However, when the senior leaders persuaded him to reconsider, he reluctantly agreed, and was appointed on probation on January 7, 1979. "I agreed to accept the post for a trial period of three months because I had never received any training for this kind of work. I was given a monthly remuneration of sixteen kilogrammes of foodgrains, of which ten kilogrammes was rice and six kilogrammes was maize," he revealed.

Till the time he became foreign minister, Hun Sen worried that his young age was a hindrance to his political goals. When he had defected to Vietnam in 1977, his Vietnamese hosts constantly doubted his claim that he was a military commander because he looked very young. And when the job of foreign minister was offered to him, he grew concerned that his age might again become an issue. In order to appear older than he was, he told a typist to record his birthdate on his personal resume as April 4, 1951.[2] By that sleight of hand, he made himself one year older.

Overnight, the revolutionary became a member of the establishment. In his own words, the new responsibilities that came with the ministerial position were often too much to cope with. "I faced lots of difficulties in understanding and grasping the complex issues of international affairs because I had no expertise. But, through training I learnt how to deal with these complexities. I was fortunate that several Cambodian leaders who had a great deal of experience and knowledge of diplomatic affairs helped me constantly. I, too, made a determined effort to study and research world affairs."

COLD WAR DIPLOMACY

Hun Sen made his international debut at a ministerial meeting of the Non-Aligned Movement in Colombo, Sri Lanka, in June 1979. He took to his new job with aplomb. "Like Cambodia, Sri Lanka was also a place of intense struggle," he remarked. "At the time we still occupied the Cambodian seat at the meetings of the Non-Aligned countries."[3] On his way to Sri Lanka, he flew to the two countries that were Cambodia's strongest allies, in order to get their blessings and support—he first went to Vietnam, and then to the Soviet Union. In Colombo, according to a bulletin of the Cambodian news agency SPK dated June 14, 1979, Hun Sen held talks with Sri Lankan officials and met officials from Vietnam,

Laos, Cuba and several non-aligned states, many of whom launched scathing attacks on the former Khmer Rouge regime. Taking the cue from them, he spoke to reporters from the *Far Eastern Economic Review* and an official Cambodian newspaper, and correspondents from several countries. He related to them the saga of the liberation of Cambodia, the long struggle, and the overthrow of the Pol Pot clique. In colourful language he condemned Pol Pot and Ieng Sary as being the "slaves of the Chinese emperor who invaded and killed more than three million Cambodians, and tortured and punished the remaining four million people who survived the genocide." After the briefing, Hun Sen showed the press a documentary film on the crimes of the Khmer Rouge.

At the time of the Sri Lanka meeting, Cambodia did not have diplomatic relations with the major South Asian power, India, whose prime minister, Morarji Desai, refused to recognise the Phnom Penh government unless Vietnam withdrew its forces. Nonetheless, "although we did not have diplomatic relations, India did not object to our presence," Hun Sen said. The Morarji government unexpectedly weighed in to support Cambodia at the United Nations in November that year. India suggested that a proposed conference on Cambodia should be attended by ASEAN and the Indochinese states, and that outside powers should be kept out, to minimise interference. ASEAN did not support the proposal because a smaller forum could easily be stage-managed by Hanoi to its advantage.[4]

The India card was important to Cambodia. It was the only non-communist country within Asia willing to support the isolated Phnom Penh government. But Cambodia's hopes were dashed when the new Indian Prime Minister Indira Gandhi rebuffed Vietnamese Prime Minister Pham Van Dong's proposal for India to extend diplomatic recognition to the Phnom Penh government.[5] Gandhi's reluctance stemmed from her concern that she would be seen to have been pressured by the Vietnamese premier to recognise Cambodia. However, Dong did manage to extract one important concession during his visit to New Delhi in April 1980— Gandhi dropped the precondition of her predecessor, Morarji, who had demanded that the Vietnamese withdraw their forces before India recognised Phnom Penh. Just three months after Dong's visit, India normalised relations with Cambodia. Hun Sen added: "After Mrs Indira Gandhi came to power in 1980, India eventually recognised Cambodia, and forged diplomatic relations." Indian Foreign Minister Narasimha Rao said that Cambodia needed all possible assistance from the international community after its "terrible ordeals." The announcement did not come as a surprise, as the Gandhi government had given an earlier assurance that it would recognise the new rulers of Phnom Penh.[6] Thus the new Cambodian government scored its first significant victory, breaking the cordon of diplomatic isolation that the West and non-communist Asia had thrown around Phnom Penh.

At home, life for Hun Sen's young family was for the first time entering a harmonious phase. His wife, however, had her reservations about his new job as foreign minister. "She was unhappy because she didn't want me to enter politics," he disclosed. "She persuaded me to abandon the post, and go back to the countryside to work as a farmer. I didn't agree with her because, at the time, I was working for the nation. But she was fed up with the suffering."

The reunited family was allotted a house fronting the Independence Monument in Phnom Penh, and they quickly settled down there. "At that time there was no residence for a foreign minister, but there were so many empty houses in Phnom Penh—everybody could choose one," he said. "I could get 300 houses if I wanted." Later, in the 1990s, as a resurgent Cambodian press went on the offensive, among other things it criticised his State of Cambodia government for illegally occupying homes and property that belonged to others. Hun Sen explained that the issue of overlapping property claims was a legacy of the Pol Pot regime that drove city dwellers from their homes and overturned the social structure. "After liberation on January 7, 1979, Phnom Penh was a ghost city without people," he explained. "Many home owners lost their lives. Nobody possessed their home ownership documents. When the people returned to the city, they chose to live in houses which were situated near their place of work. As the liberated people returned, one by one, they were resettled. This process resulted in an irreversible situation which required us to implement the principle of non-revision of borders, as experienced by the African countries after they gained independence from the colonialists. It would bring about a dangerous war between the newcomers and the previous owners if the ownership was revised, and would cause another evacuation of people across the country."

His job was never easy. His country desperately needed loans, but he could not get through the stiff-hinged door at the World Bank. Cambodia was ringed by an economic embargo enforced by most of the non-communist countries who wanted to punish the Heng Samrin government because it was supported by their chief enemy, communist Vietnam. When Hun Sen found it impossible to get international loans, his government came to depend completely on the Soviet Union, Cuba, Vietnam and, to some extent, India. "It was the period of the Cold War, ideological warfare, and a struggle between the two blocs, the West and the East," he pointed out. "The West had imposed unjust punishment on us, while the socialist countries extended their hand to help us economically and militarily in order to prevent the Pol Pot regime from returning."

Hun Sen found that his efforts to gain membership of the United Nations were blocked. "We made every effort to request the UN to give justice to the Cambodian people who had survived the genocide," he explained. "On the contrary, due to the pressure exerted by a number of countries, the representatives of Pol Pot could occupy the Cambodian seat at the UN." Tragedy degenerated into farce. The West and the non-communist Asian countries penalised Cambodia largely because it was supported by Vietnam, yet they thought it morally acceptable to continue to recognise the genocidal Democratic Kampuchea regime.

At home, the economic life of the people was completely shattered following the disastrous rule of the Khmer Rouge. There was no drinking water, no telephone service, no mail, no transport, no markets, and no money. In early March 1979, residents of Phnom Penh were forced to survive by eating roots, wild fruit, and leaves.[7] Millions of hectares of rice fields were temporarily abandoned due to the civil war. To ease the situation, the new government sometimes distributed rice and flour. It was only in August that news filtered out that the Heng Samrin government was preparing to revive the use of money and create a cash-based economy before the end of the year.

Communication lines had been all but severed. Cambodia was unreachable. Soon after Hun Sen became foreign minister, Cambodia's first newspaper since 1975 made an appearance. This state-owned paper consisted of eight pages, four of which were filled with pictures, and four with articles on the policies of the new government.[8] Just what these policies were became apparent a month later when President Heng Samrin said in an interview that his immediate tasks were to provide food, housing, clothing, and health services to the millions of displaced people who were returning to their homes after the genocide,[9] and to mop up the remnants of the Khmer Rouge. The interview was released by the government to coincide with a visit to Phnom Penh by Vietnamese Prime Minister Pham Van Dong, who became the first foreign head of government to travel to the country to meet its leaders in a public display of solidarity.

The country's former monarch, too, was making an attempt to return to political life. The first sign that Sihanouk was determined to fight his way back to power became apparent in July 1979, when he declared from Paris that he would create a parallel Cambodian government-in-exile. The Phnom Penh government labelled Sihanouk's proposed alliance with the Khmer Rouge and Son Sann as a front led by "a puppet—no more, no less."[10] Hun Sen had not forgotten that Sihanouk had briefly served as a puppet head of state of the Democratic Kampuchea regime, and had played a crucial role in the development of the Khmer Rouge. Hun Sen, then a hardline figure, rejected any idea of a dialogue with Sihanouk or Son Sann, the two exiled leaders who were on the verge of forming an alliance with the Khmer Rouge.

By this time, Hun Sen had become a fluent and forceful exponent of Cambodian foreign policy. He argued that Vietnam's liberation struggle against French and U.S. colonialism was a righteous war, and that Western imperialism had harmed the Indochinese countries. His rapid progress did not go unnoticed by his political mentors, Heng Samrin, Pen Sovann, and Chea Sim. In 1981, he was rewarded with the post of deputy prime minister in addition to his role as foreign minister. A more confident Hun Sen began travelling further afield to confer with his allies in New Delhi. It was in the company of Indian political leaders and foreign office bureaucrats that he felt most at ease and among friends. On a six-day visit to New Delhi in August 1981, he unveiled a two-stage plan to resolve the Cambodian problem through a regional conference among the three Indochinese states and ASEAN, followed by an international conference bringing together the major powers, particularly the United States and China.[11]

One month later, Sihanouk flew to Singapore, where he met Son Sann and Khieu Samphan at their first formal meeting to create a united force against the Phnom Penh government and its Vietnamese backers.[12] Phnom Penh dismissed the meeting as "only a new piece of theatre created by Beijing and Washington." It added: "The haggling among Mr Son Sann, Mr Sihanouk, and Mr Khieu Samphan, traitors to the Kampuchean people, will come to nothing because they are working in their own interests."[13] Hun

Sen quickly became the public face and voice of the Phnom Penh government, and played the lead role in countering Sihanouk's propaganda. The young foreign minister did not have the faintest idea that he was about to become one of the youngest prime ministers in Southeast Asia.

PRIME MINISTER AT THIRTY-THREE

It was the death of Prime Minister Chan Si that cleared the way for Hun Sen to take his post. In a stunningly rapid ascent up the pyramid slope of the Communist Party he was elected prime minister in January 1985, just six years after becoming foreign minister.[14] Hun Sen described his ascent as being the logical culmination of his leadership roles as a guerrilla, a commander, and later as an organiser of the united front. "Brothers in the party leadership entrusted me with the post of prime minister when Prime Minister Chan Si passed away at the end of 1984," he revealed.[15]

The new prime minister was just thirty-three years of age, and ranked fifth in the seven-member politburo of the ruling KPRP. The relatively inexperienced ex-guerrilla was elected unanimously at a plenary session of the national assembly. "It was the only instance in Cambodian history when a Cambodian leader got one hundred per cent of the secret votes of confidence," he explained. "This had never happened in the case of prime ministers Pen Sovann and Chan Si, my predecessors, who had lost a number of votes of confidence." Hun Sen was referring to the votes to elect Pen Sovann as the prime minister in July 1981, and Chan Si the next year. Sovann was a stalwart of the ruling KPRP, an offshoot of the Indochinese Communist Party (ICP), which had resisted French colonial rule and the Japanese occupation of Cambodia. The KPRP was formed after the ICP was dissolved in 1951 and reorganised into three Communist Parties for Vietnam, Laos, and Cambodia. The Cambodian party split in 1962 into pro-China and pro-Soviet factions.[16] The pro-Chinese group was led by Pol Pot. In January

1979, the split became permanent when the pro-Soviet (and pro-Vietnamese) faction under Pen Sovann replaced Pol Pot as the new leadership in Phnom Penh. Pen Sovann was elected secretary-general of the KPRP central committee at a time when the party had about sixty-five regular members. He distanced the party from Pol Pot's communist group, whom he castigated for being traitors, at the KPRP's Fourth Party Congress from May 26–29, 1981. The congress resolved to wipe out Pol Pot's "reactionary ultra-nationalist doctrine," erase personality cults, and develop a strong Marxist-Leninist party.

When Heng Samrin suddenly replaced Sovann as the party leader on December 4, 1981, the KPRP's pro-Vietnamese stance became even more pronounced. Sovann was removed in a purge, arrested, and virtually exiled to Hanoi because he was seen as not being loyal enough to the Vietnamese.[17] It was also believed that he was the victim of a personality clash with Heng Samrin. In Hanoi he spent seven years in jail, and another three under house arrest. "I was in a fifteen-square-metre cell. I was cut off from the outside world, and they only gave me five dollars a month to live," Pen Sovann told the *Phnom Penh Post* in an interview in May 1997. "Hun Sen and Say Phuthang were responsible for my imprisonment," he alleged.[18] Over in Phnom Penh, the national assembly voted to elect Chan Si as prime minister in early 1982. At the time, Hun Sen was visiting France as foreign minister. The same year he also travelled to the Soviet Union, and took a vacation on the Black Sea.

When Pen Sovann inquired why he was being jailed, he received a letter signed by Say Phuthang on February 12, 1982, accusing him of being "narrow-minded, extremely nationalistic, and against the Vietnamese." As a result, the KPRP could not let him return to Cambodia, the letter said. It was not till ten years later, in 1992, that Sovann was thought to be sufficiently re-educated and allowed to return home. He then applied for a post in his former party—now renamed the Cambodian People's Party (CPP)—but was not accepted because he was not trusted. His repeated requests to join the party were denied. Finally, in 1994, he was appointed as an advisor to a CPP branch in Takeo province. But soon the CPP began doubting his loyalty when it was rumoured that he might join the Khmer Nation Party, founded by Sam Rainsy, who was a son of Sam Sary, a senior official in the government of Sihanouk in the 1960s. As a result, Sovann lost his post. He alleged that Hun Sen had threatened to confiscate his house in Takeo and his car. Then he made several requests to the CPP to allow him to rejoin the party. "I kneel and beg to join [the CPP] by writing once or twice a year to Hun Sen and Chea Sim. Recently, I asked Chea Sim whether I could serve the CPP," he said. A desperate Pen Sovann then turned to Ranariddh's Funcinpec party, only to be spurned on account of his former Marxist-Leninist tendencies. He remained on the margins of Phnom Penh politics, harbouring feeble hopes of starting his own political party.

After the sacking of Pen Sovann in 1981, Chan Si became prime minister, but he did not live long. His death in December 1984 opened the way for another election. With two stalwarts out of the way, the party was led by a third influential personality, Heng Samrin. Suddenly the elevation of Hun Sen, a longstanding friend and ally of Heng Samrin's, was both possible and plausible. At the time of Chan Si's death, Hun Sen was in Hanoi, where he was briefing Vietnamese officials on Cambodian affairs. On his return, he was appointed acting prime minister by the party leadership in Phnom Penh. The prime-ministership was within reach. The party nominated just one candidate, Hun Sen, in the secret vote to elect a new premier. The five top leaders who vetted and shortlisted the candidates for premiership were Heng Samrin, Chea Sim, Say Phuthang, Chea Soth, and Bou Thang. Hun Sen considered them his five godfathers. None of them stood as candidates for the premiership because they already occupied the highest posts within the state and the party: Heng Samrin was the head of state; Chea

Sim was the chairman of the national assembly; Chea Soth and Bou Thang were deputy prime ministers in charge of the economy and national defence; and Say Phuthang was a key member of the politburo. Hun Sen told the authors that while Say Phuthang proposed Hun Sen's name within the party, Heng Samrin did so in the national assembly, and Chea Sim supervised the vote. "Although I was not eager for the top job, I had to accept it because their confidence had been entrusted in me," Hun Sen said. Without the support of these five men and other veteran party leaders such as Tea Banh, Sai Chhum and Sar Kheng, as well as a group whom Hun Sen dubbed the "senior" intellectuals such as Hor Nam Hong, Chem Snguon, Phlek Phirun, and My Samedi, and a younger group whom he called the "junior" intellectuals, Hun Sen's rise would have been inconceivable.

How did a man so young and inexperienced win the confidence of the Cambodian leaders? "They were aware of my capabilities, which I had demonstrated as the foreign minister," Hun Sen explained. "They reposed a lot of confidence in me [even though] at that time, among the members of the government and the party I was the youngest." As foreign minister he was acutely aware that the KPRP was a weak and wobbly entity, with a membership of fewer than 1,000 people. The largest province, Kompong Cham, had as few as thirty regular members. After he became prime minister, the KPRP held its Fifth Congress from October 13–16, 1985, a major event when party membership rose to more than 7,000. The congress unveiled the country's first Five-Year Plan (1986–90) to address the stuntedness of the economy, in which industries suffered from a lack of fuel, spare parts and raw materials. To the three sectors mentioned in the constitution—the state sector, the collective sector and the family sector—was added the private sector, which would play a central role in helping Hun Sen's government survive the years in isolation.

INSIDE THE PARTY

Political observers believed there were divisions within the party. In particular, Chea Sim's relationship with Hun Sen came under scrutiny from diplomats and seasoned journalists, who speculated that there was an intense rivalry between the two men going back to the early 1980s. The first public hints of the supposed rivalry surfaced when Chea Sim was believed to have engineered the dismissal of Khieu Kanharith as the editor of the party's newspaper. Kanharith was one of Hun Sen's closest friends and allies. Chea Sim apparently frowned upon Kanharith's frequent criticisms of government policy and his proximity to Western journalists, who sought him out for comments on the secretive party. Diplomats wagered that Chea Sim was behind the dismissal of Kanharith, and that by sacking a person close to Hun Sen, he wanted to send a message of his disapproval indirectly, without publicly confronting the prime minister. The rivalry, if it could be called that, was believed to stem from the peace talks in Tokyo, when Hun Sen is understood to have named all six members of the Supreme National Council—the body that was to run Cambodia until elections could be held—without seeking the approval of his party colleagues in Phnom Penh. Diplomats argued that there were factions within the CPP that thought Hun Sen to be extremely pro-West, and viewed him as having made too many concessions to those countries. From these perceptions, many diplomats concluded that the CPP, far from being united, was badly split.

"This speculation has been going on for more than fifteen years," Hun Sen said with a wide grin, as he began shedding light on the topic. "Before 1984, they said that there was rivalry between Heng Samrin and Say Phuthang, and between Heng Samrin and Chea Sim. A rivalry between Chea Sim and me is a no-win rivalry. If there was a no-win situation it meant that there was no rivalry. What was the rivalry for? Chea Sim is the head of the CPP and the chairman of the national assembly—both very senior positions.

What's the use for him to take the post of prime minister? Now, I am a powerful prime minister, so what is the use for me to take the post of the head of the party, and that of the national assembly?" Who was more powerful—Hun Sen or Chea Sim, we asked him. "I don't want to say who is more powerful. But everybody has their own obligation. If Chea Sim takes the post of prime minister maybe he would do better than Hun Sen."

When the rumours of a split first began doing the rounds of the capital in the late 1980s, Chea Sim was seen as a hardliner and Hun Sen as a reformist. While Chea Sim wanted Hun Sen to make no concessions to the non-communist factions at the peace talks, Hun Sen pursued a policy of reconciliation, and played a decisive role in achieving peace. Some political observers believed that a difference of opinion between Hun Sen and Chea Sim arose because the former was reputed to have the best team of economic advisors, which had come up with better economic plans than Chea Sim's team. One of the best informed analysts in Phnom Penh, Soviet embassy counsellor V. Loukianov, dismissed the gossip and said that Chea Sim did not covet Hun Sen's job. "There's no question of it. Mr Chea Sim is senior to Mr Hun Sen in the government and in the party politburo," Loukianov argued. "So, Mr Chea Sim would gain nothing by toppling Mr Hun Sen, who is his political junior."[19] In 1998, we told Hun Sen about the comments that Loukianov had made in 1990. "He was right, because Chea Sim has always been my boss," Hun Sen responded. "Even now, both Heng Samrin and Chea Sim are my bosses. There are two more people who are my bosses—Chea Soth and Say Phuthang. We can compare the CPP to a football team. The most important person in the team is the coach. If the coach is not effective, then the team cannot win. Chea Soth is a very good coach. When the German football team was defeated they did not blame the players. They blamed the coach. It is the same for the party. There is only one kind of rivalry between Chea Sim and me—golf. He has played golf for a long time, and I cannot defeat him. I am trying to beat him at the game."

Nevertheless, speculation about a power struggle between Hun Sen and Chea Sim persisted through 1992. The CIA believed that Chea Sim was the "regime's most powerful official," who was "taking a more active role in Phnom Penh's all-out effort to gain international legitimacy."[20] It was believed that Chea Sim had gained the upper hand following a constitutional amendment in April that allowed him to act as the president in the absence, or illness, of President Heng Samrin. The pecking order now was Chea Sim, Heng Samrin, and then Hun Sen. While Hun Sen had elevated his close associates to ministerial posts, Chea Sim appointed his brother-in-law, Sar Kheng, as a deputy prime minister and minister of the interior. The ruling party said in May 1992 that there was no basis to the "rumours" of a power struggle, and that the party was united. A senior Cambodian government official confided that the political trio of Hun Sen, Chea Sim, and Heng Samrin that ran Cambodia were not just comrades but close friends who liked to share a bottle of cognac. "Sometimes Hun Sen walks into Chea Sim's house, or Heng Samrin walks into Hun Sen's house, and they eat and drink together. They are the best of friends," the official said. But sceptical diplomats continued to believe that what they saw as a power struggle would hurt the party in the coming elections.

NEGOTIATING PEACE

Hun Sen had been a member of the KPRP's politburo ever since the formation of the Kampuchean United Front for National Salvation in Vietnam in 1978. When the central committee and the politburo were set up, his "godfathers" ensured a place for him. Almost a year after becoming the prime minister, he gave up the post of foreign minister in December 1986 in order to concentrate his energies on running the country and, in particular, to manage the military campaign against the Khmer Rouge.

Hemmed in by a crippling U.S. trade embargo and a ban on World Bank and International Monetary Fund loans, Cambodia faced a daunting array of economic and diplomatic challenges. By his own admission, Hun Sen found some of these issues "quite complicated," especially the management of the painful transition from a planned economy to a mixed economy and, ultimately, to an open economy. "It was imperative to find a political solution through negotiations," Hun Sen declared. "Economic reforms went along with political reforms. However, political stability had to be maintained so that economic reforms could be carried out together with the search for a political solution to end the war and bring about peace." He paused to drag long and hard on a cigarette, then sipped Chinese tea, before saying: "I will write a book about these complicated issues."

The perception of his government as a "Vietnam-installed puppet regime" made it even more difficult for him to steer the isolated country onto the path of economic reform. Although it did bother him, there was little he could do to mould the opinion of the United States, the Western allies and China, who were critical of the hard-earned liberation of Cambodia and the removal of the Khmer Rouge by the Cambodian rebels and the Vietnamese army. "Justice still prevailed in the world," Hun Sen said with conviction. "Therefore, I did not pay much attention to what [issues] were raised. I devoted much of my time to help the people to be free from poverty—our real enemy—rather than quarrelling with the press."

"It was a very complicated period," he said. "From 1979 to 1983, it was a state of total confrontation. From 1984, we entered a new phase of confrontation and negotiation. I still remember two very important men from ASEAN: the foreign ministers— Mochtar Kusumaatmadja of Indonesia, and Ghazalie Shafie of Malaysia. From the Indochinese countries, we had Nguyen Co Thach of Vietnam. We had two groups of countries—the ASEAN six and the Indochinese three. So, we had to speed up the process of negotiation."

To prevent Thailand from interfering in Cambodian affairs, and urge it to end its support of the Khmer Rouge, the Hun Sen government proposed that the Thai military play a neutral role in order to avoid confrontation. In the end, Hun Sen had a secret meeting with Thai General Chavalit Yongchaiyudh in Vientiane in late 1988, and met Prime Minister Chatichai Choonhavan in 1989. The effort was futile, as Thailand continued supporting the Khmer Rouge.

Nurtured by his party bosses, Hun Sen adopted a hard line against the resistance led by Sihanouk, while his army fought the remnants of the Khmer Rouge along the border with Thailand. The young Cambodian premier could count on the unstinting backing of his communist party chiefs. The party evolved a consensus on its domestic and foreign policy, and Hun Sen fine-tuned it. In May 1987, he rejected an overture for peace made by Sihanouk as "not new and not realistic."[21] But by October he had softened his stand, and offered the top three positions to Sihanouk in a future coalition government—head of state, deputy head of state, and prime minister. Sihanouk rejected the offer out of hand. "I would rather die in Beijing or Pyongyang than be a puppet president in Phnom Penh, a stooge of Hanoi," Sihanouk shot back from France in December.[22] He was willing, however, to return as the head of a new state run by his three-party opposition and the Hun Sen government. The angry young man gradually saw sense in the search for peace, and agreed to start talks with Sihanouk, who lived in exile in Beijing, and occasionally travelled to Pyongyang and Paris. "I did consider achieving a peaceful solution, especially with Sihanouk, since the early-1980s after the first partial withdrawal of the Vietnamese troops from Cambodia in 1982," Hun Sen said amiably.

The breakthrough occurred on December 2, 1987, when Hun Sen met Sihanouk on neutral ground in Fère-en-Tardenois, a wooded village northeast of Paris. It was the first dialogue between the sixty-five-year-old prince and the thirty-five-year-old peasant.[23] It soon became apparent that it was a dialogue of equals, between an urbane champagne-drinking prince and a nationalist schooled in the jungles of Indochina. "The decision to hold the talks was based on the view that military power could not solve the Cambodian problem, and only negotiations and national reconciliation could bring peace," Hun Sen said. Although the two adversaries had serious differences, during their talks Hun Sen put the past behind him. After six hours of eyeballing each other at the Renaissance chateau where the talks were being held, the two men reached a tentative agreement on a four-point plan to end the bloody civil war that had by now raged for nine years. (Hun Sen made it clear that he was not in France just to meet Sihanouk: he took leave of the talks to attend the French Communist Party congress, making his political leanings quite apparent.) After three days of talks, the two sides agreed to ask North Korean strongman Kim Il Sung to mediate between China and Vietnam, the main backers of the Khmer Rouge and the Phnom Penh government, respectively.[24] The fact that a communiqué, issued at the end of the talks, made no mention of the controversial presence of some 140,000 Vietnamese troops in Cambodia spoke volumes for Hun Sen's dexterity as a negotiator. The two leaders agreed to pursue talks in Pyongyang a month later. "The significance of the agreement between Sihanouk and me was to seek a peaceful solution," Hun Sen said.

Just six days after their landmark talks, however, the mercurial Sihanouk suddenly changed his mind and cancelled further peace talks with Hun Sen, calling him a "lackey of the Vietnamese" who had arrived at the talks "empty-handed and sought to score propaganda points."[25] Sihanouk's flip-flops delayed the return of peace to his country. It showed that he remained hostage to the Khmer Rouge, whom he had encouraged in the 1970s in the desperate hope that they would restore him to power, only to be disappointed

Battlefield enemies come face to face: The first one-on-one meeting between the young Prime Minister Hun Sen and Prince Norodom Sihanouk (right) in Fère-en-Tardenois, France, on December 2, 1987.

when they capitalised on his popularity with the people to capture power, and then kept him virtually imprisoned in the Royal Palace in Phnom Penh.

It became apparent during the Paris talks that Hun Sen did not have a stomach for foreign food. Ranariddh recalled a story of how he would not eat French food during the Paris talks, and that Asian food had to be arranged for him. "I do not like foreign food, except Chinese food," Hun Sen revealed. "The Cambodian nationals who lived in Paris helped cook Khmer food for me. When I travel abroad I always carry dried fish and fish sauce, which are my familiar foods." On his travels, he avoided foods rich in butter and fat because they tended to upset his stomach.

It was under the Khmer Rouge's intense pressure and criticism that Sihanouk called off the Pyongyang talks. He complained that

PHOTO COURTESY OF HUN SEN

At the talks: (sitting, from left) Son Sann, Sihanouk, and Hun Sen; (standing, from left) Sieng Lapresse, Reng Thach, Khek Sisoda, Norodom Ranariddh, Hor Nam Hong, Dith Munty, and Cham Prasidh.

he had asked Hun Sen to include the withdrawal of the Vietnamese troops in the final communiqué, but Hun Sen had responded that "such references were useless." Now Sihanouk set preconditions for further negotiations: first, he wanted to negotiate directly with the Vietnamese; and, second, the Khmer Rouge and Son Sann had to agree to meet Hun Sen.

With the talks broken off for now, Hun Sen told the Cambodians to "fight and negotiate simultaneously."[26] The loudest and harshest exchanges were those between Hun Sen and the Khmer Rouge. "The Khmer Rouge and I never agreed with each other," Hun Sen said without flinching. "I often got into arguments with the Khmer Rouge during the negotiations. I was always optimistic, and that was why I continued with the negotiations. There were lots of difficulties, but it was better than fighting."

In late 1987, Hun Sen took back the post of foreign minister in order to stamp his personal style on foreign affairs, a department that would play a critical role in managing the peace negotiations.[27] (He reassigned the former foreign minister, Kong Korm—to whom he had relinquished the position just the year before—as his assistant.) The move enhanced his stature while he was preparing for a second round of talks with Sihanouk.

Throwing the schedule into utter confusion, Sihanouk once again performed a flip-flop. He asked Hun Sen to meet him in Saint-Germain-en-Laye in France on January 20–21, 1988.[28] The rapidly maturing Hun Sen knew who his friends were. Before meeting Sihanouk he stopped over in New Delhi to talk to his ally, Indian Prime Minister Rajiv Gandhi, who had inherited his mother's warmth and affection for the Cambodians that went beyond the compulsions of their political alliance.[29] The two countries were bound by the threads of a common Hindu culture, and the Pali-Sanskrit script that the language of the Khmers was based on. The two prime ministers met for more than an hour, and discussed ways of finding peace.

In the French winter retreat of Saint-Germain-en-Laye, Hun Sen met Sihanouk for a second round of peace talks. Hun Sen quickly proved his sharpness as a negotiator when, using a gently chiding but respectful tone, he succeeded in getting Sihanouk to agree to form a two-party coalition government between the two of them, leaving out the Khmer Rouge and Son Sann.[30] The final session of their two-day talks stretched to almost five hours. In the end, Sihanouk was persuaded to drop his previous insistence on forming a four-party government that also included the Khmer Rouge. But Sihanouk rejected Hun Sen's demand that the Khmer Rouge be disbanded after Hun Sen linked the withdrawal of the Vietnamese from Cambodia to the demobilisation of Pol Pot's forces. Although much younger in years than his political rivals such as Sihanouk, Son Sann, and Pol Pot—all in their sixties—Hun

Sen grew in political stature through his participation in the peace talks. Even though Sihanouk was older, Hun Sen negotiated with him from a position of strength and equality. He represented the reformist face of the State of Cambodia, and regularly came out with a string of strong and clever statements that were crafted to make sensational newspaper headlines.

As Hun Sen left a deep impression at the peace talks, Sihanouk's son, Ranariddh, a new political recruit, was also trying to make an impact. "Often some people forget the historical reality," Hun Sen told the authors. "My counterpart in the peace talks was not Ranariddh, not Khieu Samphan, not Son Sann. Please remember that it was a negotiation between Hun Sen and Sihanouk that began on December 18, 1987, in France. At that time Ranariddh was a note-taking man, and was equal to Cham Prasidh, who was my personal secretary. During the negotiations those present were Sihanouk, his wife [Monique], and Ranariddh; and on my side I had Dith Munty and Cham Prasidh. So, they should not forget the history."

At that time, Cambodia had two governments—Hun Sen was the head of the government that ran the country, and Sihanouk was the head of a coalition government-in-exile that took the form of a resistance force. "But we did not recognise the factions in his three-party government," Hun Sen asserted. "So, besides Sihanouk the others were not my counterparts. When writing the history of Cambodia please don't forget this point. Some people want to promote the note-taking secretary in the meeting to a negotiator. History is history. We cannot readjust it." Comparisons between Hun Sen and Ranariddh were, nevertheless, drawn. "Whether he was capable or incapable I don't want to judge him," Hun Sen said. "I was born in a village. He [Ranariddh] was born in a royal palace. He got a doctorate in France. I got a doctorate in Vietnam. More people were born in villages than in the palace. If he looks down on Hun Sen he will look down on millions of people who are poorer than himself. He should not forget that I used to confront his father. When they look down on me they fall into their own trap."

From Saint-Germain-en-Laye, the sputtering on-now-off-again talks and their tired participants conducted further parleys at places such as Paris, Tokyo, Jakarta and Bogor. But as the factions were still trading artillery fire, peace was in jeopardy. The vitiated atmosphere led to an escalation of tensions. To make matters worse, Sihanouk urged China not to end its assistance to the Khmer Rouge. On the other side, the Soviet Union generously provided weapons to arm the Phnom Penh government. In June 1989, the first squadron of Soviet-built MiG-21 fighter jets, flown by Cambodian pilots trained in the Soviet Union, touched down at Pochentong Airport in Phnom Penh.[31] The Soviet military build-up was part of a plan to strengthen Cambodian defences ahead of the planned withdrawal of Vietnamese troops in September. Just before the arrival of the fighters, Moscow had delivered tanks, armoured personnel carriers, and artillery to Phnom Penh.

At this juncture, the unpredictable Sihanouk sprang yet another surprise. In August, he stepped down as the head of his political party, Funcinpec, and appointed Ranariddh as its new secretary-general.[32] Sihanouk relinquished his post in order to project himself as a non-partisan supreme leader of Cambodia, and thereby hasten the process of achieving peace.

CULMINATION OF THE TALKS

After the withdrawal of the Vietnamese forces from Cambodia in September 1989, the Phnom Penh government eventually began winning new friends. Cracks appeared in the Western policy to isolate Cambodia. By November, the Sihanouk-led resistance was alarmed, and the United States and ASEAN watched with concern as Britain, Canada, France, New Zealand, and Australia began dialogues with the Hun Sen government. France, a former colonial ruler of Cambodia, was ready to open an Alliance Francaise in

Phnom Penh to serve as an official cultural mission. Canada and Britain sent diplomats on a fact-finding trip to Cambodia. The same month New Zealand Foreign Minister Russell Marshall met Hun Sen in Ho Chi Minh City during his trip through Southeast Asia.[33] Most heartening of all to Hun Sen, the European Parliament in Strasbourg urged member states of the European Community in November to extend de facto recognition to his government.[34] It called for an end to all military aid to the Sihanouk-led opposition factions and "deplored the Chinese government's continued political, military, and economic support of the Khmer Rouge." While urging the twelve European states to intensify humanitarian aid to the Cambodian people, it advised them to isolate the Khmer Rouge army and its leaders "diplomatically and militarily," particularly in the UN. A diplomat in Phnom Penh commented: "In Washington, they're not happy with it. But on the other hand it was not unexpected, and nobody has moved towards recognition of Phnom Penh."

Ultimately, a durable peace accord was signed in Paris in October 1991. It called on the four factions to cooperate, and hold a general election in 1993. Even though the Khmer Rouge signed the agreement, it boycotted the polls. "But this [my differences with the Khmer Rouge] was not the cause of the boycott of the elections by the Khmer Rouge in 1993," Hun Sen clarified. "They did not honour any of their commitments as they were required to by the Paris peace accord."

When Sihanouk returned home to Cambodia in November 1991, after twelve years in exile, his tune had changed. "Hun Sen is a remarkable leader," he said approvingly. "He is young, intelligent, and experienced in the affairs of state. He is patriotic, and has a genuine love for his people. He has national pride. When I was young I was like him—energetic, tempestuous, violent with words. But that's youth. We all mellow with age. Cambodia is lucky to have Hun Sen. We need several Hun Sens." From calling him a "bad son," Sihanouk now referred to Hun Sen as his "adopted son." This warm feeling was dampened somewhat, however, when Khmer Rouge leader Khieu Samphan, who had been allowed back in Phnom Penh as part of the peace plan, was attacked on his return by a large mob that wanted revenge. Diplomats alleged that the Phnom Penh government might have been behind the episode, because it did little to stop the assault. Sihanouk commented acerbically that he now trusted Hun Sen "only fifty per cent."

For his part, Hun Sen added another item to his impressive curriculum vitae. He made up for a lack of formal education by completing a 172-page thesis entitled "The Characteristics of Cambodian Politics." A doctoral degree was awarded to him by Vietnam's National Institute of Politics in 1991. The poor pagoda boy who could not complete his studies now had the highest academic honour, to match his standing in the uppermost tier of political power in his country.

VI

U.S. COLD WAR POLICY TOWARD

PHNOM PENH AND HUN SEN

1982–90

WASHINGTON MAINTAINED a stance of indifference toward Cambodia after the end of the Vietnam War and U.S. withdrawal from Saigon in 1975. This indifference was a result of the Vietnam Syndrome, which symbolised U.S. reluctance to get embroiled in expensive and enervating foreign military interventions. Washington's attitude changed, however, after the Vietnam-backed Khmer revolutionaries liberated Cambodia in 1979, and then set up the PRK regime. Although lacking formal diplomatic relations with Phnom Penh, U.S. officials kept a careful watch on the PRK and its young prime minister. Both the Central Intelligence Agency and the Department of State regularly produced short and long papers on Cambodia, and U.S. presidents and officials often discussed the Cambodian crisis at meetings with their counterparts in Europe and Asia. The record of U.S. diplomatic history provides rich evidence of how Cambodia once again began to figure prominently in the Cold War rivalry, and in the triangular diplomacy between the United States, Soviet Union, and China.

GREAT-POWER RIVALRY

U.S. officials worried about Cambodia falling under the Soviet sphere of influence. Moscow had already established a foothold by its support of the PRK, warned CIA Director William Casey in July

1982, and this was cause for concern—"We've seen Soviet and proxy successes in the mid to late 1970s in Angola, Ethiopia, Cambodia, Nicaragua and elsewhere."[1]

The following month, a CIA study identified a new source of subversion besides China: "Beijing's once prominent role as exporter of violent communist revolution, however, has been assumed by a new Asian power—Vietnam. Vietnam might well become an Asian Cuba in the 1980s, encouraging and assisting sympathetic factions within Asian parties."[2] From the CIA perspective, these conclusions were backed by the evidence of Vietnam's presence in Cambodia.[3] In October 1983, speaking at Westminster College in Fulton, Missouri (where in 1946 Churchill had delivered his Iron Curtain speech, exaggerating the threat of global communism), Casey now constructed fear about Vietnamese intentions: "Vietnam, with the fourth-largest army in the world, keeps China and Thailand worried as it solidifies its position in Kampuchea."[4]

The question of how the Cambodian civil war should be resolved was emerging as a factor in the great-power rivalry.[5] The CIA painted a nuanced picture of Sino-Soviet differences in Southeast Asia, with Beijing backing the Khmer Rouge and Moscow staying steadfast in its support of Phnom Penh: "Moscow has repeatedly rejected China's conditions [for rapprochement with Moscow] that call for the Soviet Union to ... stop supporting Vietnam's occupation of Kampuchea."[6] At talks between senior Chinese and Soviet foreign ministry officials in 1982 and 1983, the Chinese reiterated their preconditions for normalisation of relations with Moscow: withdraw Soviet forces from the Sino-Soviet border, end Soviet support for Vietnam's occupation of Kampuchea, and withdraw Soviet forces from Afghanistan. Earlier, following U.S.-backed incursions into Cambodia and Laos during the Nixon presidency, the Soviets "made a strong pitch to China on the basis of proletarian internationalism in support of the Vietnamese."

In mid-1984, signs emerged of a significant change in Hanoi's military strategy in Cambodia. Vietnam broke with its traditional pattern of hunkering down in rear area garrisons during the wet season, and positioned several units along the border with Thailand, in order to pressure the Cambodian resistance forces. Hanoi's strategy consisted of driving the resistance into Thailand, constructing intricate systems of barriers, deploying its units along the border to prevent infiltration by the resistance, and building up PRK military forces. From 1985 to 1987, Hanoi deployed ten of its eleven combat divisions within Cambodia along the Thai border. These moves by Hanoi were necessary because the PRK military, the CIA argued, was "developing at a snail's pace," and "in our judgement is far from being able to assume primary responsibility for internal security."

Faced with Vietnamese military power at the border, the Khmer Rouge began building a new face in order to gain acceptance abroad, maintain the façade of a working relationship with the Non-Communist Resistance (NCR), and stay alert to any effort to "foreclose Khmer Rouge participation in negotiations and any resulting political settlement." Under "new management," the Khmer Rouge "moved to distance itself from Pol Pot, who personifies the group's past excesses," and to dismantle symbols of his power. In September 1985, Pol Pot was "retired" as supreme commander of the army. The Khmer Rouge named Deputy Prime Minister Son Sen as his replacement. A "New Look" Khmer Rouge mounted a campaign to widen its appeal among Cambodians, capitalising on Vietnam's "occasionally heavy-handed approach in Cambodia, which features forced conscription for barrier construction and service with the PRK Armed Forces, and sometimes violent reprisals against suspected resistance collaborators." The CIA worried that Vietnamese and PRK officials were "countering this activity with intensified propaganda efforts of their own," as they "strive to keep memories of Khmer Rouge brutality fresh in the minds of Cambodians while emphasizing Vietnam's exclusive role in ending this dark period and helping promote Cambodia's rebirth." But PRK propaganda was not having much impact because the "prospect of combat with the feared Khmer Rouge and a general aversion to fighting fellow Khmer make service with PRK forces all the more unattractive to reluctant conscripts and contribute to their high rate of desertion, poor morale, and abysmal performance."[7]

DIVISIONS WITHIN ASEAN

The problems that the PRK faced in recruitment were, however, more than compensated for by early signs of support from Thailand. The ASEAN states generally opposed the Hun Sen regime as a demonstration of Cold War solidarity with Washington, but there were now growing divisions within the association. U.S. State Department officials observed that "although Thailand still formally adheres to [the] ASEAN line, PM Chatichai has taken an independent position, embracing the PRK's Hun Sen and removing barriers to trade."[8] This was perhaps the first recognition by U.S. diplomats of Hun Sen's expanding profile within the ASEAN region. As Hun Sen bulked large in ASEAN diplomacy, State Department officials began framing the U.S. position on Cambodia: "We are intensifying our diplomatic efforts to achieve a negotiated settlement [among the four Cambodian factions] with three objectives—(1) verified withdrawal of Vietnamese troops, (2) prevention of Khmer Rouge return to power, (3) self-determination for the Cambodian people." Further, "We plan to enhance our assistance to Prince Sihanouk and the Non-Communist Resistance to allow them to play a key role in a settlement..."[9] U.S. diplomatic documents repeatedly clarified that all U.S. assistance to the NCR was non-lethal.

U.S. officials chose to support Sihanouk and the NCR because U.S. policy opposed Vietnamese presence in Cambodia. "Hanoi's promise to withdraw [its forces from Cambodia] by September 30 [1989] is not enough. Hun Sen and Hanoi must make real concessions on key issues of power sharing and a sufficiently strong international presence to permit a comprehensive, stable settlement."

The State Department clarified its position in June 1986: "We unalterably oppose a Khmer Rouge return to power in Cambodia. Nor do we accept unilateral PRK authority—a reward for Hanoi's aggression." Right from the point when the Cambodian factions began exploring the idea of holding peace talks, the United States and Hun Sen became Cold War diplomatic adversaries.

In December 1988, Vietnam announced that in order to settle the Cambodian conflict, it wanted to hold a second Informal Meeting in Jakarta the coming February—following the first one in July 1988—whether or not the Cambodian resistance factions participated. A CIA report noticed a difference of opinion within ASEAN on the matter, arguing that Singapore and Thailand "probably prefer to shelve the talks because they do not trust Indonesian Foreign Minister [Ali] Alatas and consider him overly deferential to Hanoi." The CIA specifically commented on the diplomatic rivalry between Thailand and Indonesia, that "Bangkok also would welcome a setback for Alatas" as it "tries to regain the lead in ASEAN diplomacy on Cambodia." Two conclusions to be drawn from these comments are that Indonesia had also become a supporter of the PRK, and that Indonesia and Thailand would soon compete to enlarge their influence within the PRK and Cambodia.[10] Thai Prime Minister Chatichai Choonhavan revealed his sympathy for communist regimes during his meeting with U.S. President George H.W. Bush in Tokyo on February 23, 1989. When Bush asked: "What kind of government does Laos have?" Chatichai replied: "A benevolent one," which was a surprising remark about the communist government in Laos, particularly because the United States and its allies consistently described Laos as authoritarian and dictatorial, and paid little respect to the national liberation struggle of the Lao people against U.S. intervention in Indochina. Chatichai told Bush that he had pressured the reluctant NCR factions to travel to Jakarta for the Informal Meetings. "We told them, if you don't all go, the meeting will be dominated by the PRK."[11]

SINO-SOVIET RAPPROCHEMENT

The normalisation of relations between the Soviet Union and China, initiated by Soviet President Mikhail Gorbachev, would ultimately shape the outcome of the Cambodian civil war. When Bush met Chinese President Yang Shangkun at the Great Hall of the People in Beijing on February 25, 1989, the U.S. president began the meeting with the comment that he was "not worried about the Gorbachev visit to China" slated for May that year because Sino-U.S. relations were strong. Yang told Bush that the attitude of the Vietnamese and the Phnom Penh government had "gone from bad to worse," and it remained to be seen whether the Soviets would make good on their consensus with China that all Vietnamese troops should withdraw from Cambodia by September 30, 1989.[12] Officials in Washington and Beijing wrongly presumed that they could dictate policy to Hanoi. The Vietnamese leadership had demonstrated, through the course of the Vietnam War, that they were powerful actors who possessed the political agency to make their own decisions.

Beijing wanted Sihanouk as the head of a future government in Phnom Penh; the CIA believed that the "Chinese also worry that PRK Premier Hun Sen's recent initiatives and his growing international stature will enhance his ability to dominate Cambodia after the Vietnamese pullout." While China sought a written Soviet commitment to install a future Cambodian government headed by Sihanouk, the Soviets insisted that they could not dictate policy to Vietnam and the PRK.[13] The Chinese and Soviet press downplayed the prospects of a breakthrough on Cambodia, ahead of a landmark Sino-Soviet summit in Beijing between Gorbachev and senior Chinese leader Deng Xiaoping.

Gorbachev's visit to China in May 1989 marked the end of the Sino-Soviet ideological dispute that had paralysed bilateral relations since the 1950s. Gorbachev and Deng discussed the future of Cambodia from their respective positions—China as a backer of the Khmer Rouge, and Moscow as a supporter of the Hun Sen government. A CIA research study, on the overlapping spheres of influence of the United States and the Soviet Union, argued that there was a new desire among Soviet leaders to help end global Cold War conflicts, but not at the cost of leaving their client states in the lurch. The study noted that "Moscow's approach to regional conflicts has changed substantially. Soviet leaders have opened a dialogue with Washington on these disputes, supported settlement processes in several regions, withdrawn from Afghanistan, and urged client states such as Angola, Cambodia, and Ethiopia to move toward negotiated settlement of disputes and conflicts." But the Soviets were not forcing their clients to accept "peace at any price." Departing from its traditional denunciation of ASEAN as a tool of U.S. policy, a 1987 Soviet broadcast praised ASEAN as a force for peace and stability in Asia.[14] Yet, the Gorbachev–Deng meeting failed to reach an agreement on Cambodia, with both sides saying they sought the "swiftest political settlement." Moscow adhered to its position that the internal problems of Cambodia should be solved by Cambodians themselves, while Beijing favoured the formation of a four-party interim coalition government headed by Sihanouk to manage the elections.[15]

Gorbachev's global diplomacy was already making China adjust its policy toward Hun Sen. Ahead of another round of Sihanouk–Hun Sen peace talks, this time in Paris in May 1989, Beijing welcomed Phnom Penh's proposal to hold general elections after the Vietnamese completed the withdrawal of their troops, but it called for strict international supervision.[16]

The Sihanouk–Hun Sen meeting helped narrow the gap between these two leaders. But more important, in the CIA's view, was Sihanouk's acceptance of the continuation of the Hun Sen regime: "They now agree that Hun Sen's administration will anchor an interim government and are working to reshape it to accommodate coalition arrangements." The Khmer Rouge, under duress, had endorsed the arrangement. The CIA warned that the negotiating arrangement Sihanouk and Hun Sen had set up was "delicate and subject to sudden collapse," but it could lead to a peace conference in July. The agency was confident Hanoi would remove its troops ahead of the conference. It believed that "Sihanouk and Hun Sen's new diplomatic momentum substantially raises the ante to the Khmer Rouge."

GROWING INTERNATIONAL STATURE

As the Cambodian factions began demonstrating a willingness to talk, Vietnam sought an exit strategy. Hanoi's new attitude of compromise was noted at a meeting between President Bush and Indonesian President Suharto at the White House on June 9, 1989. Suharto struck a note of optimism with his remark that there had been a "breakthrough" in Vietnam's "inflexible attitude" between the first and the second Jakarta Informal Meetings. "Previously they had refused to negotiate. Originally Vietnam was confident that it could solve the Cambodian problem on its own. After eight to nine years in which they have failed to achieve any encouraging results, their economy has suffered," he said, adding that Hanoi had sought outside help in solving the problem.[17] Suharto brought the topic of Hun Sen into the conversation, telling Bush about his various gestures of conciliation: "Hun Sen also made concessions: altering the Constitution, changing the name to 'Negara Kampuchea' (State of Cambodia), leaving out mention of 'Democratic' or 'People's Republic.' He accepted Buddhism as the state religion, and accepted Sihanouk as Head of the State of Cambodia."

Bush would hear words of praise about Hun Sen not just in Asia but also in Europe. French President Mitterrand told Bush: "Hun Sen is the strong point of his government. Paradoxically, we didn't choose him but he is governing well. He is benefitting from the fears of the return of the Khmer Rouge." Mitterrand described the Khmer Rouge as a "nightmare," and he did not see much of a to the Middle East, and they have permitted The Voice of America correspondent to come in, although they do continue their jamming. We are also having discussions regarding Fulbright scholars. In taking this first step, I have taken some heat, but we want to move them forward on the rights of dissidents. Time will tell. I hope that I am right. (S)

<u>General Scowcroft</u>: There is an internal struggle going on in China. (S)

<u>Foreign Minister Dumas</u>: How is Deng Xiaoping? (S)

<u>President Mitterrand</u>: Has the situation stabilized? (S)

<u>General Scowcroft</u>: No, Deng Xiaoping still has control when he wants it. He is trying to transfer power to Jiang Zemin, the General Secretary of the Party. (S)

<u>The President</u>: Li Peng is tough and has something of an anti-US streak, but even he seemed a little more positive. Du Shi Meng was pleased that Scowcroft was meeting with Jiang Zemin. (S)

<u>President Mitterrand</u>: These eighty-year-olds give us some hope. (S)

<u>Foreign Minister Dumas</u>: Did anything come up on Cambodia? (S)

<u>General Scowcroft</u>: We didn't discuss it. (S)

<u>Secretary Baker</u>: China has said no to the idea of a UN-supervised process. (S)

<u>President Mitterrand</u>: Hun Sen is the strong point of his government. Paradoxically, we didn't choose him but he is governing well. He is benefiting from fears of the return of the Khmer Rouge. For us, the Khmer Rouge are a nightmare. They would kill the negotiation. Hun Sen really needs to be taken into account by us. Sihanouk has lost lots of authority. He hopes to regain it in the field via the Khmer Rouge. (S)

<u>Secretary Baker</u>: There can be no settlement that does not involve the Khmer Rouge and China. That is an absolute fact of life. (S)

<u>Foreign Minister Dumas</u>: If you have China then you have the Khmer Rouge. China is pulling the strings. Without China, Hun Sen will be the strongest. The Khmer Rouge depends entirely on China. (S)

<u>Secretary Baker</u>: Without China, the Khmer Rouge would indeed be weak. (S)

<u>General Scowcroft</u>: But China won't cut its links to the Khmer Rouge; that is their influence in the game. (S)

<u>Secretary Baker</u>: We have differences as to the role of the Vietnamese. We believe they influence Hun Sen. The West has

"Hun Sen is the strong point of his government": A page from the Memorandum of Conversation between French President Francois Mitterrand and U.S. President George H.W. Bush, December 16, 1989.

future for Sihanouk who had "lost lots of authority." In his conversation with Bush, Mitterrand emphasised the importance of Hun Sen in Western policy-making: "Hun Sen really needs to be taken into account by us."[18]

A new milestone was reached in July–August 1989, with the convening of the Paris Peace Conference. As the talks opened, the CIA argued that Moscow showed no sign of breaking with its Indochinese allies, and that Soviet leaders were committed to the preservation of the Phnom Penh government. "Moscow is willing to accept a prominent role for Sihanouk, but not to dismantle the existing Cambodian government apparatus, and will probably demand that Hun Sen retain a position of power." The CIA documents reveal that Hun Sen was emerging as a significant challenger to U.S. policy in Cambodia, with the support of his Cold War allies in Moscow and Hanoi.

Two trends in the Cambodian conflict worried the State Department: the increasing acceptance of Hun Sen abroad, and the declining approval of the NCR by some ASEAN countries. The department argued that "since the Paris Conference, the focus on the Cambodian situation has shifted from the diplomatic arena to the battlefield," which obviously alarmed many Southeast Asian countries. As a result, the State Department observed that certain ASEAN countries "have declining enthusiasm for the NCR and are showing an incipient affinity for contacts with the Hun Sen regime."[19] Distressed by this trend, the department hoped that President Bush's meeting with Gorbachev in Malta on December 2–3, 1989, and Secretary of State James Baker's discussions there with Soviet Foreign Minister Eduard Shevardnadze would "provide an opportunity to enlist Soviet support in getting the political process moving again." At this stage, U.S. officials were proposing a UN-run Cambodia, which would "neutralize the PRK regime," an arrangement which would anyway "assure continuation of the PRK bureaucracy." Unable to alter events in Cambodia, which was by now peripheral to core U.S. interests, U.S. officials hoped to leverage Soviet assistance to influence a favourable outcome, and they were resigned to accepting Hun Sen's domination of the bureaucracy even after a plan to have the UN run the country took effect.[20]

For its part, the CIA was alarmed that Gorbachev's global diplomacy was aimed at replacing U.S. dominance in war-torn places such as Afghanistan and Cambodia with a larger role for the United Nations. Gorbachev's proposals—which the hardline Soviet leaders before him would not have offered—won much global support. The CIA warned that Soviet proposals for UN peacekeeping forces in Angola, Cambodia, and Nicaragua aimed to encourage international pressure against the United States—which supported insurgencies in these countries—and to lower the cost of Soviet commitment in these areas.[21]

In another report, the CIA struck a note of caution, warning that most ASEAN countries were in the process of switching their support from the NCR to the Phnom Penh regime. It argued that the Phnom Penh regime was "gaining stature abroad," and that while "ASEAN is divided on the Cambodia question, most of its member states are considering closer ties to Phnom Penh." It appeared that only Singapore "continues to take a vocal stand against the Phnom Penh regime," and that this "shift toward Phnom Penh [by the other ASEAN states] is not likely to slow no matter what the resistance accomplish on the battlefield."[22] In view of the accelerating acceptance of the Hun Sen regime by most ASEAN states, U.S. Assistant Secretary of State for East Asian and Pacific Affairs, Richard Solomon, put forward two proposals to the Secretary of State— (1) a power-sharing formula of a quadripartite or bipartite interim government with Hun Sen as prime minister, a state council headed by Sihanouk, and minimal power for the Khmer Rouge, and (2) the country to be under UN supervision before and after elections.[23]

THE U.N. OPTION

Solomon believed that the time had come to grasp the UN option because it was gaining the approval of all the Cambodian factions, except the Khmer Rouge: "a series of intriguing signals from Phnom Penh, Hanoi, and Prince Sihanouk suggest growing interest in exploring an enhanced UN role in a Cambodian settlement," he wrote in a memo to the Secretary of State. In particular, Solomon referred to the December 9, 1989 press interview and communiqué following Soviet Deputy Foreign Minister Igor Rogachev's visit to Phnom Penh, in which Hun Sen expressed support for Chatichai's proposal for another Jakarta meeting. Hun Sen said: "The meeting should begin with discussion based on the Namibia formula for the formation of interim authorities in Cambodia." Recognising the fact that Rogachev had expressed firm support for the Hun Sen proposal, and because the NCR did not reject the proposal, Solomon argued that this was the "time to move," because "we now have every major player except the KR [Khmer Rouge] and the Chinese expressing support for some form of a UN role." Solomon quickly issued instructions to all U.S. embassies in the ASEAN countries and in China to "express our strong interest in exploring a UN role and solicit their views on the parameters of such a UN role." He also asked U.S. diplomats to "urge the Soviets and Chinese there [at the UN in New York] to press their PRK and KR clients for greater detail."[24]

Solomon was cautiously optimistic about a future UN role in supervising a Cambodian general election, to be held after a peace accord had been signed. Exploring the structure of a proposed UN transitional authority in Cambodia, Solomon was hopeful: "Sihanouk and Son Sann enthusiastically accepted the idea. The KR have been suspicious of it. Hun Sen has agreed to consider some variation of the notion, although he undoubtedly sees a UN role as a means of maintaining the PRK essentially intact." This time—thanks to Gorbachev–Deng diplomacy to end the

Sino-Soviet dispute—the Soviets and the Chinese agreed to the idea of an enhanced UN role; they remained deadlocked, however, over the future of the Hun Sen regime. They disagreed about "the degree to which the Hun Sen regime should be diluted or neutralized," Solomon observed, and added that "the Chinese argue for total dismantling and the Soviets the maintenance of the status quo." He warned that "unless PRK administrative control is politically neutralized before elections are held, we see no possibility of a real exercise of self-determination by the Cambodian people."

Estimating that the massive UN operation in Cambodia would cost about US$2 billion to US$5 billion, Solomon believed that an enhanced UN role would help resolve the long-running civil war. He recommended that the United States "keep the pressure on the Soviets, Hanoi, and Phnom Penh by isolating them, the Soviets within the Perm Five [the five permanent members of the UN Security Council] and the other two at regional fora, such as the Jakarta meeting." He urged a strong U.S. stand against those two Southeast Asian governments: "Hanoi and Phnom Penh are seeking international acceptance and respectability, and we should make clear publicly that intransigence on the part of Hanoi and Phnom Penh on granting the UN an effective degree of authority is the main factor standing in the way of significant progress toward a settlement based on an enhanced UN role."[25] Solomon further pointed out that in spite of the success of Hun Sen's global and regional diplomacy to gain international support for his government, all was not well with the Cambodian economy. Following the withdrawal of Vietnam, "the regime in Phnom Penh is struggling on several fronts for survival."[26]

The United States and Singapore explored ways to ensure that a future Cambodian election would be held in a free and fair atmosphere. Singapore Prime Minister-designate Goh Chok Tong, on a visit to Washington, D.C. in April 1990, told senior U.S. officials: "There is a fair chance that the NCR, under Sihanouk, will win the election. If this cannot be maneuvered, the war will become a contest between the KR and the PRK, neither of which is favorable to our interests." Goh declared: "We do not think there will be a military solution. The stalemate must be maintained; this will lead people to make the compromises necessary to bring about an election." He advised that "when victory is quite near, we would be stupid to hand it to the KR or the PRK."[27] Bush's Assistant National Security Advisor Brent Scowcroft wondered if Hun Sen would respect the results of an election, if it was held under his regime. Scowcroft remarked: "Is it essential for elections that [the] Hun Sen regime withdraw from governing the country? Results from Nicaragua show that notwithstanding Ortega's control of the government and the army, he got beaten. Why wouldn't this be possible in Cambodia?" Goh replied: "The situation in Cambodia is much more complex and it is different. If Hun Sen organizes the elections, this amounts to recognition of the Hun Sen government." Scowcroft responded: "Why not bring the UN into Cambodia but do so without tampering with Hun Sen's government?" Tommy Koh, Singapore's Ambassador to the United States, suggested that "following the Nicaragua model just won't work. Neither KR nor PRC [People's Republic of China] would agree to participate in such an election because it would recognise PRK legitimacy. Without KR and PRC agreement a free election cannot take place." The U.S.–Singapore diplomatic encounter showed that U.S. officials were eager for a speedy resolution to the Cambodian crisis by bringing the UN into Cambodia. U.S. officials were resigned to the reality that the Hun Sen administration would remain in power during the proposed UN-supervised general election; they now believed that Hun Sen's administration—under UN oversight—would enable the UN to organise the elections; and they hoped that Hun Sen would respect the result of those elections as Jose Daniel Ortega, the socialist President of Nicaragua, had done when he lost the presidential election in his country just earlier that year.

The following month, the State Department deliberated on a range of diplomatic options, from recognising the Hun Sen government to weaning the NCR away from the Khmer Rouge. The department weighed four options on Cambodia—(1) continue the present policy of emphasising diplomatic means to reach a peace settlement, (2) convince the non-communists to break with the Khmer Rouge, and provide a full range of assistance to the NCR to make it independent of the Khmer Rouge, (3) "support a Nicaragua-style solution with a quick election under Hun Sen administration, with participation of UN observers," and (4) "recognize the Hun Sen government and sever all links to the NCR."[28] The State Department recommended Options 1 and 2 to Secretary of State James Baker. On Option 3, it commented that it "saw little possibility that Sihanouk would agree" and it would certainly be opposed by the Chinese and the Khmer Rouge. It further commented that "support of the weak Hun Sen regime under Option 4 would resolve nothing and lead to continued hostilities and probable KR victory. It would also mean capitulation to Vietnam and the legitimation of a foreign invasion, and would seriously damage our credibility in the region." In order to entice Hanoi, the State Department recommended that Secretary Baker should tell Vietnam what the United States was prepared to offer in order to normalise relations with Vietnam, if the Vietnamese showed flexibility in settling the Cambodian crisis: "Consider indicating willingness to meet Hun Sen when he agrees to relinquish power and join a Supreme National Council." This document reveals that while the United States was averse to the continuance of the Hun Sen government in power, it did consider recognition of that government as an option, but discarded it as unviable. The position enunciated by U.S. officials, that they were prepared to meet Hun Sen, but only after he stepped down from power and joined the Supreme National Council (SNC), was unrealistic because the Phnom Penh government had already won the support of several countries, and it was determined to remain in power. Hun Sen had explained that his government would join the SNC as a government in power, and not as a powerless political party.

At this juncture, U.S. Congressman Stephen Solarz began playing an independent role in resolving the Cambodian crisis, both in urging the State Department to discard its Cold War mindset, and by later opening a direct channel of communication with Hun Sen. Solarz told State Department official Charles Twining in June 1990 that the United States needed to "clear the air" on Cambodia to show that U.S. aid to the NCR was not ending up in the hands of the Khmer Rouge, and to push ahead with a settlement. He urged the United States to "announce that it is in the interest of a political settlement in Cambodia that we are prepared to engage in a dialogue with the SRV [Socialist Republic of Vietnam] and the PRK." Solarz advised the department that with the passage of time U.S. policy "makes less and less sense," indicating the need to begin the process of normalisation with Vietnam.[29] The following year in January, Solarz met Hun Sen for a private meeting in Phnom Penh, signalling a warming of relations with the Cambodian leader.

But U.S. policy-makers were apprehensive about Soviet assistance to the Hun Sen government. They were deeply concerned because both superpowers still regarded Indochina as lying within their own sphere of influence. Baker wrote to Shevardnadze, declaring that both the United States and the Soviet Union sought a comprehensive political settlement, and "we also agree on the need to remove great power rivalry from Indochina." He added a warning: "I am disturbed that the USSR has been providing greatly increased supplies of weapons to Hun Sen, and that Vietnam and the PRK remain intransigent with respect to a political solution." Baker cautioned his Soviet counterpart that Hun Sen's forces would not be able to overwhelm the Khmer Rouge, who were well-armed, but a Khmer Rouge victory or attrition of Hun Sen's forces would not serve the interests of the Soviet Union, Vietnam, or the United

States.[30] At the same time, Thai Prime Minister Chatichai urged Bush to "ask the Chinese to halt arms shipments to the Khmer Rouge." Bush responded: "Regarding China and the KR, I don't think we have as much leverage with China now, but I like your suggestion and we will talk to them about it."[31]

Cambodia's belligerent factions eventually signed a peace agreement in Paris on October 23, 1991, clearing the way for the UN to send in peacekeepers, who would organise a general election. The following month, the United States made a significant gesture in normalising relations with Cambodia by opening a diplomatic mission in Phnom Penh. The main opponents of the Hun Sen government, including the United States, China, and some ASEAN countries, had all come to accept the existence of the Hun Sen administration, and abandoned their earlier demand to dismantle it. Through the vexed negotiations leading to the peace accord, Hun Sen had grown substantially in stature on the international stage as his country's principal diplomat.

VII

AT CROSSROADS IN THE POST-COLD WAR

1990–93

HUN SEN'S POLITICAL BOSSES in the KPRP told him to win friends abroad, to put an end to the country's isolation in the mid-1980s. It was a difficult task for the newly installed prime minister who, in 1985, was just beginning the daunting process of reaching out to several non-communist countries in Asia and the West that had not extended diplomatic recognition to his country. Four years later, the situation remained just as grim for the PRK, despite its attempt to whitewash its image by changing its name to the State of Cambodia (SOC). Hun Sen spent nights in his Takhmau home worrying about these matters. There was little he could do to counter the press reports that routinely called his government a "pariah state." The embattled SOC needed international assistance—foreign investments and aid for infrastructure development, as well as weapons to arm the military. Hun Sen's main ally, the rapidly fragmenting Soviet Union, could no longer be counted on to supply weapons free of charge. Cambodia, moreover, was ringed by an economic embargo. The only non-communist country that supported his government was India.

PHNOM PENH'S COMMUNISTS

The Cambodian economy faced a crisis. As the Soviet Union reduced its aid, Hun Sen attempted to diversify the sources of supplies. He then played the India card. On a visit to New Delhi in October 1990, he asked the Indian government to help find a solution to the civil war. He discussed with Indian External Affairs Minister Inder Kumar Gujral the prospects for peace in Cambodia, which Indian officials said was almost within grasp. But they did not reveal much else. In private, Hun Sen asked Gujral for military aid. The request remained secret. On a visit to Singapore in 1993, Gujral, who was no longer the foreign minister but remained a member of parliament, told the authors that Hun Sen had, in fact, asked India during the October 1990 meeting to supply arms to Cambodia so that it could defend itself against its enemies, principally the Khmer Rouge. "I didn't know how to respond to Hun Sen's request because I did not know whether he had made this kind of a request to my predecessor," Gujral said. In the end, Gujral did not make a commitment to supply arms.[1] But that did not jeopardise the closeness between India and Cambodia—Indian army troops that served as United Nations peacekeepers during the elections in 1993 were even injured fighting the Khmer Rouge.

The CIA closely monitored Phnom Penh's economic problems, drawing the accurate conclusion that the Phnom Penh government was "struggling on several fronts for survival," especially after the withdrawal of Vietnam's military and civilian advisors.[2] They conceded, however, that "Phnom Penh has had a modicum of success in rebuilding the country's war-damaged economy by implementing a reform program with free market principles and the prospect of commercial opportunities is attracting the interest of neighbouring countries such as Thailand and Singapore." And because Moscow lacked the financial resources to aid Phnom Penh, it was urging the key actors in the conflict to accelerate their peace talks. Under Gorbachev, Moscow was "taking a more active role in the diplomatic maneuvering on the Cambodian issue—pushing Hanoi and Phnom Penh toward more flexibility on such matters as UN involvement."[3]

In some respects the country's isolation was self-imposed by the SOC. In 1990, there was a ban on the import of most foreign newspapers. As far as the vice-minister of culture Pen Yet was concerned, the only newspapers permitted to enter the country were those from the socialist countries. The only shop selling books in the capital, the *Librairie d'Etat* at 224 Achar Mean Boulevard, stocked several Soviet pamphlets, and no texts in English or French.

The socialist bear hug had smothered Cambodia in other ways as well. There were just nine foreign embassies in the capital, eight from the socialist bloc alone. Diplomats from the Soviet Union, Cuba, Hungary, Bulgaria, Poland, Czechoslovakia, Laos, and Vietnam were regarded as honoured guests, with access to the top leadership. In return, the communists who ran Cambodia were in theory able to extract financial aid from the European socialist bloc. But as the 1990s began, the devastated socialist bloc economies were really in no shape to bail out Cambodia.

The most powerful embassy in the capital was that of the Soviet Union, though its run-down compound was at odds with the fact. As the authors approached the electrically-operated wrought-iron embassy gate in May 1990, it swung open by itself. More Cold War stereotypes lay ahead. The authors were met by a Russian receptionist, a stern woman, and were told to wait for the only official who had been authorised to speak on behalf of the embassy. His name was V. Loukianov. Although he wore formal office attire, Loukianov was completely relaxed and, with his David Niven moustache, was so unlike the typical Soviet diplomat. In his clipped British accent, acquired at a Moscow language course, he was willing to talk about Cambodia with rare candour. The next evening, over dinner at the Hotel Cambodiana, Loukianov commented scathingly: "This is a wild place. A few people have become rich overnight. They are driving around town signing deals by the dozen, but many are signed and forgotten."[4] While a rich minority of Cambodians signed business deals with their foreign partners, and treated themselves to sumptuous ten-course Chinese banquets, an unfortunate eighty per cent of the people seldom had meat, or their favourite *pra hok* spiced fish, on their tables. "There are some truly bizarre things going on," Loukianov continued. "At this very hotel, a Cambodian flush with cash flung US$500 at the feet of a singer for singing his favourite Chinese song." Loukianov was aware of the embarrassing similarities between communist Cambodia and Leninist Soviet Union, as well as neighbouring Vietnam and Laos.

Those were hard times. The Soviet government was in bad odour at home and in Cambodia. Gorbachev's efforts to reform the bankrupt Soviet economy were faltering, making it convenient for the Cambodians to blame Moscow, in part, for their economic problems. By 1990 the Soviets had cut back severely on their trade credits. The Soviet commercial officer in Phnom Penh, Nikolay Orekhov, told the authors that his country could no longer finance the construction of ports, roads, and bridges; they would, however, continue to build printing presses at no cost, and would certainly help Cambodia set up its own circus.[5] A Cuban diplomat proudly said that Cuba's relations with Cambodia had improved: Havana had not only sent a boxing coach, but also dispatched a Hispanic professor to Phnom Penh. "A little knowledge of Spanish may help Cambodia improve its relations with the Spanish-speaking world," he benevolently remarked at his embassy.[6] The Cambodians were not amused.

The vast majority of the people, living in their fragile wooden huts on stilts in scattered villages, did not need lectures or a circus. They needed shelter, drinking water, and electricity. It was estimated that about ninety per cent of the country's estimated nine million people lived in poverty. There were no reliable statistics on national population since the last census in 1962 had recorded a population of 5.72 million. It was only in mid-1998 that a new census would reveal that the population had by then grown to 11.42 million. Many Cambodians went to bed hungry. Yim Sokan, an eleven-year-old who worked at a petrol kiosk in the city of Siem

Reap, told the authors that he was forced to work because his father, whose legs were destroyed by a landmine planted by the Khmer Rouge guerrillas, could not find a job. The young boy had to support a family of six.[7] Cambodians were a sad and broken people eager to impress outsiders, but their brave smiles could not conceal the wounds within. Many remembered the genocide, and how thousands of people living in Phnom Penh, women and children included, were tortured. Scorpions were set upon women's breasts, their nails extracted, and, if they were lucky, death came quickly by the gun. Those who survived these indignities were herded cattle-like into communes. Now times had changed. Pol Pot's Maoists were replaced by Soviet-style communists.

"Look around you, and you will see many communist partymen sitting around the bars and enjoying their whiskies," Vanna, our taxi driver, commented. The communists had begun coming out into the open in their ill-fitting business suits tailored in Phnom Penh, and were openly striking business deals with Chinese businessmen from Singapore and Thailand. "Look at them, their salary is less than US$25 a month, and yet they own houses and cars, and they dine out," he added, gesturing toward the bright lights on Achar Mean Boulevard. Much later, Mam Sophana, a Cambodian architect who was trained in the United States and had returned to help rebuild his country, explained why it was wrong to label Cambodians corrupt: "Outsiders are stupid if they point a finger at the Hun Sen government, and say, 'You are corrupt, you are no good.' They should see the reality before they talk. If these people, Heng Samrin and Hun Sen, were not brave enough, they would have given up long ago. Corruption is a very complicated word. You have to know its roots. How much salary does a civil servant get? Just US$20 a month. The government does not have the money to pay higher salaries. So, how can they survive? Let those people who say 'Cambodians are corrupt' live in Cambodia for a month, and they will know they are not corrupt."[8]

Pen Yet, the softspoken, moustachioed vice-minister of culture and information, threw up his hands in a grand gesture of helplessness at another form of corruption where the worst offenders were the rich antique-dealers who were stripping the Angkor temples of their ancient sculptures. "Cambodia has lost about twenty per cent of her ancient treasures to smugglers," Pen Yet said, shaking his head.[9] "London is the main destination for the Cambodian treasures which are sold at auctions. We are now making a list of the antique objects we have lost, and the list will be given to Interpol for action."[10]

The sharp disparity in wealth between rich and poor did not go unnoticed by the Khmer Rouge. Those who tuned in to the guerrillas' clandestine radio station were entertained by angry broadcasters criticising the Phnom Penh communists for selling out the Cambodian economy to foreign speculators. The Khmer Rouge, who had banned money and enterprise during their rule, now ridiculed the lopsided economic structure. Mak Ben, a former Khmer Rouge military commander, spoke bitterly of the Phnom Penh communists. But Mak Ben had forgotten that life during the Khmer Rouge's so-called egalitarian society had been much worse after Pol Pot had shut down the economy.

Even so, basic necessities remained scarce. Denied international loans along with diplomatic recognition, the state came to rely excessively on the Soviet Union for gasoline and fertiliser, and on Cuba for sugar. There was simply no money to pay the salaries of civil servants. As a result, the state did what other economically challenged communist governments had done at one time or another: it decided to provide state employees with subsidised goods every month—eighteen kilogrammes of rice, two bars of Soviet-made soap, and one kilogramme of sugar. All other Cambodians were left to fend for themselves. Two years later, in 1992, when the authors met Hun Sen for the first time, he candidly remarked: "When I began as foreign minister in 1979, my salary was in the form of rations—ten kilogrammes of rice and six kilogrammes of maize. Nowadays, the situation is not as pessimistic as in 1979. That is why we should not be too pessimistic, or optimistic."[11]

Rice was ever at the forefront of Hun Sen's mind; his government spared no effort to ensure that the country had enough of it. The year 1979 was in fact an agricultural disaster. With the Khmer Rouge just overthrown and the people newly liberated, there was chaos in the farms and much of the rice crop was not harvested. As a result, famine occurred. Rice stocks accumulated by the Khmer Rouge were quickly used up, and the famine was worsened by a severe drought. But the farmers were able to do the impossible. They managed to double the rice crop the following year. So while most people could not afford to eat chicken and pork, rice was soon cheaply and freely available again, sometimes supplemented by small shipments from abroad. But rice was also a time-bomb for the government. Unscrupulous local businessmen in league with Thai traders created shortages by selling the rice crop to the Thais just across the border, where it fetched a price thirty per cent higher than that fixed by the Cambodian government. The artificially created shortage pushed up the price at home, making rice too expensive for the masses. This was nothing new for Asia—from the last days of Mao Zedong to the Deng Xiaoping regime, rice was smuggled out of China to places where it fetched a higher price. A bad harvest would spell political disaster for any government that ruled Cambodia. A full-blown rice riot would ensure that the party in power would not be re-elected. Australian Lieutenant-General John Sanderson, the commander of the UN peacekeeping forces in Cambodia, believed that the nexus between rice traders and Thailand ought to be severed once and for all, for the sake of stability.

Cambodia under the Hun Sen administration was fairly cut off. Few tourists were visible on the streets of Phnom Penh, and nobody could give a straight answer as to how many had been bold enough to set foot in the war-torn land. Sam Promonea, the general-director of tourism, revealed that 16,993 tourists visited Cambodia in 1990, most of whom were Japanese, followed by the French, Germans, Swiss, and Italians. These were not rich business-class travellers, he said; most were backpackers who were quite happy living in cheap guesthouses.[12] The ban on foreign newspapers was broken at the newly opened Hotel Cambodiana in November 1990, and a few other establishments. Stacks of the *Bangkok Post,* a daily newspaper published in Thailand, were delivered to hotel guests in their rooms, albeit a day late because of delays in transportation from Bangkok.

As the Cambodian government began opening the country to the outside world, it realised that its earlier language policies were now outdated. The Russian language had been given priority in schools under the communist regime because most of the scholarships were provided by the Soviet Union and the socialist bloc. But in July 1993, the new royal government, which had come to power following elections in May that year, openly supported the use of French, and abandoned Russian. The reason was simple. France, having reopened its embassy earlier, had offered to rebuild the educational system, provided the medium of instruction was French. But France's campaign to put the Gallic language on Cambodian tongues foundered. Over 1,000 students staged a protest against the use of French as the medium of instruction for courses at the Institute of Technology in the capital. The students said that knowledge of French would not help them find jobs. Then in late 1993 Sihanouk jumped into the fray. From his hospital bed in Beijing, where he was undergoing treatment for cancer, Sihanouk wrote a paper called "National Education: To Learn French or English?" Curiously, he wrote the paper in French, but argued in support of the use of English. "This support is legitimate, logical, and realistic because in today's and tomorrow's world, English—as the language of communication and international study—has become, and will inevitably remain, a quasi-universal language," he argued. "Even the young Chinese nurses in the hospital where I am staying are conscientiously learning English." Cambodian students had nothing against French, or any other foreign language. The fact was that they felt cheated. First they had been made to learn Russian by the pro-Soviet governments of Pen Sovann, Chan Si, Heng Samrin, and Hun Sen from 1979 to 1991. At the same time, the Vietnamese backers of the regime ensured that Vietnamese was a compulsory subject. Others learnt Romanian mainly because Romanian scholarships were being offered. Now, many students realised that their learning Russian, Vietnamese, and Romanian had all been a waste, and they did not want to speak French either. By 1994, an enterprising Westerner had opened a small institute called the Banana Centre that began teaching English.

IN SEPTEMBER 1991, the Hun Sen government was gripped by a sense of paralysis. It was uncertain what its fate would be after Sihanouk's return to the Royal Palace, due in November. In anticipation of his return twenty-one years after being overthrown, Cambodian workmen toiled in the hot sun to repair and whitewash the royal residence. Numbed by decades of civil war, genocide, and poverty, there was no great mood of expectation, no talk of a grand homecoming party. Sihanouk did not have good memories of Phnom Penh because Pol Pot had kept him a prisoner inside his own palace, and restricted his movements. As a result, he could only imagine the kind of destruction that Pol Pot had unleashed. Just before Vietnamese forces rolled into the capital in 1979, Sihanouk had escaped by plane to Beijing. He left behind a city that the Khmer Rouge had systematically depopulated. During Sihanouk's rule the capital had resembled a balmy French provincial town with broad boulevards, dance halls, French restaurants, and a gracious lifestyle. All of that had been erased by the Khmer Rouge, who banned enterprise, and turned the country into a brutal laboratory for their experiment in nation building.

Hun Sen worried for his government's political future after the prince returned to head the SNC—made up of all the warring factions—as well as for the very future of Cambodian communism. Soviet embassy counsellor Loukianov noted: "Communism in Cambodia is under threat, and that is a source of worry to the leaders in the government." The Communist Party knew it had to change with the times because an historic peace accord to end the civil war would soon be signed in October. The next step would be the general election, supervised by the United Nations. The government knew that it could not possibly take on the democratic political parties headed by the Cambodian princes and their supporters at the polls. Recognising that the Cambodian people would not tolerate being ruled by failed Marxist-Leninists, Hun Sen began earnest preparations to shift the country toward a different political system from communism. The government hurriedly drafted a new constitution, watering down communism as the state ideology.

On the economic front, Hun Sen's attempts thus far to revive the moribund economy had failed to gain traction. But it would be an injustice to heap all the blame for Cambodia's monumental failures on the CPP. The real damage had been wreaked by the Khmer Rouge, who dismantled the economy, shut down businesses and factories, and murdered Western-trained Cambodian intellectuals, doctors, teachers, and scientists in their zeal to build a new Cambodia, a country without any Western influences and imbued with the Maoist vision of an agriculture-oriented society. Their dislike for money was so extreme that they had used explosives to blow up the National Bank building on Tou Samouth Boulevard. "They wanted to show their hostility against the free market," said Tioulong Saumura, a senior central banker. "It has been such a trauma." A daughter of former Cambodian army chief Nhiek Tioulong, who had served Sihanouk, Saumura had given up her job in Paris for the position of deputy governor of the National Bank of Cambodia, which paid merely US$50 a month. The Khmer

189

Rouge targetted the bank as a symbol of capitalism. It was a sharp decline for a country whose treasury buildings had covered a vast area during the reign of the Angkor kings. Saumura said decisively: "We want to turn the page. We want to write a good story, and it has to be a good story." Hun Sen had exactly the same thoughts. In 1991, he rebuilt the National Bank building exactly as it was before.[13]

Currency problems plagued Cambodia. After surviving for several years as a country without a currency—the Khmer Rouge having banned the use of money—the state had reintroduced the riel in 1980. But the new government lacked the technology, namely printing presses, to issue the currency. Thus the riel would be printed in Moscow, and every two months secretly flown into Phnom Penh among crates of vodka and caviar. The cash deliveries helped the government survive its isolation until the early 1990s. The Soviets replenished the currency, and maintained the monetary system.[14] The money would quickly be injected into the market as fresh fuel to stoke an inflationary fire. Michael Ward, a World Bank official stationed in Cambodia as a member of UNTAC, made a surprising disclosure: "As the government's deficit rises, it prints more money." The state simply used the printing press to finance the budget, as did many governments, sending inflation spiralling upwards to triple digits. Not only did the government print money, Ward revealed, the Khmer Rouge, too, issued xeroxed coupons which passed for money in the northwestern zones it controlled. After UNTAC took charge of the finances of the Hun Sen government, it ordered the state to stop printing its currency in the Soviet Union. But Phnom Penh would not admit that it flew in bills pressed in the Soviet Union. The minister concerned with the issue was evasive. Prince Norodom Chakrapong, a son of Sihanouk, who joined Hun Sen's government in 1992 as a vice-prime minister in charge of civil aviation, denied a report that UNTAC had prevented a plane-load of riels, printed in Moscow, from being circulated in

Cambodia in order to control inflation, then running at about 150 per cent. Chakrapong said defensively: "There are many other reasons for inflation, including the heavy spending by UNTAC staff, which has sent the price of food soaring."[15]

The emptiness of the state coffers and the reckless tinkering by untrained financial managers conspired to cause the riel to plunge from 4 riels to the U.S. dollar to 880 riels to the dollar in 1992, and hit a historic low of 5,000 riels to the dollar in mid-1993, before recovering to 2,500 riels in October 1994. With planned expenditure of 186 billion riels (less than US$100 million) in 1992, and a deficit of 83 billion riels, the government could do precious little to develop the country.

As a result of the withdrawal of Vietnamese forces from Cambodia in 1989, and the collapse of the Soviet Union soon afterwards, the Hun Sen government was denied direct military support by Hanoi, and economic aid by Moscow. It was a tremendous squeeze on the budget, eighty per cent of which was being funnelled into the armed forces. Most of the defence budget was spent on salaries for the army rather than on military hardware—for one good reason: if the army was not paid, it might have turned against its own government or, worse, broken away to form an organised force of rebels.

The poor people of Cambodia endured in silence the bizarre policies of their rulers. Just as some peculiar events came in the shape of a secret cargo of money flown in from Moscow, so at other times odd spectacles unfolded on the banks of the Tonle Sap.

The brown banks of the mighty river lay exposed as the water level dropped in the dry season, leaving fish and vegetation to rot under an unforgiving sun. A taxi driver pointed to a disused building on the river bank, and said: "That Sihanouk casino house. Now closing down." Norodom Sihanouk—mercurial god-prince, filmmaker, saxophone player, jazz singer, and author—came up with an eccentric scheme in the late 1960s to set up a casino in his poor country. That way, he reckoned, his people would grow richer, and the state would earn a windfall. The prince commissioned a Khmer-style building on the banks of the Tonle Sap. The clatter of the roulette tables was silenced soon enough when the prince was removed in a coup in 1970. The coup also put paid to his scheme to open a five-star hotel next to the casino. In the end, it took a Singapore company to make the prince's dream a reality. An enormous old building on the banks of the Tonle Sap was refurbished by two Singaporean businessmen and a Cambodian Chinese named Hui Keung, who divided his time between Phnom Penh and Hong Kong, and represented a new breed of Cambodian entrepreneur to emerge after the destruction of the business community by the Khmer Rouge. The trio was among the early risk-takers. They went ahead and invested capital in restoring the Hotel Cambodiana, making a long-term commitment to a country most businessmen were giving a miss.

The hotel opened in June 1990, at a time when the United States still had a trade embargo against Cambodia. The Hun Sen government capitalised on the growing presence of foreign businessmen in Phnom Penh, a bustling city which in 1990 bore scant resemblance to a communist country, even less to a country at war with itself. Lunch at the Mekong Restaurant of the Hotel Cambodiana had a carnival-like atmosphere as foreign businessmen, diplomats, journalists, and groups of Japanese and European tourists ate a French-style buffet. A mini economic boom in the capital seemed set to continue. Michel Horn, the French general manager of the hotel, predicted that his company would invest even more money in the hotel.[16] Eager to resurrect a spirit of enterprise in the people, the Hun Sen government had enacted a foreign investment law on July 26, 1989, years ahead of many other Asian countries.[17] The law provided guarantees that the state would not nationalise or expropriate foreign investments. It was a promise the state would keep, even though no formal courts of appeal existed where foreign firms could take their grievances in case of a dispute. By 1992, about US$300 million of foreign wealth would be invested in the country. Coca-Cola set up a bottling factory in Phnom Penh, and Australian businessmen were brewing Angkor Beer in Sihanoukville. Although the investment law, which bore the seal of President Heng Samrin, spelt out the level of taxes foreign firms would pay, some firms circumvented the rules, paying whatever they chose. A jungle economy took root.

Still, the embargoes hamstrung the economy, and desperate to break free of them, the Hun Sen government began selling national offshore oil assets. It awarded six oilfields near the Gulf of Thailand to foreign firms even before the peace accord was signed in October 1991. The firms made substantial investments to explore for oil in the waters of the Khmer Trough, close to the Thailand-owned Pattani Trough, which supplied most of Thailand's oil. These deals netted an income of US$6 million in 1991, and US$20 million by 1992.[18] Even earlier, a Japanese sawmiller, Okada, had inked a deal to invest US$16 million to set up mills in a venture that further denuded the endangered forests in order to ship timber back to Japan.[19] As government officials and their foreign business partners felled trees, forest cover in the provinces of Kandal and Takeo near Phnom Penh shrank from fifteen per cent in the early 1960s to zero in the 1980s. In their sanctuaries, the Khmer Rouge sold timber concessions to Thai traders with close links to the Thai military. A report by the international law firm Baker & McKenzie advised businessmen who were keen to trade with the Khmer Rouge to fill a standard business form issued by the guerrillas.

In a significant breakthrough for Phnom Penh, Australian state-run telecommunications firm OTC International signed a deal with the Hun Sen government in early 1990 to help pull his government, and his country, out of isolation. OTC's operations manager in Phnom Penh, Lindsay Harradine, said: "When we came to Cambodia in 1990 there were fewer than ten operator-assisted lines via Moscow."[20] That meant a call to London would go through three operators. "First, you'd call the local operator in Phnom Penh, who would call the operator in Moscow, who would in turn call the operator in London, who would finally connect you," Harradine explained. Diplomats were accustomed to spending hours waiting by the phone and praying that a Soviet-supplied Intersputnik satellite dish—which linked Cambodia to the outside world via Moscow—would perform. Throwing caution to the wind and treating the U.S. embargo with contempt, OTC signed a ten-year business deal with the Cambodian Directorate of Posts and Telecommunications. In effect, firms like OTC and the dozens of other foreign investors were following a policy of constructive engagement, rather than a negative policy of isolating the Hun Sen government, whom many businessmen viewed as grand liberators from the terrible genocide. For all the boldness of the deal, however, the Australian firm was helpless when confronted by the lumbering Cambodian bureaucracy. It was no secret that the phone lines were usually dead. What was not known was that the work of the Department of Posts and Telecommunications was badly hampered by governmental meddling. Despite turning a profit of 150 million riels (US$96,000) in 1990, the department remained in deep financial trouble. The heart of the problem was that government offices and state-run firms—which accounted for eighty per cent of the subscribers—continually defaulted on their phone bills. The same problem plagued other government utilities such as the water and electricity departments.[21]

Just as crippling, the country suffered from a lack of roads. Virtually none had been built after the 1930s, and what old roads there were had been subjected to incessant bombardment by the Khmer Rouge. The guerrillas resorted to literally cutting away sections of roads to make them impossible to drive on. There was no tarred road to the killing fields of Choeung Ek, about seventeen kilometres south of Phnom Penh, only a dirt track over which bullock carts, trucks, and cars squeezed past one another, whipping up a screen of dust.

The prevalent perception of Cambodia was of a country where the bullock cart was the preferred mode of transportation. But not many villagers could afford to buy a bullock, or a cart. Still, bicycles and motorcycles were becoming more visible. There were more than 5,000 cars in the cities by 1989, and as many as 60,000 motorcycles. By 1992, the car population had risen to 40,000, most of which had been brought into the country by the 22,000 UN troops, and the nouveaux riches.

Travel by rail was risky on account of bandits, possible Khmer Rouge attacks and explosions set off by landmines. There were just two rail lines, both of one-metre gauge. One was the 385-kilometre line from Phnom Penh to the Thai border town of Poipet, built in the 1940s by the former French colonial rulers, and the other was a 263-kilometre line from Phnom Penh to the port of Sihanoukville, built in post-independence Cambodia in the 1960s. On the Sihanoukville line the engine did not lead the train; it came behind a wagon meant to take the brunt of an explosion. A diplomat quipped darkly that those who travelled in the lead wagon travelled free, as a concession to the risk they took. The heavily armed guards in the compartments did not inspire much confidence either, and they were eyed with deep mistrust by the travellers.

Air travel carried similar risks. Though there were fears that Russian-built aircraft could be hit by sniper fire as they made the final approach into Siem Reap, a more real danger was the technical safety of the craft themselves. The Russians who maintained them underpaid their technical workers. Kampuchea Airlines, the flag carrier, operated a fleet of three Russian Antonov-24 propeller aircraft, two Tupolev-134 jets, and three Mil Mi-8 helicopters. Operating out of the airport in Phnom Penh, the airline flew regularly to Siem Reap and Stung Treng, and twice-weekly to Hanoi and Ho Chi Minh City. The flights to Ho Chi Minh City were almost always full, however, forcing travellers to undertake an eight-hour journey by taxi, through the border at Bavet, a river crossing, and an immigration checkpoint.

Municipal water quality was abysmal. At the Hotel Cambodiana, the water, pumped from the silted Mekong River, ran red. The city of Phnom Penh drew its drinking water from the Tonle Sap and Tonle Bassac rivers, into which it also pumped raw sewage. The water was filtered, but the three very old French-built treatment plants often ran out of chemicals, and when that happened, water was simply released to the city without being treated. Till the mid-1990s, a mere twenty per cent of the urban population could turn on a tap and get treated water. The rest had to use wells, ponds, and streams, which posed a serious health hazard. Children suffered acute diarrhoea eight times a year, on average. Like the telephone company, the water and electricity departments were cash-strapped because government offices and companies that used the services would not pay their bills.

When the Heng Samrin regime took control, it grappled with the almost impossible task of rebuilding an education system literally out of the graves of dead teachers—an entire generation of teachers had been killed off by the Khmer Rouge. Students had lost four years of education, and would lose several more, as the system was in shambles. As expected, the socialist bloc countries rushed to Cambodia's side, bringing funds and technical assistance to set up new schools and revive old ones. Some of the aid came in the shape of training for Cambodian government officials at Moscow's institutes of higher learning. As a result, Cambodian economic officials returned with outdated ideas of centralised planning and the supremacy of a command economy at a time when neighbouring Thailand and Singapore were vigorously opening their markets to foreign capital.

With just thirty per cent of its people literate, and an average lifespan of a mere fifty years, Cambodia could not possibly slip any lower into stagnation. Vietnam, which went through much longer wars against China, France, and the United States, had done much better, with a literacy rate of over eighty per cent, and an average lifespan of sixty-five years. But to give Cambodia its due, the five years of compulsory education worked wonders. A group of children in Siem Reap amazed visitors with their fluency in English, learned at a local school. They even related a fairly accurate history of Angkor Wat in six minutes, which usually got them a well-earned dollar. The country was now welcoming Cambodian scholars trained in the West, who were coming back to their homeland and raising academic standards. "The day is not far," commented a Canadian academic on attachment to the government, "when foreign students will come to the University of Phnom Penh to study Khmer history, rather than go to Yale University." It was the educated Cambodians who were filling in a shortage caused by the withdrawal in 1990 of Soviet teachers as a result of a cutback in Moscow's aid. Yet the irony was that many teachers did not report to work. Many took part-time jobs to make ends meet when salary payments became irregular.

The killing of the entire academic fraternity was rivalled in savagery by the systematic annihilation of the medical profession. When the Khmer Rouge invaded the capital on April 17, 1975, they converged on the hospitals. Doctors and nurses were forced to march toward the countryside, where they were killed. According to eyewitness accounts documented by the Heng Samrin regime, one doctor, Dr Phlek Chhat, a resident physician at the Preah Ket Mealea hospital, was arrested in Kompong Thom province; a burning torch was thrust into his mouth, and he was killed. Like Dr Phlek, hundreds of doctors never saw their families again after they were snatched that morning.[22] Meas Kim Suon, a doctor-turned-journalist, believed that by the time the Khmer Rouge completed the destruction, there were fewer than fifty doctors left in the entire country. An effort to produce doctors was launched, and by 1991 the medical colleges had produced over 700 of them.

Meas Kim Suon was one of these mass-produced doctors. Soon after he graduated in the mid-1980s, he was attached as a field doctor to the army, which was then fighting the Khmer Rouge and the Sihanoukists along the Thai border. In malarial conditions, Kim Suon treated infected soldiers, removed bullets and shrapnel from the wounded, and amputated limbs. He worked day and night until he grew tired of life in the jungle, and chose to become a journalist. He took a regular job as a guide for foreign journalists in the ministry of information, and during the run-up to the May 1993 elections began reporting for a Japanese newspaper, *Mainichi Daily News*. Kim Suon had done his bit for the country and was now doing what he liked best, explained his boss at the ministry, Leng Sochea. The authors had the privilege of working with Kim Suon as well as his elder brother Kim Heng, a senior official in the ministry of foreign affairs who was later posted to Washington, D.C. They demonstrated that Cambodia was more than capable of producing homegrown talent in times of adversity. The authors also worked with Leng Sochea in the capital and the provinces, where his array of contacts and ability to think on his feet helped enormously. After the elections, Sochea was promoted to director of the press in the ministry of information, and then he moved further up, becoming the deputy director-general of information. Both Kim Suon and Sochea were fair-skinned owing to their Chinese ancestry. "I am a half-blood," Kim Suon liked to comment with a good-natured grin.

Even though Cambodia had succeeded somewhat in rebuilding its medical profession, still, less than half the population had access to medical care, and only twenty per cent of the medicines needed were produced locally. In the mid-1980s, the government began importing essential drugs, but these were sold at highly inflated prices in the local market, further hurting a long-suffering people. While health services were free at the time, some government doctors were unscrupulous enough to charge money. A twenty-year-long civil war extracted a heavy toll on families, with limbless men numbering over 41,000, and skewing the population mix: it was believed that about sixty-five per cent of the adult population consisted of women, who singlehandedly shouldered the burden of raising their families.

Deep disorder gnawed at the core of the Hun Sen administration and its huge force of 150,000 civil servants in the nineteen provinces and two municipalities. The provinces, or *khet*, had considerable financial autonomy in raising revenue and collecting taxes, and they seldom reported their financial accounts to the capital. It was nothing new, and had happened in both China and India, where central governments faced resistance from the states. In Cambodia, the provincial governors lorded over their domains, raising and spending their revenue as they chose, with little interference from their political superiors in Phnom Penh.[23] It was believed that the provincial governors demanded such autonomy in return for loyalty to the SOC government. A large part of the problem was that it was difficult for provincial governors to communicate regularly with the central government, as phone connections were almost absent, and fax machines unheard of in the remote areas. Provincial revenues remained non-transparent till the elections in May 1993. The new government passed a law on finances, making it essential for provincial income to go straight into the national treasury in Phnom Penh. But by mid-1995, First Prime Minister Ranariddh seemed to back off from this law. In an interview with the authors he justified the old position where the states had greater financial autonomy. The volte-face suggested that Ranariddh had failed to break the stranglehold of vested interests in the provinces.

The hard times were seeing some signs of alleviation. Ten years after the Khmer Rouge regime was overthrown, the economy grew by 2.4 per cent in 1989. In 1990, it posted negative growth as a direct result of a cutback in Soviet trade credits, but rebounded with 13.5 per cent growth in 1991, 6.5 per cent in 1992, and more than 8 per cent in 1994. The news that the economy had grown by 6.5 per cent in 1992 was generally ignored by the world's press, which was chiefly occupied with criticising Hun Sen's administration. What lent credibility to the country's achievement was that the remarkable growth rate was announced by the UN, which was mandated to run the country from late 1991 to 1993. Not only did the 6.5 per cent figure go missing in action, so did the 13.5 per cent number.

Behind the burgeoning economy was the hand of an emerging Cambodian business community that had set up seventy private companies, some twelve years after the Khmer Rouge had wiped out all private enterprise. Among the new breed of bold Cambodian entrepreneurs was Leang Eng Chhin, who had left Cambodia in 1970, the year Sihanouk was overthrown. He set up a company in Singapore, made money and headed right back to Phnom Penh in 1991 to invest US$1.1 million on refurbishing the run-down White Hotel on Achar Mean Boulevard. He renamed it the Pailin Hotel after the blood-red rubies of Pailin in northwestern Cambodia, an area that remained under Khmer Rouge control. "It was all my money," he affirmed enthusiastically. Chhin was a curious mixture: he was the managing director of a Singapore firm, Tristars; he carried a French passport, was a Cambodian by birth, and did not speak a word of English.[24] There were at least 100 millionaires in Phnom Penh in 1990, and as many Mercedes cars. But Soviet diplomat Loukianov criticised the majority of the Cambodian millionaires. "I agree there are about 100 millionaires here, but they won't invest a cent in proper development," he said, bemoaning their extravagance. "They would rather buy foreign cars, villas and clothes."

Foreign investors, too, saw opportunities in Cambodia. In spite of the civil war, the ninety per cent of the country under the control of the Hun Sen government was relatively safe. No foreign businessman had been killed in Cambodia, aside from an attack on a Taiwanese businessman by bandits in the countryside, but a spate of kidnappings was enough cause for concern. The political violence that preceded the elections of May 1993 pitted the rival factions against each other, but did not affect foreigners. Kamaralzaman Tambu, the Malaysian editor of the weekly tabloid *Cambodia Times,* compared the situation with the communist insurgency in Malaya in the 1950s, a time when residents of Singapore continued to visit their relatives on peninsular Malaysia. The same Singaporeans were now the largest trading partners of Cambodia. One Singaporean businessman claimed that he had not felt the need to exercise caution before investing in the country: "The more dangerous it gets, the more business I do. I made most of my money in the most dangerous times before the peace accord was signed in October 1991." The sound of cash registers ringing in Phnom Penh was louder than the crackle of distant gunfire.

The country came to resemble a primeval economy where nothing was illegal. With government owned-firms getting into business, allegations surfaced in the newspapers about corrupt officials leasing land and public buildings to foreign businessmen, without the approval of the ministry of finance. These allegations would become another dark motif in 1992–93 when UN officials would talk about it in whispers but come up with no hard evidence to help bring the guilty to book. Still, a positive outcome was that the UN recommended the establishment of a ledger of state properties. The new money, new cars, and new villas added a grimy glitter to the capital where rotting garbage and open drains were yet another motif. Stig Engstrom, the representative of an Australian telecommunications firm, was amazed at the pace of change. "In 1988, there were only eighty foreigners in Phnom Penh, today there are about 500," he explained in 1990. By August 1991, the government had hurriedly given approval to a dozen foreign companies to build hotels at a combined cost of about US$40 million. Critics called it ad hoc, wild, and unplanned. Nonetheless, the reconstruction had started, though the peace accord was only a gleam in Hun Sen's eye.

A LONG CONVERSATION

With a fluid flick of his wrist Hun Sen jerked a packet of State Express cigarettes towards us. We declined the offer, and Hun Sen smiled knowingly, the way smokers smile at non-smokers, and lit up. We were talking to the prime minister on New Year's Day, 1992, inside a spacious meeting room within the Council of Ministers Building in Phnom Penh. Hun Sen's tanned, impassive face and soft Khmer tones did not betray a hint of fatigue from the celebration the night before.[25] The revelry in Phnom Penh had been excessive. Cambodia had little cause to celebrate. Old hatreds ran deep in spite of the signing of a peace accord in Paris in October the previous year. Although a tentative peace had returned, the Cambodian people remained abysmally poor. The accord had done little to improve their lives; instead the approximately 22,000 peacekeeping forces serving under UNTAC had caused inflation, which took rice and potatoes out of the reach of the common people.

It had not been easy to meet Hun Sen, who had a full agenda starting with a meeting with visiting U.S. Congressman Stephen Solarz. Our guide, Leng Sochea, pressed us to approach Cham Prasidh, a senior prime ministerial aide. We told Prasidh that we wanted to meet the premier. Prasidh was polite, and said that he would convey our message to Hun Sen. He told us to wait and hope for the best. About forty minutes later, an official came running towards us, and said that Hun Sen had agreed to meet us, but he did not have much time. How much time would he give us, we asked. "Oh, about forty-five minutes," he replied.

Just the previous month, Hun Sen had demonstrated profound political sagacity by predicting that his CPP would form a coalition government with the Funcinpec party after the general election in May 1993. It was a public relations master-stroke, delivered in Kompong Cham during Sihanouk's visit to the province, and was aimed at reassuring Sihanouk that his royalist party would play a major role in a future government. On that occasion Sihanouk told the people of Kompong Cham: "The last time I came to this province was in 1976. The Khmer Rouge brought me, but I didn't have much freedom."

Hun Sen did everything to please Sihanouk. He made sure that the 125-kilometre road from the capital to the province was decked with hundreds of national flags, and that the people were informed about his visit so that they would line the roads expectantly to catch a glimpse of the prince. But beneath the public relations Sihanouk was aware of the painful reality. A year earlier, he had shot a film, *My Village at Dusk*, depicting the harshness of life in a Khmer village. Sihanouk said: "I wanted to show the realities, happiness and misfortune of a Khmer village whose surrounding areas, including fields and rice paddies, are riddled with landmines; the courage, abnegation, sacrifices of some, the despair of others; the present difference in the way of life between city and country; [and] Cambodia's uncertain future in which the process of domestic reconciliation is still a precarious one."

The man we met that New Year's Day did not seem to carry the encumbrance of a traumatic past. We were in Hun Sen's palatial meeting room. Before us, he had met Solarz, the encounter signalling that the United States might soon begin the process of normalising relations with Phnom Penh. Dressed in a dark suit and a discreet tie, Hun Sen greeted us in his native Khmer language through his interpreter Uch Kiman, who held the rank of vice-minister. Though his education had been interrupted, Hun Sen had learnt to speak a little English, as well as French, and Russian. The years sat easily on him. His glowing skin and shiny black hair neatly parted down the side made him look younger than his forty years. His glass eye did tend to unnerve, however, as he had a nervous twitch. He smoked constantly, inhaling deeply before speaking, and emitting puffs of smoke with his words. There were four government officials present in the room, all taking copious notes.

What, we asked, was the biggest crisis that confronted his

country? Had his party dropped the idea of putting the Khmer Rouge leaders on trial? And did he think that the Cambodian people would, at some stage, demand a court trial for the genocidal crimes committed by them? "I believe that the idea of bringing the Khmer Rouge to trial will not be abandoned, because there are many people who would like to see justice done," he said in earnest tones. "The popular anger against the Khmer Rouge cannot be diluted." He stopped to drag on his cigarette with an air of great gravity and dignity, and continued: "Although a number of countries had subscribed to the Paris peace agreement, all of them wanted to bring the Khmer Rouge back to trial. I think we should let the next elected government decide on this." His patience was running thin with the Khmer Rouge, who had breached the peace agreement by refusing to demobilise their forces and lay down their Chinese-supplied weapons. He sounded a stern warning on that New Year's Day. "This peace agreement must be implemented completely— one hundred per cent, no less," he declared. "I know there will be difficulties, and we are sure that the Khmer Rouge will hide their weapons and army in the jungles. UNTAC will have the responsibility of carrying out this task." Hun Sen, whose government's 55,000 troops had been verified by UNTAC, with some placed in cantonments for eventual demobilisation, was convinced that the Khmer Rouge would refuse to demobilise all of their troops.

Later that week, his government would receive a major boost when U.S. President George H.W. Bush lifted the by now sixteen-year-long trade embargo against Cambodia.[26] But the U.S. gesture was not intended as a signal of support or recognition for the Hun Sen government. The lifting of the embargo was Washington's way of announcing that Sihanouk was back in Phnom Penh, and that the country would no longer be isolated. It sent a muddled signal to the business community that it was all right to do business with Cambodia, an economy still firmly controlled by Hun Sen. The Bush administration knew the economic realities perfectly well, and yet it figured that the time had come to lift the embargo because it was wrong to punish Cambodia indefinitely. It was no small victory for Hun Sen, who was given another boost when the government of Singapore, which had severed ties with Cambodia when Vietnamese troops entered Cambodia in 1979, lifted its own embargo on investments. "It is good news, and a great encouragement to hear about the lifting of the economic embargo by Singapore to encourage foreign investments here," said Hun Sen, puffing away. "I believe that we can develop our own economy only when we have foreign investments coming in very quickly." Those were happy days for Hun Sen, as Singapore emerged as Cambodia's biggest trading partner. Some Singaporean businessmen had begun investing hard currency in hotels and tourism projects even before the embargo was lifted; now they forged links directly with the Hun Sen government, which was issuing investment approvals with a vengeance. By the end of 1991, Hun Sen's government had won about US$350 million in foreign investments from businessmen in twenty-two countries, including Singapore, Thailand, France, Malaysia, and Australia. Turning to look at us and then around the room as if seeking approval, Hun Sen issued an open invitation to foreign investors: "I think we should not wait until after the elections in 1993, but rather we should start right now. After a very long war, Cambodia has become a very interesting marketplace for foreign investments, despite the fact that peace is not completely restored because the peace agreement has just been reached. But the conditions for investment have been fully implemented."

What Hun Sen left unsaid was that foreign investments could also help legitimise his government, and that foreign businessmen drawn by visions of gold served his government faithfully. They were signifiers of the successful revival of the Cambodian economy at the toughest time in Hun Sen's political career—the peace talks.

His government still lacked the funds to finance major developments, however. "According to the initial assessment made by our ministry of planning, we will need US$1.2 billion to reconstruct our infrastructure. But we have three priorities on top of all the other priorities. Our country is an agricultural one, and our farmers represent more than ninety per cent of our population. Therefore, any political party in power cannot overlook the agricultural aspects of the problem." The second priority, he said, related to the lack of transport and communications, and unless his country could quickly develop its roads, bridges, and communications, its economy would remain stunted. A third priority was to put in place electricity supplies, without which industrial output could not be raised. However, "so far we have not received any budget commitments for reconstruction," Hun Sen complained, dragging furiously on a cigarette. "The great operation of UNTAC will have to face the problem of a lack of money." Only three countries had actually contributed funds: "France has provided assistance in the restoration of our water and electricity supplies in Phnom Penh; Thailand has helped reconstruct the road from the border town of Poipet to Sisophon, and other projects as well; and Japan is in the process of discussing the reconstruction of the bridge across the Tonle Sap which was blown up in the war," he remarked. Other countries had shown a clear lack of enthusiasm. "For this reason I believe that maybe the private sector will play a major role in economic reconstruction."

Hun Sen found himself in a particularly unenviable position when his biggest ally, the Soviet Union, began self-destructing. In 1991, the Soviet Union reduced its trade credits to Cambodia from an annual level of US$100 million to a mere US$12 million. Cambodia's other faithful ally, Cuba, could not do much either because it was also severely hit by cuts in Soviet aid. Cambodia, which had relied on Soviet credits to buy Soviet oil, turned to Singapore to meet its oil needs, and Singapore oil suppliers readily cashed in on the opportunity. The collapse of the Soviet Union delivered a crushing blow to the Cambodian economy. "In the last year our trade relations with the Soviet Union have not produced anything much," Hun Sen said, carefully explaining the root causes of the economic crisis. "Our students are being shipped back from Russia, and the Russian teachers have also returned home. A number of agreements are in a difficult period. All these problems were not brought about because of any political problems between the two countries. In fact, the Russian people, and the other independent states, continue having a good consideration towards us."[27]

Nothing hurt his government more than Vietnam's decision to also pare down its assistance, much of which had already been whittled down when Hanoi withdrew its troops in 1989. But after the Soviets reduced their aid to Vietnam in 1991, Hanoi was also affected. The Paris peace agreement jeopardised any chance of a revival of Indochinese solidarity as it demanded that Vietnam and China, major players in the Cambodian civil war, should no longer interfere in Cambodia. Hun Sen pondered this point, and clarified: "Any agreement, or treaty, with Vietnam that is not in conformity with the Paris agreement will be invalidated, and other agreements that are in conformity with the Paris agreement will be continued, especially technical, scientific, and cultural agreements. We will not only continue our cooperation with Vietnam, but also with other countries." An important defence treaty with Vietnam was suspended because it was incompatible with the Paris peace accord.

Just when it seemed that Hun Sen was finally becoming more acceptable in international eyes—the withdrawal of Vietnamese troops making him appear truly independent of Vietnam—he was once again embroiled in a full-blown controversy. In the months before the signing of the peace accord, Phnom Penh was rife with talk of corruption among some of Hun Sen's ministers. But it was hearsay, and nobody could substantiate the charges. A cyclo driver, who drove us around Phnom Penh, could not resist commenting on the lavish homes the ministers lived in. "Their salaries are very low. How could they become so rich?" he said, pointing at neat rows of ministerial villas as we rode past. A junior official in the Hun Sen government remarked: "In 1979, none of them had any personal wealth, and none had houses and cars. But within ten years they have amassed tremendous wealth, and this makes us wonder how most of us have remained so poor, and these ministers have grown so rich." Sihanouk, on returning to Phnom Penh in late 1991, would note that people's lifestyles were a study in contrasts. At one extreme were the ministers and officials living in their French-style villas; at the other end were the large numbers of poor citizens who did not even own a bicycle, and earned a pittance to string body and soul together. It was too much for Sihanouk to bear, and his office released a public statement accusing the Hun Sen government of corruption. One of Sihanouk's personal aides, Julio Jeldres, made sweeping allegations that ranged from grand larceny to petty thievery. He said that the officials were selling everything from government-owned buildings and land to factories and office fixtures. The government, he charged, had failed to run its own factories, and had leased them on monthly rent to foreign companies. An official in the ministry of planning informed us that while it was true that at least sixty factories were leased to foreign investors, all the deals were above-board, and the rent was collected by the ministries. Hun Sen's response was that the biggest weapon to fight corruption was development.

As our meeting drew to an end, the battery of prime ministerial aides who were studiously jotting down his every word looked relieved. Hun Sen broke into a broad smile as we parted. Leng Sochea, too, looked visibly pleased that we had been able to meet his leader. Later, Sochea said enthusiastically: "It was incredible. Hun Sen seldom meets writers." Then he added thoughtfully: "We have to study the text of the interview carefully because he has said many things that set a new policy direction for Cambodia."

VIII

THE PEASANT AND THE PRINCES

1991–97

WITH THE PEACE ACCORD signed in Paris in October 1991, Sihanouk prepared to return home to take up his position as head of state of a unified Cambodia. Hun Sen, in a spirit of reconciliation, embraced the prince's homecoming, and thought no more of the abuse and humiliation that Sihanouk had heaped on him over the years—calling him a "lackey of Vietnam," and "his bad son." He ordered city officials to spare no effort in cleaning up the capital ahead of Sihanouk's arrival on November 14.

It was to be a grand homecoming. The changes were visible at Sihanouk's point of entry, Pochentong Airport. Gone was the run-down control tower that had looked like a relic from the First Indochina War, and in its place a freshly whitewashed structure gleamed in the sun, festooned with ribbons and crested by Sihanouk's portrait.[1] The interior of the terminal had seen the painter's brush, and sparkled white.[2] Visitors no longer sweated as they waited in long immigration lines. Ceiling fans swished overhead. Travellers' passports were stamped within minutes, and the anticipated inquisition from the customs officers no longer happened. The bureaucratic machinery appeared to be on a public relations exercise. The streets were swept so clean they looked unreal; the cyclos were instructed to avoid the main Kampuchea–Vietnam Avenue; little gardens were created in roadside niches. Phnom Penh was transformed into its former self when Sihanouk had been the chief of state until 1970.

Though he would be inaccessible to most Cambodians, the prince's presence could be felt. The Royal Palace wore a coat of yellow paint once again, and the royal flag flew above the walls. Sihanouk often emerged from seclusion to deliver a public lecture, or to open a new school or a medical dispensary. He was a changed man. Sources close to him revealed that gone were the days when he would throw lavish parties and play the saxophone for his guests. Now the parties were fewer, and more sober, though he regularly granted audiences to diplomats and foreign politicians, and gave them a sense of his vision. But he had not lost his sharp tongue. On meeting U.S. Ambassador Charles Twining, the prince warned bluntly: "I wish that the United States could avoid something like the event in 1970 when President Richard Nixon supported Lon Nol against Sihanouk. Please don't interfere in the dispute of Cambodians."[3]

The reason for the prince's sobriety was that he was now an elder statesman, and the head of an uneasy coalition of four parties. As the chairman of the SNC, Sihanouk was non-partisan and impartial, though covertly he made his likes and dislikes quite plain. In the interest of political stability, he refrained from destabilising the SNC, though he could not resist an occasional jibe. As he resumed playing a central role in national politics, his words and actions had a deep impact on Hun Sen and his policies. Hun Sen observed Sihanouk's tendency to denounce his government, but he did not react, fearing that a direct confrontation with the prince would be seen by the people as an insult to royalty.

THE YOUNG NORODOMS

The return of Sihanouk and his family members gave hope to many Cambodians. Isolated, deprived and poor, they wanted to entrust their country to the royal family, in whom they had longstanding faith. Hun Sen and his party realised that steps had to be taken quickly to counter the groundswell of support for the royal family.

Opportunity came knocking in the shape of Prince Norodom Chakrapong, a son of Sihanouk who had broken away from the Funcinpec party his father had founded. Chakrapong was displeased with the way Funcinpec was being run, and sought a meeting with Hun Sen and other CPP leaders, for exploratory talks about his political future. The talks went well, and he joined the SOC government in January 1992. His defection, a year ahead of the general election, worsened relations between him and his half-brother, Ranariddh. When it came to the pedigree of royal lineage, Chakrapong was the purer of the two. Chakrapong's mother, Princess Sisowath Pongsanmoni, was not only a member of the royal family, she was also Sihanouk's aunt. Ranariddh's mother, Neak Moneang Phat Kanhol, was a commoner. Sihanouk took four other wives besides Pongsanmoni and Kanhol. They were Princess Sisowath Monikessan, who bore him Prince Naradipo; Kanita Norodom Thavet Norleak, a member of the royal family who had no children; a Laotian woman named Mam Manivann, who bore him Princess Sucheatvateya and Princess Arunrasmey; and the Eurasian beauty Monique Izzi, who gave him two sons, Prince Sihamoni and Prince Narindrapong. Chakrapong had six siblings, some of whom had been killed by the Khmer Rouge; but Ranariddh's only sister, Princess Buppha Devi, survived.

The princes Chakrapong and Ranariddh were a study in contrasts. Ek Sereywath, a French-educated Funcinpec official, graphically compared the two: "Ranariddh is an intellectual with a doctorate, while Chakrapong is just an air force pilot. The two brothers do not get on." Longstanding rivals with serious differences, Chakrapong and Ranariddh disagreed on how Funcinpec ought to deal with the Khmer Rouge. The only similarity was the striking resemblance they had with their father, and the distinctive falsetto all three spoke in. Their quarrel became an item of public interest in 1992. Chakrapong, aged forty-seven, and Ranariddh, forty-eight, made their entry into Cambodian politics in exile. Having built up an international reputation for his role in the Cambodian peace talks, Ranariddh took over Funcinpec's leadership from his father. It was a post that Chakrapong had been eyeing, and when he did not get it, he rebelled and joined Hun Sen's government.

To gain an insight into the royal feud, the authors phoned Chakrapong's office in mid-August 1992. His son, the young Prince Norodom Buddhapong, who doubled as his assistant, readily arranged a meeting with his father the next morning at his office in the Council of Ministers Building.

Chakrapong, a swarthy man in a dark suit, walked into the room and greeted the authors effusively. He explained why he had broken away from his father's party. "I joined the royalist party because my father was the president of the party, and I wanted to eject the Vietnamese troops from Cambodia," Chakrapong said enthusiastically. "My goal, as a citizen of Cambodia, was achieved the day the Paris peace agreement was signed in October 1991, which ended the factional fighting. My father became the head of state, and my duty was over."[4] Before joining the SOC, Chakrapong had served as the deputy chief of staff and commander of an elite brigade of Sihanouk's National Army of Independent Kampuchea during the years when Sihanouk headed Funcinpec. A senior member of Hun Sen's government told the authors that soon after Chakrapong left his father's party, he tried to join the Khmer Rouge, but could not reach an agreement with them to accommodate him. He entered the CPP as a second choice. "I was the number two man in Funcinpec," Chakrapong emphasised during the hour-long conversation. It went without saying that his father was number one.

After Hun Sen appointed him a vice-prime minister, Chakrapong quickly became a household name. He was also given a high rank in the CPP's communist-style politburo, the inner coterie that ran Cambodia. By all accounts, the party intended to employ Chakrapong as a vote-puller in the elections of May 1993 in an attempt to counter the appeal of Ranariddh. Chakrapong was the only member of the royal family that the CPP had acquired, and they would be banking on him to win the hearts and minds of the voters who revered the Norodoms.

As one of five vice-prime ministers in the SOC, Chakrapong's responsibilities encompassed six ministries—civil aviation, tourism, industry, culture, education, and social welfare. The load was too much for the prince, who played a figurehead role in most ministries aside from civil aviation, where he performed well. He immersed himself in an ambitious plan to expand the national airline. Part of the reason for his interest in aviation was that he had served as a fighter pilot in the Royal Cambodian Air Force when his father was the chief of state. Sihanouk had, at the time, planned to ask the Soviet Union to provide MiG-21 fighter aircraft, but he was ousted in a coup. Chakrapong, for his part, said that he would upgrade the Cambodian national airline by leasing a Boeing passenger jet, as well as adding more air connections.

Had he embraced some form of Marxist ideology by joining the communist-style CPP? "As the blood of the royal family I would not have joined a party that was communist," Chakrapong said indignantly. The CPP was shedding its communist image, and Chakrapong's argument sounded logical. Time and again, Chakrapong used his father's name to reiterate the point that he had won paternal approval for most of his actions. "Our head of state, my father, has assured us that after the elections, our government's economic policies will not be discarded," he insisted. Chakrapong began using his power soon after he took office. When Ranariddh wanted to fly into Pochentong Airport in a private airplane, Chakrapong exercised his authority as minister of civil aviation to deny permission. Repeated requests by Ranariddh were rejected. It was an episode that Ranariddh would not forget, and he would take revenge at the first opportunity.

THE PERSISTENT PROBLEM OF THE KHMER ROUGE

Back at the Royal Palace, Sihanouk fully exploited his status as an elder statesman. Even before the Paris peace agreement was signed in 1991, he had realised that the rank that would best serve his future political ambition was not as the head of the Funcinpec party, which he had created after he was ousted from power, but as the head of state. By vacating the leadership of the political party for his son Ranariddh—who was a spitting image of his father—he gambled that his son would lead the party to victory in the elections, and pave the way for him to retake power. By being appointed—uncontested—as the head of state, he laid the foundation to achieve his goal, to be elected the president of the country, as early as 1993. It was vintage Sihanouk strategy, aimed at keeping political power within the family.

In August 1992, with nine months to go before the scheduled elections, the authors paid a visit to the Royal Palace. The quarter of the palace we caught a glimpse of was not in the best shape— paint was peeling from the walls. A gardener tended the first flowers to bloom since peace officially descended on the unfortunate land. Keo Puth Reasmey, a loyal member of Sihanouk's cabinet secretariat, agreed to deliver a letter from us to the prince. "He is very prompt in answering letters," Reasmey promised. As a matter of routine Sihanouk personally answered his mail, making small jottings in French. Reasmey told us to return in two days. Sure enough, Sihanouk had answered all the questions. All his comments in French were there on our letter, written along the margins, and squeezed between the lines. In less than a week, we received a formal letter signed by the prince on royal letterhead. Sihanouk had also taken the trouble of enclosing a document containing his thoughts on the economic reconstruction of his country. But it was his opinion on the Khmer Rouge that was the most eye-opening.

The Khmer Rouge remained the chief obstacle to Sihanouk's ambition of becoming an elected president. By refusing to demobilise their troops—as the peace accord called for—the Khmer Rouge cast a cloud of uncertainty over whether the elections could be held as planned the following May. The prince knew that leaving the Khmer Rouge out of the election would hurt national stability, by pushing the faction deeper into isolation and militancy. But asked if it would be advisable for UNTAC to hold three-party elections between only the CPP, Son Sann's Khmer People's National Liberation Front, and Ranariddh's Funcinpec party, he replied categorically: "That would be the best solution, because the Khmer Rouge leave UNTAC no other choice." It was an extreme position for a neutral head of state to take, but he believed that the larger good of the country ought not to be sacrificed because of the non-cooperation of the guerrillas. "The elections will probably be held on schedule. And, they will be held only in the non-Khmer Rouge zones," he wrote.[5] His instincts were prophetic.

November came by and nothing had changed to make the peace process any smoother. The Khmer Rouge was still holding out. The statement by the prince confirmed the widely held view that elections were not likely to be held nationwide, because the Khmer Rouge had not allowed UN peacekeepers to enter their areas of control in order to prepare for the polls. There was also the larger threat of the country being partitioned if the elections were held without the Khmer Rouge. And for their part, the Khmer Rouge accused UN peacekeepers of various lapses, such as being in league with the Hun Sen government, failing to verify the presence of Vietnamese troops disguised as civilians, and refusing to dismantle the administrative structures of the Hun Sen government. UNTAC routinely parried these accusations with its standard comments that it was not in league with any faction, that there was no hard evidence of the presence of Vietnamese troops in the country, and that the peace accord did not call for the dismantling of the Hun Sen government.

Sihanouk's sights were set beyond the shenanigans of the Khmer Rouge, and beyond the elections. Once again, he wanted to see himself ensconced as the ruler. There was a rising chorus of demands from various politicians for him to become an elected president in 1993. He was certain to be elected because there were no credible opponents in the entire slate of possible candidates. If CPP leaders Heng Samrin and Chea Sim ran against him, they were likely to meet humiliating defeat at the hands of a prince who had possessed the power of sweeping the majority vote in the country in the 1960s. The charisma still held. But Sihanouk set a tough condition. He would run for president only if the presidential poll was held before the general election in May 1993. He refused to run if the presidential election was held at the same time or after. What were Sihanouk's motives? Was he attempting to consolidate his personal grip on power before the general election? Sihanouk was beset by two worries. One, a fear that if the presidential poll were held at the same time as the general election, there was a risk that the Khmer Rouge could scuttle the entire election and dash his hopes of becoming the president. Secondly, he was genuinely concerned about political stability. Fears that the country was heading down a slippery slope to anarchy had imbued a sense of urgency to a plan to hold an early presidential poll.

ADJUSTING TO THE NEW CAMBODIA

A year after our first meeting with Hun Sen, we met him again on January 5, 1993, at the Khmer-style Chamkarmon Palace, meaning "silkworm fields," which was used to accommodate visiting foreign dignitaries. The palace was crowded with workers from non-governmental organisations, UN officials, and media men, who closed in on the prime minister. As we approached, he recognised us instantly. "How are you two?" he inquired. We asked if he had time for an interview and without hesitation he said, "Come with me. We will go and talk in private in the other chamber."[6] His demeanour was that of a man who never needed to consult his aides before making a decision about whom to meet. He walked briskly out of

JULIE MEHTA

The long interview: Author Harish Mehta interviewing Hun Sen at the Chamkarmon Palace in Phnom Penh in January 1993.

the meeting hall, through a corridor packed with diplomats and media, and entered a large room, followed by his interpreter, Uch Kiman, and a senior general of his armed forces who wore a gold Rolex watch.

It was an elegant room, but not particularly Cambodian in its decor. The floor was covered with a thick carpet that looked typically Vietnamese—a reminder of Hun Sen's close ties with Hanoi—and large paintings depicting Cambodian village life lined the walls. The Rolex-sporting general was at hand to be consulted, but Hun Sen did not need any prompting. The young village lad had matured beyond his forty-one years. He had one advantage over his political rivals: his age. On that morning, with the elections just five months away, he warned that if the polls could not be held in May it would be impossible to hold them until the year 2000. "By then, I will be forty-eight years old. But I will probably outlive many older politicians," he predicted.

It had been a tough morning for him. He had heard the news over the BBC radio that Sihanouk was threatening not to cooperate with his government, or with UNTAC. Sihanouk was reacting angrily to the recent killing of members of Funcinpec, allegedly by activists of the CPP. Diplomats believed that Hun Sen was not involved personally, and that the campaign of violence was being conducted by certain hardliners within the CPP who disliked Hun Sen's reformist agenda, and felt that he had sold out the party's interests when he signed the peace accord; they would have preferred to continue fighting to safeguard their political power, which faced the threat of the ballot box. But Hun Sen, who had weathered many political storms, was not troubled by the news that Sihanouk was laying down preconditions for his participation in the political process. Sihanouk's wish for a presidential election before the general election was not to be fulfilled.

Earlier that morning, talking to aid workers, Hun Sen had demanded the ejection of the Khmer Rouge from the peace accord, and insisted that they must be branded as insurgents and outlaws. But the country was no longer being run by his party. It was administered by UNTAC. As a result, Hun Sen lacked the authority to outlaw the guerrillas, who had walked away from the peace process and refused to disarm and demobilise their troops. Asked to describe his experience of working with UNTAC, he said thoughtfully: "We consider this an obligation that we have to fulfill within the framework of the Paris agreement. With regard to the financial aspect, we consider UNTAC's control as technical assistance. We are using UNTAC's control as a way of learning how to combat inflation, and also how to prevent our officials from committing illegal acts." He inhaled deeply on a cigarette as he waited for the next question. The CPP had honoured the peace accord by transferring five of its ministries to UNTAC control—earning Hun Sen much international goodwill—but the Khmer Rouge had not submitted itself to UNTAC. How did this anomaly impact the peace accord? Looking suddenly agitated, he said: "We are now insisting that UNTAC exercise the same kind of control over the other parties that signed the peace accord. We know that the Khmer Rouge will not comply. But if we argue that just because the Khmer Rouge will not comply, so we should also not comply, it will mean that we have fallen into the trap of the Khmer Rouge. Therefore, we insist, and demand, that the Khmer Rouge be excluded from the peace process."[7]

He then turned his ire on the parties of Ranariddh and Son Sann. "Concerning these two parties, we insist that there be similar control by UNTAC over them, particularly over their finances, because there must be no financial influence over the elections," he argued. "Right now, the question is, where do these parties get the money to spend on their political campaigns? They do not have the revenue from, for instance, rubber plantations, industry, agriculture, or taxes. So, do they get assistance from foreigners? If they do, is it in conformity with the Paris accord? Is it also in conformity with the neutral political environment which the UN wanted to create?" His biggest worry on that Tuesday morning was that the Khmer Rouge had expanded the areas under their control. Earlier that morning, a general from the CPP armed forces had explained how the guerrillas were able to dominate more areas. The Khmer Rouge had spread the word that it would carry out their threat of cutting off the hands of those who dared cast their ballots, raising fears among the people living in the countryside. UNTAC electoral officials, stationed in far-flung provinces, lived in fear as well. Hun Sen cautioned: "If we take appropriate and quick measures not to allow the Khmer Rouge to expand further, I believe the elections can be held."

The trouble was, UNTAC had spent about US$2 billion and still failed to create the conditions for voting to take place on election day, just five months away. The Cambodian and foreign press were not alone in criticising UNTAC for its failure to bring the Khmer Rouge into the peace process. Hun Sen, too, was annoyed.

"If UNTAC has no courage to carry out its mandate, and if UNTAC continues to withdraw all the time [whenever it is threatened by the Khmer Rouge], and if UNTAC does not allow us our right of self-defence [if attacked by the Khmer Rouge], then it means that the elections will face a lot of difficulties, even to the point that elections may not be held," he deduced. As an afterthought, he added: "It is still not too late. We can still find the right measures."

On that calm morning, the threat of the guerrillas seemed much magnified. We asked Hun Sen if he would give a piece of Cambodian territory to the Khmer Rouge if there was no option but to partition the country. "We cannot accept the partitioning of Cambodia," he said softly, and added: "We cannot allow insurgency either. Thailand and Malaysia have both addressed this kind of a problem, and have found a common solution." When asked whether his government would take up arms against the Khmer Rouge if it tried to recapture power using military means, Hun Sen said: "Right now there is no other force in the country apart from us that can face up to the threat of the Khmer Rouge. If we had not exercised our right of self-defence, perhaps UNTAC would already have run away from Cambodia. The other parties can only make a noise about the Khmer Rouge's actions, but they have no ability whatsoever to face them. As long as the State of Cambodia exists, as long as the Cambodian People's Party exists, and as long as Heng Samrin, Chea Sim, and Hun Sen exist, the Khmer Rouge can never bring back their regime. The people have real confidence in our party, not in the other parties." With a grin, he added: "The Cambodian people are now beginning to joke that UNTAC is running away from the Khmer Rouge faster than even the Cambodian people because they have cars and aircraft at their disposal, whereas the Cambodians only have bicycles and bullock carts."

He was visibly offended by the criticism levelled by the UNTAC report, "The Short-Term Impact of UNTAC on Cambodia's Economy," which claimed that inflation, running at about 150 per cent, was not caused by UNTAC but by his government. UNTAC blamed it for fuelling the inflation by printing money to finance the budget deficit. Hun Sen refuted the charge: "We have a domestic consensus that we must keep our spending within our revenue in order to implement our economic stabilisation policy," he explained. "For four months already we have not used the printing press to print money. And we are trying not to print any more money. UNTAC has tried to avoid its responsibility in Cambodia on the economic aspects in general. We do not name UNTAC as the main source of economic instability and inflation. But UNTAC should recognise that it has not contributed to economic stability. Its presence here, and the resulting increase in local consumption, has created the problem of rising prices. Our production remains the same, yet the number of mouths to feed has increased. Another reason for inflation is that UNTAC troops and civilians have refused to convert their U.S. dollars into the local currency before spending. This has caused a loss of confidence in our currency. This is very important politically, because a loss of confidence in our local currency reflects a loss of confidence in our policy, and has a very big impact."[8]

Would he ask the UNTAC chief, Yasushi Akashi, to order his 22,000 staff to use Cambodian riels instead of U.S. dollars? "I have raised this issue twice with Mr Akashi since August 1992, and he promised he would look into it," Hun Sen said hopefully. "Two days ago, I signed a memorandum and sent it to him, requesting that UNTAC personnel exchange ten per cent of their salaries, or revenue, intended for local consumption. So far, I have not received a reply." Vegetable sellers said that due to massive purchases by UNTAC, the price of potatoes had risen from 200 riels to 450 riels a kilogramme in December 1992. As traders began speculating, the price of rice increased five-fold. Akashi still did not respond to the emergency, and it was only in April 1993 that he told the Cambodian people that UNTAC was considering bringing extra rice onto the market.

A bigger crisis preoccupied Hun Sen. He revealed that the government would run a thirty-per-cent deficit, which meant there was no money to finance a third of development. "According to the World Bank's pledge, by 1993 Cambodia will get US$75 million in assistance, of which US$35 million will be earmarked for importing commodities for domestic consumption," he said optimistically. Smiling again, he added: "If this kind of assistance is forthcoming, our projected deficit will be reduced." While the Asian Development Bank wasted no time in approving loans to Cambodia worth over US$70 million to generate electricity and to build irrigation canals, the World Bank had shelved its plans. Even as Hun Sen was expressing the hope that the World Bank would lend money, the loan fell through. A few days later, Michael Ward, a World Bank official who worked as a deputy economic advisor to UNTAC, revealed that the US$75 million loan, though approved in principle, was blocked at the last minute. "If it became known in the capital markets that the World Bank had offloaded US$75 million in Cambodia, and if the political situation in Cambodia deteriorated, it would cause a catastrophe in the markets," he said coldly.[9] A senior World Bank official who was due to visit Phnom Penh in January 1993 suddenly cancelled his trip because the bank now regarded any loans to the country as being too risky. Another reason the loan was blocked, Ward explained, was that it had become harder for UNTAC to negotiate with Sihanouk, who was in Beijing for cancer treatment. Before the loan could be sanctioned, the prince's stamp of approval was needed, but he had declined to give his royal endorsement at that stage. It revealed his indifference to the plight of his people, who would be made to suffer a little longer.

THE ELECTIONS

Sihanouk continued writing letters around the world and releasing daily statements to the press from the three capitals on his regular itinerary—Beijing, Pyongyang, and Phnom Penh. A statement he issued from Beijing on February 8, 1993, revealed a fresh lust for power. "Due to the grave situation in my country, it is important that the president of Cambodia has the same powers as the president of the USA," Sihanouk recommended.[10] He made it clear furthermore that he was unwilling to share power with a prime minister. To allay fears that he would turn into a dictator, he added a few words of reassurance: "Of course, alongside the president there will be a Parliament, or a National Assembly." There was panic in the ranks of the CPP and Funcinpec, both of which feared that Sihanouk would relegate them to the backbenches within the national assembly. There was no doubting that if Sihanouk ran for president, he would win hands down.

Sihanouk wanted power, and it seemed that many influential people wanted him to have it. Hun Sen wanted him to run in a presidential election, and so did the UNTAC chief. After a closed-door meeting with Sihanouk on May 22, 1993, Akashi declared elatedly: "There's no doubt that he will play a very, very important role." Ranariddh said much more. After casting his ballot on May 23 in Phnom Penh, he affirmed: "My father will be given full state powers. He will not merely be a figurehead. He will really run the country."[11]

Out of the peace accord emerged the elections. In political party offices across Phnom Penh, strategists worked out their power combinations. With Funcinpec leading the vote count, the most likely cabinet line-up appeared to be Prime Minister Ranariddh, and Vice-Prime Minister Hun Sen. Another possible scenario: Emperor Sihanouk, President Ranariddh, and Prime Minister Hun Sen. This formula seemed the most acceptable as it accommodated the interests of the three principal aspirants.[12] There was a third scenario: President and Prime Minister Sihanouk, and Senior Deputy Prime Ministers Ranariddh and Hun Sen. Sihanouk would probably have revelled in both roles as the head of state and the head of government, but Ranariddh and Hun Sen were not likely to accept such a patently unfair arrangement.

In early June 1993, the victory of Funcinpec was announced. The royalist party, created back in 1981 by Sihanouk to fight the Vietnamese army, had defeated the CPP by a narrow margin. It was still a victory, and a great day for Sihanouk—a party that had fought the elections on the Sihanoukist platform had triumphed. It was clear that Funcinpec had won primarily because of the popular appeal of Sihanouk, whose name Ranariddh used widely during the campaign. Sihanouk's half-brother, Prince Norodom Sirivudh, had told the authors before the elections: "We have strong support from the people because we are the Sihanoukist party."[13]

On June 3, Sihanouk launched a "coup." He issued a statement saying that he was forming an interim government with himself as the prime minister. A few hours later the CPP came out in support of Sihanouk, thus denying Ranariddh the first opportunity to form a government as the head of the winning party. A new chapter in Cambodian history was scripted that evening. Sihanouk appointed himself prime minister and supreme commander of the armed forces, and named Ranariddh and Hun Sen his deputy prime ministers. The appointments took immediate effect. The trouble was that Ranariddh had not been consulted. Stinging allegations swirled around the capital that Sihanouk had staged a "constitutional coup" with the help of the CPP, which wanted to undercut Ranariddh by any means. In Sihanouk, the CPP found the only leader with national stature who was able, and willing, to curtail Ranariddh's power. Two hurriedly issued statements by Sihanouk and the CPP in the evening declared that the interim government—named the National Government of Cambodia (NGC)—would remain in power for three months, until the national assembly adopted a new constitution, and a new government was formed. Palace officials said that Sihanouk was confident of Ranariddh's support. A declaration by the CPP stated: "The CPP wishes to appeal to all compatriots, public servants, and all categories of the armed forces to remain calm, to be pleased with, and optimistic of, the NGC under the High Leadership of our Samdech Preah Norodom Sihanouk."

That evening, Hun Sen stepped down as prime minister of a country he had led without a break since his appointment in 1985, and his SOC government, installed in 1979 with the help of the Vietnamese, was dissolved. Sok An, the chief of cabinet of the CPP, said in quavering tones: "Yes, it is dissolved." But several questions remained unanswered. What was the true story of the attempt by Sihanouk to grab power? Was Hun Sen disappointed at having to step down? Hun Sen told the authors plainly: "Chea Sim and I had an audience with Sihanouk to beg his royal highness to set up a provisional government immediately, to save the situation. I had no reason to be disappointed, because I had made the proposal. I sent the announcement of the formation of the new government to the radio and television stations to be broadcast." The same evening, we asked the same question of Khieu Kanharith, the SOC spokesman. He said thoughtfully: "Hun Sen is happy that there were no clashes after the election results were announced." Kanharith wisely left the question unanswered.

Sihanouk's NGC was created at the end of three days of secret talks with CPP supremo Chea Sim at the Royal Palace. During the same week, Sok An told the authors that the negotiations had gone "smoothly and without disagreement." Notably, Ranariddh, who was away in Banteay Meanchey province, was not informed of the meetings. It was obvious that a deal had been struck behind his back. That night, Sam Rainsy, a rising star in Funcinpec, told the authors that he had been "taken totally by surprise" by the formation of the government. On June 3, Sihanouk spoke to Ranariddh on the phone and tried to persuade him to join the government, but the latter was not convinced. Sihanouk agonised through a sleepless night. Yet, he remained convinced that Ranariddh would eventually agree. He felt that his son would have no objections to his becoming the prime minister of an interim government because, after all, the royalist party had won the elections on the strength of the Sihanouk name. His reading of his son, as well as of the top Funcinpec leaders such as Rainsy, was completely wrong.

By giving Hun Sen an equal position in the government with Ranariddh, Sihanouk had accepted the political reality that since the army and the civilian administration were controlled by the CPP, it would have to be given a major role in government. Sihanouk believed that the formation of the NGC had defused a potentially explosive situation, which could have resulted in Hun Sen refusing to hand over power, and launching a coup against a Funcinpec government. For Sihanouk, it was the first executive post he had held since his removal in the coup of 1970. It was to be a very short tenure.

Many observers believed that the CPP had threatened to wage war if it did not get to share power equally with Funcinpec. Was it true that Hun Sen, or the other CPP leaders, had delivered such dire warnings? "This was not true," Hun Sen responded indignantly. "It was a total distortion. In fact, Funcinpec had only fifty-eight seats in a 120-member national assembly, whereas a minimum two-thirds majority—eighty seats—was required to approve the new constitution. So what could they do at the time if the CPP had refused to establish the provisional government and approve the constitution? It was complicated enough to say that it was a failure of UNTAC, which meant that the UN would have to prolong UNTAC's presence. This would have meant that the UN would have to spend more money, and the State of Cambodia government [headed by Hun Sen] would have continued in power. In this respect, they should have seen the good intentions of the CPP."

From Banteay Meanchey, Ranariddh faxed a letter to his father, asking him to explain the legal basis for the creation of the interim government, as well as the legislative structures under which the new regime would function. He also demanded that his half-brother, Chakrapong, be kept out of a future government, as the siblings had not resolved their personal differences. Sihanouk failed to come up with a reasonable response to Ranariddh's query about the legal basis for the regime. But he confirmed that Chakrapong would not be included in the NGC. Sihanouk glossed over the fact that there were no legislative structures in place under which the NGC could function.

On June 4, Sihanouk's hurriedly formed interim government collapsed, after holding power for less than a day. In a statement, he announced: "Given that some Cambodians, and some UN people, say that the NGC was born out of a constitutional coup, I renounce forming and presiding over the NGC." He added: "The only goal that I had in accepting the proposal was to avoid a bloody conflict that Hun Sen made me understand would happen. In renouncing the NGC I leave the Cambodian People's Party and Funcinpec to take responsibility for all that will happen."[14] The NGC had been shot to pieces by Ranariddh and a hawkish core within Funcinpec.[15] An aide to Sihanouk lamented: "Sam Rainsy is behind the collapse of the government. He is the Funcinpec leader who wants to keep power for himself." It was unacceptable to Ranariddh to be placed on the same level as Hun Sen, and he demanded a higher post. From being a novice during the peace talks between Sihanouk and Hun Sen in the late 1980s, Ranariddh had won the people's mandate to rule. He now believed that he possessed more of the popular mandate than Hun Sen. Ranariddh was advised by his aides that it was political suicide for Funcinpec to cede power so tamely to Sihanouk because the party had garnered six per cent more votes than the CPP. Ranariddh, for his part, refused to accept the treacherous reality that winning an election was not a guarantee of forming a government.

When his own Funcinpec party betrayed him, Sihanouk found new support in Hun Sen's party, which, to a man, backed his bid to become the prime minister, and a future executive president. In return, Sihanouk played the consummate conciliator by urging the Khmer Rouge not to attack Hun Sen's armed forces, because they were now under his direct command, saying that any attack on them would be construed as an attack on Sihanouk. Did Sihanouk betray his son's right to form the government as the victor? "The king's initiative was completely correct," Hun Sen said in retrospect. "Ranariddh should have been grateful to the king. How could Ranariddh have run the country with less than fifty-per-cent majority?"

In the coming weeks, as the rift in the house of Norodom grew wider, it would be Hun Sen's party that gained the most. Sihanouk now dropped all niceties and openly turned against Ranariddh. Appearing on state television, he told the people that Ranariddh had broken his promise to transfer power to him within twenty-four hours of winning the election. He lamented his son's disloyalty. The episode revealed the deep-rooted mistrust that Sihanouk had for his son. Under the influence of his wife Monique, Sihanouk favoured those of his children borne by her over those by his other wives. Ranariddh was not Monique's son; he was the child of a royal ballerina. Rarely did Sihanouk display fatherly love towards Ranariddh, maintaining instead a regal distance between them. It was not surprising that he denied his son his legitimate right to form a new government.

What, indeed, were Sihanouk's motives for attempting to take power? It appeared that he intended the interim government to serve as a forum to reconcile the factions under his leadership. It was also a move to pre-empt a refusal by Hun Sen to hand over power. Indeed, Chea Sim had warned Sihanouk that unless they struck a deal to share power, powerful leaders within the CPP would not agree to hand over power to the new government. There could even be bloodshed. That day, palace officials were spreading the word that Sihanouk had abandoned the formation of the NGC because "some countries in the UN permanent five opposed it." It was believed that U.S. officials were among them. For what it was worth, UNTAC chief Akashi lent his support to the NGC during a meeting with Sihanouk on June 3. Palace officials hoped that the NGC could be revived at a future meeting of the SNC. But a meeting of the SNC, scheduled for June 5, was cancelled because Sihanouk said he was "unwell," and would not chair it. In the end, by destroying his father's government, Ranariddh not only embarrassed Sihanouk but also lost face as he returned to the capital and resumed talks with the CPP to share power. Later, the members of the national assembly wrote a new constitution that required a two-thirds majority for any party to form a government. It was thus written in stone that under no circumstances could Ranariddh form a government on his own. He needed the CPP as much as the CPP needed him. Once again, Hun Sen's crafty calculations proved correct. With the collapse of the Sihanouk government, Hun Sen remained the prime minister until a new government could be installed.

Behaving just as unpredictably as his father, Ranariddh performed a volte-face on June 7, saying he was dropping all objections to Sihanouk's idea of forming a coalition government. Ranariddh declared on Radio France Internationale: "We accept and support the idea of forming this Cambodian national government under my father's presidency."[16] Ranariddh was now saying that his objections covered only minor points. "I only proposed some details to improve this government, and I said that the formation of a government must take into account the will of the sovereign people." Although Funcinpec was ahead of Hun Sen's party with a lead of six per cent of the votes, Ranariddh was candid in accepting the political realities. "One must admit that the situation in Cambodia makes it necessary to form a government of broad national union under the high presidency of my father," he clarified. Ranariddh's statement defused tensions between father and son, and patched up an enervating rift in the Norodom family. Prince Norodom Buddhapong, a son of Chakrapong, told the authors buoyantly: "It is a good development. We can move on. This is the beginning of everything after so many misses." Sihanouk's aide, Sina Than, said hopefully: "We have been expecting this news. Over the past few days there have been indications that Prince Ranariddh might reconsider his position."[17] Late at night on June 7, the authors phoned Sam Rainsy in Bangkok. He said that he had just heard the news over the Voice of America. He did not sound happy with Ranariddh's new position.

Two days later, Sihanouk gave vent to his anger, accusing UNTAC officials, the United States, and malicious newspapermen of thwarting his bid to form an interim government. On June 9, he issued a statement, crafted as usual in elegant French, and capping his gauche takeover attempt. "I absolutely refuse to undertake a similar experience in the present, and in the future," Sihanouk pledged. "I have learnt my lesson. I must, at all costs, respect the letter of the Paris accords, and avoid constitutional coups."[18] Sihanouk added pugnaciously: "It is now the duty of others—UNTAC, the UN, the USA, and others—to attempt a constitutional coup in Cambodia, if that makes them happy." A palace official told the authors that evening that Sihanouk was annoyed by a malicious newspaper report that claimed that Sihanouk, his wife Princess Monique, and his son Chakrapong were planning to "steal power from Ranariddh."

DISTRIBUTION OF POWER

The power struggle was intensifying in Phnom Penh, with Hun Sen's party dictating terms in a bid to control the lion's share of the ministries in a coalition government. It became apparent that the CPP's demands would be met because it controlled the army and police. At the same time, the CPP choreographed another drama. It sent senior army and police officers to pay their respects to Sihanouk, to shower him with blandishments, and to assure him of their loyalty. In doing so, the CPP took advantage of the rift between Sihanouk and Ranariddh, and succeeded in winning much-needed support from the former.

In a sideshow, Sihanouk conferred the country's highest military rank—five-star general—on Heng Samrin, Chea Sim, Hun Sen, and Ranariddh, more as an indication of political seniority than military power. In a decree, Sihanouk said that all the appointments were to the new Royal Cambodian Armed Forces, the name by which the armed forces were known during his rule.[19] On June 29, Sihanouk changed the name of the country and replaced the national flag in an attempt to reassert his rule and end the dominance of the Hun Sen government. "The State of Cambodia is now simply called Cambodge in French, and Kampuchea," Sihanouk announced in a royal order.[20] The national anthem, discarded since 1970, was re-adopted. But Sihanouk altered a part of the song that eulogised the king because he no longer wished Cambodia to be a traditional kingdom ruled by an absolute monarch. Ieng Mouly, a newly-elected MP from the Buddhist Liberal Democratic Party, told the authors: "The prince has made these changes because he wants to give a fresh start to a new government which will be represented by an older royalist flag and national song, and Sihanouk will become a legitimate head of Cambodia."

A twelve-member constituent assembly drafted two versions of a future constitution, and sought Sihanouk's views on the provisions for his role in it. But Sihanouk had flown out to his residence in Pyongyang. Ranariddh and Hun Sen were forced to fly there to visit him in September 1993, carrying with them the two drafts, one of which provided for establishing a constitutional monarchy. Ranariddh supported the restoration of the monarchy, whereas Sihanouk, still hankering for power, wanted a greater executive role. After talking to the two co-premiers, Sihanouk gave his approval to the national assembly to adopt the draft of the constitution creating a constitutional monarchy, and agreed to be king.

But just hours after the co-premiers returned to Phnom Penh on September 3, Sihanouk sent them a fax saying he had changed his mind. He explained that he wanted to avoid creating a controversy: "If we discuss the problem of the monarchy, and the nation, we will be responsible for [creating] a new division in our nation." Two days later, he sent a message to the national assembly, rejecting the decision to appoint him the king. It would be better, he advised, to follow a constitutional path that was neither a monarchy nor a republic. Ranariddh was not just perplexed by his vacillating parent, he was annoyed. Palace officials argued that Sihanouk had never wanted to become king again, and that the co-premiers were trying to foist the monarchy on him.

And then on the night of September 24, 1993, Sihanouk surprised his countrymen by taking the oath as king in an elaborate ceremony at the yellow-spired Royal Palace.[21] Earlier that morning, he had approved and signed the constitution that returned him to the throne but restored only a few of the powers that had been snatched from him in the coup twenty-three years before. Dressed in regal Khmer finery—a white tunic with gold buttons set off by purple knee-length silken pants—a dapper seventy-one-year-old Sihanouk and his consort, Monique, were named king and queen. The man who had sought absolute power had settled for a lesser role as a constitutional king, which brought with it ceremonial power over the armed forces, and the authority to appoint and dismiss cabinet ministers. These, however, were powers he would never be allowed to exercise. The country was now being run by two prime ministers. That afternoon, as he greeted the thousands of people who gathered outside the palace gates to catch a glimpse of their beloved king, he cut a vulnerable figure standing alone on the palace balcony, shielded from the searing sun by a royal parasol carried by an official bearer.

Two weeks after his restoration to the throne, Sihanouk was back in Beijing, where he was operated on by Chinese doctors to remove a malignant tumour close to his prostate. Cambodians were dealt a shock when he revealed that the tumour was cancerous. Protracted treatment delayed his return to Phnom Penh, and his health was precarious enough for him to write to the government in October 1993, saying his death was near. This set off fears that the country's stability would be shaken, because he was seen as the only leader capable of keeping the political factions within the coalition from destabilising the government. As the constitution did not specify a line of succession to the throne, his death or serious illness was expected to spark a controversial battle for succession.

He also worried about the well-being of his wife after his death. "After my death, which is not unforeseen, the royal government, and the National Assembly of Cambodia, will please allow my widow, Queen Monique Sihanouk, to live the rest of her life in the Royal Palace, in the house currently occupied by my secretariat, and where my venerable deceased mother, Queen Sisowath Kossamak, lived before being unjustly chased out of the Royal Palace by the leaders of the Lon Nol coup in 1970." If the house was not available, he requested that she should be allowed to live in what was now the residence of the members of his secretariat. "It was a house I was so familiar with since 1989 when I had first visited the palace," he said, referring to his return to his country.

Soon, however, King Sihanouk put himself on a collision course with the very people who had supported his ascent to the monarchy—Ranariddh and Hun Sen. On May 7, 1994, he called for new elections with the participation of all parties, including the Khmer Rouge. Or, he said, the guerrillas should give up the areas they controlled in exchange for a role in the government. In recent weeks, fighting between the Khmer Rouge and government forces had escalated after the guerrillas recaptured the ruby-rich town of Pailin. The government, fighting the guerrillas with its back to the wall, dismissed the king's idea out of hand. The government neither had the money to organise another election nor could it provide security for an election campaign and ensure that all the factions—Khmer Rouge included—were disarmed. The UN, with many competing demands on its money, could not afford to finance another poll either.

Next, Sihanouk himself began to work the ground in another attempt at taking power. The king declared in an interview that he was ready to assume power for "one to two years" to save his country from chaos. Hun Sen was shocked, and he wrote a letter to the king asking him to clarify his statement. "What I want now is clear information whether your highness wants to be the prime minister?" Hun Sen asked. He was outraged by the king's allegation that he was an obstacle to peace because he did not wish to give a role in the government to the Khmer Rouge. Hun Sen said that he was so upset at being considered an obstacle that he considered resigning. In a letter to the king, a copy of which took up a full page in several Cambodian newspapers, Hun Sen sounded indignant: "I was shocked at the point where Sihanouk said that he would not retake power without the support of Hun Sen, or the CPP, because the king does not want bloodshed to fight a secession led by Hun Sen. This sentence weighs very heavily on me."[22]

Sihanouk was not alone in denouncing Hun Sen. Sam Rainsy, too, opposed moves to outlaw the Khmer Rouge. Despite Rainsy's opposition, a bill outlawing the Khmer Rouge was passed by a majority in the national assembly. What many Cambodians found objectionable was Sihanouk's offer to make Khieu Samphan a vice-president at a time when the guerrillas were battling government forces in Pailin, and had shown their intentions by taking three Westerners hostage. The king replied to Hun Sen on June 18, explaining, "I would like to clarify to your Excellency that I have no intention to act as prime minister in Cambodia. I am an old man and suffer serious illness."[23]

PRINCE VERSUS PRINCE

One of Sihanouk's staunch supporters, who had taken umbrage at the king's political marginalisation, was Prince Sirivudh, his half-brother, who served as the foreign minister. On October 25, 1994, the authors telephoned Sirivudh at his residence in Phnom Penh,

JULIE MEHTA

A staunch Sihanouk loyalist: Prince Norodom Sirivudh, at his office in Phnom Penh in January 1993.

and he asked us to come and see him right away. We found him sitting in his first-floor library, typing a letter of resignation to his boss, Ranariddh. Why did he wish to resign after just fifteen months in office? "I am leaving because I don't agree with a lot of things. An idea of His Majesty Norodom Sihanouk to set up a national reconciliation council between the government and the Khmer Rouge was not accepted. Moreover, the king had proposed some solutions to resolve the problems between the government and a Thai firm, but the king's ideas were not accepted." Hammering the keys of his old manual typewriter, Sirivudh added: "To be honest I did have problems with Mr Hun Sen, in particular. I did not have problems with Prince Ranariddh, who is my boss and the president of the

235

Funcinpec party. But I cannot work with Mr Hun Sen. He insulted King Sihanouk by writing him a six-page letter. I could do nothing about this, and I was frustrated." Was he more loyal to the king than to the government he worked for? "The government is loyal to the king," he explained. "We are a kingdom here. But we have found that the suggestions of King Sihanouk are not taken into consideration at all."[24]

We had met before. In January 1993, with his name tag pinned on his shirt pocket, Sirivudh had looked more like a company executive than an aspiring politician. Sirivudh's story in short: In the 1990s he had "opposed U.S. imperialism in Indochina," he said candidly.[25] He took refuge in France, where he worked, and wanted to return to Cambodia in 1976, but was "unaware of the genocide being committed by the Khmer Rouge at the time." He waited three years, and joined Sihanouk's movement in 1979, the year the Khmer Rouge was ousted from power. Sirivudh then spent much of his time in the jungles on the Thai–Cambodian border fighting shoulder to shoulder with his nephews, Ranariddh and Chakrapong. Sirivudh was the first among the Norodoms to return to Phnom Penh from the border in November 1991, just a month after the signing of the Paris peace agreement.

Sirivudh bristled as he spoke about Cambodia's million mutinies. He said that UNTAC had failed in its mission to protect his people: at least twenty of his partymen had been gunned down by political opponents. The authors then asked Sirivudh how the royal family had viewed Chakrapong's defection from the royalist party. "We were disappointed with Prince Chakrapong when he left us, and joined the government of Prime Minister Hun Sen," Sirivudh said in dismay. "But Prince Chakrapong was also disappointed with Funcinpec." He then revealed Hun Sen's strategy to lure young princes away from the royalist party: "When I returned to Phnom Penh in November 1991 Hun Sen offered to arrange to get my house back, and he offered me a car. I refused, because I

*A rebellious Norodom: Prince Norodom
Chakrapong, at his office in Phnom Penh
in August 1992.*

wanted to win the elections and then take my property." Sirivudh
implied that Chakrapong had gladly taken the perquisites of high
office offered by Hun Sen.

As the minister of civil aviation, Chakrapong had flown frequently to Southeast Asian capitals on business. He was instrumental in launching the national carrier, Kampuchea Airlines, funded
by a Malaysian businessman. But soon, Chakrapong's rising star
began to fade. His sudden decline and fall was his own doing. On
June 10, 1993, within days of the announcement of the results of
the elections, Chakrapong and a cabal of CPP leaders—including
Sin Song, the minister of the interior, and the governors of seven
eastern provinces—refused to accept the victory of the royalists led

by Chakrapong's arch-rival, Ranariddh. Rebels under Chakrapong formed a self-styled Samdech Euv Autonomous Zone (SEAZ), as a sort of breakaway state. Samdech Euv, a term of respect that meant "Papa King," was often used to describe Sihanouk. Chakrapong used his father's name in the hope of legitimising the SEAZ. At any rate, it appeared that the rebels were trying to subvert the results of the elections, for which Cambodians had turned out to vote in overwhelming numbers. For a few troubled days in June it appeared that the country would be partitioned when province after province broke away. The rebel provinces were Kompong Cham, Kratie, Prey Veng, Svay Rieng, Mondulkiri, Ratanakiri, and Stung Treng—the rural heartland from which the CPP drew its power.

The secession embarrassed Hun Sen. It appeared that the rebels had acted with his approval because one of the rebel leaders was his brother Hun Neng, the governor of Kompong Cham. To quash the rumours and defuse the crisis, Hun Sen drove to Kompong Cham accompanied by his aide, Uch Kiman, to persuade his brother to abandon the move to break up the country. Earlier, Hun Neng had expelled UNTAC forces and Funcinpec officials from the province. Hun Sen succeeded in his mission, and Kompong Cham abandoned the autonomous zone. After a week of uncertainty this was the first sign that the autonomous zone was collapsing. With Kompong Cham back in the fold it was likely that Prey Veng and Svay Rieng would also abandon the secession. Predictably, those two provinces gave up the struggle a couple of days later. The remaining rural provinces followed suit and, within days, the movement was dead. Chakrapong's hamfistedness lay exposed. Hun Sen suffered a considerable loss of face as the rebels were from his party. He admitted that they were a group of "misled people."[26]

A few hours after the formation of the autonomous zone on June 10, a senior army officer, who served as an UNTAC peacekeeper, told the authors that he had received intelligence information that Chakrapong was planning to escape to Vietnam in order to avoid being arrested. True enough, on June 15 Chakrapong did flee to Vietnam. For its part, Vietnam said that it was unable to prevent Chakrapong from entering the country. The foreign ministry in Hanoi said that it had no information as to his whereabouts in Vietnam. Meanwhile, Chakrapong and Sin Song resigned their seats in the national assembly.[27]

Chakrapong's version of the story of his rebellion emerged in early July 1993, when the authors met him at his residence in Phnom Penh.[28] What had he hoped to achieve by forming the autonomous zone? "The results of the election were full of irregularities," he remonstrated. What irked him was Ranariddh's refusal to share power. "My father proposed setting up an interim government with himself as president, supported by two vice-premiers, Hun Sen and Ranariddh," he argued. "But Ranariddh's party said that they alone should take power because they had won the elections. My father reminded Ranariddh of his election strategy that 'voting for Funcinpec was like voting for Sihanouk.' But everybody stuck to their stand. Akashi said that the election was free and fair, and he dismissed the irregularities as minor. If something similar happened in Japan, it would not be a small thing." Chakrapong explained that the people in the villages were unhappy with the results of the elections. "People in many provinces were angry about the irregularities," he declared. "Everybody thought what I was doing was impossible. All the leaders had lost control. The only man who could solve the problem was Prince Sihanouk. I want to set the record straight. When I said that I was setting up an autonomous zone, people thought it was a separate country. I called it an autonomous zone in the name of my father. So how could they accuse me, and General Sin Song, of separating from the country? It was not true." Not only had Chakrapong been abandoned by his party for having rebelled, but Ranariddh urged Sihanouk not to include Chakrapong in a future government, and Sihanouk agreed. "How could my brother say that at a time when we were trying to forge national reconciliation?" Chakrapong argued. "What kind of national reconciliation is that? Before Prince Ranariddh made his demand I had already told my father that I did not want to participate in the government. But Ranariddh also demanded that Hun Sen should not participate. But now Hun Sen is in the government."

How had Chakrapong managed to win the support of the governors of the seven eastern provinces, and convince them to break away? "I love the people, and they knew me well, and had confidence in me." He hypothesised: "Had I continued my campaign for one more day, a lot more provinces would have joined me." Why did he abandon the idea of forming an autonomous zone? "I had to stop because I had no access to the mass media," he reasoned. "My mistake was that I did not have a radio or TV station through which I could explain what I was doing. I stopped when I saw that everybody had apparently agreed to solve the problem in Phnom Penh through Prince Sihanouk." Had he received Sihanouk's blessings to form the autonomous zone? "My father did not know anything about the autonomous zone," he clarified. "I was alone with Sin Song."

Chakrapong spoke bitterly about the treatment he had received at the hands of the CPP. "I was betrayed. Maybe I will leave the party. I was very loyal to the party, but I was very sad that my party is not united. I was very sad that I was sacrificed by my party. I served them with all my heart, but I don't like to be betrayed. I would like to see the CPP defend their members because all of us are responsible. Why only sacrifice Chakrapong and Sin Song for the sake of the so-called national reconciliation? Why sacrifice us to please Funcinpec? I don't know whether I will remain in the party. But I was very disappointed that my party changed its position quickly. It doesn't have a firm stand." The betrayal hurt him deeply. "I was very surprised that the CPP was not standing by me. When I joined the CPP I thought they were reasonable and united, and would help each other. But now I have begun to understand what some people in the CPP are all about. One day when I come back into active politics I will tell you the entire story."

"My father said over the radio that autonomous zones were nothing new. Even the Khmer Rouge had its autonomous zones where UNTAC was not allowed to enter. The only thing that he asked of me was not to indulge in violence. What I did was very peaceful. My movement did not involve the army or the police. It was supported just by the people. I did not kill any UNTAC personnel. But the Khmer Rouge, in their autonomous zone, had killed more than twenty UNTAC people. My approach was non-violent, like Mahatma Gandhi. I followed the people, and they were the ones who demonstrated."

Was the idea of forming an autonomous zone a plot hatched by the CPP leaders, who may have wanted Chakrapong to do so in order to manoeuvre themselves into a stronger position to bargain for a bigger role in the government? Laughing, Chakrapong said, "I have heard about this. I cannot talk about it now. But maybe, one day, I will talk. One day, I will tell you what happened. I am responsible for what I did."

Why did he go to Ho Chi Minh City after the autonomous zone collapsed? His sudden departure had been interpreted as an escape, and damaged his image. "Being an army man, I made deceptive moves," he explained. "I took my ninety-year-old grandmother to Ho Chi Minh City, that's all. I only stayed for a couple of hours in Vietnam. I never 'escaped' to Vietnam, as the press reported it. What was the need for me to go to Vietnam? Cambodia is a big country, and I had lived in the jungles for more than ten years." After coming back from Vietnam, Chakrapong stayed in Prey Veng city for a day to meet Hun Sen, who had rushed to him with a message from Sihanouk. "And then I came back. I would not have come back without his message," Chakrapong said firmly. What was Sihanouk's message? "To come back for the sake of national reconciliation," he added. When the controversy had blown over, Chakrapong went to see his father in the capital on June 18. "My father was very happy to see me and Sin Song," he said elatedly. "He then offered me the post of four-star general."

If Hun Sen had not pursued the rebels all the way to the eastern provinces to persuade them to abandon their reckless agenda, the continuing rebellion would have jeopardised the formation of the coalition government. From being an asset to the CPP, Chakrapong became a liability. Hun Sen told the authors: "Prince Chakrapong and General Sin Song did it themselves. Both of them arrested me on June 2, 1993, and tried to force me to resign as the prime minister so that they could hold power, and oppose the results of the election. Afterwards they led, and formed, the autonomous zone. It was I who solved these problems, and prevented fighting and bloodshed."

In an interview in May 2001, Hun Sen told the authors about the arrest. He had kept it confidential until then, and out of the public domain. "Nobody knows how I suffered since 1993," he said sadly. He had been arrested for three hours, he said. If he had not been clever enough, he could have been in grave danger of losing his life. "It is much better not to write this story," Hun Sen began, but then decided to reveal the entire episode. Smiling broadly, and drawing hard on a cigarette, he said: "I would like to talk a bit about the results of the 1993 general election."

The plot ran along the following lines. On June 2, 1993, Hun Sen called a meeting at his house, where he stressed that his party must recognise the results of the election. But two key CPP officials, Chakrapong and General Sin Song, refused to do so. The next day, Hun Sen held a closed-door meeting of his senior partymen because the conflict between Chakrapong and Ranariddh could not be resolved. Then, Sin Song, Hun Sen's old friend, agreed to recognise the election results. It left Chakrapong as the only holdout. Suddenly, at about noon, Chakrapong barged into the closed-door meeting. Petulantly, he insisted that if Ranariddh kept him out of the government—which indeed Ranariddh was intent on doing—he would not recognise the results. Hun Sen declared the meeting closed, and left the room.

He went to his brother-in-law's house, which was close to the CPP headquarters. Sin Song followed him there. Sin Song advised Hun Sen that the CPP must make concessions and at the same time demand some high posts in a future government. He suggested that the CPP should give the position of head of state to Sihanouk, but in return the party should ask that the position of the commander-in-chief of the armed forces be given to Chakrapong. Hun Sen told Sin Song that the CPP could not make such a concession because the post of the commander-in-chief was always held by the head of state. He reasoned that if the CPP gave the position of the head of state to Sihanouk yet took away the post of commander-in-chief from him, then Sihanouk and the international community would see it as an illegal act. Another complication was that if Chakrapong held the post of commander-in-chief, then Ranariddh would refuse to take part in the government, because they disliked each other. Eventually, Hun Sen advised Sin Song to break for lunch. The meeting was to resume at 4 p.m.

While Hun Sen was at lunch, his mobile phone rang. It was Sin Song. He suggested to Hun Sen that they should all meet at his house because it was quiet there, and that he had a new formula for sharing power. As his house was not far away, Hun Sen went there with only a driver and a bodyguard. On arriving at the house, Hun Sen found only three people present—Chakrapong, Sin Song and Pol Saroeun, the commander-in-chief of the armed forces. Hun Sen noticed Saroeun's face was clouded in confusion.

Sin Song declared that he was staging a coup. "I have to arrest you as a brother," he told Hun Sen. Hun Sen took in the words calmly. Then he asked Chakrapong and Sin Song what type of military force they were using to carry out their coup. They replied that they were using the army and the police. Hun Sen told them that it was not possible for them to use the army and police against him, and that it would lead to bloodshed. "I told them it's not good to stage a coup," he recounted. "I told them it would be better to do it the following way: that at 6 p.m. I would make a statement to announce my resignation on television and radio. Then the national assembly of the State of Cambodia would have to meet immediately to select Chakrapong as the prime minister." On hearing that he would become prime minister, Chakrapong remained quiet. That gave Hun Sen the opportunity to call other CPP leaders, and ask them to come to Sin Song's house. When all of them had gathered, Hun Sen declared that the coup plotters did not recognise the results of the election. He said he would resign and that they would have a new prime minister. The CPP leaders attending the meeting did not agree with Hun Sen's proposal, however, and the "coup" fizzled out.

Eventually, Hun Sen ordered a special unit to move to his house along with three armoured cars. This was the unit that provided protection to the city and served as his personal bodyguard. "So, I've always had to take care of my security," he said bluntly. "At the same time, we were able to monitor Sirivudh's phone conversation of his attempt to kill me, too. There remained many people that would like to kill me."

A year after his failed secession, the rebellious Chakrapong got into trouble, again. The trio of Chakrapong, Sin Song and General Sin Sen—all CPP members—were accused of trying to engineer a coup against Ranariddh and Hun Sen in early July 1994. A truckload of rebels was seen moving into Phnom Penh, but they were quickly disarmed before they could put their plan into action. Within minutes it was all over. It was believed that Chakrapong had launched the coup plot after the CPP stripped him of his status as an elected MP. But there was more to it than met the eye. Chakrapong had been drawn into a larger power struggle.

Ranariddh, with no love lost for his half-brother, had been searching for ways to end his political career. At the same time, Hun Sen's CPP was trying to muster support to pass a law outlawing the Khmer Rouge that had been introduced in the national assembly but could not be passed for several months due to lack of support from Funcinpec. They struck a deal. Hun Sen would support strong action against Chakrapong and, in return, Ranariddh would give Hun Sen's party the necessary support to pass the law. A section of the CPP initially resisted the move to punish Chakrapong too severely, but after internal discussions, the disciplined and secretive CPP reached a consensus to sacrifice him, as he had become a political liability. Winning Funcinpec support to ban the Khmer Rouge was of much greater importance to the CPP than the future of Chakrapong. The CPP worried that Funcinpec, a former battlefield ally of the Khmer Rouge, was reluctant to outlaw the guerrillas, and that many of its MPs were good friends with Khmer Rouge officials. The time to strike a deal to ban the Khmer Rouge arrived when the guerrillas inflicted a humiliating military defeat on the Royal Cambodian Armed Forces, and thwarted their bid to capture Pailin and Anlong Veng, located in the Dangrek Mountains in the north of the country.

Soon after the arrest of the coup leaders, Hun Sen feared that the trio had wanted to establish a new government and appoint a new head of state to replace King Sihanouk. Hun Sen revealed: "In his first confession Sin Song said, in a letter, that the coup was aimed at destroying the government, which he called an anarchist government, in order to set up a temporary national liberation government." But Chakrapong disagreed vehemently. He insisted that the coup was a fiction, a convenient excuse concocted by the government to get rid of him. "How could just 200–300 soldiers pull off a coup, when Phnom Penh was such a heavily defended town?" Moreover, there was no bloodshed, or exchange of fire, as reported by co-interior minister Sar Kheng. To make the coup theory even more ludicrous, none of the soldiers involved were prosecuted, he said.

The end to Chakrapong's short and flamboyant political career came with his deportation to Malaysia.[29] Sin Song was kept under house arrest in the Cambodian capital. There was now no threat to Ranariddh from any member of the royal family. Hun Sen argued: "The exile of Chakrapong was carried out according to the proposal made by King Sihanouk. It was also of use to Ranariddh because these two princes were not on good terms."

Chakrapong had left Cambodia, but the reverberations of his abortive coup continued to be felt in Phnom Penh. The government closed down a popular Khmer-language newspaper, *Morning News*, in early July, for linking Sar Kheng—a brother-in-law of CPP leader Chea Sim—with the coup plotters. While the editor, Nguon Nonn, was censured, the government banned ministers from talking to the media about investigations into the attempted coup. The leak had to be plugged, and the government's plumbers were hard at work.

Cambodia was a forgiving place. It had embraced former Khmer Rouge guerrillas such as Hun Sen, Chea Sim, and Heng Samrin as its present-day leaders, and there seemed no reason why Chakrapong would not ultimately be forgiven in the same spirit. Chakrapong remained a pariah till November 1997, when Sihanouk pardoned him. In a conciliatory mood, Hun Sen agreed to the king's proposal to rehabilitate his wayward son. But Hun Sen remained wary of Chakrapong. The trump card that Hun Sen and his CPP colleagues thought they had spotted in Chakrapong when they inducted him into the party had nearly cost them the game.

IX

THE COALITION

1993-97

To his parents Hun Sen would always be a carefree pagoda boy even though by now he had played variegated roles—that of a Khmer Rouge guerrilla, a liberator, a communist, the SOC's leading diplomat, and a peace negotiator. He had always managed to snatch victory, or avoid defeat, at the end of each act of the political drama. As he learnt the intricacies of his trade, he made up for a lack of formal education with earthy, rustic common sense, and a strong belief in what was right for his country.

The political maturing of Hun Sen had culminated in the signing of the Paris peace accord in 1991, which brought in their wake 22,000 peacekeepers of the UNTAC, who arrived in Cambodia in late 1991 to organise the general election of May 1993. Dozens of political parties mushroomed in the summer sun, and took to the campaign trail.[1] Peace prevailed until the royalist Funcinpec party began opening its party offices across the country.[2] UNTAC senior official Reginald Austin, who was in charge of organising the poll, bemoaned the use of political violence and intimidation and levelled very specific accusations: "As Funcinpec made headway with voters in areas controlled by the CPP, the CPP grew suspicious and began harassing the other parties. The worst political violence happened in Prey Veng province, which used to be a very peaceful place."[3] Till that time, UNTAC lacked hard evidence against Hun Sen's CPP, which deflected the blame for many violent incidents onto the Khmer Rouge. The true extent of the political murders would only emerge months later, seriously implicating both the CPP and the Khmer Rouge and, to a lesser extent, Funcinpec.

The results of the poll were announced in early June 1993. Funcinpec won fifty-eight seats, the CPP fifty-one.[4] CPP stalwart Chea Sim cried foul, and wrote a series of letters to the UN complaining of electoral fraud.[5] UNTAC disputed some of the charges, accepted others, but claimed broad success for the mammoth election.

The election symbolised Hun Sen's first defeat. The verdict was devastating, yet truthful and telling. It was not outright rejection, though. The people still trusted him and his party enough to give them fifty-one seats in the national assembly, and viewed him as their saviour from the genocide. But they also wanted to give Ranariddh's royalists a chance to rule, and improve their lives. They sent Hun Sen the crushing message that he had not done enough to extricate them from appalling poverty. For the new democrat, the political reality was sobering, and brought with it a sense of being wronged. The old rage was ignited. "About 1,000 ballot boxes had their padlocks broken, and a large number of ballots were found scattered outside the boxes," Hun Sen gravely told the authors. "These irregularities led to the conclusion that the elections were not fair." He believed that UNTAC policies had worked against his party. "UNTAC had made two amendments to the electoral law without consulting the SNC," he said. These amendments gave the political parties the right to sign and seal the ballot boxes, and set up safe havens to store the boxes at night. As a result, the parties may have been given ample opportunity to cheat by exchanging the ballot boxes.[6] He regarded as unfounded the allegations that the CPP had harassed other political parties ahead of the election. "This was just not true," Hun Sen reacted sharply. "I would like to ask why, after the elections, did they consider it a free and fair poll? Because the CPP lost, they no longer used the word 'intimidation.' But if the CPP had won they would have retained this word. What an injustice against us!" He added presciently: "The same thing will happen to us in the next election in 1998."

Hun Sen accepted defeat. He saw in his loss the imprint of his past mistakes. He knew that he would have to turn his failure into success by working harder to help the rural poor. He began taking contributions from donors and investing the money in building schools, roads, and irrigation canals throughout the country. They came to be known as "Hun Sen Road," "Hun Sen School," and "Hun Sen Canal." His charitable deeds drew uncharitable protests from Ranariddh's royalists, who lacked the stamina to keep up with Hun Sen's reconstruction programme that changed the face of entire villages. Ranariddh's work in the villages paled by comparison. The royalists debased the reconstruction process, accusing Hun Sen of buying the support of the villagers with his largesse. Their cynicism, however, did not convince the poor villagers who had come to regard Hun Sen as one of their own.

Owing to the pressures of national politics and tense negotiations, Hun Sen's health occasionally gave cause for concern. When he visited Singapore in December 1993, he had more than diplomacy on his mind. First, he wanted to meet Singapore's leaders, and secondly, he needed a medical check-up. It was a routine scan for the stressed politician who used to faint frequently at the peace talks in the 1980s. In 1994, when the authors unexpectedly met him on a flight from Phnom Penh to Singapore, Hun Sen broke into a smile, and revealed that he would undergo an operation at a Singapore hospital to remove a small growth in his back. "It is nothing serious. I will live long, very long," he predicted.

From the tears of defeat flowed the rage and renewed power of Hun Sen. With his setback at the polls, he was, to all eyes, a loser. But in Cambodia the winner of an election does not necessarily exercise power. Under a power-sharing arrangement, Funcinpec and the CPP formed a coalition government. Although Ranariddh took charge as First Prime Minister, he could not control the vast

Hun Sen's ally and adversary: Prince Norodom Ranariddh addressing village folk in Khum Veal, Kompong Speu province, in October 1994.

provincial administration that was run by the party of Second Prime Minister Hun Sen. Too small and too thin on the ground, Ranariddh's party was no match for the CPP's pervasive network of army commanders, police chiefs, and governors, most of whom had fought alongside their leader in the war of liberation against the Khmer Rouge. The powerful provincial figures were handpicked by Hun Sen, and they remained loyal to him.

Ranariddh and Hun Sen worked hard at building the facade of a cohesive government and, for a time, they succeeded in presenting a united front. The co-premiers even went abroad on joint official visits and praised each other unstintingly. But it was just a brittle facade, doomed to crack under pressure. Ranariddh grew increasingly frustrated with the awesome power of the CPP, compared to which his Funcinpec was minuscule. Hun Sen was always on edge because he had to control a vast country on a small budget; Ranariddh was concerned that his party was unable to manage its own affairs, let alone run the country. One of Ranariddh's complaints was that, even as First Prime Minister, he could not get his party officials appointed to posts in the ministry of information, or as judges—two departments that were monopolised by the CPP.[7] Hun Sen protested the allegation, arguing that "Ranariddh forgot the difference between public and political functions. These officials work for the public, which is neutral. They do not serve the policy of a political party. They serve the policy of the royal government as a whole. Further, the judges should be independent, and should not be appointed by political parties, or the government."[8] It sounded like a self-serving argument.

When the authors asked if he had a serious conflict with Ranariddh over sharing ministerial portfolios, Hun Sen brushed off the suggestion: "We do not have such an arrangement. By and large the two prime ministers are responsible for the whole country. We work things out through a consensus." Asked whether the two parties in the coalition government would turn against each other sooner or later, he argued: "I am the one who is involved in these matters. I don't think there will be any differences. We have the same ideas, and almost the same thinking. Our domestic policy, foreign policy, and policies on the remaining problems, including the Khmer Rouge, are all the same. So, I don't think there is anything that should cause the two parties to split. It is felt within the country, and outside, that the two parties have to work together— not only for today, but for many more years."

Although Hun Sen exercised de facto control over the government, within his own party his authority and political style was being questioned and criticised. A congress of the CPP, held in 1996, generated speculation that factions existed within the party. Hun Sen quickly scotched the rumours. "The CPP is a most democratic party," he explained. "Party members dare to express their opinions, and criticise other party members who commit mistakes. We cannot say that there are divisions in the CPP, but we can say that there are people who dare to express their opinions. The CPP is more democratic than other political parties." It was alleged that the CPP was funded by rich Cambodian businessmen, but Hun Sen dismissed these suggestions: "The CPP gets its funds from the donations and contributions made by a large number of party members. This kind of an allegation is slanderous." Hun Sen's argument that the CPP was a democratic party was convincing, up to a point: while the party allowed internal dissent at congresses, it would not tolerate a direct threat to party stability. Party members often went so far as to criticise Hun Sen, who was also CPP vice-president. At a CPP Congress in February 1997, several delegates are believed to have questioned Hun Sen about his expensive rural development programmes and his outspokenness. A senior CPP military official urged Hun Sen to work more with the party, and not just on his own, ahead of the commune and national elections.[9] Yet, there were no serious rifts within the party, and there was no threat to Hun Sen's positions within the party or the government.

WAR OF THE COALITION PARTNERS

Eventually, a falling-out between the two prime ministers seemed imminent. How did relations with Ranariddh sour? Hun Sen explained the genesis of the crisis within the coalition: "Tension in the coalition government broke out when Ranariddh decided to seek a military balance between Funcinpec and the CPP on January 20, 1996, and [made inflammatory statements] at the Funcinpec Congress in March 1996. I did not have any personal contradictions with Ranariddh, but Ranariddh did betray his partners in the royal government by illegally smuggling weapons, clandestinely building up his forces, holding secret talks with the outlawed Khmer Rouge, and infiltrating troops, many of whom were Khmer Rouge soldiers, into Phnom Penh."

By 1996, Ranariddh's Funcinpec had fragmented. The party had been weakened by the sacking of finance minister Sam Rainsy from the government in 1994, and from the party in 1995, as well as the arrest and exile of foreign minister Norodom Sirivudh in 1995. At the Funcinpec Party Congress in March 1996, Ranariddh mounted a scathing attack on his coalition partner, the CPP. The congress had begun on a harmonious note, with Ranariddh even inviting Hun Sen to attend the opening session, where banners in the meeting hall proclaimed, "Long Live the Funcinpec–CPP Alliance." Yet, no sooner had Hun Sen departed from the session than Ranariddh denounced the idea of sharing power, and accused the government of being a puppet of the Vietnamese. He then threatened to withdraw from the coalition. He also began making overtures to Sirivudh. The CPP saw in this a double game that was intended to destabilise the coalition.

As Funcinpec built up its forces, Ranariddh imported almost three tonnes of weapons to arm his soldiers. The weapons were secretly imported in Ranariddh's name as "spare parts." When the container was inspected at the southern port of Sihanoukville, the authorities found rockets, AK-47 assault rifles, handguns, and ammunition. General Choa Phirun, the chief of the department of materials and technique of the ministry of defence, said that Ranariddh's "spare parts" were imported without the knowledge of his department, and without the approval of the general staff, the ministry of defence, the commanders-in-chief, or the royal government. Ranariddh grew more radical, promoting hardliners such as Serey Kosal and Nhiek Bun Chhay to higher posts in his military. And when a state-owned television station refused to air a broadcast by Serey Kosal, it was attacked with rockets and assault rifles. As he lost influence within his government and among his partymen, who could not tolerate his imperious style, Ranariddh grew frustrated, and needed to forge an alliance with other Cambodians to shore up his political base and recruit troops that could stand up to the forces loyal to Hun Sen.[10] There was only one way to accomplish this impossible task. He had to turn to the Khmer Rouge for help.

The final provocation was a secret pact between Ranariddh and the Khmer Rouge that was signed in early July 1997. According to a *Phnom Penh Post* report in May 1998, secret Khmer Rouge documents confirmed suspicions that Ranariddh was again joining forces with his old battlefield allies.[11] The documents were authenticated on May 19 by Pich Chheang, a former Khmer Rouge ambassador to China, and by Yim San, a commander of the Khmer Rouge Division 980. In one of the documents, a Khmer Rouge official states: "Ranariddh's boat is sinking in the sea, but our boat is not. We have to help him but the way we help is to offer him a stick— not a hand, not an embrace, not to let him cling to our boat, or we all die. We have to play a trick." A Khmer Rouge official, Ta Tern, was quoted as saying: "The Front is not important. Signing to join the Front obtains us legitimacy. Once we are legitimate the world will want to help us... The Front is only a transition to grab forces, not to go to die, but to grab forces and fight the *yuon* [a pejorative word for the Vietnamese]." The Khmer Rouge had accepted Ranariddh's overtures to join his National United Front—though only with the intention of strengthening itself to later seize power to complete its aborted peasant revolution.

THE NEWS ALWAYS arrived late in Vung Tau. A quiet beach resort in southern Vietnam, Vung Tau, known as Cap Saint Jacques during French colonial rule, was swept by cool sea breezes blowing in from the South China Sea the year round. Vung Tau's beaches were, at the time, undiscovered and unspoilt by tourists. Only a few Russian oil-rig workers and their wives lounged on deckchairs. Time stood perfectly still. The newspapers were a day old, sometimes two. And it was not too far from Cambodia. For these reasons it was Hun Sen's preferred holiday spot.

Hun Sen, Bun Rany, and their children were sleeping in their suite after a relaxed day on the beach, when, in the early hours of July 5, 1997 the ringing of a mobile phone woke him. Groggily,

Hun Sen picked up the phone. The caller was a member of his staff in Phnom Penh, who informed him that Ranariddh's troops were digging in for an offensive against government forces. Cutting short the family vacation, Hun Sen flew back in his helicopter to his country residence in Takhmau at about 10 a.m. the same day.

Unlike in Vung Tau, the news arrived early in Phnom Penh. As Hun Sen listened to a Voice of America radio broadcast, and read the news reports over the following days, he was surprised and amused that the media had suddenly elevated him to the status of a strongman. "It is not yet correct to call me a strongman," he told the authors after the event. In a calm tone, he added: "I will recognise that I am a strongman when I succeed in eliminating the poverty of the Cambodian people and bring peace, economic development, and security to Cambodia."

Hun Sen's holiday in Vung Tau was not a state secret. As had been the practice, the two prime ministers, Ranariddh and Hun Sen, were expected to inform each other and the Council of Ministers in advance about their travel plans. Hun Sen had notified the government that he would be on vacation in Vung Tau from July 1–7. Ranariddh, on the other hand, did not tell the government when exactly he would go abroad. He originally said that he would depart for France on July 9, but he abruptly left the country, in secret, on July 4 just before the fighting began.

As the sound of artillery, mortar, and automatic weapons shattered the serenity of the slow-paced capital, many Cambodians feared that the civil war had returned. They could not understand why the fighting had broken out. Those who tuned into the Voice of America listened to Ranariddh accusing Hun Sen of launching a coup d'etat against him. The government dismissed the charges. It said that if Hun Sen had intended to stage a coup he would not have been holidaying abroad, he would have been present in the capital to manage the action. Rather, the fighting was orchestrated and launched by Ranariddh, who was in Phnom Penh on the eve of the clashes. And, having done so, Ranariddh had fled to safety in Bangkok just hours before the fighting broke out. Ranariddh's version of events was the exact opposite: he had done nothing illegal or provocative; Hun Sen's forces had attacked first.[12]

The prelude to the clashes, the government said, was the "illegal" formation of two Funcinpec military strongholds—a garrison at Wat Phniet in Kompong Speu province, and the movement of forces to an area near the residence of General Chao Sambath, a senior Funcinpec commander. When the government received complaints from officials in Kompong Speu that an "illegal" garrison had been set up there, it asked Funcinpec General Nhiek Bun Chhay to relocate his troops to the barracks at the Tang Krasang base in Phnom Penh. The general refused. All the troops belonging to the Cambodian factions were supposed to have been merged with the Royal Cambodian Armed Forces (RCAF), but this understanding was often breached. On the night of July 4, the RCAF chief of staff, General Ke Kim Yan, tried to get Nhiek Bun Chhay to shut down the illegal garrison, and move his troops. The latter kept stalling. An ultimatum was issued to Nhiek Bun Chhay to shut his base by 5.30 a.m. on July 5.[13] There were no signs of closure. At 6 a.m., Ke Kim Yan ordered that the base be surrounded, and at 6.30 a.m. RCAF troops entered and disarmed the illegally-recruited troops.

At the same time, the residence of General Chao Sambath had turned into a mini-garrison. Repeated attempts to get his troops to surrender their weapons failed. After the illegal forces in Kompong Speu were disarmed, troops under Nhiek Bun Chhay's command, based at Pochentong Airport, seized the airport on July 5, and shut it down. They arrested several airport officials. At about 5 p.m. reinforcements from Nhiek Bun Chhay's Tang Krasang military base moved to the airport to reinforce their position. The seizure of the airport was seen by the government as a hostile act aimed at preventing Hun Sen from returning from Vung Tau.

The same morning, Hun Sen appeared on state television. He

told the people to remain calm, and urged the troops to return to their barracks. At about 3 p.m., parts of Phnom Penh witnessed gunfire. As the military police approached the residence of Chao Sambath, they came under fire from within, and from nearby buildings. Military police then used a T-55 tank in a show of force, but the rebels blew up its tracks with anti-tank rockets. As the area was heavily populated with civilians, the military police could not retaliate until the residents had left their homes.

Soon afterwards, the two sides clashed at three places: the residence of Nhiek Bun Chhay, Pochentong Airport, and Tang Krasang military base. People cowered in fear as their city reverberated with the sound of DK-82 mortars, DK-75 guns mounted on armoured personnel carriers, and 100-mm guns mounted on tanks. Only as night fell over the burning city did the thundery sounds of gunfire finally cease. The stunned city dwellers breathed a sigh of relief.

Hun Sen and his national commanders did not sleep that night. They hunkered down to review the situation. Hun Sen's training as a guerrilla commander was put to use as he took charge. In the early hours of the morning of July 6, a decision was taken to launch mopping-up operations. But Ranariddh's forces did not give up, and they went on the offensive. Two columns of Funcinpec tanks and troops moved out of the Tang Krasang base at 4 a.m. and rolled towards the capital. The government reacted by throwing a cordon around the house of Chao Sambath, and tried to prevent the two tank columns from entering the city. On the way to the city, Nhiek Bun Chhay's forces captured an arms warehouse where most of the weapons imported by Ranariddh were stored. When his forces reached the outer limits of the city, their advance was blocked by government forces. The superior forces of Nhiek Bun Chhay were pitted against the military police. In this perilous situation, Hun Sen ordered his elite bodyguards to rush from Takhmau to join combat because the other RCAF units were already deployed in the city, and the provincial units were too far away to be recalled in time. At 9.30 a.m. bodyguards attached to Regiment 70, backed by three tanks and three armoured personnel carriers, reached the line of fighting to support the military police and the special forces. Two government tanks were destroyed in the morning battles.

A new front opened in the afternoon. The forces deployed at Ranariddh's residence and its periphery began firing. Forces belonging to Funcinpec General Serey Kosal attacked the house of government minister Sok An but were repulsed. Next, government forces attacked Ranariddh's residence and forced the troops barricaded inside to surrender. At 2.30 p.m. Ranariddh's forces, positioned within his Funcinpec party headquarters near the Chroy Changva Bridge, fired on government forces that were deployed close by. Ranariddh's forces were overwhelmed quickly. The final assault on the Tang Krasang base began around 3.30 p.m. when reinforcements were rushed to assist Hun Sen's bodyguards. Forces from Military Region 2 arrived after completing their operations against the Funcinpec party headquarters. Brigade 444 from Military Region 3, backed by six tanks, drove down from Kompong Speu. Together they attacked Nhiek Bun Chhay's position from the rear, inflicting heavy casualties on their adversary. By 6 p.m., troops of Brigade 444 had captured the residence of Chao Sambath, and by 7 p.m. Ranariddh's forces were in scattered retreat.[14]

On August 6, Ranariddh was stripped of his parliamentary immunity, and replaced as First Prime Minister by a vote in the national assembly.[15] He remained in Bangkok, loath to return to Phnom Penh to face charges in a military court for illegally importing weapons.[16] After months of uncertainty, during which Hun Sen insisted that if Ranariddh returned he would be taken straight from the airport to jail, Hun Sen relented and proposed an amnesty for him. Ranariddh was ultimately given a royal amnesty by Sihanouk.

After the military takeover Hun Sen told the authors: "Ranariddh is in conflict with the law. The court will have to decide his case according to the law. I have never considered Ranariddh my enemy, therefore I proposed an amnesty for him over the sentence that was passed by the court. We did not take strong action against Funcinpec but against an extremist group led by Ranariddh, and a number of his generals." But several ominous questions remained. Surely the killing of more than forty Ranariddh supporters could have been avoided? "I did not want the fighting to happen, but Ranariddh and his generals did not give us any other option," Hun Sen responded. "It was inevitable that there would be casualties on both sides, as well as among the people." Was the destruction of Ranariddh's residence an intentional act, or did the troops get carried away in the heat of the moment? "Fighting always causes damage to human life and property, whether it belongs to individuals, or to political parties," Hun Sen said calmly. "It is better not to cause the fighting."

Hun Sen's calculated gamble had shown that he could overthrow an elected national leader, even if it meant being denied aid by the United States or membership of ASEAN in the short term. Not a single country labelled Hun Sen's action a coup. But Ranariddh said: "We must call a cat a cat. It was a coup, of course." For his part, Hun Sen told the authors: "I was displeased when people said that I had staged a coup because, at the time, all my children had come back home from New York and Singapore, and my mother was with me. If I was to stage a coup I would not call my children back home, and keep my mother in the house around which the fighting was going on."

In response to the overthrow of Ranariddh, the United States merely suspended two-thirds of its US$35 million in annual aid. The administration of U.S. President Bill Clinton stopped short of calling it a coup,[17] as doing so would have rendered any future aid to Cambodia illegal under U.S. law, which banned funds to any regime resulting from a putsch. The process of resuming aid would have become tangled in endless congressional debates, and the ultimate sufferers would have been the Cambodian people. Japan refused to cut its US$70 million in aid, while China, ASEAN, Australia, and the European Union were not entirely averse to the emergence of a strong leader who would, they hoped, finally ensure national stability.[18]

A major setback to Hun Sen was the refusal by ASEAN to admit Cambodia into its ranks at its ministerial meeting on July 10, 1997.[19] Visibly disappointed by ASEAN's double standards in admitting Myanmar despite the human rights abuses committed by the military junta and denying membership to Cambodia, Hun Sen turned to China for support. He paid obeisance to Beijing by shutting down Taiwan's representative office in Phnom Penh after accusing it of supporting Ranariddh. China's embassy in Phnom Penh said that it appreciated the shift to a one-China policy.

With Ranariddh in self-imposed exile, Sihanouk lent his support to the duo of Hun Sen, who remained the Second Prime Minister, and Ung Huot, who was appointed First Prime Minister by a vote in the national assembly on August 6. Moreover, Sihanouk did not endorse his son Ranariddh's bid to represent the country at the United Nations. Instead, he approved the names of officials appointed by the powerful Phnom Penh pair.[20] Sihanouk did not condemn the military clashes that had led to Ranariddh's overthrow. "The king is neutral, and above all political parties," Hun Sen told the authors. "Furthermore, their majesties, the king and queen, have as many as eleven million children who have always called on them as father and mother, grandfather and grandmother. Therefore, it is certain that the king will not take sides with one man against another. It is the generous heart of the king that I clearly understand."

While France and Japan supported Hun Sen, the United States wanted to see the return of Ranariddh.[21] "The current tendency is to open the door for all political parties and politicians, including Ranariddh, to participate in the polls," Hun Sen told the authors. "The royal government has done everything possible in this direction. In the near future, I will make every effort to have the forthcoming elections held in a free, fair, and democratic manner, and without intimidation," he said earnestly.

EVEN AS THIRTY-NINE political parties registered to contest the general election in July 1998, the most powerful personality was clearly Hun Sen, who appeared to have positioned himself to lead his country well into the next century. Backed by a fiercely loyal military and civil administrative network, and protected by his bodyguards, the youthful leader seemed impervious to any future coup d'etat.

"It was on this basis that I advised Ranariddh, and all the leaders, that if they would like to topple me militarily they would have to wait for ten or fifteen years," Hun Sen explained. "They would have to wait until the people I recruited had retired, because ninety per cent of the generals and the young officers are my people. The deputy governor of Siem Reap is a two-star general, whom I recruited. The people who have been sharing [power] with me are now spread throughout the country. They would not turn the gun against me. They would not refuse to carry out an order if Hun Sen gave that order. It's a big mistake on the part of Ranariddh. I advised Ranariddh that if he would like to score a victory over Hun Sen he would have to play smarter politics than Hun Sen. It would be dangerous for him if he launches any military adventure. Out of twenty-four hours in a day we needed only eleven hours to put an end to the incident."

X

THE HUNS

1975–98

As HUN SEN TIGHTENED his control over Cambodia, his elder brother Hun Neng dominated the politics of Kompong Cham, the rice bowl of the country. Governor of the province, Hun Neng was an extremely reclusive man whose life remained cloaked in secrecy ahead of the general election.[1] While voters were casting their ballots in Kompong Cham early in the morning on May 25, 1993, Deputy Governor Lay Sokha commented cheerfully: "We will win the election. We have two teams—team A, and team B in reserve." Why two teams? Well, if one team was killed the other would live to contest the election, argued Sokha, who had assisted Hun Neng since 1985. The CPP would win because Hun Sen had visited the province four times that year which, he believed, was an indicator of the good work his supreme leader had done. When the authors requested an interview with Hun Neng, Sokha seemed surprised. "Impossible. He does not meet writers."

AN ELDER BROTHER

The cordon around Hun Neng seemed impenetrable. Back on the road we decided to make contact through an Indian Army battalion that was based in the province. We stopped under a tree beside the Mekong River. Minutes later, a patrol jeep of three Indian Army soldiers, their heads covered with sky-blue UN bandanas, approached. We flagged them down, and asked for directions. They asked us to follow them. A ten-minute ride through narrow roads choked with dense foliage brought us to a clearing where a dozen prefabricated houses stood, exposed to possible Khmer Rouge attacks on three sides. Kompong Cham was a stronghold of the guerrillas, who had bases in fourteen of the fifteen districts. There, we met the battalion commander, Colonel A.N. Bahuguna. We told him that the purpose of our visit was to meet Hun Sen's older brother, Hun Neng. The colonel knew him personally, so he summoned his Cambodian liaison man, and asked him to go to Hun Neng's residence with a request for an appointment for the same afternoon. An hour later, the liaison man reappeared with the news that Hun Neng's secretary had turned down our request because the governor was busy. Undaunted by the rejection, we set off for the governor's house. An army jeep dropped us outside a sprawling red-tiled hacienda-style mansion with armed guards outside and inside. We walked up the stairs to an ostentatious living room lined with black faux-leather sofas, an outsized television set, and Khmer paintings covering whitewashed walls.

We found Hun Neng sitting there, alone. The brothers bore a striking resemblance, except that Hun Neng was slightly taller, and did not wear spectacles. At forty-one, he was three years Hun Sen's

HARISH MEHTA

An elder sibling: Hun Neng, the governor of Kompong Cham province, in a 1993 photograph taken at his provincial residence.

263

senior. In a well-tailored grey safari suit, Hun Neng did not look like a provincial figure from a small town.

As he started talking, it became clear that they were not just siblings; they were brothers-in-arms who were facing a tough election campaign to keep the CPP in power. To the Hun brothers the electoral battle for Kompong Cham was not an ordinary contest. It was a do-or-die effort to retain control over the province where they were born, and thus they deployed their strongest leaders here: Hun Sen, Hun Neng, and Chakrapong. The CPP stalwarts were being opposed by Funcinpec's Sirivudh. With an expansive sweep of his arm, Hun Neng said with conviction: "The reason why we will win the election here is that the people have no faith in the Khmer Rouge. Kompong Cham is the province where they committed their most terrible genocidal crimes. The people have not forgotten." Hun Neng related a story to reinforce his claim. "A car dealer in Phnom Penh has wagered that if our party loses the election he would give away free cars," he said without any trace of doubt. "So confident is he of our victory. The reason why the people will vote for us is that they are suspicious of the Khmer Rouge, and of parties linked with them."[2]

A few days earlier, Ung Huot, a political advisor to Ranariddh, had expressed the opposing view. He had said with certitude that Funcinpec would win in Kompong Cham. This perception challenged conventional wisdom that the Hun brothers were the favourites as they controlled much more than Kompong Cham: their influence spilled over into neighbouring Prey Veng and Svay Rieng provinces, which together with Kompong Cham sent thirty-four members to the national assembly, and comprised thirty-three per cent of the registered voters in the country. Confident of their roots and connections in the three provinces, the Hun brothers were aiming to win the majority of the vote. "That," explained Colonel Bahuguna, "is the political significance of these three states." Kompong Cham's political importance as a major rice-producing province was its strategic location at the confluence of two rivers, the Mekong and the Tonle Sap. Its commercial importance was that the traditional trade route to Vietnam ran through it. At the time it seemed that the only negative factor that could muddy Hun Neng's ambitious economic plan to transform Kompong Cham into a significant producer of agricultural commodities was the presence of the Khmer Rouge.[3] But Colonel Bahuguna discounted their ability to inflict damage after a recent violent encounter with the Indian Army had scared the guerrillas, who had kept a low profile since then.

Hun Neng's rise coincided with the meteoric ascent of his younger brother. Hun Neng had experienced harsh treatment at the hands of the Khmer Rouge—jailed by them in the mid-1970s, punished, and exiled to the hills of Kompong Thom for nine months. His crime: he was the brother of Hun Sen, who had betrayed the Khmer Rouge. According to a family member, Hun Neng was forced to perform hard labour at a site in Kompong Thom, where the Khmer Rouge was constructing a large dyke: "They wanted to kill him through hard work. He was given no food, and made to work very hard. He was reduced to skin and bones." Like his brother, Hun Neng was a revolutionary. He had helped Hun Sen raise the Cambodian forces that, together with the Vietnamese troops, eventually overthrew the Khmer Rouge in 1979. While Hun Neng played an important role in mobilising military forces in Kompong Cham, Hun Sen sought refuge and political asylum in southern Vietnam. Reminiscing about the past, Hun Neng began talking about the liberation of Cambodia from the Khmer Rouge. "In 1979, Hun Sen's forces and my forces met on the left and right sides of the Mekong River, and then got together to launch an attack on the Khmer Rouge," he recalled. Hun Neng defended his brother and his CPP colleagues who were being denounced by their political rivals as ex-Khmer Rouge cadres. "Ranariddh accuses Hun Sen, Heng Samrin, and Chea Sim of belonging to the Khmer Rouge in the 1970s, but they were never really a part of the guerrilla movement because all three had fallen out with the Khmer Rouge in the 1970s," he clarified.

Hun Neng went on to study economics in Phnom Penh, and served as an economic advisor to the local government of Kompong Cham. He rose to become the chief of a district, and in 1985 was appointed governor of the province—the same year that Hun Sen became prime minister. Owing to his background in economics, Hun Neng took a keen interest in the provincial economy, and was a member of the powerful central committee of the CPP. The afternoon we met him, he voiced his concerns over the negative propaganda war being waged by Funcinpec—it declared that if it won the elections it would cancel the business contracts the Hun Sen government had entered into with domestic and foreign companies. "The Voice of America had broadcast this warning," Hun Neng said disapprovingly. "Some people were conducting this propaganda campaign to discourage investors from coming to Cambodia." As the interview came to an end, Hun Neng asked us to return to his province someday, and write about its flourishing economy.

Later that week, Hun Neng's confidence was shaken. On Saturday, May 29, early election results showed the CPP trailing in four provinces: Funcinpec was ahead in the constituencies of Phnom Penh, Pursat, Sihanoukville, and Kratie.[4] By midday on Sunday, however, the CPP had regained ground in the see-saw battle, and led Funcinpec in seven constituencies, while Funcinpec was ahead in five. When the final results came in, Funcinpec defeated the CPP by a slender margin of six per cent of the vote. A diplomat, insisting on anonymity, explained: "It was more a negative vote against the Hun Sen government rather than a positive vote for Ranariddh. It was an indictment of the way the State of Cambodia government had ruled since 1979." Ranariddh's political manager, Ung Huot, said jubilantly: "When people come out to vote in such large numbers it usually signals that they want a change."

The feared bloodbath did not happen, and Cambodia's first elections since the 1960s turned out to be less violent than expected. Nor did Hun Sen impose a Burma-style solution by imprisoning the victors of the poll. He and his party chose the pragmatic option: to share power with Ranariddh. While Ranariddh was the public face of the government, real power resided with Hun Sen, Chea Sim, and Heng Samrin.

As for Kompong Cham, Hun Neng remained its governor. Yet, many Cambodians viewed him as being too authoritarian, and aloof from the needs of the people. In the end, he was a provincial figure, lacking the national appeal and the vast power of his illustrious brother.

THE HUN HOUSEHOLD

The prime-ministership changed Hun Sen's tastes. He now lived in a palatial home, where he held political meetings, hosted foreign government officials, entertained Cambodian guests, and played

Hun Sen's fortress-like country home: The sprawling three-storey mansion in Takhmau, south of Phnom Penh, was built in 1997.

267

golf at a specially-constructed mini course on his lawn. He still made the effort to spend time with the family on simple pleasures such as feeding the pelicans that lived on his private lake, playing volleyball, and watching movies on video.

His taste in food remained very traditional, very Khmer. He only relished food cooked by his wife. "So discerning is his palate that he can tell instantly if Bun Rany had cooked a certain dish," a family member commented.[5] Her menus were uncomplicated. At breakfast, it was always rice with some dried fish and fish sauce accompanied by a cup of black coffee. For lunch and dinner, he ate a dish of bamboo shoots with pork, or fish spiced with *pra hok* cooked with bananas. His favourite fruit was longan. In the evenings, he enjoyed a couple of pegs of Hennessy cognac mixed with Coke. Bun Rany had engaged a few cooks at the prime ministerial residence. They prepared the ingredients, and waited for her to come into the kitchen and cook up a quick dish. The Hun family did not like to mix sugar with salt, unlike the Thais, who had a penchant for mixing the two, for instance combining chilli-hot noodles with sugar.

The family worried about Hun Sen's smoking. He had smoked forty cigarettes a day since his guerrilla days, and found no reason to stop. His children tried to get him to quit. He set himself many deadlines, but failed each time. "He does not take too many puffs. At the most he takes four of five puffs of a stick, and lets it burn out," explained his brother-in-law, Nim Chandara.

Another constant were old friends. His sense of loyalty to the people who had supported him in his guerrilla days remained strong. In the jungle he had been so popular that many mothers adopted him as their son, and many young women took him as their brother. When these adoptive mothers and sisters began arriving at his home in Takhmau, Hun Sen greeted them warmly, swapped old stories, and shared food and cigarettes. But Bun Rany felt that the never-ending stream of visitors was an invasion of their privacy,

PHOTO COURTESY OF HUN SEN

*An emotionally charged meeting: Bun Rany in her
reception room at the Hun Takhmau country home in
December 1997, with co-author Julie Mehta.*

leaving no time for the family. She protested to Hun Sen, but he
told her he could not turn his back on the people on whom he had
relied during his years as a guerrilla. Sometimes, when the house
was overflowing with people, he would tell Bun Rany to send the
children to the home of his sister, Hun Sinath, who took pleasure
in taking care of them.

Bun Rany and Hun Sen lived as normal a life as possible, with
their college-going children coming in and out of the house whenever they were home for the holidays. Bun Rany talked about her

children and their powerful father. "He is very soft with the children," she said devotedly. "When they were small they would come into his bed, and he would horse around with them."

The Hun children constantly worried for the safety of their father. "They used to fret a lot when he went abroad on his trips," Bun Rany said tenderly. "Especially when they were very young they used to be sick at being separated from him." The family valued its closeness after years of suffering and separation. "The children would not stay in a separate room when they were young," she said. "They used to come and sleep with us. Only when they grew up did they have their separate rooms. This was especially true of the last three children, who still like to come and jump into our bed." But Bun Rany was realistic about bringing them up with the right amount of discipline. "Both of us cracked the whip when we had to," she explained. "But we've been fairly lucky with them because they have been obedient kids most of the time. They were sent to school pretty early—when they were five years old. They didn't really know how to fool around with other kids because they got a large dose of discipline pretty early on at home. I only recall one time when their father hit Manet and Manith when they were travelling together. By and large, we have only had to guide them along, and never had to really reprimand them."

The years of suffering together with her first surviving child, Manet, had forged a special bond between mother and child. "I love all my children equally, but I feel a special bond with him because of what we shared. "It was a hard life for Manet. When I was pregnant with him we only got to eat fish paste and porridge. We hardly ever had the luxury of vegetables or meat. I feel the most sympathy for him," said Bun Rany. "Manet is a really unique kid. He's the only one of my children who's cried when I've given him a new shirt," she said adoringly. The boy would burst into tears because he had seen his parents suffer so much. He shared their pain. "Manet had always been at the top of the class, or in the worst case, second or third. As a child he was self-driven," said the proud parent. A determined child, Manet surprised his parents by taking computer training and Thai language lessons in addition to his usual work-load. "Manet never went out partying, or asked us for money at any point," she said appreciatively. "Before going to New York he sat for an exam in Cambodia and topped the charts in mathematics." Hun Sen was proud of Manet, who won financial aid to study at West Point Military Academy in the mid-1990s. Manet graduated from the academy in May 1999, and a rapturous Hun Sen flew to the United States to attend the graduation ceremony.[6]

Hun Sen's political career took a toll on the time the family spent together. "We did not have much time to really hang around with them, but they've turned out pretty good kids," she said approvingly. But she was concerned about her daughter, Maly, who studied in Singapore. "I do occasionally worry about my daughter because she does not live with me. And I know that she is under strict supervision under her uncle who is more of a disciplinarian than I am." The woman who came through the Khmer Rouge slaughter said gratefully: "I think we are lucky that despite the separation and enormous stress we have remained a fairly happy and functional family."

Hun Sen's extended family had endured mixed fortunes.[7] His elder brother Hun San worked as a director of transportation in the ministry of communications from 1979 till the early 1990s, when he met with a road accident. A motorcycle enthusiast who enjoyed long journeys on his machine, Hun San was riding in the city when he was hit by a car. He suffered serious injuries to his head, and was unable to work. Hun Sen's sister Sengny married Meas Sovanndy, who worked as a deputy director in the border police department and had previously been a driver for Nhek Huon, one of the four men who had escaped to Vietnam along with Hun Sen in 1977. Another sister, Sinath, married Nim Chandara, who worked as a vice-director in the ministry of the interior, and was in charge of the department of bodyguards. His youngest sister, Thoeun, remarried after her husband died; her second husband, Keo Sokleng, worked as a bureau chief in the economic police department.

Hun Sen's father, Hun Neang, loved his son intensely, but sometimes had his differences with him. For years, Hun Neang worked hard at building a high school in a rural area, but he was disappointed when Hun Sen suggested to him that the school should be named after King Sihanouk. Hun Neang protested, saying that he had put much effort into the school. Hun Sen did not broach the subject for some weeks. When Hun Sen persisted, Hun Neang relented, and the school was eventually named after Sihanouk. A family member said that Hun Neang was not happy with his son's decision.

His parents continued living in his well-guarded mansion in Phnom Penh after Hun Sen moved into his country home in Takhmau in 1989. As a result of the armed clashes on the streets of Phnom Penh in July 1997 between the forces of Hun Sen and Ranariddh, his mother's health was affected, and she was moved to Calmette Hospital in Phnom Penh. She turned seventy-seven that year, and his father seventy-five. Hun Sen's voice broke as he said, "According to the doctor, my mother could not live more than six months. She was given a lot of treatment, but the doctor gave her no more than six months." She died in early 1998. A childhood friend of Hun Sen's, Chhim You Teck, who worked as a medical assistant at the Calmette Hospital, said that his mother suffered from a serious liver ailment. The Hun family honoured the passing of his mother by mourning for a month. Hun Sen cancelled all appointments, and postponed an interview with the authors.

A YOUNGER SISTER AND HER HUSBAND

The tiny village of Peam Koh Sna, located within the rice fields of Kompong Cham, loomed large in the national consciousness, as it was the birthplace of Hun Sen. It was also the birthplace of

From ideologue to academic: Hun Sen received an honorary PhD in law from Iowa Wesleyan College in October 1996.

his younger sister Hun Sinath, as well as their other siblings. The plucky young Sinath took to her studies like a fish to water but her education was interrupted by the civil war. She joined the maquis in 1971, and was assigned to work as a nurse in a hospital in the same area where Hun Sen later commanded a Khmer Rouge guerrilla regiment. Her medical unit followed Hun Sen's fighting forces as they fanned out to engage Lon Nol's troops in battle. Brother and sister stayed in close touch during this troubled period. The Angkar arrested her soon after Hun Sen escaped to Vietnam. She was forced to perform hard labour. Her supervisors pointed fingers at her, and broke her spirit by calling her an enemy. They accusingly said her brother was half-Vietnamese. Over in Vietnam, Hun Sen was worried about his family, and he planned a secret search and rescue mission. In late 1977, he led a special team from Vietnam to the family home in Kompong Cham, but he could not locate the

273

family. "When he found nobody he burned the house. He thought that nobody was alive," said Nim Chandara, the man who later married Hun Sinath. It appears that he burned down the house so it would not fall into the hands of his enemies.

Nim Chandara was born in Takeo province, where his father was a school teacher. When he was eleven years old his father moved to Svay Rieng province, close to the border with Vietnam. Later, the scholarly family decided to leave the province because it lacked schools. They moved to Phnom Penh so that the children could go to high school and university. Chandara studied at the faculty of medicine in Phnom Penh, and completed the second year of his medical studies in 1975. During the Pol Pot years the family was forced to move back to Takeo province. His father and his elder brother, a doctor, were killed by the Khmer Rouge in 1977. After liberation, Chandara stayed on in Svay Rieng, where he had many good friends and happy memories. But his city friends called him back to Phnom Penh. He returned and joined the Sixth Battalion in January 1979. His life took a sudden twist on February 2, 1979, when Hun Sen visited his unit, and requested that the educational records of all the soldiers be shown to him. On seeing Chandara's certificates, he realised that he was highly educated, and immediately took him out of the unit.

Hun Sen asked Chandara and a group of soldiers to search for his family. "First, we found his father and Sinath in Stung Trang," Chandara recollected. "The difficulty was that everybody had been separated. Then we found Thoeun and Sengny, and at the end we found his wife, Bun Rany." Hun Sen's father had wisely kept a low profile: "He was smart and kept his identity secret. Hun Sen's mother was also very smart. She had a lot of Muslim and Chinese friends. She was also in the Stung Trang area, but lived separately," Chandara explained. Hun Sen's older brother Hun San had been forced by the Khmer Rouge to build homes in Kompong Cham, while his sister Sengny stitched clothes for the Khmer Rouge in the same province.

After liberation, Sinath eventually completed her education through the 1980s, and went on to study the Thai language and Thai culture. Chandara worked hard for Hun Sen, who grew to trust him. Unexpectedly, in 1979, Hun Sen asked some ministry of foreign affairs officials to arrange Chandara's marriage with his sister, Sinath. "On April 3, 1979, Hun Sen asked us to get married, and we were married on April 9, just six days later," Chandara said elatedly.

Chandara was later sent to Germany, and he took German language courses for a year. "Hun Sen wanted me to become a diplomat, but I didn't like the job," he said. "I told him that I wanted to become a pilot." After returning from Germany, Chandara worked in the foreign ministry for a short while before moving to the department of immigration in the ministry of the interior, where he helped Hun Sen with his security. Soon after Chakrapong failed to engineer a coup in July 1994, Hun Sen moved Chandara to the bodyguards' department, an elite unit that took care of the security of Cambodian leaders. There is much evidence to show that Hun Sen took a personal interest in the lives of not just his immediate family, but also of his extended family and friends.

BROTHERHOOD OF THE SOIL

To Hun Sen, family meant not just relationships based on birth or common law; it signified a wider web of friendships beyond the narrow meaning of family. These friendships were important because they sustained him during long periods of isolation. "After I was married I seldom met my wife and children," Hun Sen explained. "Not until 1979 did I have a family reunion. But a good deed always brings a return, and although I was separated from my parents and family, I enjoyed the love and sympathy of the people and friends who looked after me. It was because of them that I could survive." And, when Kim Chreng, a monk who had taken care of Hun Sen and the other pagoda boys, passed away in 1990, Hun Sen was saddened. But he could not attend the funeral on account of heavy fighting in the Khmer Rouge stronghold of Pailin in the northwest. He donated money for the funeral.

Some of his closest friends were those he had made in his days as a Khmer Rouge commander, especially the four defectors who had ventured with him into Vietnam, and others whom he hand-picked to serve the party and the state. And, when one of his loyalists would betray him, Hun Sen would still extend his hand in friendship because he valued friendship above all else.

Back on June 21, 1977, the four Khmer Rouge guerrillas who had accompanied Hun Sen across the border into Vietnam feared they would be shot dead by Vietnamese border guards. It was a risk worth taking. They were escaping from Pol Pot's clutches into the jaws of communist Vietnam. The four men—Nhek Huon, Nuch Than, San Sanh, and Paor Ean—wept as they crossed the tense border. They left their lives in the hands of their leader, Hun Sen. Their worst fears came true: they were incessantly interrogated by the Vietnamese military authorities; they were thrown into jail in the Vietnamese province of Song Be. They were prepared to die. But Hun Sen prevailed, and was able to convince the Vietnamese to help him raise a liberation force. When the Khmer Rouge was overthrown in 1979, the four men drove into Phnom Penh victoriously as war heroes. Their hardship and suffering did not go unrewarded by their mentor. In spite of the great gulf created by the passage of time, Hun Sen still remained friends with the four.

One of the escapees, Nhek Huon, was elevated to a senior post in the military in Phnom Penh in 1979, where he stayed till the early 1980s. He was then moved to take command of the western battlefield from 1983 to 1985, but was recalled after suffering a severe attack of malaria. He was then transferred to the Second Regional Military command in Kompong Cham as the second-in-command.

But because of failing health, he was reassigned to a desk job in Phnom Penh where he formulated military strategy. A second defector, Nuch Than, was appointed the head of the youth wing of the CPP, a post Hun Sen had relinquished in his favour. Afterwards, Nuch Than was appointed the deputy general-director of a state-owned rubber plantation, but he did not last long in the job. Talking about the third follower, San Sanh, Hun Sen said with a hint of pride in his voice: "In the assault against the Khmer Rouge in 1979, San Sanh was the head of a battalion that confronted the Khmer Rouge in the front lines in Battambang province." San Sanh was transferred to the ministry of commerce in 1980, and rose to become a director in the inspection department. The fourth escapee, Paor Ean, was rewarded with the post of the head of military logistics in Phnom Penh. Later, he left the country for the West.[8] Even though these four men who had rallied behind Hun Sen in his time of need were no longer a part of the power structure, Hun Sen continued to greatly value their friendship.

Hun Sen built up a vast network of supporters based on principles of allegiance, fidelity, and friendship. His recruitment policy would pay dividends. He first constructed a support base within the military, and then broadened it to encompass the civilian administration. Having handpicked his key generals, colonels, and majors, he began expanding his support structure as early as 1977. By the 1990s, he had appointed loyalists as governors of provinces. His civilian and military recruits controlled the entire country through a nationwide network that remained faithful to its leader. He would enlist these devoted recruits to perform a variety of military and intelligence functions. He candidly remarked: "So, people might say that Hun Sen has a strong intelligence network in the country, and that there are Hun Sen's people [planted] in the other political parties, and that Hun Sen could defeat the Khmer Rouge through the intelligence strategy."

One of his loyalists, Ung Phan, was appointed minister of

transport, communications, and posts.[9] Ung Phan grew ambitious and tried to set up his own political party as a challenger to the ruling KPRP. He was expelled from the KPRP, and imprisoned for seventeen months in Phnom Penh's T-3 Jail in May 1990 for setting up an underground organisation while still being a member of the ruling party.

The government made a stunning revelation in a radio broadcast on July 31, 1990: "The party central committee decided to expel Ung Phan from the party central committee and the party, because he betrayed the party and the nation's historic tasks."[10] It added that his actions caused a split in the forces opposing the Khmer Rouge that was fighting the government along the Thai border. The expulsion came at a meeting of the sixty-five-member central committee held from July 23–30. Along with Ung Phan, at least five other government and military officials were arrested for trying to form a separate, pro-democracy party. The radio broadcast declared that the state had foiled a coup plot, but it did not identify the plotters. The broadcast affirmed that the constitution allowed the freedom of association, but it clarified that the communist party was the leading political entity in the nation. After Ung Phan's release Hun Sen still considered him a friend, and forgave him. In early 1992, Hun Sen presented a silver Toyota Crown saloon car to Ung Phan.

Yet Ung Phan refused to remain silent, and mounted yet another challenge to the government. By this time, the political environment in the country had changed vastly: the rigid one-party state was gradually being replaced by a multiparty system. A new liberal-democratic system was being created by UNTAC against the backdrop of an alarming rise in political murders by unknown assassins. Mistakenly thinking that democracy had finally taken root, Ung Phan bravely announced the formation of Cambodia's first independent association to protect human rights. But some powerful people did not like what he was doing, and he was shot in the neck and shoulders three times by unidentified gunmen when he was driving with his infant son in his silver saloon car from Takhmau to Phnom Penh in January 1992. The bullets narrowly missed the child, and a badly injured Ung Phan was rushed to a local hospital where he gradually recovered. The surgeon who operated on him said that Ung Phan had told him that he did not hold the government responsible for the attack. Suspicion lingered that some people in the government, or close to the government, were behind the attack. After being discharged from hospital, Ung Phan was placed under the personal protection of Hun Sen.[11] When Hun Sen brought the badly shaken forty-one-year-old Ung Phan to his Phnom Penh residence out of sympathy, he was criticised by some of his partymen for helping a man who had betrayed the party.

The irrepressible Ung Phan then joined forces with Ranariddh's Funcinpec party, an act that severed his links with Hun Sen and the ruling party. He was appointed a deputy prime minister when an interim coalition government was formed in June 1993, and he travelled to Malaysia and Singapore to encourage Malaysians and Singaporeans to invest in his country.[12] But Ung Phan's tenure with First Prime Minister Ranariddh ended in April 1997 when he accused Ranariddh of incompetence, and said that he was unfit to lead Funcinpec and the nation. Hun Sen's CPP quickly denounced Ranariddh, and expressed its support for Ung Phan's demand to sack Ranariddh. The fracas brought out into the open the festering conflict between the two main coalition partners, Funcinpec and CPP. But Ung Phan still admired and respected Hun Sen. In 1995, the duo built a high school in Svay Rieng province simply called "Hun Sen-Ung Phan High School." Ung Phan tried to prove his loyalty by providing Hun Sen with vital information about a plot to assassinate Hun Sen that was allegedly launched by Foreign Minister Prince Sirivudh in 1995. Finally, Ung Phan broke away from Funcinpec in April 1997.

It was apparent that Ung Phan had again grown close to Hun Sen, and that the CPP was using him as a tool to divide the already fractious Funcinpec leaders. Ung Phan played a role in preparing the government's case against Prince Sirivudh, who was accused of plotting the assassination of Hun Sen.[13] When the case against Sirivudh was heard in a Phnom Penh court, the most significant piece of evidence against the prince was a deposition by Ung Phan in which he claimed that Sirivudh had told him that he would kill Hun Sen. By this time Ung Phan had fallen out with Ranariddh. He accused Ranariddh of fomenting instability by ordering that Funcinpec achieve military parity with the CPP. Ung Phan alleged that the creation of a Funcinpec-led National Front alliance, ahead of the general election, was a de facto coup d'etat. According to Nim Chandara, Ung Phan and Hun Sen remained good friends. "Hun Sen is a very forgiving person," said Chandara. "He has a large and soft heart."

XI

TAKING CHARGE

1995–99

MANY CAMBODIANS QUESTIONED Hun Sen's commitment to democracy because of his government's tough action against Prince Sirivudh, who had resigned as the foreign minister in 1994, and was believed to have serious differences with both Hun Sen and Ranariddh. In November 1995, Sirivudh was placed under house arrest for allegedly plotting to assassinate Hun Sen. Sirivudh denied the charges, but the ministry of the interior said that it possessed "convincing evidence" implicating Sirivudh in the plot. The ministry produced an audiotape of a conversation that Sirivudh had allegedly had with a journalist. The journalist later amended his version of events, and said that Sirivudh might have been joking when he had made incriminating references. Human rights groups and diplomats warned that Cambodia was reverting to a repressive state. Cambodian lawyers said that Sirivudh could face a ten-year jail term if he was found guilty.

Sihanouk did not want Sirivudh to face trial, and three weeks after his arrest he offered a solution: exile Sirivudh to France and save him from the indignity of a trial. The proposal was quickly accepted by Hun Sen and Ranariddh, both of whom saw it as an opportunity to remove a political opponent from the scene almost painlessly. Critics alleged that the government was bringing trumped-up charges to exile a rival. Sirivudh won support for his cause in several European countries, and some U.S. senators threatened that the arrest could derail Cambodia's efforts to win most-favoured-nation trading status. Hun Sen stood firm, warning the United States not to interfere in Cambodian affairs. Eventually, by 1996, Cambodia did win the trade benefits, and the Sirivudh affair was all but forgotten.

RUN-UP TO THE 1998 ELECTIONS

In November 1997, the Hun Sen camp began preparing for general elections—eight months before they were due. Sitting in his fortress-like home in Takhmau, Hun Sen declared that his country was open for business again. Foreign investors who had withdrawn in panic after Ranariddh was overthrown in July that year were returning: the sale of one offshore oilfield alone was valued at US$36 million. In a signal that businessmen viewed Hun Sen's leadership as a source of stability, five international oil companies agreed to explore for gas and oil in waters off the coast of Sihanoukville. Beaming, Hun Sen declared that more than US$100 million worth of investments had been approved. At the same time, however, opposition leader Sam Rainsy was warning investors to avoid Cambodia. Visibly offended, Hun Sen told the authors: "We were accused by the Americans of not having any respect for human rights. We have a free press and a multi-party democracy. I don't think any country could teach Cambodia about human rights. They can be teachers on economy and technology, but not on politics, human rights, and democracy. I feel that human rights in Cambodia are at their peak. But they come from America to teach us about human rights and democracy, and I don't want to be their student."[1]

At this time the government was concerned about the emergence of Pol Pot from a life of secrecy, following his interview with the U.S. journalist Nate Thayer. Hun Sen had toppled Pol Pot in 1979, but he had failed to put an end to his movement. Why had he been unable to capture the guerrilla chief? "If people want Pol Pot to stay alive he will stay alive," Hun Sen said. "If they want to put an end to him, that will be his end. There were people who hated

Pol Pot, but they also wanted him to stay alive. Pol Pot should have come to an end in 1979, but how could he stay [politically alive] for so long? It was because those who hated him had supported him. If there was no one to support Pol Pot, if there was no one to take him to the United Nations, if there was no one to help him set up the tripartite coalition government, then that would have been his end. We should put an end to Pol Pot, but unless the others join us, we cannot. It's the same for Ranariddh. He relies on Pol Pot to fight. Pol Pot has attached himself to Ranariddh, and those who protect Ranariddh also protect Pol Pot."

But on April 15, 1998, in the forests of Anlong Veng, the seventy-three-year-old Khmer Rouge leader suffered a massive heart attack and died. His body was found by his wife, who had come to his bed at night to arrange his mosquito net. The architect of the genocide had lain close to death for weeks, isolated, despised, and mistrusted by his own cadres, who had put him on trial for murdering one of his trusted colleagues. Now he lay dead with an expression of deep hurt on his wrinkled and bloated face. His death denied Cambodians an opportunity to prosecute the leader of the genocidal regime.

When the authors met Hun Sen again in early June 1998, just a month before the elections, he was brimming with confidence, while the opposition could hardly conceal its fear. Funcinpec had split into nine factions, and its MPs belonged to as many different parties. Hun Sen used simple maths to show that his party would win, and that the fractured Funcinpec would lose: "Now we have fifty-one seats in the national assembly. Divide it by one. What is the result? Another party has fifty-eight seats. Divide it by nine. What is the result?" This equation made Hun Sen confident of winning most of the seats in the 122-member national assembly.

What would happen, we asked, if the two parties were to win almost the same number of seats as they did in 1993? Would the CPP agree to form a coalition? Hun Sen said yes, adding pragmatically:

"If we win a majority, even a two-thirds majority, we will still set up a coalition government."

The most significant change was that the system of two prime ministers would cease after the July poll; a single prime minister would take office, as set out in the constitution. The new premier would be named from the party that won most of the seats, and not from an alliance of parties that together commanded the largest number of MPs. Even here, Hun Sen had no fears. The strongest challenger to the CPP was a four-party National United Front set up by Ranariddh, Sam Rainsy, Son Sann, and a smaller party. In a gesture of goodwill Hun Sen declared: "If we do not have enough seats, we will get [the prime minister] from the other parties."

The election in 1998 was more complex than the election of 1993. Yet it cost much less. UNTAC had spent more than US$2 billion on a two-year exercise to organise the last poll, but the 1998 election, organised by the Cambodians themselves, cost merely US$32 million in funds—contributed by the European Union, Japan, China, and South Korea, with the UN providing a little. Whereas the last election had featured twenty parties, there were thirty-nine parties registered in the 1998 poll. The number of constituencies had increased from 120 to 122 with the addition of Anlong Veng and Kep—two areas formerly held by the Khmer Rouge.

STRONGMAN'S GRIP

Hun Sen did his calculations over and over. The answer was the same every time: the CPP would win the elections in July 1998. Yet, beneath the bravado of the arithmetic Hun Sen was beset by the fear that his party could lose. The concerns were very real. Opinion polls showed Funcinpec and CPP running in a blood-spattered photo finish. Hun Sen worked hard to modernise his obsolete party. The strongman went into cyberspace in late 1997, when his party posted a homepage on the Internet in order to soften its image and broaden its appeal.[2] The idea to start a website was proposed by the party's central committee, following fierce fighting in Phnom Penh earlier that year that led to the overthrow of Ranariddh. Few people in Cambodia had seen the website owing to a scarcity of computers, but the party said it was aimed at winning friends among Internet surfers around the world.

Hun Sen's critics alleged that the CPP was intimidating voters and attacking the opposition, and that the opposition was denied access to state-run media. As the campaign limped towards its closing days, the CPP received a sudden scare when Hun Sen was rushed to hospital for an emergency appendectomy. The surgery prevented him from addressing public meetings in the critical phase of the campaign. But he returned within days to cast his own ballot at a polling station. The chess player who had learnt the intricacies of the game at a backstreet barbershop had held resolutely on to the board. He saw the election as a game with four set-piece battles: the registration of voters, the actual polling, the counting of the votes, and the formation of the government.

It was a bittersweet victory. His party won a majority of the votes but lost in two of his strongholds—Kompong Cham province, where he was born and where his brother Hun Neng was the governor, and Kandal province, where he lived. It was a personal disappointment for Hun Sen that he failed to win the support of the people in his own provinces even after raising development funds for them. The humiliation in Kompong Cham and Kandal lent credibility to the election, to the fact that it was not rigged. The smoothness of the polling process laid to rest the allegations of widespread intimidation. The European Union, Japan, Australia, and the United States endorsed the conduct of the election as generally free and fair.

The CPP won an impressive 41.4 per cent of the votes, Funcinpec garnered 31.7 per cent, and the Sam Rainsy Party a respectable 14.3 per cent.[3] The outcome came as a surprise, as earlier predictions had indicated a tight three-way race. The voters

285

showed their preference for Hun Sen, and declining confidence in Ranariddh and Rainsy. This was easy to understand. Since the 1993 election, Hun Sen had spent millions from his party's funds to build schools, hospitals, and irrigation canals across the country. His style was simple, yet it touched the people who came to regard him as one of their own. He sat down with them in their rice fields, smoked a cigarette or two with them, and discussed their problems. On the other hand, Ranariddh's image was hurt by his attempt to import weapons, and his controversial alliance with the Khmer Rouge, while Rainsy's excessively negative tone had begun to jar on many people, particularly the Khmer business community, which was disappointed by his frequent warnings to foreign investors to avoid doing business in Cambodia. Too long had the country been hurt by false hopes and arrested development. A new reign of peace was always just around the corner. A new era of plenty was always about to emerge. But then, something terrible would always happen to plunge the country back into the depths of despair.

After the July election it appeared that the country had a fresh chance to make a new beginning under a powerful leader. But there were many obstacles in the strongman's way. Ranariddh and Rainsy, having the lost the election, discredited the entire polling process. While the CPP had performed better than expected, it still fell short of the two-thirds majority necessary to form a government that could survive a vote of confidence. This forced Hun Sen into a coalition. He offered to form a government with Ranariddh, but the prince spurned his offer, claiming that the election was rigged. The complaints of the opposition were investigated by the election authorities and found to be lacking in merit. In the end, the protests of Ranariddh and Rainsy were discounted by most diplomats. The 800 international observers and 20,000 local election officials argued that while the existing administrative structures favoured the CPP, they could find no evidence of massive rigging. They said they did not detect fraud. Even U.S. officials described the election as "a successful exercise in national self-determination." Out of the 5.4 million registered voters, ninety per cent had actually cast their ballots, and a majority had shown their preference for Hun Sen. The result was a blow to Ranariddh and Rainsy, who, diplomats said, were unwilling to accept any result other than their own victory.

For Hun Sen the electoral triumph underscored an even greater victory: he had won legitimacy in the eyes of his own people. He had sacrificed an important chesspiece in the 1993 election when he agreed to form a government as a junior partner to First Prime Minister Ranariddh. From then on, a series of rapid moves had succeeded in consolidating his power while wearing down his opponents: the firing of Sam Rainsy; the exile of Sirivudh; the breaking up of the Khmer Rouge via an expedient alliance with one of its top leaders, Ieng Sary; the military takeover in 1997; and the successful execution of elections that were as free and fair as possible. Now that left only one potential threat, Sihanouk. But this danger was swiftly neutralised. The ailing king openly acknowledged Hun Sen's status as a strongman, and treated him with respect. After the overthrow of his son Ranariddh, Sihanouk had stopped supporting him, instead backing Hun Sen's claim to the UN seat. When Ranariddh refused to form a government after the results of the July poll were announced, Sihanouk put his support behind Hun Sen. The king urged his son, and Rainsy, to form a coalition government with Hun Sen in the larger interests of the nation. In early August, after remaining in the shadows for weeks, Sihanouk attempted to break up the fracas with a suggestion to host talks between the three main parties and the National Election Commission (NEC), which had organised the poll.[4] It had little effect on the opposition parties.

As the chorus of protests by Ranariddh, Rainsy and their supporters escalated, and as their demands for a recount, even a repoll, resonated in the quiet boulevards of the capital, the emerging strongman drew comfort and confidence from the support that the international community had given him.[5] The Philippines' Foreign Secretary Domingo Siazon urged Hun Sen and Ranariddh to set up a coalition as a first step towards being accepted as a member of ASEAN. "It would be highly immoral, or irresponsible, for the political leaders of Cambodia not to form a government only because of their individual ambitions," Siazon argued. French President Jacques Chirac added: "The international observers assessed the election as free and fair. These elections were at first a success for Cambodia, and the Cambodian people. It is today essential that the country's main political forces work in respect of the will expressed by the Cambodian people."

On September 1, the NEC officially declared the CPP the winner of the election. The results showed the CPP winning more than two million votes, which gave the party sixty-four seats in the assembly; Funcinpec finished second with 1.5 million votes, resulting in forty-three seats; the Sam Rainsy Party came third with almost 700,000 votes, or fifteen seats. Rainsy, in particular, did not relish the result of the election. He urged Cambodian soldiers to turn their guns on Hun Sen, and suggested that the United States should attack Hun Sen's headquarters with missiles and smart bombs. The U.S. embassy in Phnom Penh protested his comments, which many diplomats saw as a ploy to provoke Hun Sen into violence so that the entire election would be discredited.

When the Constitutional Council—the highest appeals body, which was stacked with Hun Sen's sympathisers—rejected opposition demands for a recount of the votes, some 15,000 supporters of Ranariddh and Rainsy took to the streets. Incited by Rainsy's chauvinistic anti-Vietnamese rhetoric, a group of protestors set ablaze a monument marking the Vietnamese liberation of 1979. The government did not intervene to break up the mass sit-ins at Phnom Penh parks, fearing it would be accused of subverting the democratic process. But its hand was forced when an unknown attacker threw a grenade into Hun Sen's city residence on September 7. His father was at home but nobody was injured and little damage was done. Hun Sen grew more concerned about the safety of his family. Clashes broke out as the police moved in to disperse the protestors, who were camping in public places. Several protestors were wounded, and a Buddhist monk was believed to have been killed. Hun Sen remained calm in the face of the protests, knowing that it was mere posturing, aimed at strengthening the opposition's bargaining stance at talks to form a new coalition government. Even while the protests were going on, at least four Funcinpec members were eyeing the portfolio of tourism minister.

Hun Sen's reading of the post-election situation was accurate. By mid-September, Ranariddh and Rainsy dropped all demands concerning the election except two—an accounting of all used, unused, and reserve ballot papers, and the use of a different formula to determine the allocation of assembly seats. They alleged that the seat-allocation formula had been illegally changed before the vote to favour the ruling party. To remind the opposition that he was the winner of the election, Hun Sen warned that the CPP had three options—to form a coalition government with Ranariddh's Funcinpec; to amend the constitution in order to do away with the two-thirds majority rule and govern alone (toward which he had already gathered enough signatures from the newly elected deputies to the national assembly)[6]; or simply extend the life of his existing government.

Victory had a predictable effect on Hun Sen. He began to think and plan like a prime minister even before he had been formally installed. He pledged to appoint an "economic government" to stabilise the currency, control inflation, and reduce the budget deficit. The embattled riel gained in value after his victory, and businessmen predicted that an era of plenty had finally arrived. The currency strengthened to 3,000 riels to one U.S. dollar from around 4,200 riels before the elections, largely due to renewed hopes for stability. In an interview with the *Asian Wall Street Journal,* he made

289

a surprising confession: he accepted the criticism that rampant logging had ravaged his country, and promised no longer to rely on revenue from felling trees. He spoke about halving the size of the armed forces now that the Khmer Rouge was not a threat—his country could no longer shoulder the burden of paying for more than 200,000 security personnel, and at most the armed forces should be capped at 70,000 men, he declared.

The former guerrilla had finally been legitimised after winning the election, and now he was confident that Cambodia would become a member of ASEAN by December 1998.[7] "I will travel to Hanoi with two options: the first possibility is that, after being officially admitted, we will participate officially in the summit. The second possibility is that we would travel there to be officially admitted," he said. Sensing that a breakthrough was close at hand, Hun Sen wrote to Thailand's Prime Minister Chuan Leekpai, requesting membership of ASEAN. In his letter, he affirmed: "Cambodia has always had a strong commitment for ASEAN membership to achieve ASEAN's founding vision of all ASEAN states in one ASEAN family." ASEAN consisted of nine countries, and once Cambodia became the tenth member, the vision of the ASEAN Ten would be realised, he appealed. It was in that spirit that he asked Chuan to press his case at the meeting of ASEAN foreign ministers in New York at the end of August.[8] Hun Sen was disappointed once again. ASEAN rejected Cambodia, the foreign ministers explaining that they had delayed admission because a legitimate government had not yet been formed.[9]

THE EVENT THAT Hun Sen's family constantly worried about occurred on September 24, 1998. While he was being driven to Sihanouk's residence in Siem Reap ahead of the swearing-in of MPs at Angkor Wat, unknown assailants fired a B-40 rocket at his car.[10] The rocket missed the motorcade and hit a house just ten metres from Hun Sen's vehicle, killing a twelve-year-old boy and injuring three others. Hun Sen was not hurt. "This was clearly an attempt to kill me," he declared. (This was not the first time an attempt had been made on his life: in 1996 two snipers fired at his car as it passed by a garment factory in Kandal city; a bullet hit the helmet of a motorcycle outrider, who was wounded; Hun Sen, unharmed, continued on his way.)

Police chief Hok Lundy accused the opposition of the attack: "The leaders of Funcinpec and Sam Rainsy Party always say that the army and police should kill Hun Sen, and then they threw two grenades at Hun Sen's house. They have used various means to kill Hun Sen and we believe that Sam Rainsy was the leader. Yes, we are one hundred per cent sure that the opposition parties were behind it, and they cooperated to kill him." Rainsy and Ranariddh both said they knew nothing of the attack. Later, three rockets were discovered near the scene of the explosion. Police said that the hand-propelled rockets were remote-controlled, and that because of heavy rain the day before only one cluster had exploded. A cryptic note was found in a battery pack: "The King Bee will eliminate all the nation's dictators gradually. Today the nation's main dictator must be finished." Hun Sen linked the attack to the one on his residence earlier that month and offered a US$200,000 reward to the attackers if they would name their ringleader. "If the opposition leaders do not instruct their forces to stop conducting activities which threaten my life, they would die after the most severe suffering. For a snake, if we don't hit it on the head it can still move and bite back. So we must hit it on the head, not its tail," Hun Sen warned. "Killing Hun Sen will not put an end to the problem. It will make it worse. I feel that if Hun Sen dies, the deaths of the opposition leaders would not be far behind. If the leaders of the opposition have advised their people to conduct this type of act, I think their future will not be good." He cancelled his attendance at an official reception following the swearing-in of the MPs, and left by helicopter. The next day both Ranariddh and Rainsy departed in haste to Bangkok, leaving their party officials to voice fears that the government was expected to take tough action against them. Police said they were pursuing two suspects, one of whom was a former Khmer Rouge fighter linked to the Sam Rainsy Party.

THE FEAR OF REBELLION within his party forced Ranariddh to accept the offer of forming a coalition with Hun Sen. The prince had seen Funcinpec splinter into several factions, and was aware that his schoolmasterly tone was disliked by many influential party officials, some of whom had held secret talks with the CPP in order to explore what role they could play in a future government. Sihanouk, too, urged Ranariddh to compromise. The monarch realised that if his son did not form a coalition government he would further wreck the royalist party. Prak Sokhonn, an advisor to Hun Sen, commented: "One day Ranariddh says he will join the coalition, the next day he says he won't." On October 7, Hun Sen declared that his government would continue in office until a deal could be reached with Ranariddh. He told his ministers and civil servants that they should continue doing their jobs until replacements were selected. But the Sam Rainsy Party complained that several ministers, who had failed to win back their parliamentary seats, had no right to continue in office.

Finally, an intervention by Sihanouk proved decisive. The CPP and Funcinpec broke the deadlock, and negotiated a complex deal on November 14 to form a government.[11] Rainsy was left out of the arrangement. Hun Sen would be the prime minister, and Ranariddh would become the president of the national assembly. In order to accommodate CPP leader Chea Sim, a senate would be created, to be headed by him. Under the deal, the CPP took the choicest ministries—foreign affairs, finance, commerce, agriculture, and telecommunications. Funcinpec took the ministries of justice, information, and civil aviation, and a couple of less important portfolios.

It was apparent that Hun Sen had managed to strike a deal with

Ranariddh by giving Funcinpec influential positions in the government. As a result, Funcinpec was no longer a vocal opposition party, and had more or less been co-opted by Hun Sen. Yet, Hun Sen remained insecure. To strike the compromise, the CPP had to double the number of ministerial and deputy ministerial posts in order to accommodate a lot of people. The new top-heavy government imposed an unbearable cost on the treasury. It was forced to find new ways to cut costs and boost revenue. No longer could civil servants import cars tax-free. Their salaries were to be taxed, and their mobile phones taken away. Hun Sen led by example: he slashed his entourage of advisors from more than 100 to just ten.

On November 30, Prime Minister Hun Sen and his unwieldy new coalition government won a vote of confidence in the national assembly.[12] Within days, the UN awarded Cambodia's seat to representatives of Hun Sen.[13]

Cambodia's entry into ASEAN, however, was not as easily won. In early December, the leaders of Singapore, Thailand, and the Philippines blocked its accession. The three countries first wanted to see the creation of a new senate. Vietnam, Malaysia, Indonesia, and Myanmar, on the other hand, strongly backed the immediate entry of Cambodia, throwing ASEAN's prized consensus-oriented approach into jeopardy. But ASEAN left the door open to Hun Sen.[14] He was invited to attend the ASEAN summit in Hanoi in December 1998 as a guest—an opportunity he used most effectively. In a shrewdly crafted speech, he made a strong pitch for his country to join the regional group, painting a favourable picture of his country.[15] The Cambodian general election was held on time, he declared, with the participation of thirty-nine political parties, and a voter turnout of more than ninety per cent. He trumpeted the fact that the election was hailed as free and fair by international observers, and even described by some foreigners as a "miracle on the Mekong." He basked in the afterglow of Funcinpec and the CPP forming a coalition government, and the

*Two strongmen: Myanmar leader General Than Shwe being greeted by
Hun Sen and Bun Rany during his official visit to Phnom Penh in 1996.*

*Improving relations with Thailand: Hun Sen meeting former Thai
prime minister, Chatichai Choonhavan, in Bangkok in 1997.*

pact between the two parties in setting up a common political platform to strengthen political stability. Moving to the state of the
nation, he argued that the economy had grown by two per cent in
1997, in line with global and regional trends. In the same year the
economy of Thailand had contracted by 1.7 per cent after being
hit by the Asian economic crisis. Foreign and domestic investment
in Cambodia reached US$800 million in the first nine months of
1998, maintaining the same level as the previous year, he explained,
underlining the point that confidence in his country had not waned
after the bloody takeover. He used the continuing Asian economic
crisis to argue that ASEAN needed to strengthen its cohesion in
order to battle the challenges that had impoverished Southeast
Asians. He pledged that Cambodia would push forward with its
market reforms and create a liberal and transparent legal system,
because joining ASEAN was a priority. The ASEAN heads of government, listening intently, were apparently moved by Hun Sen's
rustic sincerity. Four months later, Hun Sen's dream came true in
just the way he wanted. Cambodia finally joined ASEAN on April
30, 1999 in Hanoi, the political heartland of his strongest ally, to
whom he owed his political rise.[16] Cambodian Foreign Minister
Hor Nam Hong and nine other ASEAN foreign ministers signed a
declaration formally inducting Cambodia. For Hun Sen it was the
ultimate trophy after a frustratingly long search for political legitimacy. His former enemies in ASEAN had finally embraced him.

ROLE IN THE KHMER ROUGE

A dark cloud that loomed persistently over Hun Sen's career was
the speculation that during his years as a Khmer Rouge commander
he had carried out the instructions of his seniors to kill innocent Cambodians. From 1975 to 1979, the Democratic Kampuchea
regime starved, tortured, and killed about 1.7 million people in the
urban and rural areas. The victims of the genocide were Cambodia's
Buddhist monks and ethnic minorities such as the Vietnamese,

Chinese, Thai, and Cham Muslims. "It is better not to ask me, but to ask the people who live in those areas [where the killings took place]," Hun Sen placidly told the authors, in reaction to whether he had blood on his hands. "I don't want to respond to any allegations, but the people know the truth. The people in those areas criticise Sihanouk, but they don't criticise Hun Sen. They support Hun Sen. Is there any reason for the people to love a man who carried out killings? The people will have memories of my stay in those areas. Please go to those areas and see for yourself." An independent investigation into the genocide, funded by the U.S. Department of State, and conducted by Yale University scholars, had failed to come up with any evidence implicating Hun Sen in the killings.

The facts supported Hun Sen's case: his influence in the Khmer Rouge was confined to the military. As a young army officer, Hun Sen was not required to develop connections with the ruling political cadres. He never met Pol Pot, Nuon Chea (who served under Pol Pot as deputy secretary of the Communist Party of Kampuchea), or Khieu Samphan (who headed the State Presidium of Democratic Kampuchea). He did meet Ieng Sary once, in late 1972, when Sary entered the liberated zone. Sary, at that time, worked for Sihanouk as a special overseas envoy.

Through the mid-1990s, Hun Sen developed a new, albeit controversial, strategy to break up the Khmer Rouge, by encouraging its top leaders to defect to the government. From a force of 50,000 fighters at the peak of Pol Pot's regime, Khmer Rouge numbers were whittled down to about 4,000 in 1993, and to just about 1,000 in 1997. Hun Sen devised their fragmentation by granting amnesty to Sary, thereby splintering them into smaller factions that sought similar deals to escape punishment. The amnesty given to Sary was not irreversible. As Cambodians clamoured to bring Khmer Rouge leaders to trial, the amnesty seemed only a temporary reprieve, a typically Hun Sen-style feint, to break up the guerrillas.

When Khieu Samphan and Nuon Chea surrendered to the government in December 1998, the Cambodian media, civil society, and state officials were debating the contentious issue of a court trial. The duo added insult to injury when they said "sorry" for their crimes against humanity, and then promptly retreated into the cool comfort of their US$105-a-night rooms at the deluxe Royal Phnom Penh Hotel, when they should have been jailed in the city's T-3 prison. Yet another Khmer Rouge general, Ta Mok, also known as "the Butcher," remained on the loose, raising new fears that if he was allowed to run free in the jungles he would be able to rebuild his vanquished forces and again come to control a swathe of Cambodian territory. More ominously, bands of Khmer Rouge people might rally around him, and turn into bandits who would terrorise the people.

Hun Sen insisted that Khieu Samphan and Nuon Chea face a court trial. Even the government's severest critic, Sam Rainsy, lent his backing to Hun Sen's proposal. Some Cambodians argued that it was pointless to exhume the issue, and that the best way to heal the nation was to abandon the idea of holding a trial. But it would set an immoral precedent for an unconscionable crime, and take the country down a dangerous road. If anything, the way to heal the wounded people was to bring the buried past out into the open, to confront it boldly, and set an example by punishing the guilty. Equally, it was of crucial importance that a trial be held in a Cambodian court. The Cambodian tragedy was, to a large extent, a result of the U.S. destruction of Prince Sihanouk's neutral regime. It was U.S. President Richard Nixon's secret bombing of Cambodia that inflamed Khmer anger, and set the stage for fanatics such as Pol Pot and the Khmer Rouge to emerge. Pol Pot despised the West for destroying his country, and in his zeal to wipe out all Western traces from Khmer society he killed his own people. The relentless U.S. bombardment of a poor country and its dark role in destabilising

Sihanouk had stripped Washington of the moral authority to sit in judgment on the travails of modern-day Cambodia.

The trial of Khmer Rouge leaders was in danger of being scuttled by several countries that played a clandestine role in backing Pol Pot. In their attempt to overthrow the Hun Sen government in the 1980s, China, many Western countries and ASEAN had backed the Khmer Rouge. China, in particular, publicly opposed holding a trial because its support for the guerrillas would be documented and placed in the public domain. It would be yet another travesty of justice if the narrow self-interest of a few countries—to keep the lid shut tight on their reprehensible support for the Khmer Rouge— was allowed to derail a trial.

There were many who argued that Hun Sen should also be brought to trial because he was part of the Khmer Rouge until he defected to Vietnam in 1977. Yet, the fact was that he was not a decision-maker in the Khmer Rouge: he was a military commander who had fled when asked to attack innocent people. Investigators had anyway found nothing to implicate him.

XII

PLANNING THE ROYAL SUCCESSION

2001–2003

IN THE INTERESTS OF ensuring political stability, Hun Sen prepared a comprehensive plan in 2001 to select a successor to the
throne after the death of King Sihanouk. He had kept the documents in a drawer in his Boulevard Suramarit office. One of these
documents was a confidential copy of a draft law that specified how
the Council of the Throne, a committee of senior leaders, would
function to choose a new king in the event of Sihanouk's demise.[1]
The draft law was kept secret because Cambodian politicians were
reluctant to bring it up for discussion while the king lived. When
the opposition leader Sam Rainsy requested the national assembly
to consider drafting the law and debating the issue of royal succession, he was turned down. Some politicians believed that a debate
on the law would be tantamount to tempting fate. "It would be like
cursing the king to die soon," a member of parliament commented.

Hun Sen, however, discreetly prepared a draft law. He kept it
in a state of readiness because the constitution gave the Council of
the Throne just one week to select a new king. He aimed to avoid
the occurrence of a "throne-crisis" that was expected to follow the
death of Sihanouk. A crisis was likely because the law on the functioning of the Council of the Throne would not be in place at the
moment of the king's death. The fact that a new king was to be
installed within a week had led the CPP leader to prepare a draft
law in order to ensure a smooth royal succession. The authors asked
Hun Sen if he really had a draft law under lock and key in his

299

drawer. He nodded in confirmation. He did not deny the existence of the draft. The strongman had chalked out the process of succession in a confidential dossier: the options, and the names of possible successors.

In the year 2002, many Cambodians worried about the impact of the death of Sihanouk on the country: all Cambodians, who adoringly called him Papa King, were expected to go into a state of deep mourning. While the public grieved, the Hun Sen government would have three options immediately after the death of the king. First, the national assembly would adopt the law on the functioning of the Council of the Throne. The king would be chosen in keeping with the spirit of the constitution. Two of Sihanouk's sons were possible candidates for kingship—Ranariddh and Sihamoni. Their nominations would be in keeping with the constitutional requirement of allowing only a male heir descended from the bloodlines of Kings Ang Duong, Norodom, or Sisowath to succeed Sihanouk. Hun Sen heard the above analysis offered by the authors. He said it matched his own view.

The second option was proving to be more difficult to implement. This was to make Sihanouk's wife, Monique, the queen. But this option required the constitution to be amended. Hun Sen argued that the constitution could be altered so that the wife of the last king was made eligible to become the queen. The initiative to amend the charter could be taken by Hun Sen, or the president of the national assembly, on the suggestion of one-fourth of the assembly members, and passed by no less than two-thirds of them. When the authors asked Hun Sen if this option also lay locked up in his office drawer, he did not deny it. Again, he agreed with this view of how the throne-crisis might be resolved.

The third option grew out of the throne-crisis itself. If efforts to select a new king via the first and second options failed, Cambodia would appoint an acting head of state, but not a king. The appointment of an acting head of state would prolong political uncertainty and could even shake the stability of the coalition government.

The preferred options were the first and second. But if Ranariddh and Sihamoni ruled themselves out of the race to become king, the second option of amending the constitution to make Monique the queen would also find acceptability because the Cambodian people knew her well. Many Cambodians, including Hun Sen, believed that she could rise to the occasion in order to play the role of a senior statesman to help reconcile the constantly bickering political parties. Her prospects, however, were dim because she was a commoner, and not from the families of Ang Duong, Norodom or Sisowath. Many Cambodians felt it was possible to get around the problem by adding a few words to the constitution to include the wife of the last king on the list of the eligible candidates. The authors asked Hun Sen if he favoured the option of making Monique the queen. He said he did.

Foreign diplomats based in Cambodia were of the view that Ranariddh's future in public life was not in doubt. In mid-2002, an Asian diplomat commented that since his prospect of becoming the prime minister was not bright, he may like to become the king. When the authors presented the diplomat's view to Hun Sen, he thoughtfully commented: "I am not sure what Ranariddh would like to be in the future. What I know for sure is that he would like to see the development of Cambodia, too. Whether he would like Cambodia to be developed when he becomes the prime minister, or as king, I am not sure. So, it's subject to his attitude." In a sudden burst of English, Hun Sen quoted a proverb to reinforce the point that it was not enough just to have prime ministerial ambitions. He uttered half the proverb in English, half in Khmer. He had acquired enough English to know its oldest sayings, and had translated them, in his mind, into Khmer. "An English proverb goes—if wishes were horses, beggars would ride," he said with a smile. "Even if we want to be the prime minister, we cannot become the prime minister if we don't win the election. If we wish to have both, we could lose both, too. If he wants to be the prime minister, he must face tough competition from all the political parties. If he loses the competition to become the prime minister, he ultimately has the chance to become the king because the Council of the Throne has realised that already. I still remember one incident, after my visit to Jakarta in June 1999. I read a magazine on the plane and saw an interview given by Prince Ranariddh, in which he said Hun Sen would decide who would be the next king. A month before that there was a letter sent by a person known as Rumrith to the king, and the king responded to Rumrith. Actually the king and Rumrith were the same person. He said the choice of who would be the king is subject to the strongman, that he would have as king who he liked," he added, clearly relishing Sihanouk's approval of his governance.

The strongman revealed much about his style of working with friends and foes. "I asked Prince Ranariddh to tell me what he would like to be," he explained. "Because, then I would plan the scenario the way he would like it to be. I once told him in 1994 that he should prepare himself to become the king. I told him straightforwardly. It seems he respects my analysis. I asked him, 'Who would be an able person to reconcile the political parties, if there was a conflict?' Among all the sons of the king, he is the most able man. This is the way I spoke to him, straightforwardly, that he had better get himself prepared. This was not just for him but for his children, too. I told him that it was not in my interest or profit at all because I am not a candidate to become the king. I just would like to have a respected king so we can enjoy stability. However, we always wish our King Sihanouk to live a long life. But we are sure that we are not immortal."

He did not want to be seen as the arranger of Ranariddh's ascension to the throne. "It would be said that I did it [i.e. help to make him king] because I did not want any competitor [in national politics]," he clarified. "Sometimes others view our good intentions negatively. Sometimes our good intention for Prince Ranariddh to be the king is seen as removing Ranariddh from politics because I am supposedly afraid to compete with him. Some politicians are making this kind of an analysis. So I prefer the [king's] wife to become the [future] queen, so I can still stay in competition with Ranariddh and work as a partner with him. Nowadays I would like to compete with a strong rival, not a weak one, otherwise we cannot know our own strength."

Would the people accept Monique as queen, owing to her Franco-Italian parentage? "She has Italian blood, but Italian with French citizenship," Hun Sen said reassuringly. "But in Cambodia ninety-eight per cent of the people do not know that. Her activities do not show any trace that she is foreign. She is in an even better position to represent Cambodian women than Cambodian women themselves." Would Hun Sen rather see the queen become a future monarch? "I would rather have this option than the first one," he said decisively. "She is not involved in politics. She is in a better position than the others."

The widening power of Hun Sen enabled him to enlist the services of politicians belonging to several political parties. Many of his political adversaries, realising they could not fight him, decided to join him. He was influential in allocating ministerial and senior government positions not only to members of his own party but also to those in Funcinpec who had formed a coalition government with him in 1998. Given his vast influence over King Sihanouk and his party's control over every aspect of the state, Hun Sen emerged a kingmaker.

The Cambodian Constitution, adopted in 1993, clearly spelled out that the monarch was to be elected, and that an incumbent king could not name a successor. In the event of the death of the king, the president of the national assembly would become the head of state. Ranariddh, being the holder of that post till at least the elections of 2003, would automatically become the acting head of state were his father to die. The acting head of state would remain in office until the Council of the Throne nominated a successor, who would be a male of more than thirty years of age. The council consisted of the president of the national assembly, the prime minister, two senior Buddhist monks of the Orders of Mohanikay and Thammayut, and the first and second vice-presidents of the national assembly and the senate. It was no coincidence that most of them were supporters of Hun Sen and his party, and had an interest in ensuring that a future monarch wielded minimum power, and that he played the role of a reconciler were the political parties to fall out.

LE STRONGMAN

King Sihanouk was aware of Hun Sen's influence, and he used Franglais to describe Hun Sen as *"le strongman."* The appellation amused Hun Sen immensely, especially as it came from the lips of the king himself. He enjoyed all the attention the king lavished on him. Hun Sen commented earnestly: "My king sometimes calls me *le strongman*. In some matters he says, 'It is up to the strongman.' Sometimes when we talk about who would replace him as king after his death, he says that is subject to the strongman."

Apart from Ranariddh, Sihamoni, and Monique, other names expected to appear on the council's shortlist were Norodom Sirivudh, Norodom Chakrapong, and Sisowath Chivanmonirak. The chances of a Sisowath becoming king were not particularly good, in view of the presence of influential Norodom family members in the lineup. At this time, Sihanouk's advisors worried that the monarchy was being relegated to the status of a museum relic. They were intent on keeping the monarchial tradition alive. Ranariddh revealed his dilemma in conversation with the authors: "Of course, as a human being I am facing a great dilemma. I don't want to praise myself that everyone acknowledges that among the members of the royal family, maybe I am the only one who..." he said, leaving the sentence unfinished, but implying that people generally believed that he was the fittest person to become the next king.

"But at the same time Funcinpec needs me, and I am still fighting for the victory of my party, but it is up to the people," Ranariddh added realistically.

Ranariddh was a tired figure after the 1998 election. His overthrow a year earlier had forced him right back into an alliance with Hun Sen and, in yet another setback, he was soon to suffer a minor stroke for which he sought medical care in Singapore. As the head of the party that came second in the elections, he took the post of the president of the national assembly. He may have secretly aspired to become a future king, but there was the unresolved question: who would succeed him as the party leader?

Ranariddh was unwilling—understandably—to directly address the issue of the succession to the throne, and so he argued: "On the contrary, we should take advantage of the very good health of His Majesty the King, and we are very lucky [he is with us]. As Buddhists, we cannot talk about the succession because we will have to talk about death, and we must not. The reality is that the king is in very good health. I should take advantage of the good health of His Majesty the King who represents unity and peace, in order to strengthen my party." Ranariddh was being polite. The king was not in good health. He had suffered a long bout with cancer, and was often in Beijing for treatment, rest and recuperation in the rapidly gathering twilight of his brilliant, if controversial, political career. His return to the monarchy was not quite on his own terms. He had wanted his comeback to be no less spectacular than the ascension to power of Charles de Gaulle. He wanted full presidential powers. Alas, he had to settle for the role of a king who was a figurehead. Awakened from a nightmarish past, Sihanouk found his present not particularly calming. One of his principal worries, the future of his wife, returned to haunt him. He fretted that after his death the government would cast her out of the palace, just as the Lon Nol regime had evicted his mother Queen Sisowath Kossamak Nearireath from the palace.

If Sihanouk had a successor in mind, he did not reveal a name. He, nonetheless, provided strong clues about his preference. There was more to Sihamoni accompanying his parents on their overseas trips to Indonesia and Malaysia than a mere holiday. His presence in the royal entourage suggested he was being prepared for future kingship. It was possible that Sihamoni was being groomed and closely identified with the palace so that he would become king, and take care of his mother and ensure that she was not turned out of the palace. But Sihanouk confounded political observers when he named Ranariddh as his successor in a 1996 interview with the *Cambodia Daily*, which quoted him as saying that Ranariddh was the "one proper candidate to succeed him." On seeing the report, Sihanouk turned around and denied it, calling it "truly stupefying," quickly quashing his embarrassing throwaway comment, and adding that he had not named a successor.[2]

The succession issue reappeared in August 1997, with Sihanouk saying he intended to have Sihamoni succeed him, instead of Ranariddh, who had been overthrown a month earlier and had sought refuge in Bangkok and France. It was not for Sihanouk to make his choice, for he was forbidden by the constitution from doing so. Sihanouk was not a kingmaker. Sihamoni's candidacy, however, found favour with Hun Sen and Chea Sim, who thought he would pose no threat of becoming an alternative power centre. True to their calculations, ballet dancer Sihamoni had no interest in politics, thereby fulfilling both the constitutional requirement and Hun Sen's desire to keep the king out of politics. Neck and neck in the race was Ranariddh, who vacillated between wanting to become king and staying on in politics. In late 2002, he unequivocally said that his name should be withdrawn from any list of potential kings, revealing that he intended to remain in charge of his political party.

The potential successors were aware that the kingship did not bring with it political power, or a large purse. Sihanouk relied almost entirely on his allowance from China, and on the use of residences in that country and in North Korea. But a future monarch would not be guaranteed any such largesse. Those benefits were exclusively granted to Sihanouk owing to his unusually close personal relationship with Zhou Enlai and Kim Il Sung. Sihanouk and Monique were believed to have supplemented the foreign financial aid with their own business investments. Ranariddh, however, had no personal links with the Chinese or North Korean leadership. He may even have antagonised Beijing with his outbursts against China's military and financial support for Pol Pot. Cash-strapped North Korea was hardly in a position to finance the expenses of a future Cambodian king. Ranariddh realised that by staying on in politics, he would wield what power he could claim. As king, he would be bereft of power. Then, there was an unlikely candidate, Chakrapong, who had been exiled for allegedly plotting a coup, and was pardoned and allowed to return to Cambodia in 1998, four years after the event. He set up a small airline, and appeared to keep himself out of politics.

Hun Sen remained on cordial terms with most members of the royal family. Yet he did not consider them his friends. Had his relationship with Ranariddh improved? "Normally I do not seek to be friends with the royal family because it is not easy to do so," Hun Sen said candidly. "It is difficult, starting from using the words [of respect]. By the way, if the royal family members are politicians they should remain politicians; if they are royalty, they should remain royalty. One of the king's daughters [Buppha Devi] is the minister of culture, so she has to sit according to her rank. The Royal Palace has its own hierarchy, but in the government she has to sit in accordance with her rank. The government has its own hierarchy. For example, one of the Thai princes was a pilot, and after flying he came back and was respected as a member of the royalty by everyone. We cannot do it that way. That's their way. By the way, they are not involved in politics, so it is acceptable to their people. Even though they are from the Cambodian royal family, I am the prime minister, and I cannot go and show my respect to them."

The ever-mercurial Sihanouk sent shock waves rippling across his country in March 2003 when he said that he was prepared to abdicate if the national assembly approved of it. The monarch seemed to be speaking out of a sense of deep hurt at suggestions that he was planning to seize political power. He promised he would not enter politics. Explaining his latest desire to quit the throne, Sihanouk announced in a French-language statement that he had "no political intentions or ambitions that certain compatriots and foreigners unjustly ascribe to me." He declared: "Assigning to me the desire to govern Cambodia 'from beyond my throne' is proof of injustice and of an unacceptable contempt with respect to me." He clarified that he would step down only if more than half the members of the national assembly asked him to do so, adding that parliamentary sanction was necessary so that he would not be held responsible for any negative fallout from his abdication.

IN CAMBODIAN POLITICS, gestures spoke more powerfully than words. As voting to elect the leaders of the country's communes got underway in early February 2002, Hun Sen refused to cast his ballot. Critics argued that kings did not vote as they wished to remain neutral, but politicians must vote in order to set a good example. Some observers asked: did Hun Sen believe that he was the king? Was he so confident that his party would sweep the elections that he did not need to cast his vote? Hun Sen countered: "I do not want to be the monarch even if I was selected. If I did, it would be an act of betrayal. I protect the monarch and I went to the forest to struggle because the monarch was ousted."

The choice of Sihanouk's successor was in his hands, he declared, as was the very survival of the monarchy. Without his support, Sihanouk would not have been restored to the throne in 1993, he added for effect. "I don't want to be the king, but I have the right to establish the king, to select the king and to protect the king. If Hun Sen casts a veto and there is no consensus, the monarch will not be selected. If there is no consensus and Hun Sen does not vote, there will not be a king." At any rate, the controversy of his not voting played out for about a week. Chea Sim, Ranariddh and Rainsy cast their ballots. Hun Sen argued that he had refrained from voting because he wanted to remain neutral, and that he was unfairly accused of wanting to be the king.

XIII

EMBRACING DEMOCRACY

2002

HUN SEN HAD REINVENTED HIMSELF after overthrowing an elected prime minister and winning an election in 1998. He was now determined to gain acceptance as a democrat—however shunned, and however reluctant—in the eyes of critics who remembered his beginnings as a battalion commander in the military ranks of Pol Pot's Democratic Kampuchea. He aimed to demonstrate that the elections to the rural communes, or clusters of villages, on February 3, 2002, would complete the task of introducing democracy at all levels of the long-suffering society. His government's true colours showed through in a string of political killings that marred those universal commune elections, the first to be held since independence from France in 1953.

VIOLENCE AT THE POLLS

It was with good reason that human rights groups and a truncated political opposition alleged that the campaign to elect the leaders of 1,621 rural communes was not free and fair. The poll was sullied by the mysterious killing of as many as twenty-three candidates and activists, most from the opposition, whose deaths—not surprisingly—were not investigated, and the intimidation of many more.[1] The government came under fire for showing scant respect for democracy. The slayings took place in areas where the incumbent CPP faced its most serious threat from popular opposition candidates. The communes had been run by chiefs appointed by the Hun Sen government when it took power in 1979, after having overthrown Pol Pot. A note of caution must be sounded at once that Hun Sen was not thought to be behind the killings: he had pleaded for peace and harmony. Rather, the wave of violence was thought to have been unleashed by some of his party officials. They were loath to face the test of the ballot box. The fifty-year-old Hun Sen had a problem in getting his petulant rank and file to avoid violence at a time when the government was overwhelmed by the sheer scale of the enterprise—more than 75,000 candidates ran for more than 11,200 council seats in communes, and more than four million voters, out of a population of twelve million people, cast their ballots. The long-expected reduction in the number of political parties had happened: thirty-nine parties took part in the general election of 1998, but only eight fielded candidates in the commune poll.

In what was widely described as a Hun Sen landslide, his party won 1,598 communes, representing ninety-eight per cent of the seats, or sixty-two per cent of the vote. His brilliant performance upset the calculations of the most seasoned analysts, most of whom had expected him to win no more than seventy per cent of the seats.[2] When all the votes were counted, the Sam Rainsy Party won thirteen communes, and the royalist Funcinpec picked up just ten. Hun Sen had no complaints about the polling process. Neither did Rainsy, who suddenly looked like a leader of national stature. Yet, Kent Wiedemann, the resident U.S. ambassador to Cambodia, was far from impressed. Half of the killings were politically motivated, he claimed. Wiedemann was shocked at the government's denials. "It's appallingly irresponsible on the part of the government, insulting almost, and dismissive of the international community's concerns expressed to the government time after time after time, when it is unwilling to accept the fact that there were some political killings," he argued.[3]

No stranger to being criticised by U.S. officials, Hun Sen went on the defensive, dismissing complaints that the elections fell short

311

of international standards, and questioning the very nature of the so-called international standards. "I don't understand. International standards exist only in sports. If your understanding about it is poor, go back and study it," he shot back. Some countries were wary of signalling approval of the polls, fearing that if they did, they would be criticised for supporting Hun Sen. The European Union, having described the general election of 1998 as "credible and acceptable," tried to avoid using the terms "free and fair" to classify the commune poll. Diplomats, nonetheless, generally welcomed the election as measured progress for democracy. One allegation would have stung Hun Sen the deepest: the charge by independent Cambodian monitors that his party had bought votes in at least 128 districts on the day before the election. In some places, entire communities were given donations and gifts for their support, they declared; in others, individuals were given money for votes. Tep Ngorn, the cabinet chief for the CPP, denied the allegations.

Back at the centre of power in Phnom Penh, the former pagoda boy and the prince had taken a journey together—from distrusting allies to enemies, and finally to coalition partners again after the election of 1998. When Hun Sen and Ranariddh agreed to form a coalition government, Ranariddh and his party officials were careful not to make the same "mistakes" even though that meant playing a subservient role to the CPP. Most Ranariddh officials were happy with this arrangement; Hun Sen had given them ministerial posts and they were relieved to get back into power after a year in exile. Hun Sen remarked that he worked very well with Ranariddh within the government and the national assembly.

Hun Sen told the authors about his recent meeting with Ranariddh: "We talked about the work to be done. I think both of us had a bitter experience because of the conflict, therefore we had to find a way to work together. I just talked it over with Prince Ranariddh, that we had to play the role of elder brothers, mobilising all the younger brothers to work together. This was my recommendation to him so that he could mobilise Funcinpec, that was divided into nine groups." Hun Sen, as prime minister, did not wish to put Ranariddh in an embarrassing position when dealing with former Funcinpec officials. He did not wish to undermine Ranariddh when he appointed ex-Funcinpec people to government posts, because Ranariddh may not have been on good terms with his former colleagues, who could have grown closer to Hun Sen than to Ranariddh. In order to foster a cordial working relationship between the coalition partners, Hun Sen offered a word of advice to Funcinpec leaders: "But this recommendation can only be accepted by Prince Ranariddh, and not by other Funcinpec officials. Therefore, Funcinpec still remains divided—Ung Huot, Loy Sim Cheang and others have still not come together. These are the internal affairs of other parties, and we should not intervene. I requested them for only one thing—there should not be any revenge, because the government needs stability. Several former members of Funcinpec were still given high posts. Therefore I would like Prince Ranariddh to accept my recommendation to mobilise the younger brothers."

Ranariddh's relationship with Sam Rainsy, a former Funcinpec official, was an uneasy blend of cordiality and tension, six years after co-premiers Ranariddh and Hun Sen fired him as finance minister, paving the way for his subsequent removal from the royalist party. "From the outside, from what I have seen, it is still a bitter relationship," Hun Sen said in a rare comment on the Ranariddh-Rainsy relationship. "But according to some secret information about Rainsy's meetings, it seems he still bears thoughts of revenge against Ranariddh. Ranariddh used to complain to me that Rainsy would not tolerate him." Ranariddh's Funcinpec did not attach much credibility to Rainsy through 2001. Senior Funcinpec leaders who now occupied important government posts saw Rainsy as a maverick opposition member with not much of a future. Ranariddh even praised the "mature attitude" of his party officials who had chosen not to confront Hun Sen in the commune election. "We must not directly confront them, we must work with them, or else no good can come of it," Ranariddh told the authors ahead of the commune election. When campaigning began, the parties of Hun Sen and Sam Rainsy presented the rural people with their ideas for development. Ranariddh's party chose not to campaign directly against Hun Sen; the timid strategy led to Funcinpec's defeat. Voters withdrew support from Ranariddh upon seeing the party not actively challenging Hun Sen.

In the end, Rainsy's party gained by the diffidence of Ranariddh and his party. Having won thirteen communes, a victorious Rainsy saw a glimmer of hope: might he be the runner-up in the general election in 2003? He declared that he would consider a coalition government with his longtime rival Hun Sen and other CPP leaders, if his party performed well in those elections. CPP Honorary Chairman Heng Samrin lent support to Rainsy's idea, saying that a coalition with him was possible. If a coalition was established, it would be at the expense of Ranariddh's party, which was at present in a coalition with the CPP. That remark of Rainsy's prompted Ranariddh to warn that the monarchy, reinstalled in 1993 after a hiatus of over two decades, could be threatened if his royalist party was not in the government. "We don't know if we are moving towards a coalition between the CPP and the Sam Rainsy Party. Maybe the royalists will be a minor political force, and maybe it [the CPP-Rainsy coalition] will be a threat to the monarchy. But we do not know until 2003," Ranariddh warned.[4] He still defended his coalition with Hun Sen as being essential for stability, but he may have baulked at the enormity of the task of reviving his dispirited party from within.

XIV

THE WIDENING CLAN

1999–2003

In THE FERTILE MIND of the pagoda boy, folk tales ran free as mudfish swimming in the Mekong: gnarled old trees came to life, illuminations lit the night sky, holy men flew through the air on rain clouds. Such images seized the imagination of the child growing up along the fecund banks of the mighty river, in places with magical names like Kompong Cham and Svay Rieng. The strongman would carry them inside his head like so many secret chants.

THE WORLD OF SPIRITS AND FOLKLORE

One of Hun Sen's beliefs was that his granddaughter, Hun Mana's daughter, Tep Thida (meaning "Angel"), was a reincarnation of his mother. His acceptance of the law of reincarnation grew out of the richness of the folk stories of Cambodia's villages and a shared heritage with India; ideas such as these grounded the people firmly to their sacred red earth. After his mother passed away in 1998 at the age of seventy-nine, she was reincarnated as his granddaughter in 2000, sixteen months later, he declared with certainty. "My granddaughter looks one hundred per cent the same. She uses the same left hand as her great-grandmother. Nobody else in my family uses their left hand, except my granddaughter," he asserted with a finality that could only come from complete belief. He made these revelations sitting in the plush ministerial lounge at Pochentong Airport in Phnom Penh, while he awaited the arrival of Singapore's Prime Minister Goh Chok Tong in May 2001.[1] Few knew that his stranger-than-fiction life had a supernatural side. Many who heard his stories fell under their spell; those who harboured doubts did not risk challenging them. Before his mother died she had undergone a surgical operation; remarkably, the baby had a birthmark at the exact same spot on her abdomen. "When my father, who is still alive, talks about old stories, this sixteen-month-old child gets very angry," Hun Sen told the authors with passionate conviction. "These incidents started when she was three months old. Whenever anybody my mother knew comes to the house, the infant looks and smiles at that person. Everybody believes that the Dalai Lama was reincarnated, but a reincarnation has also happened in my family."

"At meal times, unless we play the song of Tum Teav, the child will not eat. Unless I play the song 'Pagoda Boy,' the child will not sleep," he said, referring to Tum Teav, a Cambodian love story like *Romeo and Juliet*, and the "Song of the Pagoda Boy," whose lyrics he had written. Tum Teav, he added, referred to an area where Bun Rany had lived and harvested paddy under the Khmer Rouge. Eyes brimming with tears, he talked about the similarities between grandmother and grandchild. "Among all her children, I was the one that my mother pitied the most because I was separated from the family. She lived with me for eighteen years before she died," he said, his voice dropping to a whisper. Listening to him, it did seem that his belief in reincarnation was an article of faith, and not some unproven hypothesis. "Many unique things have happened in the life of my family," he added.

Khmer mysticism similarly surrounded the arrival of his son Manet. It was around 11 p.m on the night of October 20, 1977, Hun Sen recalled. Not far from the house where Bun Rany was in labour was a *chrey* tree that had stood there for hundreds of years. Near the tree was a small hut in which, Hun Sen believed, a magical power resided. In the darkness of the night, his family members saw lights flying out of the tree and the hut, to other places beyond. Then, lights flowing from other directions converged on the tree.

Returning to his pagoda boy roots: Hun Sen and Bun Rany celebrating Kathina in 1996. During the festival, Cambodians donate money and materials to Buddhist monks and to their pagodas.

The light from the tree, being only about seventy metres away, bathed their home in silvery bursts at the time when Bun Rany gave birth to Manet. "Five hundred people saw the light. That was when Manet was born. Some of the people who witnessed the event are still alive," he said, now speaking rapidly in an effort to keep pace with the speed with which his memories were rushing back. The child suffered malnutrition when his mother was held captive by the Khmer Rouge, and Hun Sen worried that his son's intellectual development would be affected. But he turned out to be a brilliant student. Hun Sen believed this was due to the blessings of the powerful lights that attended his birth.

The humble souls living in the villages of his home province of Kompong Cham hung on to every word their fortune-tellers uttered. Just before the birth of Hun Sen, a monk who doubled as a fortune-teller predicted that a future national leader would be born in the Kompong Cham area. Keo Nam, a resident of Dey Loeu village in the same province told journalist Eric Unmacht the following story: "The monk said that one person in the commune would be a leader, a strong man in Cambodia. We did not believe him at the time because Hun Nal was not even born."[2] The monk's prophecy appeared to be accurate. Young Hun Nal, who later changed his name to Hun Sen, was to become the strongman whose coming was foretold.

Fortune-tellers were to play a remarkably important part in Hun Sen's life. He believed that the rain god intervened to save his life during the rocket attack on his car in Siem Reap in 1998. "Before I went to Siem Reap, my brother-in-law had a dream. Something told him that I did not pay enough attention to Preah Ang Khmau, who is a god with a black body. I did not know where this Preah Ang Khmau was. When we asked the locals, we discovered that Preah Ang Khmau was in the province of Siem Reap." Hun Sen went to the temple of Preah Ang Khmau to pay his respects. There, he consulted a fortune-teller's book. He placed incense sticks on the powerful words written in the book, he said, and the book delivered a message. "It read like this: 'There was a king who condemned a man to death, but it was fortunate the man was not killed, and the man later became a powerful person,'" Hun Sen revealed, with clear-eyed belief in the sacred. He then recounted the events of the night before the rocket attack. "It was strange that night that it rained from 3 a.m. to 9 a.m. Maybe because of the rain, the four rockets that were fired at my vehicle did not go off. Only one rocket exploded. I saw with my own eyes one rocket flying just twenty centimetres in front of the windscreen of my car." He looked to his right and saw a cloud of thick smoke in the bushes, where the explosive had just been launched from. "It seems there is some great power, somebody, or something, that always follows and takes care of me," Hun Sen told the authors. His driver slammed on the brakes, but he urged him to quickly drive out of harm's way. "Then I cancelled my trip, and paid my respects to the king," he said with relief.

The audacious attack and the miraculous escape caused such alarm within the family that Bun Rany further tightened his personal security. She was the main decision-maker in these matters. She advised him not to drink water or eat food that had not been properly inspected. She allowed him to play golf at the club, but she would not let him shower or eat there, unless there was an official ceremony and the food had been properly inspected. "Because we cannot control the water used in the clubhouse, I think her recommendation is good. Manet's comments on my security were minimal because he is a man and he knows my character and attitude well, that I do not like to go to many public places," he clarified.

Manet advised his father to improve the living standards of the people, and save them from the heavy hand of the government. He told him that he was most concerned about the mistreatment of the people by the authorities. He thought his father's security depended on the people, and therefore he wanted the people to love and respect him. Once Manet wrote him a letter marked "Confidential," advising him to send his staff to crosscheck reports of incidents, rather than believe the reports sent to him. "I used to be a soldier, and he was also an army man, so he does not talk much about security," Hun Sen said with a knowing smile. "As for the rest of the children, I am more concerned about their security rather than them being concerned about my security."

Hun Sen accepted these dangers as a consequence of his position. "A politician's life is uncertain, and we have to learn from the experience of other world leaders," he told the authors. "I still remember what Sonia Gandhi [wife of slain Indian Prime Minister Rajiv Gandhi] told my wife, that she had to take care of my security. Politicians are not permanent."

Hun Sen revealed that a terrorist group had tried to assassinate him in 2000. The group, which called itself the Cambodian Freedom Fighters (CFF), consisted of nineteen members including Cambodians and a U.S. citizen, and was headquartered in Long Beach, California. In November 2000, it staged a series of attacks in Phnom Penh in an attempt to overthrow the government. At least eight people died and fourteen were injured in the street-fighting, but the coup ultimately failed. "We know that the hit-man and some others are now in custody, awaiting court trial," Hun Sen said. Some members of the group had come to Phnom Penh, he added, and then they moved to the relative safety of Battambang and Banteay Meanchey on realising that the authorities knew about them. The coup-plotters were eventually sentenced to jail terms ranging from five years to life imprisonment.[3] With a mixture of disgust and disdain, Hun Sen said the terrorists would have liked to kill him. Some politicians who could not defeat him in the polls had to resort to such tactics, he argued. "If they could not get rid of Hun Sen, then there was no chance for them to succeed in their plan. [But] I am not just a target for anyone to shoot at. I have my ways of survival. I am not a moving target for people to shoot at." With a deep sigh Hun Sen quoted a Cambodian proverb: "The trap never forgets the bird; but the bird forgets the trap." Mixing metaphors and puffing blissfully on a cigarette, he added: "I am like a cat that has been scalded by hot water, so I have to be careful of cold water, too. So, when I am the target of their attempted attack, I have to think how I can survive. I have been thinking that when I am in power, I will not allow anyone to treat me badly."

Shrugging off the real and imagined threats to his life, Hun Sen grew in confidence. By 2001, he was moving freely around the capital, playing golf at suburban clubs and visiting the homes of friends and relatives. The Huns moved out of their rural fortress-like home in Takhmau after several years. They felt safe enough to move back into their city residence fronting the Independence Monument at

41 Boulevard Suramarit. "Takhmau is a nice place to live, and I would like to return there. But I cannot because my father and grandchild live in the city. Also, it is a bit far from the golf course. The time spent travelling from Takhmau to the golf course is so much that we will have less time to play," he quipped. For a man who spent his mornings at the golf club, he still put in long hours at work. He had just finished reviewing a speech he would deliver a couple of days later at an ASEAN tourism meeting. Normally, his aides wrote his speeches but he would not just stand up and read what they had written. He would review a speech in order to inject his own ideas into it. He was concerned that Cambodian culture was being forgotten, and that the waves of tourists flooding in were getting a distorted image of the Cambodian people. "Foreign tourists who come to Cambodia spend time and money to find out what is Khmer, what is Cambodian. It's a bit strange that some restaurants showcase foreign cultural products to foreign tourists," he argued. "So, it's a waste of money to send our dancing troupes abroad to show our Cambodian culture."

He began to think of himself as a strongman, as the threats to his life receded into the background. He explained what sort of Southeast Asian strongman he really was: "The war is now over. We've failed to develop our nation. There is a strongman. Some may think that a strongman is fearsome, but I am not that type of a strongman." Was he upset with the title of the book, *Strongman*? "During the golf game I played with His Excellency Goh Chok Tong [in May 2001], he called me strongman from the first to the eighteenth hole. So it has become just a name."

THE SONGWRITER

A thick pile of handwritten manuscripts lay importantly on his desk. The Khmer script was scrupulously neat, written in black ink in the hand of the strongman himself. Leaving the conference table where he was talking to the authors, he walked to the desk and

PHOTO COURTESY OF HUN SEN

Strongman in print: Hun Sen holding a copy of Strongman
*(1999 edition), with authors Harish and Julie Mehta, at the
Shangri-La Hotel in Bangkok in 2000.*

picked up two manuscripts from the heap. "Maybe it's time for me to stop writing. I have been writing too much," he said, referring to the more than 250 songs he had penned. "During the Cambodian New Year, I did not have time to go out because I was spending my time writing. I do not remember exactly how many songs I have written." Hun Sen's musical repertoire had grown in just a few years. He was prolific and had produced about twenty compact discs, each with twelve or thirteen songs.

There was another, unknown, side to the poet: he had been secretly working on the script for a play based on his life. "I've given the original copy of the play to the playwright," he said, settling back in his seat, and rifling through a photocopy. "I have stayed awake late at night, recalling my past struggles for a radio play. I have hardly slept in the last three months," he said without a trace of tiredness. He produced his best work between 10 p.m. and 1 a.m. The ninety-five-part radio play, *The Sun Under the Light of the Full Moon*, by playwright Huy Vesna, was broadcast on four local radio stations. The playwright had read the first edition of *Strongman* and had been inspired to write a play based on it in the Cambodian language. But when Hun Sen heard the play on the radio, he felt there were gaps; the playwright did not know many things about his life. He decided to intervene. He then rewrote the play, describing the course of his life, so the playwright could use it in his script. "Some places, I wrote in red ink. It describes my life but it is written for the purposes of art," Hun Sen said, sounding less like a strongman and more like a man of culture. The play was being turned into a dramatic novel. "But it is different from a novel because in a drama music is played and there is a soundtrack. I also recommended which songs should be played. I am now turning myself into a dramatist, a playwright. This is not strange to me because back in 1971 I used to write dramas, and direct people how to act, and I used to act myself." A movie company from Thailand was interested in making a film on his life, but Hun Sen had told them he would review the script first in order to ensure it was not too long or too short, and that if the actors were not good enough he would withhold approval to shoot the film.

As he wrote his stories, the stories helped him remember what he had gone through. His writings included the twenty-two days he was imprisoned in Vietnam. "But we could not get Vietnamese actors, so we just described it," he said.

HABITS AND TASTES

Hun Sen had trained his body to function on little or no sleep. From his days as a callow youth in the maquis, he slept as little as an hour or two at night. His willpower helped him stay awake through hot, cold, or rainy nights, sometimes huddled inside a trench, or wrapped around the roots of a banyan tree, or cleaved to a pile of fishing nets in the bottom of a wooden dugout boat to hide himself from the enemy as he kept watch. Some nights, he would shut his eyes for no more than an hour. As a young foreign minister, when the pressure of work increased, he stayed up all night reading books on diplomacy and papers on international affairs in order to educate himself on the job he was tasked with. In 2002, at age fifty, his sleep pattern had not changed. As always, he turned in at 1 a.m., only to rise at 3 a.m. He would awaken in high spirits, eager to read and get ready for a round of golf. Oddly enough, even though he had been taking sleeping pills for fifteen years, the drugs had failed to induce sleep for longer. "Some people say that sleeping pills affect your nervous system. Just don't believe them because they help you to rest," he explained. "I find no difficulty even though I take only one or two hours' rest."

After a light breakfast, his practice was to sit down to read the documents his aides sent him. If he could not read over breakfast, he would run his eye over them while being driven to his office in the Council of Ministers Building. On other days he worked at his office at home. The flood of papers never seemed to subside. "Even if I have this much work, they keep adding more for me," he said, raising his arms high above his head. Often he would be buried under so many documents that he could not break for lunch till 2 p.m. He would only allow himself the luxury of a fifteen-minute nap to help soothe his left eye, the artificial one. Sometimes Bun Rany took him away from the office to have lunch. When he broke for lunch also depended on one other factor. "It is also subject to the officials in my cabinet: how much they can tolerate me," he added, using humour.

His simplicity perplexed the people around him. His family and aides found that it was very easy to take care of him. They sometimes wished he would be a little more demanding. "No need to order food from the best place, I can eat anything that is offered," he said. Giving little thought to his personal comforts, Hun Sen worked without breaks. He would not eat dinner at a fixed time, refusing to leave office until all the papers had been read, discussed, and signed. "I don't have a regular time for dinner. Sometimes, there are thirty pieces of paper for me to read before I can make a decision. But when I finish those thirty papers, they bring me another stack," he said in a tone of mock complaint. With large stacks of documents to read every day, did he find the time to meet Bun Rany for dinner? "We would be in a difficult situation if we did not have meals together—whether I wait for her or she waits for me. But most of the time, she waits for me," he said with a smile.

Growing up in the village, he had developed a fondness for local Cambodian food, and later grew to like Chinese food as well. He was partial to a type of Cambodian soup cooked with banana. He knew this dish well from his days as a soldier, when he used to make it. Even when he was promoted to a higher rank, everyone in the regiment had to take turns to cook for the group. "I knew very well that when it was my turn to cook, I would prepare this type of soup," he said, proud of his ability to cook local food. His family was aware of his few requests, that he was fond of pickled green pineapple and cucumber, and dry and sour fish. Sometimes his lunch consisted of only pickled green pineapple and rice. He liked fish that had a strong, distinctive smell and flavour—a lingering taste from childhood. Of the two fish preparations, *pra hok* and *pa ok,* he preferred the former, not just because it was cheaper and a lot more odorous than *pa ok.* Cambodians generally liked *pra hok* more also because it was a lifesaver during famine: it could be stored in its dried form for about two years. "You can eat *pa ok* at most four times a month, you won't like it more often. But you can eat *pra hok* thirty days a month. We have *pra hok* for twenty days, and *pa ok* for ten days," he said, making a rare reference to the topic of food, in which he had little interest. He drank two cups of coffee daily, one in the morning and one in the afternoon—but not because he liked it. His doctor had prescribed the regimen to keep his blood pressure stable.

Hun Sen's earthly attachments were to his children, not to food or to drink. Daughter Mana lived in a house right behind his Phnom Penh residence. It was not close enough. "We would like her to be with us, but she prefers to be on her own. Therefore, we have to sometimes bring the grandchild here. Maly is now grown up, and she seems to have a talent for the English language. She is now with her sister Hun Mana—and they are speaking in English to each other," he said in disbelief. He broke off in mid-sentence to say, "You could take a picture of me with my granddaughter, but my wife has taken her out somewhere."

ON THE LINKS

On May 12, 2001, Hun Sen invited Harish to the Royal Phnom Penh Golf Club. "It will be a game among ASEAN One, Plus Three," he said. "I am the ASEAN One, and the Plus Three are the ambassadors of China, Japan, and South Korea." The reference to the Plus Three represented the three non-Southeast Asian partners of ASEAN. With a handicap of fifteen, Hun Sen could drive just as powerfully as the Plus Three diplomats and his Cambodian compatriot, Phnom Penh Governor Chea Sophara. Clad in specially tailored trousers with his "Dragon Team" logo embroidered on it, he played with panache, ferocity and good humour, undaunted by having only one functioning eye.

After hitting his ball into at least one sand bunker, he could not resist a smoke. He lit up his staple State Express. "I do a lot of work here at the golf course," he said, referring to his preference for conducting global diplomacy on the rolling greens. There were two golf courses in the vicinity, one close to Phnom Penh, and the other in Kompong Speu. Hun Sen remarked: "Both our courses have communications links with the city, and I can sign

PHOTO COURTESY OF HUN SEN

Preparing himself for golf diplomacy: Hun Sen
taking his first swing at a golf course in Kompong
Speu province in 1998.

a decree or a document at the course, no problem. Once I signed a letter to United Nations Secretary-General Kofi Annan about setting up a tribunal to bring the Khmer Rouge leaders to justice right here." A couple of days earlier, he had paired up with Prime Minister Goh of Singapore against the duo of Singapore Foreign Minister Shunmugam Jayakumar and Cambodian Foreign Minister Hor Nam Hong. Till then, Hun Sen had not played with any other ASEAN prime minister, an anomaly he had wished to rectify urgently. Golf had also helped somewhat to rebuild bridges among Cambodia's rival politicians. He had played Ranariddh three or four times. "Ranariddh plays very well. He's been playing for a long time. He's played five or six years more than me," said Hun Sen, who had been playing for about eight years.

For him, golf was not just a health workout that had helped

lower his cholesterol. It was a passion, evident in the way he looked after his Hiro Honma clubs. "I take care of my clubs like my children," he said with enthusiasm. "I don't leave it to other people to take care of my things. I am from the military. I don't depend on my soldiers. Now when I play golf I feel like a young army man."

That morning under an unforgiving sun, Hun Sen perspired profusely. "Water," he said pointing at damp patches on his shirt. He then turned to an aide, who whispered something to him. "It is perspiration," Hun Sen clarified. His English language skills had improved considerably. If his ball fell short of a hole, or found a bunker, his partners encouraged him. "Hit harder, Strongman," they cheered. "Strongman is trying," he replied. His constant jokes and playful jibes at friends made the mood at the course very light-hearted. He made bets with one of his Cambodian compatriots. The players stuffed a couple of dollar bills into every hole. The winner took all. Hun Sen won some, and lost some.

BUN RANY'S SOCIAL AGENDA

Bun Rany had flown back just that morning from an exhausting official trip to Shanghai and Beijing, but she emerged from her bedroom looking none the worse for travel. Dressed in a silk *sampot* and a Khmer-style blouse rimmed with fine green-and-gold piping, she hugged Julie warmly.[4] We sat on finely carved Khmer chairs. Glass cabinets behind us contained an array of precious items gifted by heads of state and visiting dignitaries. A replica Tang-dynasty horse was reflected in the well-polished mirrors lining a large showcase. "Very nice to see you," said the slim and youthful-looking forty-seven-year-old. Bun Rany spoke so softly that at times we strained to catch the nuances.

On that afternoon, May 15, 2001, diplomats in Phnom Penh were praising her moving speech at a meeting of the Cambodian Red Cross. She had performed well in her years heading the organisation as its president. The four-year term was demanding, but her

328

sincerity in supporting the causes of the world body, and her famil-iarity with charitable work and needs of the underprivileged, had won the hearts of the Cambodian people and the international com-munity. "If we consider ourselves to be in high places, without the support of the people, it is meaningless," Bun Rany said modestly. "So when I work for the Red Cross it is the same driving princi-ple, that if we are in a position of power we should be humble, not extravagant. If you're rich and you don't help the less privileged, then it seems pointless to be rich and be deprived of the opportu-nity to assist the poor and be appreciated." One of her board mem-bers, the wife of an ambassador, paid her a lavish compliment: "She never uses a script when she addresses the Red Cross's fundraising rallies. Facts and figures are at her fingertips. Her natural ability to speak so charmingly, packing in so much information, has been very impressive." Occasionally, she might make a few jottings of some statistics, but usually she did not need any notes because she was aware of the work being done. She did a lot of it herself. Several members of the board found her so effective that they urged her to stay on as president for another four years. "My board members insist that they will elect me, and should I refuse, they threaten to hold a demonstration in front of my residence," she said with a giggle.

Long before she took charge of the Red Cross, Bun Rany was involved in developmental work in creating centres in support of orphans and the poor, and victims of humanitarian disasters. She tended to react quickly to natural calamities, rushing to a disas-ter area, and remaining there round the clock. She would hold monthly meetings with the general secretary and board members in Phnom Penh, as well as in the provinces, to make sure she was kept informed of the progress of her projects.

Before she took the helm, the Cambodian Red Cross was buf-feted by damaging press reports alleging that a former president and several board members had kept inaccurate financial records, and that funds were misappropriated. Bun Rany's tenure as president was very different. "I decided right at the beginning that transparency and accountability would be two central principles that I would scrupulously uphold as president of the Red Cross," she explained. "The money received from the donors in my time is put straight into the central bank of the country. It is all clear, since it is money that really belongs to the people." She introduced a system of presenting the funds to Queen Monique as soon the money was collected. The queen, in turn, would hand the money right back to Bun Rany, who would transfer it to a representative of the national treasury present at the charity functions. This representative would make a public announcement of the donations received and funds raised to the non-governmental organisations and other participants at the fundraisers. Three days after the fundraiser, Bun Rany would call a meeting with the wives of the foreign ambassadors based in Phnom Penh, and inform them of the money collected. They, in turn, would share their takings of the funds they had collected by selling goods at their stalls at the charity bazaars. "We're able to record everything openly, so everyone knows exactly what we have made and there's no opportunity for any misunderstanding," she clarified. "The funds collected at such bazaars come from people who want to know, and have a right to know, where their money is being spent." The money was then allocated to various activities of the Red Cross—sixty per cent earmarked for disaster relief, a certain percentage for drought relief, and a portion for development projects. "We cannot use these funds to buy sofa sets, for instance," she said with a laugh, emphasising the point with her hands.

She employed her management skills to protect her husband. The prime minister had waxed eloquent about the layers of security his wife had spread around him, and the very stringent curbs on his eating, drinking, and even showering at the golf club. All she allowed him to do was play the game and walk the course, and come back home. By her own admission, she had even written a note to her husband telling him "he should be truthful and fair, and be committed to what he had promised to do and not do." Hun Sen's gregariousness and his penchant for mixing freely with people gave her sleepless nights. "The danger of being shot at and the danger of being poisoned are the two crucial issues for his safety," she said firmly. She knew, of course, that it was not a special problem just for her husband, and that security was a common concern for all Cambodian leaders. "Once you stand in a very high position, you are exposed to the strongest winds. You don't know who really likes you and who doesn't. You may not die instantly if someone has poisoned your food. You can die after some months if you are continuously poisoned or can be taken very ill," she explained.

Bun Rany was not upset when she came in for criticism by the media. "I do not pay any attention to the media," she emphasised. "I don't really care what they say. They have a right to write whatever they wish. I have to keep my own goals in view and do my job—try to reduce the poverty of the people by providing training and jobs. Whatever the Western media says doesn't bother me too much, and I don't let it pressure me because I get relief from the support of the people. There are people who like to 'make' the news. They are professionals at making the news. So my ambition is that my people have enough to eat, enough clothes to wear, and a roof over their heads. That is all. I do believe it is the democratic right of the media to write what they want. But if they lie too many times, people will not believe them anymore. As for my personal feelings, I have never really felt like the wife of a prime minister, but always like an ordinary citizen. And I try my best to help the people."

Brushing off media controversies, she plunged even deeper into the task of uplifting her poor compatriots. She derived pleasure and satisfaction from having established vocational training centres for women in Phnom Penh and Kandal. The women learned the craft of making wedding dresses and ordinary

All the Huns: A family photograph taken in 1997: (from left) sons Manet, Manith and Mani, Hun Sen, Bun Rany, and daughters Maly and Mana.

PHOTO COURTESY OF HUN SEN

Family day at the waterfalls: Bun Rany with granddaughter Tep Thida in 2001.

clothes at the centres and then went out and found good jobs. "In Kandal province, for instance, we had two centres. Now we have only one, because the women from one of them all got jobs!" she said with a happy laugh.

She had changed since our first meeting. From the hesitant smile and a cluster of Khmer sapphires on her fingers, she had become far more relaxed and forthcoming. She now wore an elaborate diamond pendant, ring, and bracelet. When asked about her secret to looking trim, she explained: "I never diet. But after my gall bladder operation, I avoid all fat." She was quick to notice the beams of recognition on the authors' faces upon recognising the familiar faces of the wives of cabinet ministers Sok An and Tea Banh among her photographs. "I don't play golf, you know, but two ladies who are really excellent golfers are Madame Sok An and Madame Tea Banh," she said with a giggle.

AT HOME

Bun Rany's granddaughter Tep Thida was the love of her life and her constant companion. Thida's mother, Mana, lived with her husband just behind the Hun residence. The closeness made for easy accessibility for the granddaughter to curry favour with the grandparents. In fact, by her own admission, four-year-old Thida spent almost all her waking hours with her youthful grandma or grandpa. "Only when she falls asleep do we send her home," Bun Rany said adoringly.

Closer to home, Bun Rany's understated concern for others was apparent even in the big move she agreed to in 1999, from the vast, open countryside and plush interiors of the Takhmau residence to the somewhat more austere and limited scope of the house in town, on Boulevard Suramarit. Did she miss the rolling greens and the sweeping staircase of the Tiger's Den? "It's not as if we never go there anymore, you know," she said gently, adding that it was the sensible thing to do, not to have to commute such long distances. "But more than that, it was concern for my father-in-law and my mother that clinched it. They are very old. I spoke to my husband and told him that if anything should happen to them we could never get here from Takhmau on time." Hun Sen's father Hun Neang lived in the same house, in a room just beside his son's. Bun Rany's mother, Sieng Ly, lived right behind their house, where she was cared for by Bun Rany's youngest sister, Lynn Sitha.

In the Hun living room, we sat among piles of family photographs spread out on the lace table-covers. Bun Rany loved taking photographs, mounting them in albums, and presenting them to her father-in-law, who always admired her handiwork. She described the photographs of a recent family visit to Kirirom, a hill station towering 675 metres above sea level, set amidst pine forests in the Elephant Mountains, and situated 112 kilometres southwest of Phnom Penh. There were photographs of daughter Mana in jeans, and little Thida and her other friends. She spoke candidly about the clan.

Mana went to school in Phnom Penh and had many friends there, yet she often spent time with her mother. Mana had been very keen to learn French, so she pursued that interest in college, first in France and then in the United States. When she came home for her holidays five months later, her father, in his usual convincing manner, made her see things differently and "persuaded" her to get married. She still went ahead and studied for a degree in Phnom Penh. Her husband, Meng Kom Phak, was a businessman dealing in petroleum, with a financial interest in the Khmer oil firm, Tela.

Second son Manith was engaged to Dy Chindavy, the daughter of the Chief of Police, General Hok Lundy. Chindavy, nicknamed Sros (meaning "pretty"), was studying in Melbourne at the time. Though Manith was only twenty, he had managed to get his father to agree to the marriage. He told his parents he was in love with

Chindavy, and that he could not live without her. Bun Rany, however, would have preferred Manith to get his college degree first. Her husband, she explained, was very soft on the children; he gave in to their requests easily. "But it's not just me who wanted Manith to finish his education. Manet too, being the older brother, would have preferred Manith to get married after he was financially independent and was able look after himself and his family. For me, I would be happy if Manith and his wife would get their degrees. That would be enough for me. She is a good girl," Bun Rany said. The wedding took place on January 1–3, 2002.

Maly, the youngest of the Hun children, began her studies in France. While holidaying in Malaysia, she realised that French was hardly spoken in Southeast Asia. She was disappointed, and asked to be allowed to study English in Singapore at the United World College. "After she lived in Singapore for a while, her sister would tease her about her saying *lah*, *lah*, *lah* [a Singaporeanism]. So, after UWC, she wanted to go off to the U.S. Because of the change of schools, she lost a couple of years."

Her eldest, Manet, was at that time a twenty-four-year-old graduate student at New York University, where he lived on a monthly allowance of US$600 from his parents. He still managed to save some of the money and shared it with his less fortunate friends. "Even though he may not have much money, he gives it to his friends. His uncle gives him money, and he takes it and helps his friends. This is his nature," Bun Rany said with a mixture of pride and resignation. Manet, in turn, attributed this trait to the example set by his mother, and the encouragement he received from his parents to help challenged students. Over lunch at the authors' home in Bangkok in the summer of 2003, he said his mother had instilled in him a sense of love, respect, and compassion toward others. She, like his father, taught the children "the value of people's hearts," he explained, not their material wealth or status. She encouraged him to make friends regardless of their social class and status, and to learn from their experiences, because many of them faced greater hardships than he did.

Manet completed his master's degree in economics in January 2002. His thesis was on the land distribution mechanism in Cambodia. He wanted to register for his PhD in fall that year, before returning to his country to work in the field of development economics to help the poor. He spoke with passion about working to uplift his countrymen and women and raise their living standards, and of his apprenticeship at the World Bank in Washington, D.C., during a break in his semester. As an economist, Manet was clear about staying out of politics. His father thought likewise. "I would like to be the last member of my family who was involved in politics," Hun Sen said firmly. "I would rather see him working as an assistant to a politician, helping in national reconstruction, and not become a politician himself. I feel he cannot be a merchant or businessman because he does not care much for profits. It seems he is interested in study, in research, in making recommendations rather than doing things himself."

Not only was Manet a young economist, he was also a trained soldier, a graduate of West Point. His father was aware of his son's talent and expertise, and even saw a future for him in the Royal Cambodian Armed Forces. "He can be a person within the mechanism of the administration of the armed forces," Hun Sen clarified. "He can do neutral work without involving himself in politics. I would prefer him to be a good economist, and if he enters the army, he would concentrate on the economy. I've prohibited my children from getting into politics, but I've encouraged them to enter civil society and humanitarian organisations."

On this point husband and wife were in agreement. "I've talked to Manet about it, but he doesn't say much about the issue," Bun Rany said emphatically, her voice rising unexpectedly. "We don't want our children or their spouses to be involved in politics," she said decisively. "Not any of them. I want them to be in business. Although I don't know exactly how they feel about my wishes, I really hope they do not enter politics." This sentiment was nowhere clearer than in the role she wanted for the child she had shared the most difficulties with, Manet. She recognised in him an extremely gifted son. "Most of my children have a natural aptitude to study and do fairly well, but none is as intelligent as Manet," said a very partial mother. The Hun children possessed an urge to help and a readiness to give, which seemed a common trait imbibed from both parents. "The kids would hide their clothes and distribute them to their friends without my knowledge," she said appreciatively.

THE GROOMING OF THE
MANET GENERATION

2003

HUN MANET WAS BORN four months after his father's escape to Vietnam, at a particularly difficult time for his mother. Having escaped to Vietnam, Hun Sen could not be present by her side when she gave birth in October 1977. Her terrible ordeal during pregnancy—the pangs of hunger as she got only rice porridge and fish paste, and the relentless abuse from Angkar officials who punished her because she was the wife of a "defector"—became even more severe in the months leading to the collapse of the Khmer Rouge regime, when she hid in the countryside with her young son, concealed her identity, and faced prolonged malnutrition. In these difficult circumstances, the mother did everything to protect her child. As a child, Manet grew very close to his mother because they suffered so much hardship together. Hun Sen explained: "Compared to the other children, Manet has a deep feeling of love for his mother because he was the only breast-fed child. The rest were bottle-fed." He added: "He is a clever son."

For the twenty-six-year-old Manet, the distant past was difficult to reconstruct in the course of a four-hour interview with the authors in Bangkok in 2003. "I was too young to remember much of the time my mother and I spent alone before coming to Phnom Penh. Just about the only thing that I could remember when I got to Phnom Penh for the first time was the fact that I called my father

'Pou,' which means Uncle in Khmer. It took me a little while to begin calling him Dad."[1]

Manet spoke passionately about his childhood years in the Hun household, a time when his parents instilled strong Khmer values in their young children. "My parents have taught and shown us the value of hard work and dedication. Whenever they have time, they tell us about the struggles they faced. They even took us to the villages to see the real conditions of the villagers and also their real lives when they were growing up. By doing these things, they wanted to remind us not to forget what one can do and become with hard work, given the opportunity to do so."

Manet's memory of his boyhood years was much clearer, however, especially after his father came back with the liberation forces from Vietnam and became the foreign minister. How did life change when his father became a prominent politician? "Growing up with my father holding these positions was both an exciting and challenging experience for me, as it was for my brothers and sisters," Manet said, as he opened up about his parents' expectations. "Compared to many people I was very fortunate, with my father playing an important role in the country. It gave us a sense of privilege and recognition that many kids did not have." Such recognition, however, came with pressure and responsibility, and the children felt obliged to maintain discipline. "It was our responsibility to our parents to not do anything that could hurt their reputation and make them unhappy. It was the very least that any of us could do to repay them. As my father began to take on higher positions and a bigger responsibility for the country, more attention and thus more pressure was put on us."

The uncertain and chaotic nature of Cambodian politics had a strong emotional impact on the children. "Very often, I had to put up with unimaginable news and information directed against my family, particularly my father. Fortunately, we were able to adapt and overcome these things over time. All of these comforts and difficulties helped define, sharpen and, to a certain extent, toughen my perspectives on life."

Manet's mother played an influential role in his life as a child, and he admired her inner strength for having lived through the genocide. "She instills in me a sense of love, respect, and compassion towards others." The young man's candid comments on his parents revealed a great deal about the values his parents espoused. "She encourages and supports me in helping my friends who are in need. Throughout my high school years, and even now, I have supported several of my friends who were, and are, in grave need of assistance, by providing financial and other help to them so that they can continue to stay in school instead of quitting school in order to work to earn money to support their families, or simply because they don't have the means to continue. They are smart and have great potential, but just happen to be less fortunate than I am." Manet derived a sense of satisfaction by providing assistance to his friends in need. "It is these values my mum and my dad want me and my siblings to have. I wish I could help more people, but it is impossible to do so with the limited resources we have."

He clarified some common misconceptions associated with being the son of a powerful couple. "Being my father's son, some people have a tendency to think that I can pass all my classes and get whatever I want without having to do much, or even do anything. It is very frustrating for me to hear such comments after all my hard work. On the other hand, it gives me strength and incentive to work hard in order to prove them wrong. I believe that producing actual results is the best way to counter such comments, or allegations."

When he was studying in middle and high school in Phnom Penh he very rarely saw his father happy. "My parents, particularly my father, were under constant stress and pressure from working for the country. He worked very hard and would not stop working even when he was very sick. The very least I could do to help them was by doing something to make them happy, by studying hard and getting good grades." As a result of his efforts, Manet often topped his class. "The few times I saw him smile and look happy were when I handed him my monthly grade reports at the end of the month and my annual grade reports at the end of the year, to get his signature."

He became the first Cambodian to graduate from the U.S. Military Academy at West Point in 1999. In the fall of that year he attended graduate school at New York University, and earned his PhD in Economics from the University of Bristol in 2008-2009. His doctoral degree positioned him to focus on economic issues on his return to Cambodia. He also worked for a while at the World Bank.

He had to face "two main challenges" before gaining acceptance to West Point. His entry was certainly not guaranteed. "The first challenge was to meet and exceed very high standards of academic and physical requirements. The second challenge, and probably the more difficult of the two, was to convince my father to let me go to West Point. He allowed me to get the training and be part of the military, but under one condition: that I finish my economics degree first, because he believed that it was much more important for the country in the immediate term. Thus, I had to present him with a convincing plan to get his permission." West Point, fortunately, provided the opportunity to train both in the military and pursue studies in economics. Eventually, he succeeded in getting his father's permission because his father, too, was eager for him to obtain a broad-based education in the United States that would prepare him for a future role in the Cambodian military, and in national economic development.

Manet explained his reasons for attending West Point: "Growing up with my dad, who used to be in the army, and a lot of people around me, for example the guards, and relatives who were also part of the military, I became very interested in the military

341

since I was a kid. I liked the training, the discipline, the team work, and the challenge which I would deal with in the army." For these reasons, he was willing to take up any training opportunity, even a short one, regardless of whether he got accepted at West Point. He did not have much idea about West Point, about its military traditions as a premier leadership training institution, until after he reported on the first day, when he had a chance to talk to professors and cadets about the school. "All I knew before then was that West Point was a good military school where I could learn all aspects of military and leadership training while pursuing my regular studies in economics."

Upon arriving at West Point he faced a major culture shock. "Everything West Point represented was alien to me. Rules and regulations governing what we must and must not do, physical challenges and mental pressures, such as hazing, were not anything most of us had dealt with before. I had to face a few other challenges such as language and cultural problems." Although he had studied the English language and had attended college for about a year before he went to West Point, his comprehension and communication was not good enough for the West Point environment. "I was able to adapt to it as time went by. Culture shock was a problem for me initially. I was born and raised in a culture completely different from all of my friends, whom I had to stay and interact with almost the entire time. This sometimes produced an uncomfortable interaction between me and my friends. As time went by, I learned to adapt and overcome most of these cultural constraints and improve my interaction with all my friends." For instance, like his father, Manet liked *pra hok* and dry and salted fish, but living in New York as a graduate student, he developed a liking for American and spicy Indian food.

Hun Sen attended his son's graduation at West Point in May 1999, and watched the ceremony with pride as the young man, dressed in a traditional gray jacket with red sash and sabre at his side, received his diploma. He was among the 934 graduating cadets.[2] "Graduation was a big day for me," he said. "Like the rest of my friends, I was very glad to know that I had made it through the four years of challenges, and that I had earned my right to leave as an academy graduate. It was also a big day for me because it was the day when my parents, my grandfather (who had just had an operation not long before that), my sisters and brothers, and many other friends of the family were able to come together to celebrate."

After West Point, he enrolled in the master's degree programme in economics at New York University, where the intellectual atmosphere was markedly different from the military academy. "The academic work is rigorous as well as interesting, and I have more time to study and fulfill my assignments as compared to West Point, where most of the time was allocated to doing other duties. What helped me with my studies at NYU were the time management skills and the ability to prioritise assigned tasks that I had picked up at West Point."

Manet worked briefly at the World Bank, gaining valuable experience that he intended to use in carrying out economic development work in Cambodia in the near future. "Despite my short time at the World Bank, I have been able to learn different types of policies concerning development issues, which is the main focus of my study. I have understood the benefits and challenges associated with the bank's activities in developing countries, including Cambodia. This knowledge and experience will help broaden my knowledge and enhance my ability to achieve my ultimate goal of contributing to the development of Cambodia."

Manet drew important lessons from his exposure to the American way of life, with its focus on individual rights and responsibilities. "I like the way that people can have the freedom and opportunity to do anything they want, provided their actions do not interfere with others and do not break any laws. Such freedom creates an environment for promoting innovation and creativity. I also like the fact that there are enforcing mechanisms to ensure that people exercise their freedom with a great deal of responsibility."

His American education enriched him because of its "tolerance for diversity," its emphasis on "looking at things from different angles and perspectives," and widespread public participation in the political process. "However, for such a system to work properly, certain conditions need to be in place. People's basic needs, such as food, clothing, healthcare and education, must be met, to give them an incentive to participate in the process. If people are poor, they will not care about politics or anything else besides their daily survival. They can also become targets of manipulation by some special-interest elements through the use of financial incentives. The public needs to be educated and aware of their rights and responsibilities, so that they are not manipulated by political or special interests to serve any particular interests. Unless regulatory mechanisms are in place, the idea of democracy and freedom will be just a dream and can become a source of social conflict and instability. This would apply to any country, including Cambodia."

Manet believed that the perceptions of Americans about Cambodia, and about Hun Sen, were slowly changing for the better, but most foreign media reports were still negative. "People's perception of my father and Cambodia are shaped by the media, which is, for most people, the only source of information about the country. Unfortunately, in the past and even now (although there have been some positive changes) most of the news about Cambodia reported in the foreign media has been negative. They tend to focus their reports more on problems and less on positive developments that are taking place inside Cambodia. The most effective way to change such perceptions is by improving communication, and by disseminating balanced information abroad about the actual Cambodian situation through the use of media. Tourism, too, is a good mechanism to achieve the same goal of spreading the word on real development in Cambodia, thus helping to change outsiders' perceptions of the country. Under the current conditions, I believe perceptions will change, although it will take time."

As the eldest of a rising Hun generation, Manet did not wish to impose his ideas on the younger siblings. "I personally think that telling and instructing my brothers and sisters to do what I want them to do with their lives is not the most effective way to get their compliance, and sometimes can even produce resistance. I would allow them to walk their own paths while I would be there to give them advice and suggestions and all the help they need. They will make the final decision on what to do with their lives. I think this is part of their self-development—being able to make their own decisions and learn from their past mistakes for their future." That said, he advised his siblings "not to take things for granted and do the best they can to utilise the time and opportunity that they have now," to continue educating themselves "in order to be independent and be able to fulfill their future roles and responsibilities for their lives, their families, and society," and "to work towards achieving one goal: obtaining the skills and ability to support their families without external assistance from others."

Although he was the eldest child, his parents did not appear to have pressured him to start a family, as many Asian parents did. "On the family issue, I don't think I will be ready for it anytime soon. I would rather wait until I finish all my education, find a stable job, and be confident about assuming responsibility for the family."

His immediate plans were to complete his master's degree, and then pursue his PhD in economics, which would take between three to five years. "After that, I will be going back to Cambodia. My ultimate goal is to use what I have learned abroad to help with the development of Cambodia and improve the standard of living of

the Cambodian people." It was obvious that a new Hun generation was taking shape, as Manet had made clear that he intended to
return to Cambodia after completing his studies, and that he was
determined to improve the lives of the people.

AN EVENTUAL VALIDATION

1990–2013

NEITHER A TRANSITIONAL nor a transient figure in Cambodian politics and diplomacy, Hun Sen became one of the longest-serving heads of government in Southeast Asia. Having reached the age of sixty in 2012, he served notice that he hoped to remain in politics till he turned ninety. The leaders of the ruling CPP—Chairman Chea Sim and Honorary Chairman Heng Samrin, as well as the members of the party's Central Committee and Standing Committee—had consistently supported Hun Sen's leadership of the government. The reason for their preference was that he had demonstrated that under his command the party had improved its performance in elections, and his vigorous foreign policy had won many friends and allies abroad. There was, if not a powerful logic driving his political longevity, then logic nonetheless.

Hun Sen and his senior CPP colleagues brought about a significant change in national politics: they ended the domination of politics by the Cambodian royal family and the Phnom Penh elite who had been educated in France or under the French education system—people such as Sihanouk, Pol Pot, Khieu Samphan, Son Sann, Ranariddh, and several others. Born in a village and espousing strong rural values, Hun Sen's earthy outspokenness resonated powerfully with common Cambodians.

This book has demonstrated that Hun Sen worked assiduously to maintain a long tenure in power by carefully crafting a strategy to (1) build consensus for his foreign and domestic policy within the ruling KPRP, the SOC, the CPP, and the Royal Government of Cambodia, (2) build a network of supporters among senior officials within the CPP and government, (3) develop close links with the military, and (4) develop broad international support among countries in the West and Asia in support of his foreign and domestic policy objectives.

He began his political career in diplomacy and not in national reconstruction. He functioned as his country's leading diplomat for at least six years before he emerged on the national scene. His diplomacy ranks first among his various achievements. Even after he became prime minister, his major contributions were in global diplomacy as a peace negotiator during the talks with Sihanouk. Yet, he did not practise national politics in isolation from international affairs: he combined both, and was able to project his domestic agenda on the foreign stage in order to convince the international community of the seriousness of his economic and social reforms, and he was able to gain support for his foreign policy within the party and government. He earned the confidence of his party by successfully negotiating the Paris peace agreement and winning membership of ASEAN.

In the end, he was more successful as an international diplomat than as a domestic reformer. His diplomacy in Jakarta, Tokyo, and Paris deftly outmanoeuvred the West and ASEAN, which had demanded that the SOC be dismantled ahead of the general election of 1993. Hun Sen wore out his opponents by skilfully making concessions on small issues, and refusing to compromise on major ones. Eventually, when the peace agreement was signed in Paris, the governmental structures of the SOC remained intact, and Hun Sen stayed on as prime minister. He had conceded little to his international and domestic opponents. His concession to agree to hold a general election reflected the changing global order in the post-Cold War world: because the Soviet Union was rapidly disintegrating, he could no longer count on the Communist bloc for economic

PHOTO COURTESY OF HUN SEN

*Steering through troubled waters: Hun Sen guides his boat across a
waterway in Koh Tmey commune, Saang district, Kandal province,
in 1995.*

and military support, and he now needed to integrate his country
with the West and with Asia's dynamic economies, in order to gain
investments and aid. The fact that Sihanouk was fond of Hun Sen
helped immensely, and their personal chemistry was noticed by foreign diplomats, who were beginning to recognise Hun Sen as a
legitimate national leader.

Hun Sen's second contribution lay in his formulation and preservation of core national security interests, and his refusal to compromise on those interests: his belief that Cambodia needed to
maintain Vietnam as its closest foreign ally, and to keep the border
with Vietnam stable and peaceful. The special relationship with
Vietnam was a lynchpin of Phnom Penh's foreign policy during
the Cold War, at a time when China backed the Khmer Rouge,
and the United States seemed uninterested. And because Hanoi
could not provide all the economic and military aid that Cambodia

349

needed to fight the Khmer Rouge and the NCR along the Thai–Cambodian border, Phnom Penh turned to the Soviet Union as its principal aid donor and ideological ally. The Moscow–Hanoi–Phnom Penh axis worried the United States, China, and ASEAN. Hun Sen kept Phnom Penh within the axis throughout the Cold War, but after the demise of the Soviet Union he made an effort to steer Cambodia closer toward Western Europe and ASEAN, all the while keeping his core national security interest at the front and centre. Many Cambodians did not approve of Hun Sen's links with Hanoi because they perceived Vietnam as an enemy whom they denounced in racist language. Hun Sen was not deterred by these xenophobic outbursts. He believed that Vietnam had waged a long war of resistance against U.S. intervention in Indochina, and he offered ideological support to Vietnam's national liberation struggle and to Hanoi's effort to prevent the U.S. installation of a neo-colonial regime in South Vietnam.

A third aspect of Hun Sen's tenure in power was his national development effort. He deserves praise for creating the conditions to attract foreign investment and reviving the national economy during a most difficult period of the Cold War, when Cambodia faced a U.S. economic embargo. Along with Ranariddh and other Cambodian leaders, he shares praise and blame for the partial success and partial failure of those efforts. While Hun Sen is indeed a strongman, he is not like other strongmen who have used dictatorial methods. He has not imposed martial law and suspended civil rights, and his government has enacted one of the freest press laws within Southeast Asia. He has grappled with the problem of economic construction, but his record is mixed.

Hun Sen worried about corruption within the government and the unjust practice of government officials and powerful businessmen seizing land belonging to the rural people. He admitted that corruption existed within the government, and he issued dozens of warnings, threatening corrupt officials with dire consequences.

Corruption, however, was so entrenched in parts of Cambodian society that he could not combat it single-handed. In February 1999, he warned: "I will fight all the corrupt officials before I leave my position. I don't think they are more hardline than the Khmer Rouge that I have already dismantled."[1] At a closed-door CPP Congress of 200 delegates in June 1999, he admonished his party: "If there is any official who commits wrongdoing, he must change, or else be expelled."[2] Despite his warnings, corruption was not eliminated. In order to set an example, he declared his personal wealth in 2011. He submitted an envelope containing a statement of his assets to the Anti-Corruption Unit (ACU), and he told state officials to declare their assets before the deadline of April 7.[3] "Today, I have performed my obligation as a person under the law about fighting against corruption," he said, clarifying that he had no other sources of income except his monthly salary of 4.6 million riels or US$1,150. "My salary is little, but the state covers all my expenses, so the wage is enough for me." ACU chairman Om Yintieng revealed that 24,854 officials in the state's thirty-seven institutions were required to declare their assets by the deadline.

Yet, Hun Sen's CPP remained popular among voters primarily because of the party's widespread development efforts to install irrigation canals, build roads, bridges and highways, and provide essential services such as water and electricity to rural and urban communities. He drew legitimacy from the ability of the CPP to perform well in general elections. The CPP won the general election in 2003, but failed to secure the majority vote necessary to govern alone. After nearly a year of political deadlock, Hun Sen took office in July 2004, following an arrangement between the CPP and Funcinpec to share at least some power.

A series of significant events occurred on Hun Sen's watch, all of which strengthened his hand. In August 2004, the national assembly ratified Cambodia's entry into the World Trade Organisation. In October 2004, King Sihanouk abdicated and was succeeded by

351

his son Sihamoni, who anyway was Hun Sen's preferred candidate. In December 2005, opposition leader Sam Rainsy, in exile in France, was convicted by a Cambodian court of defaming Hun Sen and sentenced to nine months in prison. In February 2006, Rainsy received a royal pardon. (Eventually, in September 2010, Rainsy was sentenced in absentia to ten years in jail after being found guilty of manipulating a map to suggest Cambodia was losing land to Vietnam.) In October 2006, Funcinpec, the junior partner in the ruling coalition, dropped Ranariddh as its leader, signalling the marginalisation of the once-powerful prince. And, when Khmer Rouge leaders were eventually brought before a Cambodian court, Hun Sen kept his distance from the court proceedings in order to demonstrate that he was not influencing its work. The trials progressed fitfully, and in July 2007, a UN-backed court tribunal began questioning suspects about allegations of genocide by the Khmer Rouge. In September, the most senior surviving member of the Khmer Rouge, Nuon Chea, known as "Brother Number Two," was arrested and charged with crimes against humanity. In November, the genocide tribunal held its first public hearing to listen to a bail plea from former prison chief, Khang Khek Ieu, better known as Comrade Duch. In February 2009, Duch went on trial in Phnom Penh on charges of presiding over the murder and torture of thousands of people as head of the Tuol Sleng prison camp. In July 2010, Duch was given a thirty-five-year jail sentence following a verdict that found him guilty of crimes against humanity. In March 2013, senior Khmer Rouge leader Ieng Sary, known as "Brother Number Three," died at the age of eighty-seven, unpunished for his crimes of genocide. Later that month, the tribunal ruled that the eighty-six-year-old Nuon Chea, who suffered from heart ailments and hypertension, was fit to stand trial, along with Khieu Samphan.

After a long tenure in power, Hun Sen triumphed at last. He eventually demonstrated that his development efforts were instrumental in delivering a resounding electoral victory that had eluded him till then. In the general election of 2008, the CPP won a clear majority—largely because Cambodia was undergoing an economic boom and many Cambodians were prospering. Domestic political parties accepted the poll verdict, as election monitors and several countries declared the election to be free and fair. The U.S. embassy in Phnom Penh declared: "Cambodia's National Assembly election was freer than any election previously held in the country, and the vast majority of Cambodia's registered voters were able to express their will in a more open atmosphere than before."[4]

Firmly ensconced as prime minister, Hun Sen encouraged his children to assume positions of power. Manet was appointed deputy commander of his father's personal bodyguard unit in September 2010. In January 2011, he was elevated to two-star military general—a move the *Bangkok Post* described as the first step in his anointment as his father's successor.[5]

The process of grooming a new generation of leaders had begun when Hun Sen appointed his daughter Mana as one of his assistants in September 2008. Veteran government spokesman Khieu Kanharith argued that Mana's appointment was based on her position as general manager of a local television station, Bayon TV, and that she would assist the prime minister in writing "proper reports."[6] Earlier in February 2004, Mana had started a new airline, First Cambodia Airlines, in collaboration with a group of local and foreign executives.[7] The airline was forced to shut down just six months into business owing to rising fuel prices and costs of operation.[8] Hun Sen's second son, Manith, served as deputy chief of his father's cabinet and as deputy secretary-general of the National General Secretariat for Land Disputes.[9]

Although his other children occupied senior positions in the administration, most Cambodians believed that the person being groomed as his successor was Manet. In a speech at a ceremony marking Manet's promotion to the rank of major-general, Minister of Defence Tea Banh argued that Manet's military qualifications at

West Point had prepared him to lead a new generation of military officers within the Royal Cambodian Armed Forces. "This school is recognised internationally for its distinction in political science, law and military affairs, and in his new position, Manet must use the skills he has learned," Tea Banh declared. Hun Sen, too, defended Manet's military promotion in January 2011, arguing that his son was well-qualified for the role. In a speech broadcast over national radio, he said: "Hun Manet joined the army in 1994. He has been in the army for sixteen years, and there is promotion within the army ranks."[10] Clarifying the need for a younger generation to assume positions of authority, he said: "We have to let the younger generation take over our work and ensure that our achievements are protected and that forces of evil who want to destroy our achievements are stopped."[11]

By 2011, many CPP leaders believed that their party ought to actively encourage the elevation of a new generation of younger colleagues to senior positions in the government. Hun Sen was not alone in appointing his children to middle- and senior-level positions. Members of the Cambodian royal family had frequently done the same. Son Sann's son Son Soubert had held several positions in public life, and the sons of Foreign Minister Hor Nam Hong and Social Affairs Minister Ith Samheng both worked at the cabinets of their respective ministries.[12] Lon Rith, a son of former Khmer Republic President Lon Nol, founded the Khmer Republic Party, and expressed the hope that his father's name would boost his political fortunes.[13]

Manet's promotion coincided with border conflict with Thailand over a disputed area near the ancient Preah Vihear Temple. In February 2011, Thai and Cambodian forces exchanged fire across the disputed border. Hun Sen called for the UN to send in peacekeepers, and Manet was given command of military operations against Thailand. Manet demonstrated his military acumen when he commanded a battle on the night of February 6, which the Thai army believed was Cambodian retaliation for the loss of their forces in an earlier battle and "slight damage" to the Preah Vihear Temple. Thai army officers also argued that Hun Sen intentionally placed Manet in command of Cambodian soldiers because "Hun Sen wanted his son to get credit and recognition from the Cambodian people, to pave the way for him to be promoted in the army." According to them, Hun Sen was implementing a long-term plan to make Major-General Manet the chief of the armed forces, and to later succeed him as the head of government. They believed that Hun Sen had used his son as a military link between Phnom Penh and Washington, which gave Cambodian forces access to U.S. military aid and training, including U.S. anti-terrorism tactics. In July 2011, the International Court of Justice ruled that both Thailand and Cambodia should withdraw their troops from the disputed area around Preah Vihear.

The old guard of Cambodia was indeed being replaced by younger men. The death of King Sihanouk on October 15, 2012 in China was widely mourned by Cambodians not just because they had a historical and emotional bond with the man they revered as Papa King, but also because his departure had an impact on the future of the monarchy and national politics.[14] Hun Sen and King Sihamoni travelled together to Beijing to bring home the body of the former king; they embraced and wept as they boarded the plane.[15] Hun Sen grieved privately before breaking down in tears in front of hundreds of journalists on November 20, saying that he was "overwhelmed" by the outpouring of sympathy from world leaders for the deceased king.[16] Indicating that he was filled with pride at hosting the meetings of ASEAN—which were attended by eight world leaders, including U.S. President Barack Obama and Chinese Premier Wen Jiabao—he said that he regretted that Sihanouk had been unable to see his country on the international stage. "I am sorry I could not hold back my tears," Hun Sen said. In order to memorialise the king, who had died at the age of eighty-nine, he announced that a four-metre tall bronze statue of Sihanouk would be placed at Dragon Park, near the Independence Monument in Phnom Penh, and October 15 would be designated as a national holiday. Some critics argued, nonetheless, that without the moderating presence of Sihanouk, Hun Sen and the other CPP leaders would function without restraint, for while Sihanouk had possessed the stature to comment freely on issues of national importance, Sihamoni played a strictly neutral role and kept out of politics, as prescribed by the constitution.

At this time, Hun Sen's attention was focused on pressing issues of global diplomacy. The U.S.–Cambodia relationship appeared, to the detriment of both countries, to have remained trapped in the era of the Cold War. An opportunity for both countries to begin afresh presented itself when Obama visited Phnom Penh in November 2012 to attend the ASEAN and East Asia Summit Meetings, becoming the first serving U.S. president to visit the country. In his closed-door meeting with Hun Sen, Obama urged the Cambodian leader to ensure that Cambodian elections were free and fair, and that political prisoners were released.[17] Many Cambodians were mystified why Obama raised the issue of elections when the U.S. embassy in Phnom Penh had earlier certified that the last election was the freest the country had seen. The Obama–Hun Sen meeting was "tense." They shook hands before their meeting, but Obama did not smile, indicating that their encounter lacked warmth and good humour. Afterwards, senior Cambodian official Prak Sokhonn placed Obama's remarks in perspective: Obama had raised human rights issues, but only because he had been asked to do so by U.S. congressmen. In response, Hun Sen thanked Obama for his "frank" comments, but he clarified that "he was the victim of a campaign" to distort the facts about human rights and democracy in Cambodia. Sokhonn explained that Hun Sen told Obama that Cambodia had a better human rights record than some of its neighbouring countries in ASEAN. Sokhonn declared: "Through a campaign of slander, it would seem as though Cambodia is a bad student, worse than Myanmar, that a teacher that was asked to help Myanmar has become a bad person," a reference to Phnom Penh's assistance to Yangon. A talented and experienced negotiator, Hun Sen explained to Obama the harsh realities of life in Cambodia, which Sokhonn paraphrased as follows: "Samdech [Hun Sen] made it clear that in Cambodia there are no political prisoners [and that political prisoners do not exist] just because there is a report and a protest demanding the release of all political prisoners." Sokhonn clarified that Hun Sen argued that while there were no political prisoners in the country, politicians who broke the law were punished in accordance with the law.

Obama brought up the issue of the displacement of some 400,000 people from their land because the government had granted concessions to private mining and agricultural firms over the past ten years. Hun Sen told Obama that such reports were exaggerated, and that the government had only forcibly evicted people from land in very rare cases—where they had illegally encroached upon the land.

For his part, Hun Sen requested that Obama reduce Cambodia's debt of US$400 million, plus interest, to the United States, which dated back to the U.S.-backed Lon Nol regime in the 1970s. Cambodian officials argued that most of the U.S. funds were spent by Lon Nol in waging war against the Cambodian people. Hun Sen proposed that Cambodia would pay back thirty per cent of the debt, plus interest of one per cent, and that the Cambodian government would spend what it would have repaid the United States on developing the country's capacity in education, demining, and culture. Hun Sen mounted a strong defence of his policies, and told Obama of his desire to deepen the relationship with the United States.[18] There were, indeed, persuasive grounds for the United States to reciprocate because a survey by a U.S. organisation dedicated to the promotion of democracy had shown that Hun Sen's governance enjoyed widespread legitimacy. An opinion poll conducted by the International Republican Institute in December 2011 revealed that eighty-one per cent of the 2,000 Cambodians polled had said that Cambodia was "generally headed in the right direction."[19]

It became clear that the ruling CPP was charting a new political course. The CPP confirmed speculation about the entry into national politics of the new generation of the Hun family, and the young sons of top party leaders. In February 2013, the party revealed that a CPP committee had recently met to finalise a list of party candidates who would run in the general election of July 2013, and that the list included two of Hun Sen's kin. Hun Sen's youngest son, the thirty-year-old Hun Mani, and son-in-law Dy Vichea, who is married to Hun Mana, were running in the election from Kompong Speu and Svay Rieng, respectively.[20] Besides Mani and Vichea, the CPP had nominated the sons of at least four of its leaders as candidates for the position of MP: Minister of the Interior Sar Kheng's son Sar Sokha, and CPP Second Vice-Chairman Say Chhum's son Say Sam El. A son of Deputy Prime Minister Sok An, and a son of Supreme Court President Dith Munty, were also in the race for a national assembly seat.[21] Hun Sen defended the nominations of his kin, and the sons of other CPP leaders. In March 2013, he commented that critics had misunderstood the nomination of family members of CPP leaders in the general election as an attempt to create a political succession. "When the CPP prepared its candidate lists, they were leaked to the media and some people mistook it as creating a dynasty," Hun Sen said. "We don't just make the appointments, they [the candidates] must be qualified." In defence of the younger generation now on the verge of making their political debut, he clarified: "No one starts their work when they are old."[22] It appeared to be a complete turnaround from his former position that he would not permit his children to enter politics; now he was encouraging his kin to do just that.

By 2013, Hun Sen had been in power for twenty-eight years. His promise, that he would remain in politics till the age of ninety, remains in the public record. His good health and excellent performance in the general election of 2008 have positioned him to contest at least four more national elections. Yet, as Khieu Kanharith has cautioned on more than one occasion: "This is Cambodia. Anything can happen here."

NOTES

INTRODUCTION

1. There are several books on the history of twentieth-century Cambodia, but none of them focus on Hun Sen. See Ben Kiernan, *How Pol Pot Came to Power: Colonialism, Nationalism, and Communism in Cambodia, 1930-1975* (New Haven, CT: Yale University Press, 2004), 254, 311; Philip Short, *Pol Pot: Anatomy of a Nightmare* (New York: Henry Holt, 2004), 379; David P. Chandler, *The Tragedy of Cambodian History* (New Haven, CT: Yale University Press, 1991), 162; Evan Gottesman, *Cambodia After the Khmer Rouge: Inside the Politics of Nation Building* (New Haven, CT: Yale University Press, 2003), 47-48; Craig Etcheson, *After the Killing Fields: Lessons from the Cambodian Genocide* (Lubbock, TX: Texas Tech University Press, 2005), 13, 30-31; Elizabeth Becker, *When the War was Over: The Voices of Cambodia's Revolution and its People* (New York: Simon and Schuster, 1986), 333-334; and Nayan Chanda, *Brother Enemy: The War after the War* (San Diego, CA: Harcourt Brace Jovanovich, 1986), 198, 217.

2. Memorandum of Conversation, President Bush's Meeting with President Francois Mitterrand of France, St. Martin, December 16, 1989, George Bush Presidential Library, College Station, Texas. http://bushlibrary.tamu.edu.

A SHORT HISTORY OF CAMBODIA

1. The name Funan may have come from the Khmer word *phnom*, meaning "mountain" in modern Khmer, and *bnam* in ancient Khmer, from a Chinese root word.

2. Some scholars have argued that evidence of Indian influence on Khmer culture is seen in four Sanskritised inscriptions, including an Indian-influenced medallion, dating to 152 C.E.: see George Coedès, *The Indianized States of Southeast Asia* (Honolulu: University of Hawaii Press, 1968), 17; and D.R. SarDesai, *Southeast Asia: Past and Present* (Boulder, CO: Westview, 2010), 22. Evidence of Indianisation has been collected by L'Ecole Francaise d'Extreme-Orient, which has listed more than 900 inscriptions in

361

Sanskrit and Khmer: see Lawrence Palmer Briggs, *The Ancient Khmer Empire* (Bangkok: White Lotus, 1999), 4. Sanskritised inscriptions from the Angkor Borei region, dated 612 C.E., further confirm the Indianisation of Khmer culture: see Malcolm MacDonald, *Angkor and the Khmers* (Singapore: Oxford University Press, 1987), 34–36.

3. SarDesai, *Southeast Asia: Past and Present*, 22–23.

4. R.C. Majumdar, *Hindu Colonies in the Far East* (Calcutta: Firma KLM, 1991), 182.

5. Interestingly, though, these dynasties maintained strong and consistent diplomatic ties with China by sending rich tributes to the Chinese court. There is some evidence, for instance, that a successor of Kaundinya, possibly Jayavarman I, referred to by Chinese chroniclers as Cho-ye-pa-mo, sent merchants to Canton to promote trade between 420 and 478 C.E., during the Song period.

6. The lineage of Jayavarman II is perhaps the most debated issue in the ancestry of Khmer kingship. Little is known about this man. There is a staggering lack of inscriptions from his reign, and Majumdar and Briggs agree that inscriptions of his reign reveal nothing about his governance, and Chinese histories, too, say nothing about him. Though generally believed to have been installed as monarch in 802 C.E. on Mount Mahendra, there is a strong possibility of him being present in the region of Prey Veng as early as 790 C.E. However, it was only an eleventh-century inscription from Sdok Kak Thom that linked Jayavarman II definitely with the Sailendra dynasty of Indonesia, before he returned to Cambodia. Most of the evidence shows that he was made a prisoner and taken to Java when the monarch preceding him was killed by the Sailendra rulers of Java. See Majumdar, *Hindu Colonies in the Far East*, 189–90; and Briggs, *The Ancient Khmer Empire*, 82.

7. Ian Mabbett and David Chandler, *The Khmers* (Oxford: Blackwell, 1996), 88.

8. Coedès, *Angkor and the Khmers*, 10.

9. SarDesai, *Southeast Asia: Past and Present*, 30.

10. See Marie Alexandrine Martin, *Cambodia: A Shattered Society* (Berkeley, CA: University of California Press, 1994), 29–33; David P. Chandler, *A History of Cambodia* (Bangkok: Silkworm, 1993), 141; SarDesai, *Southeast Asia: Past and Present*, 118; and Milton E. Osborne, *The French Presence in Cochinchina and Cambodia* (Bangkok: White Lotus, 1997), 31–32.

11. Chandler, *A History of Cambodia*, 153–59; and Martin, *Cambodia: A Shattered Society*, 35.

12. Harish C. Mehta, *Cambodia Silenced: The Press Under Six Regimes* (Bangkok & Cheney: White Lotus, 1997), 3, 7, 17, 29–33; Martin, *Cambodia: A Shattered Society*, 48–54; and Chandler, *A History of Cambodia*, 159, 163–68, 175.

13. Milton Osborne, *Sihanouk: Prince of Light, Prince of Darkness* (Sydney: Allen and Unwin, 1994), 30; and Martin, *Cambodia: A Shattered Society*, 50.

14. Norodom Sihanouk with Bernard Krisher, *Sihanouk Reminisces: World Leaders I Have Known* (Bangkok: Editions Duang Kamol, 1990), 47–48. Also see Chandler, *A History of Cambodia;* Martin: *Cambodia: A Shattered Society;* and Mehta, *Cambodia Silenced.*

15. Sihanouk, *Sihanouk Reminisces*, 71; and William Shawcross, *Sideshow: Kissinger, Nixon, and the Destruction of Cambodia* (London: The Hogarth Press, 1994), 64.

16. Taylor Owen and Ben Kiernan, "Bombs Over Cambodia," *The Walrus,* October 2006; and Shawcross, *Sideshow.*

17. Sihanouk, *Sihanouk Reminisces*, 30; David P. Chandler, *The Tragedy of Cambodian History: Politics, War, and Revolution Since 1945* (New Haven, CT: Yale University Press, 1991), 197–215; and Osborne, *Sihanouk: Prince of Light, Prince of Darkness*, 209–14.

I: DAYS IN THE KOMPONG AND THE PAGODA

1. The sub-section "Child of the Full Moon" is based on an extended audio interview conducted by Harish and Julie Mehta in Siem Reap in December 1997. It also draws upon Julie Mehta's interview with Bun Rany in Phnom Penh in December 1997. To explore the early life of Hun Sen, the authors interviewed Chhim You Teck, a medical assistant at Calmette Hospital in Phnom Penh in June 1998. The sub-section "Pagoda Boy" is based on the authors' interview with Hun Sen in Siem Reap in December 1997. Details of Hun Sen's early life are based on interviews with Path Sam, a school teacher in Phnom Penh, and Chhim You Teck in Phnom Penh in June 1998. Julie Mehta's interview with Bun Rany in Phnom Penh in June 1997 sheds new light on the travails of the suffering people of Cambodia.

2. "Cambodia's Hun Sen Reveals Personal Details, True Age," Kyodo News, June 6, 1993.

3. The Cambodian Riel–U.S. Dollar exchange is based on the *Statistical Yearbook for Asia and the Far East, 1969.* Also see "Cambodian Riel Devalued," Reuters, November 1, 1971.

11: DEEP INSIDE THE MAQUIS

1. The authors' conversations with Hun Sen in Siem Reap brought alive his memories of his days in the maquis and his first experience of combat against a U.S. Army unit inside Cambodia. In her interview with Julie Mehta, Bun Rany talked about how she secretly joined the maquis without informing her parents. The section "Romancing Rebels" is based on the authors' interview with Hun Sen and Bun Rany in Phnom Penh, December 1997.

2. For further reading on the language and sayings of the Khmer Rouge, see May B. Ebihara, Carol A. Mortland, and Judy Ledgerwood, *Cambodian Culture Since 1975* (Ithaca: Cornell University Press, 1994). Specifically see John Marston's essay, "Metaphors of the Khmer Rouge."

3. Hun Sen told the authors: "[The loss of my first child] influenced me to compose a song entitled, "The Suffering of the Wife Being Separated from Her Husband," which narrated the agony of a couple being forced to stay apart." He began composing in 1989, and wrote the words for more than 100 Cambodian songs. Some of his songs were about his impoverished childhood in the countryside. His favourite was "The Life of the Pagoda Boy." A line from the song captured his own angst: "Don't be disappointed with the rich children—the pagoda boy will have a bright future." Audio tapes of his sorrowful ballads became bestsellers in Phnom Penh in the mid-1990s, and the radio channels constantly replayed them. Also see Seth Mydans, "When He Writes a Song, Cambodia Better Listen," *New York Times,* July 15, 1998. The article quotes Hun Sen as saying: "I can't sing and I can't play an instrument. But I can write." Mydans reports that sometimes the urge to write a song strikes Hun Sen on an airplane or a helicopter, and he scribbles on scraps of paper. He wrote love songs such as "The Dark Skinned Woman of Krang Yoen," and lyrics extolling peace and human rights.

4. Hun Sen told the authors in Phnom Penh in December 1997 about his estrangement from the brutal policies of the Khmer Rouge, and his abortive plan to stage a rebellion against Pol Pot within Cambodia.

5. Hun Sen recalled that his forces confronted a U.S. army unit commanded by Geoffrey Blume. After peace returned to the country in the 1990s, Blume returned to Cambodia as a businessman and served as a charter member of the Rotary Club of Phnom Penh in 2003.

6. Kiernan, *The Pol Pot Regime,* 267–71.

7. For details of the executions of Chen Sot and Kun Deth in the Eastern Zone in the 1970s, see *Genocide and Democracy in Cambodia,* edited by Ben Kiernan (New Haven: Yale University Southeast Asia Studies, 1993).

8. Kiernan, *The Pol Pot Regime*, 370.

9. Chanda, *Brother Enemy*, 197.

III: ESCAPE TO VIETNAM

1. In interview with the authors, in Phnom Penh, December 1997.

2. As far as the authors can gauge, the only scholar to have offered a couple of facts about Hun Sen's escape to Vietnam is Ben Kiernan in *The Pol Pot Regime,* 371: Kiernan records that Hun Sen crossed the border with a few of his troops, that the Vietnamese gave the hungry escapees enough rice to eat, and that he was held in detention for twenty-two days.

3. For further reading on the plight of Cambodian women, see Ang Choulean, *Sahakum Khmae Neu Srok Barang Neng Preah Buddhasasana,* "The Cambodian Community in France and Buddhism" (Paris: Culture khmere, April-September, 1981); Chanthou Boua, "Women in Kampuchea" (Bangkok: UNICEF, 1981); and Judy Ledgerwood, "Analysis of the Situation of Women in Cambodia" (Phnom Penh: UNICEF, 1991).

4. See Henri Locard, *Pol Pot's Little Red Book: The Sayings of the Angkar* (Bangkok: Silkworm Books, 2004), 179–81. Locard explains that by singling out Cambodians who were collaborating with the Vietnamese, the Khmer Rouge underscored their belief that it was acceptable to kill such Cambodians, who possessed Vietnamese minds and souls. Xenophobia was a component of Khmer Rouge racialised ideology that encouraged killing an enemy that was physically Cambodian and yet had allegedly betrayed his or her national identity to adopt the identity of the hegemonic enemy. Locard provides a variation of this saying: *khluen khmae khue kbal yuen,* "Cambodian bodies with Vietnamese brains."

5. Hun Sen continued his long interview with the authors, talking about how he was rebuffed repeatedly by the Vietnamese when he asked them for political asylum. They asked him to seek refuge in Thailand, but he refused, and eventually managed to convince the Vietnamese to grant him political asylum.

6. Kiernan, *The Pol Pot Regime,* 373.

7. Chanda, *Brother Enemy,* 196.

8. Kiernan, *The Pol Pot Regime,* 374–75.

9. For details on border clashes between Pol Pot's forces and the Vietnamese Army, the authors consulted news reports by the Vietnam News Agency and Phnom Penh Radio. Also see "Khmers Hit Tay Ninh, says Hanoi," United Press International, February 2, 1978.

IV: LIBERATION WAR AGAINST THE KHMER ROUGE

1. In interview with the authors, in Phnom Penh, December 1997.

2. Stephen J. Morris, *Why Vietnam Invaded Cambodia: Political Culture and the Causes of War* (Stanford, CA: Stanford University Press, 1999), 101–2.

3. Kiernan, *The Pol Pot Regime*, 375–76; and Chanda, *Brother Enemy*, 255.

4. Chanda, *Brother Enemy*, 255.

5. See Carlyle A. Thayer, *The Vietnam People's Army Under Doi Moi* (Singapore: Institute of Southeast Asian Studies, 1994).

6. Radio Hanoi, December 4, 1978; and "Hanoi Front to Topple Pol Pot," *New Straits Times,* December 4, 1978.

7. "Viets Cross the Mekong," Radio of Kampuchean National United Front, January 3, 1979; "Rebels Take Phnom Penh," Radio Hanoi, January 7, 1979; and "13 Vietnam Divisions Leading War," *New Straits Times*, January 8, 1979 (based on a *New York Times* report).

8. "UN Support for Pol Pot," *New Straits Times,* January 12, 1979.

9. "Hanoi Turning Cambodia into a Vietnam, says Paper," Agence France-Presse, June 20, 1983. This report quoted Vietnamese Defence Minister Van Tien Dung, who had helped Hun Sen raise a rebel army, as praising the Cambodian armed forces on the occasion of their Revolutionary Army Day.

10. "Phnom Penh Run by a Vietnamese Committee, says Paper," Agence France-Presse, May 2, 1986.

11. Morris, *Why Vietnam Invaded Cambodia,* 224; Martin, *Cambodia: A Shattered Society,* 217; Gottesman, *Cambodia After the Khmer Rouge,* 45; and Becker, *When the War was Over,* 444.

12. Hun Sen candidly told the authors during the interview in Phnom Penh in June 1998 that his government would not have survived without the assistance of the Vietnamese. For further reading on the Vietnamese Army's operations in Cambodia, see Thayer, *The Vietnam People's Army Under Doi Moi.*

13. "Chinese Hold the Key to Total Pullout, says Co Thach," Reuters, June 21, 1983.

14. "'Viets May Pullout Before '90,' says Rajiv," *New Straits Times,* December 3, 1995.

15. Chanda, *Brother Enemy,* 303.

16. "Vietnam's Exercise in Illusion," United Press International, May 14, 1983; and "350 Newsmen Ask to Cover Viet Pullout," Agence France-Presse, September 17, 1989. Reporting on a partial Vietnamese withdrawal in May

1983, United Press International correspondent Paul Anderson wrote: "After witnessing the departure of the Vietnamese troops from Phnom Penh, journalists had the option of flying to the Vietnamese border in helicopters at US$220 each, or travelling by bus to see the soldiers cross the frontier. Only the first of two helicopters managed to arrive for the gala ceremonies. The buses were the victim of disorganisation and late starts. The second helicopter was the victim of greed. Eager for hard currency, the Cambodians had oversold the second 'copter, causing such a delay in Phnom Penh that the ceremonies were over before the journalists even departed."

17. "Cambodian Diplomacy: Beginning the End Game?" Directorate of Intelligence, Central Intelligence Agency, page 8, June 15, 1989. Refer to this declassified document online at http://www.foia.cia.gov/browse_docs.asp

18. National Intelligence Daily, December 5, 1989, page 7, Central Intelligence Agency. Accessed online http://www.foia.cia.gov/browse_docs_full.asp

V: ASCENT OF A PEASANT TO POWER

1. In interview with the authors, in Phnom Penh, June 1998.

2. "Cambodia's Hun Sen Reveals Personal Details, True Age," Kyodo News, June 6, 1993.

3. "Mr Hun Sen, Foreign Minister of Kampuchea, Arrives in Colombo," Sarapordarmean Kampuchea (SPK), June 7, 1979.

4. "Indian Draft Threatens ASEAN Move," *New Nation,* November 13, 1979.

5. "Dong's India Mission Fails," *New Nation,* April 10, 1980.

6. "Indira's 'Yes' on Ties with Samrin," *New Nation*, July 8, 1980.

7. "Residents of Phnom Penh Eating Roots," Agence France-Presse, March 25, 1979.

8. "Khmer's Daily," United Press International, January 27, 1979.

9. "Heng Outlines Priorities," *New Nation,* February 17, 1979.

10. "Sihanouk Expects to Lead Exile Government," Agence France-Presse, July 15, 1979.

11. "Heng Samrin Regime's 2-Stage Plan," Agence France-Presse, August 27, 1981.

12. "Sihanouk Hopeful," *Business Times,* Singapore, September 4, 1981.

13. "'Piece of Theatre,' says Phnom Penh," Reuters, September 3, 1981.

14. "Hun Sen Elected Prime Minister," *Straits Times*, January 15, 1985.

15. During the long interview in Phnom Penh in December 1997, Hun

Sen spoke about his rapid ascent to the position of prime minister after the death of Chan Si.

16. "Revolutionary Party in Power," *Straits Times*, May 1, 1979. For more on the KPRP, see "The Kampuchean People's Revolutionary Party," Joint Publications Research Service, Southeast Asia Region, April 10, 1987.

17. "Cambodia Party Boss Pen Sovann Sacked," *Sunday Times*, Singapore, December 6, 1981.

18. "Pen Sovann Out to Settle Old Scores," *Phnom Penh Post*, May 1997.

19. For more on Hun Sen's rumoured rivalry with Chea Sim, see Harish Mehta, "Cambodia's Ruling Party Dismisses Talk of Power Struggle," *Business Times*, May 15, 1992; and Charles P. Wallace, "A Humble Populist Hero Emerges in Cambodia: Chea Sim, the Communist Party's No. 2 Official, is Gaining Wide Popularity," *Los Angeles Times*, September 18, 1990.

20. National Intelligence Daily, July 11, 1991, CIA. Accessed online http://www.foia.cia.gov/browse_docs_full.asp.

21. "Cambodia Dismisses Sihanouk's Overtures," Associated Press, May 29, 1987.

22. "Phnom Penh Offers Top Posts to Sihanouk," United Press International, October 25, 1987.

23. "Sihanouk Opens Paris Talks with Hun Sen," *Straits Times*, December 3, 1987.

24. "Cambodia: Kim Wanted as Mediator," Reuters, Agence France-Presse, United Press International, December 5, 1987.

25. "Sihanouk Cancels Talks," Agence France-Presse, December 11, 1987.

26. "We must Fight as well as Negotiate: Hun Sen," United Press International, December 13, 1987.

27. "Hun Sen Takes Back Foreign Minister's Post," United Press International, Agence France-Presse, December 30, 1987.

28. "Sihanouk Picks France for Further Talks," Reuters, January 3, 1988.

29. "Rajiv and Hun Sen Discuss Cambodia," *Straits Times*, January 15, 1988.

30. Paul Wedel, "Rise of a Rural Revolutionary," *Straits Times* (reported by United Press International) February 7, 1988; and "Positive End to Paris Talks Despite Discord," Reuters, Agence France-Presse, January 22, 1988.

31. "Heng Samrin Gets Squadron of MiG-21s," United Press International, June 22, 1989.

32. Tan Lian Choo, "Sihanouk Steps Down as Head of His Political Body," *Straits Times*, August 28, 1989.

33. "Western Overtures to Phnom Penh Worry Resistance, U.S." Agence France-Presse, November 22, 1989.

34. "EC Urged to Recognise Phnom Penh Regime," Agence France-Presse, November 24, 1989.

VI: U.S. COLD WAR POLICY

1. Remarks of William J. Casey, Director of Central Intelligence Agency at the Smithsonian Resident Associates Program, National Gallery of American Art, Washington, D.C., July 15, 1982, Central Intelligence Agency online. http://www.foia.cia.gov/search.asp

2. "The Soviet Union and Non-Ruling Communist Parties: A Research Paper," (SOV 82-10110X), August 1982, CIA online.

3. Ibid. The U.S. agency was impartial in its analysis: it believed that it was an "anomaly" that the ousted Democratic Kampuchea government was "internationally recognized," and that the guerrilla organisation possessed 30,000 to 35,000 armed combatants. It argued that with "military assistance from Beijing, the DK is fighting Vietnamese occupation forces and the Vietnamese and Soviet-backed regime now controlling Cambodia."

4. Remarks of William J. Casey, Director of CIA at Westminster College, Fulton, Missouri, on October 29, 1983, CIA online.

5. "Sino-Soviet Exchanges, 1969–84," (EA 84-10069), April 1984, CIA online.

6. Ibid.

7. "The 'New Face' of the Khmer Rouge: Implications for Cambodian Resistance: An Intelligence Assessment," May 1987, CIA online.

8. "Cambodia Background," Memo from M.W. Marine to D. Lambertson, June 20, 1986, Freedom of Information Act (FOIA) Released Documents, U.S. State Department, online at http://foia.state.gov/SearchColls/CollsSearch.asp.

9. Ibid.

10. National Intelligence Daily for December 29, 1988, CIA online.

11. Memorandum of Conversation (Memcon), Meeting with Prime Minister Chatichai Choonhavan of Thailand, Ambassador's Residence, Tokyo, February 23, 1989, George Bush Presidential Library, College Station, Texas. http://bushlibrary.tamu.edu

12. Memcon, President Bush's Meeting with President Yang Shangkun of China, February 25, 1989, Great Hall of the People, China, George Bush Presidential Library.

13. "Sino-Soviet Relations: The Summit and Beyond," May 9, 1989, CIA online.

14. "Trends in Soviet Policy in the Third World under Gorbachev," (SOV 89-10021X), March 1989, CIA online.

15. Trends, Foreign Broadcast Information Service, May 24, 1989, CIA online.

16. National Intelligence Daily for Friday, April 28, 1989, CIA online.

17. Memcon, President Bush's Meeting with President Suharto of Indonesia, Cabinet Room, June 9, 1989, George Bush Presidential Library.

18. Memcon, President Bush's Meeting with President Francois Mitterrand of France, St. Martin, December 16, 1989, George Bush Presidential Library.

19. "The Cambodian Issue and Malta," Memo, Richard Solomon to Secretary of State, November 20, 1989, FOIA Released Documents, U.S. State Department, online.

20. Ibid.

21. "Gorbachev's Approach to United Nations: Image Building at U.S. Expense?" September 1989, CIA online. Moreover, the CIA believed that "another major goal of Gorbachev's promotion of UN peacekeeping is to counter U.S. global presence and dominance," and that "Gorbachev has pursued this goal by putting forward initiatives that would replace U.S. presence with that of the United Nations."

22. National Intelligence Daily, Tuesday, December 5, 1989, CIA online.

23. "Cambodia Concept Paper: Policy Options," Memo, Richard Solomon to Secretary of State, November 29, 1989, FOIA Released Documents, U.S. State Department, online.

24. "Cambodia: Signs of Movement," Memo, Richard Solomon to Secretary of State, December 18, 1989, FOIA Released Documents, U.S. State Department, online.

25. "Cambodia: Our Current Perm Five Initiative," From M. Zinoman, February 22, 1990, FOIA Released Documents, U.S. State Department, online.

26. "Cambodia: Prospects (deleted) The Problems As We See Them – Economic Reforms," December 29, 1989, CIA online.

27. Memcon, Meeting with Goh Chok Tong and U.S. officials Brent Scowcroft, et al, Scowcroft's Office, Washington, D.C., April 16, 1990, George Bush Presidential Library.

28. Briefing Memorandum, Desaix Anderson to Secretary of State, May 8, 1990, FOIA Released Documents, U.S. State Department, online.

29. "Congressman Solarz on Cambodia," Memo by Charles Twining, June 14, 1990, FOIA Released Documents, U.S. State Department, online.

30. Letter from James Baker to Eduard Shevardnadze, undated, FOIA Released Documents, U.S. State Department, online.

31. Memcom, Meeting between President Bush and Prime Minister Choonhavan, Oval Office, June 14, 1990, George Bush Presidential Library.

VII: AT CROSSROADS IN THE POST-COLD WAR

1. Authors' interview with Indian Minister for External Affairs Inder Kumar Gujral, Singapore 1993.

2. "Cambodia: Prospects (Deleted) The Problems as We See Them – Economic Reforms," December 29, 1989, page 1–6, CIA online.

3. "USSR–East Asia: Moscow Realigning its Policy," Directorate of Intelligence, May 1990, CIA online.

4. Authors' interview with Soviet Union embassy counsellor V. Loukianov, Phnom Penh, May 1990.

5. Harish Mehta, "State of Soviet Economy Causing Problems for Cambodia," *Business Times,* October 25, 1991.

6. Ibid.

7. See a series of reports by Julie Mehta: "Angkor At Last," *Straits Times,* October 10, 1992; "The Great Cambodian Hope," *New Paper*, Singapore, May 20, 1993; "Thrilling Fields," *Straits Times*, December 19, 1992; and "Cambodia Goes through Slow, Uncertain Growth," *Straits Times*, March 16, 1994.

8. Harish Mehta, "Straddling Two Worlds," *Business Times,* October 23–24, 1993.

9. Harish Mehta, "Country Acts to Stop Theft of Ancient Treasures, *Business Times*, September 30, 1991.

10. The country, Pen Yet said, had more than 1,000 ancient monuments, and it was these places the smugglers were raiding. Shaking his head, he said that Cambodians stole antiques and sold them to foreigners, who earned vast profits on the world markets. Smugglers were not the only threat. The civil war had taken its toll as well, with militant factions stealing antiques to buy weapons. The Khmer Rouge had been blamed for decamping with gold and silver antiques from the Silver Pagoda, located within the Royal Palace in Phnom Penh. Some Cambodians dismissed the allegation that the Khmer Rouge had pilfered the antiques. The guerrillas, they argued, were disciplined

and completely incorruptible. There were exceptions: Khmer Rouge leader Ta Mok was found in possession of rare sculptures taken from Angkor Wat. When the Cambodian army attacked Ta Mok's residence in 1993, it found a treasure trove he had left behind in a hurry to escape.

11. Harish Mehta, "The Political Maturing of Hun Sen," *Business Times*, January 8, 1992. Based on an interview with Hun Sen on January 1, 1992.

12. Harish Mehta, "Peace Dividend: How Much of a Gamble is Cambodia," *Singapore Business* magazine, April 1992.

13. Harish Mehta, "Golden Girl of Cambodian Banking," *Business Times*, June 11–12, 1994.

14. Harish Mehta, "UNTAC has Tough Job Keeping Tabs on Cambodian Currency," *Business Times*, February 12, 1993. The authors interviewed World Bank/UNTAC official Michael Ward in Phnom Penh in February 1993 on the state of the economy. Also, see "U.S. may Establish Contacts with Phnom Penh to Ensure Fair Polls," *Sunday Times,* Singapore, July 22, 1990.

15. Harish Mehta, "UN Troops in Cambodia Send Prices Soaring," *Business Times,* August 12, 1992.

16. Harish Mehta, "Cambodiana Investment's Expansion," *Business Times,* September 5, 1991.

17. Law on Foreign Investment in Cambodia (State Council No 58 KR), decreed on July 26, 1989.

18. Harish Mehta, "Cambodia Settles Dispute over Oilfields with Thailand," *Business Times*, July 9, 1992.

19. Harish Mehta, "Sawmiller Okada Plans Four Factories in Cambodia," *Business Times,* September 25, 1991.

20. Harish Mehta, "No Hang Ups in Phnom Penh, Mate," *Business Times,* March 22, 1994.

21. See "Cambodia: Agenda for Rehabilitation and Reconstruction," World Bank, East Asia and Pacific Region, June 1992.

22. See *Report by a Group of Cambodian Jurists, People's Revolutionary Tribunal held in Phnom Penh for the Trial of the Genocide Crimes of the Pol Pot–Ieng Sary Clique* (Phnom Penh: Foreign Languages Publishing House, 1990).

23. Harish Mehta, "Phnom Penh Must Forge New Accord with Provinces," *Business Times,* March 10, 1994.

24. Harish Mehta, "Return of the Native," *Singapore Business* magazine, April 1992.

25. The section "A Long Interview" is based on an interview with Hun Sen conducted by Harish Mehta on January 1, 1992 at the Council of

Ministers Building in Phnom Penh. For more on Hun Sen's views on his country, and its international relations, see two reports by Harish Mehta in the *Business Times:* "The Political Maturing of Hun Sen," January 8, 1992; and "Cambodia Needs US$1.2 Billion Urgently for Reconstruction," January 3, 1992. For more on Cambodia's economy, see "The Short-Term Impact of UNTAC on Cambodia's Economy," (Report by the Economic Advisor's Office, UNTAC, Phnom Penh, December 21, 1992). For information on the spate of violent attacks during the 1993 elections, see the UNTAC document, "Incidents of Political Violence, Harassment, and Intimidation," covering the election campaign period from March 1, 1993 to May 14, 1993. For further details about Sihanouk's films, see www.norodomsihanouk.org.

26. Harish Mehta, "Cambodia Welcomes Lifting of U.S. Embargo," *Business Times,* January 6, 1992.

27. Harish Mehta, "State of Soviet Economy Causing Problems for Cambodia," *Business Times,* February 1992.

VIII: THE PEASANT AND THE PRINCES

1. This section is based on a series of interviews that the authors conducted with Prince Chakrapong in November 1992, State of Cambodia spokesman Khieu Kanharith in May 1993, deputy UNTAC force commander French Brigadier-General Robert Rideau in May 1993, Prince Norodom Sirivudh in January 1993, Hun Sen in December 1997, and Sam Rainsy on the telephone in Bangkok in June 1993. Also see a series of reports by Julie Mehta in the *Straits Times*: "I Survived Pol Pot," March 1, 1994; and "Age Old Khmer Dance Revived," March 1, 1994; and "Apsaras in Angkor," *The Nation,* January 17, 1999.

2. Harish Mehta, "My, What a Facelift for This Lady," *Business Times,* January 4, 1992.

3. "Sihanouk Warns U.S. Against Interfering or Trying to Oust Him," *Straits Times,* November 20, 1991.

4. Harish Mehta, "Princes in Politics," *Business Times,* September 3, 1992.

5. Correspondence between Prince Norodom Sihanouk and Harish Mehta. Sihanouk, in his letter dated August 16, 1992, answered several questions posed by the author in his letter dated August 14, 1992.

6. This section is based on an interview with Hun Sen conducted by Harish and Julie Mehta on January 5, 1993 at the Chamkarmon Palace. It also contains a series of interviews Harish Mehta conducted with Hun Sen on July 2, 1993 on the lawns of the Royal Palace; on December 17, 1993 in

Singapore; on October 20, 1994 in the National Assembly; in December 1997 and June 1998 at his Takhmau home.

7. Harish Mehta, "Evict Khmer Rouge from Peace Process: Hun Sen," *Business Times,* January 6, 1993.

8. Harish Mehta, "UN Troops in Cambodia Send Prices Soaring," *Business Times,* August 12, 1992; and Harish Mehta, "UNTAC Has Not Curbed Inflation Nor Stabilised Currency: Cambodia," *Business Times,* January 5, 1993.

9. Harish Mehta, "World Bank's US$75 Million Loan to Cambodia Falls Through," *Business Times,* February 5, 1993.

10. "Cambodian President Should Have Same Powers as U.S. President: Sihanouk," Agence France-Presse, February 8, 1993.

11. Authors' interview with Ranariddh, May 23, 1993.

12. Harish Mehta, "Jockeying for Power in Cambodia," *Business Times,* June 3, 1993.

13. Harish Mehta, "The Rise of another Norodom in Cambodia," *Business Times,* January 28, 1993.

14. Harish Mehta, "Sihanouk Government Collapses in Face of Resistance from Funcinpec Hardliners," *Business Times,* June 5, 1993.

15. Ibid.

16. Harish Mehta, "Ranariddh Agrees to Back Sihanouk's National Govt," *Business Times,* June 8, 1993.

17. Ibid.

18. Harish Mehta, "Sihanouk Refuses to Form Interim Govt," *Business Times,* June 10, 1993.

19. Harish Mehta, "Hun Sen Appointed Five-Star General in Surprise Move," *Business Times,* June 22, 1993.

20. Harish Mehta, "Sihanouk Changes Country's Name, Flag," *Business Times,* July 30, 1993.

21. "Sihanouk Resumes Cambodian Kingship, Ratifies Constitution," Associated Press, September 25, 1993.

22. Mark Dodd, "Hun Sen to King—Clarify Political Intentions," Reuters, June 22, 1994.

23. Ibid.

24. Harish Mehta, "The King is Being Ignored," *Business Times,* October 26, 1994.

25. Ibid.

26. Harish Mehta, "Hun Sen Refuses to Hand Over Power, Six Provinces Break Away," *Business Times*, June 11, 1993; and Harish Mehta, "Kompong Cham Decides Against Seceding after Hun Sen Visits Brother," *Business Times,* June 15, 1993. Also, see "To Whom it May Concern," and "The Cambodian 'Coup d'Etat': Fact or Fiction?," a press release posted on the Internet by Chakrapong on August 27, 1994; and "Memorandum of Opinion," posted on the Internet by Chakrapong on August 28, 1994.

27. Harish Mehta, "Cambodian Secession Fails, Chakrapong Flees to Vietnam," *Business Times,* June 16, 1993; and Harish Mehta, "The Week When Cambodia Almost Broke Up," *Business Times*, June 16, 1993.

28. Harish Mehta, "Chakrapong's Bid to Secede—The Inside Story," *Business Times,* July 10–11, 1993.

29. Trouble shadowed Chakrapong all the way to Malaysia. He and his family reached the Malaysian capital of Kuala Lumpur, where they stayed with a personal friend. The Malaysian government allowed Chakrapong to enter the country based on a request made a year earlier by Sihanouk to let him stay in Malaysia after his attempt to form a breakaway zone. On July 6, Chakrapong urged the Malaysian government for permission to live in the country and, at the same time, denied involvement in the abortive coup the previous week. Chakrapong made his appeal in a letter to Malaysian deputy prime minister Anwar Ibrahim. But Anwar said that Malaysia could not let Chakrapong stay until it had conferred with the Cambodian government. Less than a week later, the Cambodian government expressed its unhappiness over Chakrapong's continued presence in Malaysia. Not unexpectedly, the Malaysian government, which wanted to maintain good relations with Ranariddh and Hun Sen, told Chakrapong to leave the country He was asked to migrate to a third country, and was given enough time to do so. While France and a couple of other countries were asked to accept him, the Malaysian authorities hoped that Chakrapong would leave before a visit to Malaysia in August by Ranariddh and Hun Sen. Chakrapong was a shattered man, who spoke bitterly about being first "forced out of Phnom Penh" and then Malaysia. He sought refuge in Thailand, but complained that he was "once again compelled to leave Thailand where my wife and child are Thai nationals." Under pressure from Phnom Penh, even the Thais would not allow him to stay. "Since leaving Phnom Penh I have resolved to settle down to a quiet life with my family, but the Cambodian authorities had, instead, sought to banish me from everywhere I went, as a fugitive," he said sorrowfully. "I could not even enjoy a simple life of a husband to my wife, and a father to my

children." By the end of July 1994, France opened its doors to Chakrapong, releasing Malaysia and Thailand from a diplomatic predicament.

IX: THE COALITION

1. This chapter is based on interviews with Hun Sen conducted by the authors on January 5, 1993 at the Chamkarmon Palace; on July 2, 1993 on the lawns of the Royal Palace; on December 17, 1993 in Singapore; on October 20, 1994 in the National Assembly; and in December 1997 and June 1998 at his Takhmau home.

2. For further readings on UNTAC, see the forty-nine-page UN document, "Agreements on a Comprehensive Political Settlement of the Cambodian Conflict," Paris, October 23, 1991.

3. Harish Mehta, "Road to Democracy Full of Potholes—and Landmines," *Business Times,* February 16, 1993.

4. Harish Mehta, "Funcinpec Captures Lion's Share of Seats in Hun Sen's Stronghold, Leads by 6% Overall," *Business Times,* June 8, 1993.

5. Harish Mehta, "CPP Demands Re-poll in 4 Areas or It Will Not Accept Results," *Business Times,* June 8, 1993; and Harish Mehta, "Hun Sen's Military Officers, Troops Reject Poll Result," *Business Times,* June 9, 1993.

6. For the full text of Hun Sen's objections to the general election, refer to his statement delivered to the SNC at its June 10, 1993 meeting in Phnom Penh.

7. Harish Mehta, "Two-PM System Must Go," *Business Times*, June 4, 1996.

8. The narrative in this section is culled from an interview Harish Mehta conducted with Hun Sen in Phnom Penh in December 1997, and an earlier interview with Prince Ranariddh in May 1996.

9. "CPP Congress: Hun Sen Rapped on Style While Party Expands," *Phnom Penh Post,* February 7, 1997.

10. "Support Plunges for Ranariddh in Party Division," *The Nation,* February 2, 1998.

11. "Prince's Khmer Rouge Deal Laced with Treachery," *Phnom Penh Post*, May 22-June 4, 1998. The Khmer Rouge papers were obtained by *Phnom Penh Post* reporters on May 15, 1998 in Choam, some fourteen kilometres from Anlong Veng, at a house next to Pol Pot's, and near the burnt-out remains of his funeral pyre.

12. "Heavy Fighting Rages Amidst Civil War Fears," *Straits Times*, July 7, 1997; "Evidence Against Ousted PM Found," Agence France-Presse, July 20,

1997; and "Ranariddh Fears Another Civil War," *Bangkok Post*, July 20, 1997.

13. Hun Sen explained the background to the fighting, and the overthrow of Ranariddh, in an interview with the authors in December 1997. The events surrounding the military overthrow of Ranariddh are based on official documents issued by the Cambodian government, and on statements made by Ranariddh and opposition leaders who described his removal as a coup, and an illegal act. See "White Paper: Background on the July 1997 Crisis" (twenty-seven pages); and, "Crisis in July: Report on the Armed Insurrection—Its Origins, History, and Aftermath" (eighty-four pages). Both papers were issued by the Cambodian Ministry of Foreign Affairs. Also, see a statement issued by Hun Sen on July 13, 1997 explaining the causes of the fighting, and the need to maintain stability.

14. Harish C. Mehta, "Cambodia," *Regional Outlook Southeast Asia, 1998–99* (Singapore: Institute of Southeast Asian Studies, National University of Singapore, 1998), 18–21.

15. "Cambodia will Elect New First Premier Today," *The Nation,* August 6, 1997.

16. "Ranariddh Opts Out of Civil War," *Bangkok Post,* July 19, 1997; and "Ranariddh Gives Up Armed Fight," *Thailand Times,* July 19, 1997.

17. "U.S. Condemns Hun Sen for Cambodian Violence," *Straits Times,* July 10, 1997.

18. "Ranariddh Meets Top ASEAN Team," *Straits Times,* July 19, 1997.

19. "ASEAN puts off Cambodia's Entry," *Straits Times,* July 11, 1997.

20. "Sihanouk Appoints Co-Premiers to UN," *Bangkok Post,* September 6, 1997; and Nate Thayer, "The Resurrected," *Far Eastern Economic Review,* April 16, 1998.

21. "U.S. Refuses to Recognise New Cambodian First PM," *Straits Times,* July 18, 1997.

X: THE HUNS

1. Harish Mehta travelled to Kompong Cham on May 25, 1993 by a UN helicopter, and he conducted a rare interview with Hun Neng at his residence in Kompong Cham. The same day, he also interviewed three other officials in the province: Deputy Governor of Kompong Cham Lay Sokha, Indian Army Colonel A.N. Bahuguna at his battalion headquarters, and Funcinpec political campaign manager Ung Huot.

2. Harish Mehta, "Hun Brothers Fighting the Ranariddh Wave," *Business Times,* May 31, 1993.

3. Harish Mehta, "Kompong Cham to be Developed if Hun Sen's Party Wins," *Business Times,* May 26, 1993.

4. Harish Mehta, "Funcinpec Snatches Slim Lead over CPP," *Business Times,* June 1, 1993.

5. This section is based on an in-depth interview with Bun Rany conducted by Julie Mehta in Phnom Penh in December 1997. Further information about the family was provided to the authors in an interview with Nim Chandara, a brother-in-law of Hun Sen, in Bangkok, May 1998.

6. "Cambodia's Hun Sen to Witness Son's West Point Graduation," Reuters, May 23, 1999.

7. Information about Hun Sen's siblings was provided to the authors by Nim Chandara in an interview in Bangkok in May 1998.

8. Background information on the four Khmer Rouge defectors who escaped to Vietnam with Hun Sen in 1977 was provided to the authors by Nim Chandara. Further information about the defectors was given to the authors by Hun Sen via fax in January 1999.

9. Information about Ung Phan was provided to the authors by Nim Chandara in an interview in Bangkok in May 1998.

10. "Cambodia's Ruling Party Expels Traitor Minister," *Straits Times,* August 1, 1990.

11. "Former Minister Ung Phan Placed under Hun Sen's Protection," *Straits Times,* January 31, 1992.

12. "Cambodian DPM to Visit Singapore," *Straits Times,* August 6, 1993.

13. "New Spat may be Last Straw for Cambodia Government," *Straits Times,* April 17, 1997.

XI: TAKING CHARGE

1. This chapter is based on interviews the authors conducted with Hun Sen in December 1997 and June 1998 at his Takhmau home. Also, see Hun Sen's six-page statement delivered at the ASEAN ministers' meeting in Hanoi on December 15, 1998.

2. "Cambodian Strongman Hun Sen Enters Cyberspace," Agence France-Presse, December 2, 1997; and "'Conciliator' Hun Sen Launches His Campaign," *Bangkok Post,* April 30, 1998.

3. "Hun Sen Officially Declared Winner," Agence France-Presse, September 2, 1998.

4. "Sihanouk Ready to Try and End Turmoil," Agence France-Presse, August 3, 1998; and "Ranariddh Eyes Vote Row Compromise," *Business Day,*

August 3, 1998; Barry Wain, "Ranariddh Must Play the Statesman," *Asian Wall Street Journal,* September 4, 1998; "Opposition Vows Not to Give Way," *Bangkok Post,* September 10, 1998; and "Cambodia Foes Agree to Talk," *The Nation,* Bangkok, September 23, 1998.

5. "Cambodia Vote Protest Continues as Calls Grow for Reconciliation," Agence France-Presse, September 4, 1998.

6. "Hun Sen Set to Alter Law for Solo Rule," Agence France-Presse, August 28, 1998.

7. Barry Wain, "ASEAN, UN, Will Admit Cambodia, Hun Sen Says," *Asian Wall Street Journal,* September 1, 1998.

8. "Hun Sen Asks Thailand to Lend a Hand," *Bangkok Post,* September 7, 1998.

9. "ASEAN Rejects Cambodia Yet Again," *The Nation,* Bangkok, August 25, 1998.

10. "Hun Sen Escapes Unhurt in Rocket Attack on His Car," Agence France-Presse, September 25, 1998; and "Hun Sen Blames Political Rivals for Angkor Wat Rocket Attack," Associated Press, September 25, 1998.

11. "Hun Sen Presses for Global Endorsement," *Bangkok Post*, October 27, 1998; "Coalition Deal Ends Three-Month Stalemate," *Bangkok Post,* November 14, 1998; Dominic Faulder, "The King Comes to the Rescue," *Asiaweek,* November 27, 1998; and "King Praises 'New Unity,' Reconciliation," *Bangkok Post,* November 15, 1998.

12. "Rivals' Share of Power Uneven," Agence France-Presse, November 23, 1998; and "Hun Sen Wins Stamp of Approval," *Bangkok Post,* December 1, 1998.

13. "Annan Hails New Cambodian Coalition," Reuters, December 2, 1998.

14. Lee Kim Chew, "Yes to Cambodia, But Timing Not Fixed," *Straits Times,* December 16, 1998.

15. "Sihanouk Asks ASEAN to Admit Cambodia," Kyodo, December 4, 1998; "Committee Credits UN Seat to Hun Sen," Agence France-Presse, December 6, 1998; and "Cambodia's Quick ASEAN Entry Hopes Dashed," *The Nation, Bangkok*, December 15, 1998.

16. "Cambodia Becomes Part of ASEAN," *Bangkok Post,* May 1, 1999.

XII: PLANNING THE ROYAL SUCCESSION

1. This chapter is based on an interview the authors conducted with Hun Sen at his office at 41 Boulevard Suramarit on May 11, 2001.

2. "Cambodia: Sihanouk Denies Naming Son as Successor," Dow Jones Newswires, March 13, 1996.

XIII: EMBRACING DEMOCRACY

1. "Cambodia's Election Effort Seen as Damaged by Deaths and Intimidation," Agence France-Presse, January 28, 2002.

2. "Ruling Party Dominates As Opposition Does Well in Cambodian Polls," Agence France-Presse, February 4, 2002.

3. "U.S. Criticises Cambodia Violence," Associated Press, February 7, 2002.

4. Chhay Sophal, "Cambodia Coalition may Threaten Monarchy: Prince," Reuters, February 8, 2002.

XIV: THE WIDENING CLAN

1. This chapter is based on an interview the authors conducted with Hun Sen and Bun Rany at Pochentong Airport, and later at Hun Sen's office at 41 Boulevard Suramarit on May 11, 2001.

2. Eric Unmacht, "Hun Sen at a Juncture on Rough Road to Democracy," *Bangkok Post*, March 13, 2002.

3. Reach Sambath, "Court Finds 18 Cambodians, U.S. Citizen, Guilty of Rebel Attacks," Agence France-Presse, February 28, 2002.

4. Bun Rany gave the authors a rare four-hour interview on May 15, 2001. Having known the authors for several years, she opened up her entire life to them, and was happy to discuss her husband's security, her own work as the President of the Cambodian Red Cross, and the lives of their children.

XV: THE GROOMING OF THE MANET GENERATION

1. The authors conducted a long interview with Hun Manet at the authors' residence in Bangkok in April 2003. They were given full access to Manet. They conducted a series of interviews with him, the first of which was a four-hour session in Bangkok; thereafter, they communicated with him via telephone and email between New York, where Manet lived, and Bangkok.

2. "Commencement; West Point Graduates include Ruler's Son," *New York Times*, May 30, 1999.

XVI: AN EVENTUAL VALIDATION

1. "Hun Sen Pledges to Fight Corruption After Successful Tokyo Trip," Agence France-Presse, February 28, 1999.

2. "Clean Up, Hun Sen Tells Party as Local Polls Near," Agence France-Presse, June 27, 1999; and M.H. Tee, "Hun Sen Might Have to Redesignate Some Key Lieutenants to Placate International Community," *The Vision,* Cambodia, October 21, 1998.

3. "Cambodian PM Declares Assets to Anti-Corruption Unit," Xinhua, April 1, 2011.

4. "U.S. Praises Cambodian Election as the Most Free," Associated Press, August 1, 2008.

5. Sam Rith, "Hun Sen's Son Gets Post," *Phnom Penh Post,* September 28, 2010; Vong Sokheng, "Premier's Son Earns Military Promotion," *Phnom Penh Post,* January 4, 2011; and Wassana Nanuam, "From the Barracks—Strongman Father Dreams of Glory for 'Heroic' Son," *Bangkok Post,* February 10, 2011.

6. Cheang Sokha, "PM Appoints Own Daughter to Assist Him in New Govt," *Phnom Penh Post,* September 10, 2008.

7. "Cambodian Prime Minister's Daughter Launches New Airline Venture," Associated Press, February 24, 2004.

8. "New Cambodian Airline Suspends Operations in Face of Rising Costs," Agence France-Presse, August 17, 2004.

9. May Titthara, "Hun Sen's Son to Manage Land Dispute," *Phnom Penh Post,* June 28, 2012.

10. "Cambodian PM Defends Son's Military Promotion," Agence France-Presse, January 20, 2011.

11. Vong Sokheng, "Premier's Son Earns Military Promotion," *Phnom Penh Post,* January 4, 2011.

12. Cheang Sokha, "PM appoints Own Daughter to Assist Him in New Govt," *Phnom Penh Post,* September 10, 2008.

13. Sebastian Strangio, "A Political Dynasty in the Making? Meet Lon Rith," *Phnom Penh Post,* May 2, 2008.

14. Thomas Fuller, "Cambodia, Mourning, Casts an Eye to the Future," *New York Times,* October 17, 2012.

15. "Selected Impromptu Comments During the Handing-out of Land Titles for People in the Province of Kompong Chhnang's Rolea Pa District," October 27, 2012, Cambodia New Vision, www.cnv.org.kh.

16. "Hun Sen Weeps, Dodges Questions as Asian Summits End in Cambodia," Kyodo News, November 20, 2012, and "Pride, Exhaustion Drive Cambodian Leader to Tears," Associated Press, November 20, 2012.

17. Kuch Naren and Zsombor Peter, "Obama Presses Hun Sen on Human Rights," *The Cambodia Daily,* November 20, 2012.

18. Grant Peck, "Obama Meets with Asia's Longtime 'Strongman,'" Associated Press, November 19, 2012.

19. "IRI Releases Survey of Cambodian Public Opinion," May 10, 2012, International Republican Institute, www.iri.org.

20. "Prime Minister's Kin to Run in Cambodian Elections," Associated Press, February 20, 2013.

21. Meas Sokchea, "It's Going to be a Family Affair at the Upcoming Election," *Phnom Penh Post*, February 21, 2013.

22. "Hun Sen Defends Son's Nomination," Radio Free Asia, March 3, 2013.

BIBLIOGRAPHY

ARCHIVAL AND DOCUMENTARY RESOURCES

National Security Archive, Washington, D.C.
George H.W. Bush Presidential Library, College Station, Texas
U.S. Department of State, Freedom of Information Act Released Documents
Central Intelligence Agency (declassified documents)
National Library, Cambodia
World Bank (selected reports)
UNESCO (selected reports)
UNTAC (selected reports)
Ministry of Foreign Affairs, Cambodia (selected reports)

MEDIA CITED

Agence France-Presse, *Asian Wall Street Journal, Asiaweek,* Associated Press, *Bangkok Post, Business Times* (Singapore), *Cambodia Daily, Far Eastern Economic Review,* Kyodo News, *Los Angeles Times, Nation* (Bangkok), New China News Agency, *New Nation, New Straits Times, New York Times, Phnom Penh Post,* Phnom Penh Radio, Reuters, Sarapordamean Kampuchea, *Straits Times, Sunday Times* (Singapore), *Thailand Times, The Walrus,* United Press International, Vietnam News Agency.

BOOKS AND PUBLISHED TEXTS CITED

Ang, Choulean. *Sahakum Khmae Neu Srok Barang Neng Preah Buddhasasana.* "The Cambodian Community in France and Buddhism." Paris: Culture khmere, April–September, 1981.

Becker, Elizabeth. *When the War was Over: The Voices of Cambodia's Revolution and Its People.* New York: Simon and Schuster, 1986.

Briggs, Lawrence Palmer. *The Ancient Khmer Empire.* Bangkok: White Lotus, 1999.

Chanda, Nayan. *Brother Enemy: The War After the War.* San Diego, CA: Harcourt Brace Jovanovich, 1986.

Chandler, David P. *The Tragedy of Cambodian History*. New Haven, CT: Yale University Press, 1991.

———. *A History of Cambodia*. Bangkok: Silkworm, 1993.

Chanthou, Boua. "Women in Kampuchea." Bangkok: UNICEF, 1981.

Chou Ta-Kuan. *The Customs of Cambodia*. Bangkok: The Siam Society, 1992.

Coedès, George. *The Indianized States of Southeast Asia*. Honolulu, HI: University of Hawaii Press, 1968.

Ebihara, May B., Carol A. Mortland, and Judy Ledgerwood. *Cambodian Culture Since 1975*. Ithaca, NY: Cornell University Press, 1994.

Etcheson, Craig. *After the Killing Fields: Lessons from the Cambodian Genocide*. Lubbock, TX: Texas Tech University Press, 2005.

Freeman, Michael, and Roger Warner. *Angkor*. Boston, MA: Houghton Mifflin, 1990.

Gottesman, Evan. *Cambodia After the Khmer Rouge: Inside the Politics of Nation Building*. New Haven, CT: Yale University Press, 2003.

Kiernan, Ben. *How Pol Pot Came to Power: Colonialism, Nationalism, and Communism in Cambodia, 1930–1975*. New Haven, CT: Yale University Press, 2004.

——— (ed.). *Genocide and Democracy in Cambodia*. New Haven, CT: Yale University Southeast Asia Studies, 1993.

Ledgerwood, Judy. "Analysis of the Situation of Women in Cambodia." Phnom Penh: UNICEF, 1991.

Locard, Henri. *Pol Pot's Little Red Book: The Sayings of Angkar*. Bangkok: Silkworm, 2004.

Mabbett, Ian, and David Chandler. *The Khmers*. Oxford: Blackwell, 1996.

MacDonald, Malcolm. *Angkor and the Khmers*. Singapore: Oxford University Press, 1987.

Majumdar, R.C. *Hindu Colonies in the Far East*. Calcutta: Firma KLM, 1991.

Martin, Marie Alexandrine. *Cambodia: A Shattered Society*. Berkeley, CA: University of California Press, 1994.

Mehta, Harish C. "Cambodia: A Year of Consolidation." *Southeast Asian Affairs 1996*. Singapore: Institute of Southeast Asian Studies, National University of Singapore, 1996.

———. *Cambodia Silenced: The Press Under Six Regimes*. Bangkok and Cheney: White Lotus, 1997.

———. "Cambodia." *Regional Outlook Southeast Asia, 1998–99*. Singapore: Institute of Southeast Asian Studies, National University of Singapore, 1998.

Mehta, Julie B. *Dance of Life: The Mythology, History, and Politics of Cambodian Culture*. Singapore: Graham Brash, 2001.

Morris, Stephen J. *Why Vietnam Invaded Cambodia: Political Culture and the Causes of War*. Stanford, CA: Stanford University Press, 1999.

Osborne, Milton E. *The French Presence in Cochinchina and Cambodia*. Bangkok: White Lotus, 1997.

"Report by a Group of Cambodian Jurists, People's Revolutionary Tribunal Held in Phnom Penh for the Trial of the Genocide Crimes of the Pol Pot–Ieng Sary Clique." Phnom Penh: Foreign Languages Publishing House, 1990.

SarDesai, D.R. *Southeast Asia: Past and Present*. Boulder, CO: Westview, 2010.

Shawcross, William. *Sideshow: Kissinger, Nixon, and the Destruction of Cambodia*. London: The Hogarth Press, 1994.

Short, Philip. *Pol Pot: Anatomy of a Nightmare*. New York: Henry Holt, 2004.

Sihanouk, Norodom, with Bernard Krisher. *Sihanouk Reminisces: World Leaders I Have Known*. Bangkok: Editions Duang Kamol, 1990.

Thayer, Carlyle A. *The Vietnam People's Army Under Doi Moi*. Singapore: Institute of Southeast Asian Studies, National University of Singapore, 1994.

LIST OF INTERVIEWS

The authors conducted twenty hours of face-to-face interviews with Hun Sen over a period of nine years (1992–2001). These are broken down as follows. Six hours of interviews were conducted by Harish Mehta between 1992 and 1994, when Hun Sen spoke about the enervating civil war, the genocide, and the phlegmatic process of economic reconstruction:

1. On January 1, 1992 at the Council of Ministers Building, Phnom Penh (with Julie Mehta).
2. On January 5, 1993 at the Chamkarmon Palace, Phnom Penh (with Julie Mehta).
3. On July 2, 1993 on the lawns of the Royal Palace, Phnom Penh.
4. On December 17, 1993 at the Westin Stamford Hotel, Singapore (with Julie Mehta).
5. On October 20, 1994 at the National Assembly, Phnom Penh.

Further interviews with Hun Sen were conducted by Harish and Julie Mehta as follows:

6. On December 3, 1997 at Nokor Kok Thlok Hotel, Siem Reap.
7. On December 5, 1997 at Hun Sen's residence in Takhmau, Kandal.
8. On December 6, 1997 on a helicopter trip with Hun Sen to Prey Veng.
9. In June 1998, at Hun Sen's residence in Takhmau, Kandal.
10. Hun Sen provided written answers to several questions—the last of these responses coming over the fax machine in January 1999.
11. On May 11, 2001, the authors interviewed Hun Sen (and Bun Rany) at the VIP lounge at Pochentong Airport, Phnom Penh.
12. On May 11, 2001 at Hun Sen's office at 41 Boulevard Suramarit, Phnom Penh.
13. On May 12, 2001 at the Royal Phnom Penh Golf Club (conducted by Harish Mehta).

Interviews

Interviews conducted with Bun Rany, Hun Manet, and Hun Neng:

1. Julie Mehta interviewed Bun Rany for four hours on December 7, 1997 in Phnom Penh.
2. Julie Mehta interviewed Bun Rany for four hours on May 15, 2001 in Phnom Penh.
3. Harish Mehta conducted an interview with Hun Sen's brother, Hun Neng, during the general election, on May 25, 1993 in Kompong Cham.
4. The authors conducted a four-hour interview with Hun Manet in April 2003 in Bangkok.

Interviews with members of the extended Hun family, and political and non-political actors:

1. The authors interviewed Hun Sen's brother-in-law, Nim Chandara, in May 1998 in Bangkok.
2. Harish Mehta conducted a series of interviews with Hun Sen's school teachers, school friends, and pagoda boys who lived with him at the Neakavoan Pagoda in Phnom Penh.
3. Harish Mehta interviewed the following members of the royal family: (1) Prince Norodom Sihanouk answered questions in writing on August 16, 1992, (2) Prince Norodom Chakrapong in August (with Julie Mehta) and November 1992, (3) Prince Norodom Sirivudh in January 1993, and October 1994, (4) Prince Norodom Ranariddh in April 1993 and May 1996, and (5) Prince Norodom Buddhapong in August 1992.
4. Harish Mehta interviewed the following officials (in Phnom Penh, unless otherwise stated): (1) Cambodian Minister of Culture and Information Pen Yet in May 1990, (2) Cambodian General Director of Tourism Sam Promonea in May 1990, (3) Soviet embassy counsellor V. Loukianov in May 1990, (4) Australian telecommunications executive Stig Engstrom in May 1990, (5) businessman Leang Eng Chhin in January 1992, (6) CPP spokesman Khieu Kanharith in May 1993, (7) UNTAC Deputy Force Commander French Brigadier-General Robert Rideau in May 1993, (8) Sam Rainsy by phone in June 1993, (9) Kompong Cham Deputy Governor Lay Sokha on May 25, 1993 in Kompong Cham, (10) Indian Army Colonel A.N. Bahuguna

on May 25, 1993 in Kompong Cham, (11) former Indian Minister for External Affairs Inder Kumar Gujral in 1993 in Singapore, (12) architect Mam Sophana in October 1993, (13) Deputy Governor of the National Bank of Cambodia Tioulong Saumura in May 1993 (with Julie Mehta), (14) Khmer Rouge spokesman Mak Ben at a press conference in May 1993, (15) UNTAC financial official Michael Ward in January 1993, (16) UNTAC force commander Australian Lt.-Gen. John Sanderson in May 1993, (17) *Cambodia Times* editor Kamaralzaman Tambu in May 1993.

INDEX

Akashi, Yasushi 39, 221, 223, 228, 239
Ali Alatas 167
Ang Duong 52, 64, 300–301
Angkar 75–76, 78, 82, 84–85, 87, 89, 90, 92, 94, 97–98, 100, 107–9, 273, 338
Angkor Empire 48, 50–52, 190
Angkor Thom 22, 51
Angkor Wat 12–13, 48, 51–52, 290, 185, 197
ANKI (National Army for an Independent Kampuchea) 40, 42, 212
Anlong Veng 245, 283, 284
Annan, Kofi 327
ANS (National Army of Sihanouk) 40
anti-colonialism 29, 53–55, 146
Anti-Corruption Unit 351
ASEAN see Association of Southeast Asian Nations
Asian Development Bank 222
Association of Southeast Asian Nations (ASEAN): Cambodia's membership of 25, 31, 40, 259–60, 288, 290, 293–95, 321, 326–27, 348; divisions within, 166–67, 172–73; relations with PRK/SOC, 43, 137, 141, 145, 153, 160, 179, 260, 350; Soviet Union and, 169; Summit (2012) 355–57; support for Khmer Rouge, 128–30, 298; United Nations and, 174
Auriol, Vincent 55
Austin, Reginald 247
Australia 129, 160, 193, 205, 260, 285

Bahuguna, A.N. 263–65
Bak Touk High School 69
Baker, James 172, 177–78
Bangkok 21, 120, 167, 187, 230, 256, 258, 292, 294, 306, 322, 335, 338
Banteay Meanchey 44, 225–26, 320
Bardez, Felix Louis 53
Battambang 44, 53, 131, 277, 320
Bavet 195

Bayon 22, 52
Beijing 27, 34, 58, 123, 154, 168, 187–88, 222–23, 232, 305, 328, 355
Blue Khmers 74, 93
Bogor 160
Bora (Madame) 21
Bou Thang 97, 119, 148–49
Boulevard Suramarit residence 11, 21–22, 127, 142, 272, 279, 288, 291, 299, 320, 326, 333–34
Britain 43, 160–61
Buddhism 40, 49, 71, 170, 295
Buddhist Liberal Democratic Party 40, 231
Bun Rany (Bun Sam Hieng): early life of, 64–65, 71, 75; escape from the Khmer Rouge, 108; family of, 65, 71, 75, 77, 108, 126; first-born's death, 88–89; home life of, 127, 268–70, 324–25; humanitarian work of, 328–33; Hun Sen and, 28–29, 45, 78–87, 89–90, 124–27, 142, 274, 290, 319, 330–31; life after liberation of Phnom Penh, 125–27; Manet and, 90, 107, 270–71, 316–17, 335–37, 338, 340, 353; as maquis member, 75–80, 87–90; as Red Cross president, 328–30; in Siem Reap, 13; treatment by Khmer Rouge after Hun Sen's defection, 107–9, 125–26, 316, 338; in Vung Tau, 254–56
Bun Sam Bo 13, 21
Bush, George H.W. 23, 167, 170–72, 179, 204

Calmette Hospital 272
Cambodia: anthem of, 231; bombing by U.S. Air Force, 27, 57, 60, 91, 93, 297; early history of, 48–51; flag of, 231; factions in the 1960s, 74; France and, 26, 47, 53–54, 55–56, 63; isolation of, 24, 180–82, 186, 193, 204; language policies of, 187–88; life expectancy of, 196–97;

Cambodia (*cont'd*): population of, 183, 199; *see also* Democratic Kampuchea, Khmer Republic, People's Republic of Kampuchea, State of Cambodia

Cambodian Freedom Fighters (CFF) 31, 320

Cambodian People's Party (CPP): at 1993 elections, 215, 224–28, 248, 266–67; at 1998 elections, 48, 282–90; at 2008 elections, 353; Chakrapong and, 212–13, 236–37, 240–46; in coalition with Funcinpec, 30, 202, 226, 229–30, 249–61, 267, 279, 286–88, 292–93, 312; congresses of, 251–52, 351; dominance of, 20, 31, 351; divisions within, 150–52, 218, 251–52; genesis of, 41; Hun Sen's synonymity with, 18–20; Internet presence of, 284–85; new generation of, 354, 358; political violence attributed to, 218, 247–48, 285, 310–11; power network of, 250–51, 277, 303, 348; Sam Rainsy and, 39, 284, 314; Sihanouk's relationship with, 19, 223, 230; Pen Sovann and, 147–48; youth wing of, 277

Cambodian riel 65–67, 144, 190–91, 221, 289

Canada 55, 160–66

Cap Saint Jacques (Vung Tau) 254–56

Casey, William 163–64

Central Intelligence Agency (CIA) 23, 135, 137–38, 152, 163–70, 172–73, 181

CGDK *see* Coalition Government of Democratic Kampuchea

Cham kingdoms 48–49

Cham Prasidh 157, 159, 202

Chamkarmon Palace 216–17

Chan Si 119, 146–48, 188

Chao Sambath 256–58

Chatichai Choonhavan 154, 166–67, 174, 179, 294

Chavalit Yongchaiyudh 154

Chea Sim: 35; CIA's view of, 152; as Hun Sen's mentor/friend, 145, 148, 152; Khmer Rouge and, 265; leadership of CPP, 41, 150, 216, 220, 225, 228, 246, 248, 347; in liberation war against Khmer Rouge, 96, 117–19, 124; generalship conferred on, 231; as interior minister, 128; as National Assembly chairman, 148–50; power struggle with Hun Sen rumoured, 150–52; as Senate head, 292

Chea Sophara 326

Chea Soth 118–19, 148–49, 151

Chem Snguon 149

Chen Sot 96

Chenla 49–50

Chhim You Teck 69–70, 272

China: ASEAN and, 326; Cambodian elections and, 177, 284; Cold War and, 163–64; relations with PRK, 145, 179; Soviet Union and, 164, 168–69, 175; support for Khmer Rouge, 155, 160–61, 164, 168, 179, 298, 307, 349; support for Vietcong, 57

Chinese migration into Southeast Asia 50

Chirac, Jacques 288

Choa Phirun 253

Choeung Ek 194

Chuan Leekpai 290

Chup 126

CIA *see* Central Intelligence Agency

civil administration/bureaucracy of Cambodia 59, 172–73, 184–85, 199, 226, 261, 277, 292–93

civil war in Cambodia 24, 27, 30, 71, 93, 120, 155, 164, 168, 175, 181, 198, 200, 207, 273

Clinton, Bill 57, 259

Coalition Government of Democratic Kampuchea (CGDK; the government-in-exile) 29, 37, 40, 128, 130, 145, 159

Cochin China 52

Cold War: effects on Cambodia, 24, 58, 143, 349–50; perceptions of Hun Sen during, 18, 23–24, 172, 177; U.S. policy towards Cambodia, 163–79

Colombo 140

commune elections of 2002 *see under* elections

communism in Cambodia 55, 182–85, 189, 192

Communist Party of France 55, 155

Communist Party of Kampuchea (CPK); 36, 40, 73, 75, 95–98, 111, 296 *see also* Khmer Rouge

Comrade Duch (Khang Khek Ieu) 32, 352

Constitution 170, 226, 229, 231–33, 284, 300, 303

Constitutional Council 38, 288

corruption 59, 64, 184–85, 201, 207–8, 350–51

Council of Ministers 255

Council of Ministers Building 202, 212, 324

Council of the Throne 18, 299, 302, 304
CPK *see* Communist Party of Kampuchea;
    Khmer Rouge
CPP *see* Cambodian People's Party
Cuba 141, 143, 164, 182–83, 185, 206

de Gaulle, Charles 55, 305
Dee Yon (Hun Sen's mother) 63, 65–66, 69,
    272, 315–16
Democratic Kampuchea (DK) 27, 41, 107,
    111–13, 118, 122, 124, 144–45, 298, 310; *see
    also* Khmer Rouge
Deng Xiaoping 168–69, 186, 174
Department of State (U.S.) 163, 166–67, 172,
    177–78, 296
Desai, Morarji 141–42
Dey Loeu 318
Dien Bien Phu 121
Dith Munty 157, 159, 358
Dy Chindavy 334–35
Dy Vichea 358

Ea Samnang 68
Eang, Darryl 21
Eastern Zone 90, 96, 117–18
economic development of Cambodia 59, 149,
    192, 200, 206, 208, 255, 295, 341, 343, 345,
    350, 353
education in Cambodia 137, 196–97
Ek Sereywath 211
elections: commune election (2002), 20, 31,
    308, 310–14; general election (1993),
    20, 24, 30, 37, 41–43, 47, 150, 161, 169,
    173–76, 181, 189, 201–2, 205, 213, 216–17,
    223–25, 238, 247–49, 262–67, 283–84,
    287; general election (1998), 20, 25,
    37, 48, 249, 261, 282–90, 293; general
    election (2003), 48, 314, 351; general
    election (2008), 32, 48, 353, 359; general
    election (2013), 22, 358
electoral fraud, allegations of 248, 286–89,
    312
embargo against Cambodia 24, 143, 153, 180,
    192–94, 204–5, 350
embassies in Phnom Penh 182–83, 187, 260
English language 187–88, 197, 203, 301, 326,
    335, 342
Engstrom, Stig 201
European Community 161

European Parliament 138, 161
European Union 284, 285, 312

Fère-en-Tardenois 154, 156–57
First Cambodia Airlines 353
First Indochina War 209
foreign investment in Cambodia 24, 180,
    192–94, 200–201, 205, 282, 286, 295, 348,
    350
France: colonial rule of Cambodia, 29, 40,
    42, 52–53, 55, 146, 160, 195; education
    of Cambodia's elite in, 347; Hun Sen
    and, 147, 160, 205–6, 260; monarchy
    questioned, 18; Sihanouk and, 26, 54–57;
    Vietnam and, 52, 55
Free Khmer movement 74
French Communist Party 55, 155
French language 187–88, 203, 334–35
French literature 20
French Resistance 72
Funan 48–50
Funcinpec: 41; at 1993 elections, 215, 219,
    223–24, 227, 239, 247–48, 264, 266; at
    1998 elections, 283–90; at 2002 commune
    elections, 20, 311; at 2003 elections, 351;
    Chakrapong's defection from, 211–12,
    236–37; in coalition with CPP, 24,
    30, 37, 226, 229–30, 249–61, 267, 279,
    286–88, 292–93, 312; formation of, 41;
    fragmentation of, 252, 283, 292, 313; as
    member of coalition government-in-
    exile, 29; military strongholds, 256–58;
    Pen Sovann and, 148; relationship with
    Khmer Rouge, 211; Sam Rainsy and, 39,
    252, 313; Sirivudh and, 38
FUNK (National United Front of
    Kampuchea, the maquis, *q.v.*) 41, 72
FUNSK see Kampuchean United Front for
    National Salvation

Gandhi, Indira 141–42
Gandhi, Mohandas 56, 241
Gandhi, Rajiv 133, 158, 319
Gandhi, Sonia 319
genocide *see under* Khmer Rouge
Ghazalie Shafie 153
Goh Chok Tong 175, 315, 321, 327
golf 14, 151, 268, 319–20, 324, 326–28, 330, 333
Gorbachev, Mikhail 168–69, 172–74, 181, 183

government-in-exile 29, 145; *see also* Coalition Government of Democratic Kampuchea

Gujral, Inder Kumar 181

Gulf of Thailand 193

Gulf of Tonkin 50

Ha Tien 116

Hanoi 36, 118, 132, 147–48, 175, 195, 290, 293, 295

Harradine, Lindsay 193

Heng Samkai 118

Heng Samrin: 35; government of, 128, 130–31, 143–44, 184, 188, 193, 196, 267; as Khmer Rouge member, 246, 265; leadership of CPP, 41, 150, 216, 220, 314, 347; leadership of KPRP, 137, 147–48, 152; liberation of Cambodia from Khmer Rouge, 24, 28, 96–97, 112–13, 117–20; as mentor and friend to Hun Sen, 145, 148–49, 152

Hinduism 49–50, 158

Ho Chi Minh 29, 56

Ho Chi Minh City 44, 105, 111, 115, 118, 124, 161, 195, 241

Ho Chi Minh Trail 56

Hok Lundy 291, 334

Hor Nam Hong 149, 157, 295, 327, 354

Horn, Michel 192

Hotel Cambodiana 182, 187, 192, 196

Hou Youn 127

Hui Keung 192

human rights 129, 260, 278, 281–82, 310, 356–57

Hun Maly 326, 332, 335

Hun Mana 315, 326, 332–34, 353, 358

Hun Manet: advice for siblings, 335, 345; birth of, 90, 316–17, 338; Bun Rany and, 90, 107, 270–71, 316–17, 335–38, 340, 353; compassionate nature of, 335–37, 340; early life of, 126, 270, 338–39; education of, 21, 271, 335–36, 340–41, 345–46; groomed as father's successor, 353–55; Hun Sen's security and, 319, 353; in interview, 21, 335, 338–46; in the military, 22, 271, 336, 341, 353–55; politics and, 336; World Bank stint, 21, 336, 341, 343

Hun Mani 22, 332, 358

Hun Manith 270, 332, 334–35, 353

Hun Neang 62–63, 272, 274, 316, 321, 334

Hun Neng 17, 36, 62, 123, 238, 262–67, 285

Hun San 62, 271, 274

Hun Sen: admiration for Sihanouk, 58, 64, 71, 73, 93; appointment of associates to political posts, 152; assassination attempts on, 97, 244, 280, 288, 290–91, 318–20; beliefs of, 25, 61, 315–19; birth of, 26, 61, 140, 318; Bun Rany and, 45, 78–87, 89–90, 113, 124–26; children of, 28, 88–89, 270–71; common touch of, 16, 20, 286, 347; coups against, 242–46, 275; defection to Vietnam, 24, 45, 58, 97–99, 100–115, 117, 124, 140, 265, 271, 273, 276, 338; as deputy prime minister, 29, 145, 224; detention in Song Be, 105–7, 109, 276, 323; dietary habits/tastes of, 20, 110, 156, 268, 325–26; disappointment with Sihanouk, 66, 68; doctorates of, 22, 162, 273; early life of, 13, 17, 60–71, 99; education in Phnom Penh, 58, 61, 63, 65, 70; family of, 61–66, 68, 94, 273–74; as foreign minister, 24, 26, 29–30, 124, 127, 132, 139–40, 142, 144–47, 149, 152, 158, 185, 324, 339, 348; "godfathers" of, 148, 152, 154; grooming of children for leadership, 353–54, 358; as guerrilla commander, 82, 90–93, 95–97, 273, 276, 295, 310; as guerrilla fighter, 62, 70, 72–73, 79, 93, 247, 268–69, *see also* maquis; hatred of the Khmer Rouge, 74, 93; health of, 115, 249, 285; international standing of, 135, 168, 170–72, 179, 348; interrogation by Vietnamese, 102–5, 109–10, 276; in interview, 13–15, 17, 21–22, 60, 202, 208, 216–17, 283; Khmer Rouge cadres and, 92; as Khmer Rouge member, 13, 23, 27–28, 58, 73, 91, 246, 295–98, 310; as kingmaker, 18, 302–4, 306, 308–9; language skills of, 15, 203, 301, 328; literary interests of, 64; loss of eye, 27, 82, 94, 130, 203, 324; mistrust of Vietnam, 98–99; misunderstood as Vietnamese "lackey," 128, 130–38, 155, 209, 273; name changes, 61–62, 73; as pagoda boy, 67–70, 247, 276, 315; peace negotiations with Khmer Rouge, 157; peace talks with Sihanouk *see* peace

talks; as Pink Khmer, 74; as playwright, 322–23; political asylum in Vietnam, 109–11, 114; political awakening of, 64; power struggle with Chea Sim rumoured, 150–52; as prime minister, 24, 30, 32–33, 36, 38, 47–48, 60, 69, 146, 149–50, 152, 172, 180, 227, 229, 255, 260, 265, 267, 289, 293, 308, 348, 353; on Ranariddh, 159–60, 261, 301–2, 307, 312–13, 327; recruitment of armed forces, 110, 113–14, 121, 123, 265; romantic desires of, 77–78; rumoured dead, 125–26; school-building fervour of, 18, 68, 249, 279, 286; secret rebellion against Khmer Rouge, 90, 94; sleep habits of, 323–24; smoking habit of, 13, 20–21, 110, 202–3, 268, 326; as songwriter, 19, 22, 321–23; sporting interests of, 64; "strongman" appellation, 18, 30, 60–61, 255, 287, 302, 304, 321, 328, 350; suffers malaria, 103, 106; turns against Khmer Rouge, 90, 93–94, 139; Ung Phan and, 278–80; wooed by Lon Nol regime, 94; working habits of, 324–25
Hun Sengny 62, 271, 274–75
Hun Sinath 62, 269, 271, 273–75
Hun Thoeun 62, 272, 274
Huy Vesna 322

Ieng Mouly 231
Ieng Sary 32, 92–93, 120, 124, 141, 287, 296, 352
Ieng Thirith 32
India: ally of Cambodia, 24, 133, 141, 143, 145, 158, 180–81; diplomatic relations with, 141–42; independence from British, 56; shared heritage with, 315
Indian Army 181, 262, 265
Indian migration into Southeast Asia 48–50
Indochinese Communist Party 42, 55, 146
Indonesia 153, 167, 170, 178, 293, 306
inflation 190–91, 202, 218, 220–21, 289
infrastructure development in Cambodia 194–95, 206, 249, 351
International Monetary Fund 153
Issarak 35, 62–63
Ith Samheng 354

Jakarta 160, 167, 170, 174–75, 302, 348

Japan 55, 193, 206, 259–60, 284–85, 326
Japanese occupation 42, 54, 61, 129, 146
Jayakumar, Shunmugam 327
Jayavarman II 22, 50–51
Jeldres, Julio 208

Kambuja 50
Kambuja Monthly Illustrated Review 57
Kampot 44, 123
Kampuchea Airlines 195, 237
Kampuchean People's Revolutionary Council 35, 124, 139
Kampuchean People's Revolutionary Party (KPRP): 35, 41–43, 146–47; congresses of, 29, 137, 147, 149; expulsion of Ung Phan from, 278; Pol Pot's leadership of, 55; politburo of, 146, 149, 151–52; membership drive, 149
Kampuchean United Front for National Salvation (*Front uni national de salut du Kampuchea*, or FUNSK; United Front) 28, 41, 43, 118–20, 122, 139, 152
Kampuchean United Front for National Salvation, Solidarity and Liberation 117; *see also* Kampuchean United Front for National Salvation
Kanchanaburi 50
Kandal 14, 44, 113, 193, 285, 291, 331, 333, 349
Kandol Chrum 112
Kanita Norodom Thavet Norleak 211
Ke Kim Yan 256
Keo Nam 318
Keo Puth Reasmey 216
Keo Sokleng 272
Kep 284
Khang Khek Ieu (Comrade Duch) 32, 352
Khek Sisoda 157
Khieu Kanharith 150, 225, 353, 359
Khieu Samphan 32, 36, 92–93, 114, 128, 145, 159, 162, 234, 296–97, 352
Khmer Empire 19, 48, 51–52
Khmer Issarak 62–63
Khmer language 203
Khmer Nation Party 20, 148
Khmer People's National Liberation Front (KPNLF) 29, 37, 40, 42 128, 145, 215, 219
Khmer Republic 27, 57, 354
Khmer Republic Party 354

Khmer Rouge (Communist Party of Kampuchea, *q.v.*): 56, 73–74; at 1993 elections, 161, 177, 215, 219–20; attacks on Vietnam by, 28, 94, 101, 112, 117; breaking up of, 59, 287, 296, 351; brutality of, 77, 89–90, 93–94, 107, 165, 184, 188, 295; business dealings of, 193; China's support for, 155, 160, 168, 179, 307; class ideology of, 77, 86–87, 94; destruction of economy, 144, 185, 188–90, 192, 200; destruction of education system, 137, 196; destruction of infrastructure, 195; destruction of medical system, 197–98; ethnic "cleansing" policy of, 95, 295–96; fighting PRK/SOC government, 134, 152, 154, 166, 178, 181, 198, 227, 234, 278, 350; genocidal regime of, 15, 21, 23–24, 27, 29, 36, 41, 58, 60, 100, 111, 128, 130, 141, 184, 189, 204, 236, 264, 295; guerrilla currency of, 190; international support for, 130, 133, 139, 161; killings carried out by, 94, 108, 126, 274; leadership of the maquis, 27, 73–74; as member of coalition government-in-exile, 29, 37, 40, 128, 145; movement to overthrow Lon Nol, 58, 93; the NCR and, 42, 176, 178, 350; new face of, 165; outlawing of, 234, 245, 252; overthrow of, 15, 17, 28, 43, 60, 120–24, 130, 153, 186, 188, 265, 276; peace negotiations/accords and, 158, 161, 169, 173–74, 204, 214–15, 218–19; purging of commanders, 96–97; secret talks with Ranariddh, 252–54; Sihanouk's support for, 58, 74; starvation of Cambodians under the regime of, 95, 101, 104, 109; strongholds of, 200, 215, 219–20, 233, 241, 263–65, 276, 284; take Phnom Penh, 27, 58, 82, 94; trial of leaders, 31, 32, 204, 297–98, 327, 352; UN seat occupied by, 29, 130, 143–44; uprising against, 24, 118–20; view of Hun Sen, 139; *see also* Angkar (the political bureau of the party's central committee)
Khmer Serei 74
Khmer Trough 193
Kiernan, Ben 95
Killing Fields (Choeung Ek) 194
Kim Chreng 276
Kim Il Sung 155, 307

Kingdom of Kampuchea 54
Koh Kong 44, 131
Koh Thmar village 100
Koh Tmey 349
Koh, Tommy 176
Kompong Cham: 26, 35–36, 44, 113, 118, 121, 149, 202–3, 238, 264, 274, 276; Bun Rany and, 64, 81, 87, 126, 273; Hun Neng and, 36, 238, 262–67, 285; Hun Sen and, 26, 61–62, 65–66, 68, 78–79, 81, 82, 100, 116, 126, 263, 272–73, 285, 317–18
Kompong Chhnang 44, 53
Kompong Speu 44, 250, 256, 258, 326, 358
Kompong Thom 36, 44, 197, 265
Kong Korm 158
KPNLAF (Khmer People's National Liberation Armed Forces) 42
KPNLF (Khmer People's National Liberation Front) 29, 37, 40, 42 128, 145, 215, 219
KPRP *see* Kampuchean People's Revolutionary Party
Kratie 44, 91, 113, 116, 118, 238, 266
Kroch Chhmar 45, 64–65, 71, 75, 84, 95
Krom Ngoy 64
Kuala Lumpur 128
Kun Deth 94, 96

landmines 86, 100, 125, 184, 195, 203, 357
Lang Xinh 103
Laos 29, 50, 141, 167, 182
Lay Sokha 262
Le Duc Anh 34, 115, 122, 130, 133
Le Duc Tho 118, 130, 132
Leang Eng Chhin 200
Leng Sochea 198, 202, 208
liberated zones 92, 94, 118, 120, 296
liberation from the Khmer Rouge 41, 116–38, 153, 163, 250, 265
Loc Ninh 44–45, 96, 100, 103
Lon Nol 27, 41, 47, 57–58, 67, 72–75, 78, 92–94, 111, 210, 233, 273, 305, 354, 357
Lon Rith 354
London 185, 194
Loukianov, V. 151, 182–83, 189, 200
Loy Sim Cheang 313
Luong Preah Sdech Kan 64
Lycée Indra Dhevi 26, 63, 65, 70
Lycée Sangkum Reastr Niyum 69

Lynn Kry 65, 126
Lynn Sitha 334

Mak Ben 185
Malaya 49, 201
Malaysia 201, 205, 219, 249, 279, 293, 306, 335
Malta 172
Mam Manivann 211
Mam Sophana 184
Mao Zedong 56, 186
Maoism 40, 56, 184, 189
maquis (National United Front of Kampu-
    chea) 23, 41, 72–99, 72, 74, 77, 93, 273
Marshall, Russell 161
Meas Kim Heng 198
Meas Kim Suon 197–98
Meas Sovanndy 271
Mekong River 48, 50, 61, 68–69, 87, 94, 114,
    116, 120, 139, 196, 262, 265, 315
Memot 45, 87–88, 94, 97, 100
Meng Kom Phak 334
Mitterrand, Francois 23, 170–72
Mochtar Kusumaatmadja 153
Mon people 50
Mondulkiri 44, 116, 238
Monique Izzi 159, 211, 228, 230, 232–33,
    300–301, 303–5, 307, 330
Moscow 163, 190, 194, 196–97
Muslims 15, 24, 95–96, 296
My Samedi 149
Myanmar 49–50, 260, 293, 294, 357

Nagara Vatta newspaper 53
Napoleon III 52
National Army for an Independent
    Kampuchea (ANKI) 40, 42, 212
National Bank of Cambodia 37, 67, 189–90
National Election Commission 287–88
National Government of Cambodia (NGC)
    42, 224–30
National United Front (1997) 254, 284
National United Front of Kampuchea *see*
    maquis
NCR *see* Non-Communist Resistance
Neak Moneang Phat Kanhol 211
Neakavoan Pagoda 26, 66–70
Neu Kean 70
New Delhi 145, 158, 181
New York 21, 271, 290, 341, 343

New Zealand 160–61
NGC *see* National Government of Cambodia
Nguon Nonn 246
Nguyen Co Thach 132, 153
Nguyen Van Linh 130, 134
Nguyen Van Thai 137
Nhek Huon 100, 271, 276
Nhek Tioulong 189
Nhiek Bun Chhay 253, 256–58
Nicaragua 164, 173, 176–77
Nim Chandara 268, 271, 274–75, 280
Nixon, Richard 91, 164, 210, 297
Non-Aligned Movement 140
Non-Communist Resistance (NCR) 42, 165,
    166–67, 172–76, 178, 350
Norodom I 52–53, 300–301
Norodom Arunrasmey 211
Norodom Buddhapong 212, 229
Norodom Buppha Devi 211, 307
Norodom Chakrapong 38, 190, 211–13, 237,
    226–27, 229, 230, 236–46, 267, 275, 304,
    307
Norodom Naradipo 211
Norodom Narindrapong 211
Norodom Ranariddh: 37–38; at 1993
    elections 24, 224–26, 238–39, 266–67;
    at 1998 elections, 284, 286–89; at
    2002 commune elections, 209; arms
    imports, 253, 257–58, 286; candidate
    for kingship, 300–307; coalition with
    Hun Sen, 24, 30, 37, 226, 229–30,
    249–61, 267, 279, 286–88, 292–93, 312;
    conferred generalship, 231; in exile, 31,
    260; as First Prime Minister, 30, 47,
    199, 249, 255, 258, 279, 287; at golf, 327;
    Hun Sen on, 159–60, 261, 301–2, 307,
    312–13, 327; leadership of Funcinpec, 30,
    37, 41, 160, 214–15, 224, 249, 305, 352;
    military offensive against government
    forces, 255–58; ousting of, 13, 24, 30, 37,
    48, 60, 258–60, 282, 284, 287, 305–6;
    at peace talks, 156–57, 159, 212, 227;
    relationship with Chakrapong, 38,
    211–13, 226–27, 236, 239–40, 242–46;
    relationship with Sihanouk, 31, 41, 160,
    211–12, 214, 224–29, 230, 239–40, 258;
    secret negotiations with Khmer Rouge,
    252–54, 283; Ung Phan and, 279–80
Norodom Ranariddh Party 38

Norodom Sihamoni 19, 32, 211, 300–301, 304, 306, 352, 355

Norodom Sihanouk: abdication of, 19, 26, 32, 34, 47, 56, 308, 351; ailing health of, 18, 222, 232–34, 287, 305; ANKI and, 42, 212; ascension to throne (1941) 34, 41; China and, 160, 168, 306; colour-coding system for political factions devised by, 74; death of, 19, 25, 33–34, 299, 355–56; develops casino, 192; in exile in Beijing, 27, 58, 154, 161; family of, 38, 60, 211, 235, *see also* royal family; as filmmaker, 203; France and, 26, 54–57; as head of NCR, 175; as head of NGC, 42, 224–30, 239; as head of SNC, 189, 210, 212; high life of, 66; homecoming (1991) 161, 188–89, 204, 208–10; Khmer Rouge and, 56, 58, 93, 145, 155–56, 188, 233–36, 298; as leader of coalition government-in-exile, 40, 128, 134, 144–46, 154, 156, 159–61; leadership of Funcinpec, 29, 41, 160, 224; maquis fronted by, 72, 75, 91, 93; Mitterrand on, 172; overthrow of (1970): 17, 23, 27, 34, 41, 47, 57–58, 70, 72–75, 103, 192, 226, 233, 308; peace talks with Hun Sen *see* peace talks; Pol Pot and, 55; presidential ambitions of, 214–16, 218, 222–23, 227, 231, 234; relationship with Hun Sen, 18–19, 161–62, 209–10, 302, 304, 349, 356; relationship with PRK/SOC government, 218, 233–36; relationship with Ranariddh, 31, 41, 160, 211–12, 214, 224–30, 239–40, 258; return to throne, 30, 34, 231–32, 305, 308–9; Sangkum era of, 37, 56–57, 69, 74, 91; in Second World War, 54; sends agents into Neakavoan Pagoda, 70; succession after, 299–309; support for North Vietnamese guerrillas, 26–27, 56–57; United Nations and, 174, 177; United States and, 56–57, 166, 210

Norodom Sirivudh 38, 224, 234–37, 244, 253, 267, 279–82, 287, 304

Norodom Sucheatvateya 211

Norodom Suramarit 26, 56

North Korea 155, 307

North Vietnam 27, 28, 56, 99

Nou Thol 94

Nuch Than 100, 276–77

Nuon Chea 32, 92–93, 296–97, 352

Obama, Barack 33, 355–57

Olympic Stadium, Phnom Penh 69

Om Yintieng 351

Or Lu 96

Orekhov, Nikolay 183

Ortega, Jose Daniel 176

OTC International 193

Pach Chhoeun 53

Pailin 200, 233–34, 245, 276

Pali 49, 158

Paor Ean 100, 276–77

Paris 36–38, 55, 154, 160, 169, 189

Paris peace accord 30, 41, 43, 134, 161–62, 172, 174, 179, 189, 193, 201–2, 204, 207, 209, 212, 214, 218–19, 223, 247, 348

Path Sam 70

Pattani Trough 193

peace talks between Hun Sen and Sihanouk, et al 30, 132, 154–62, 169–70, 179, 181, 205, 249, 348; *see also* Paris peace accord

Peam Chi Laang 81

Peam Koh Sna 26, 61, 63, 87, 272

Pen Sovann 35, 42, 118–19, 124, 128, 145–47, 188

Pen Yet 182, 185

Penn Nouth 91

People's Republic of Kampuchea (PRK; renamed State of Cambodia SOC in 1989, *q.v.*): 43, 124, 180; economic reforms and policies of, 136, 149, 153, 350; economic troubles of, 143–44, 149, 153, 175, 180–83, 189, 205; international recognition of, 137–38, 141–42, 152–53, 160–61, 173, 175, 177, 180, 185, 204–5; military campaign against the Khmer Rouge, 152, 154, 178, 181, 198, 234, 278, 350; military expenditure of, 191; misunderstood as puppet regime, 153; Soviet military support for, 60, 178, 180, 213, 350; support from socialist countries, 24, 143, 182, 187, 196, 348; United Nations and, 74, 181; Vietnam and, 29, 42, 131–36, 155

Pham Van Dong 141, 144

Philippines 129, 293

Phlek Chhat 197

Phlek Phirun 149

Phnom Penh: departure of Vietnamese troops from, 134; depopulation of, 143, 188; diplomatic/cultural missions in, 160, 182, 187; foreigners in, 186, 201; glory days of, 209; Hun Sen and, 26, 58, 65, 99, 124, 126, *see also* Boulevard Suramarit residence; infrastructure, 194–96; Khmer Rouge taking of, 27, 58, 77, 94; liberated, 123, 188; military clashes of July 1997: 255–60, 272, 285, 287, 295; protests of Sept 1997: 288–89; Pol Pot's return to, 55; site of Khmer capital, 49, 52
Pich Chheang 254
Pink Khmers 74, 93
Pochentong Airport 12, 124, 160, 195, 209, 213, 256, 315
Poipet 195, 206
Pol Pot (Saloth Sar): 36; attacks on Vietnam, 117; attempt to kill Hun Sen, 97; China and, 111–12, 307; class ideology of, 86–87; coup against, 34, 36, 283; death of, 30, 36, 283; education of, 36, 55; fall of, 17, 36, 58, 124, 165, 282–83; fear of Muslims, 95; Hanoi and, 111–12; kills defectors on repatriation, 93, 105, 107; leadership of Khmer Rouge, 27, 40, 42, 47, 75, 86, 91–92, 146–47, 296; Maoism and, 56, 184; overthrow of, 114, 116, 118, 120, 122–124; peace talks and, 158; PRK/SOC government and, 130, 132, 134, 141; purges ordered by, 28, 96, 110; Ranariddh and, 283; regime of, 84, 92, 101, 283, *see also* *under* Khmer Rouge; United States and, 129, 297; writings of, 20
Pol Saroeun 243
Ponhea Krek 35, 45, 87
Prak Sokhonn 11–13, 17, 292, 356
Preah Ang Khmau 318
Preah Chinavong 64
Preah Thinnavong 64
Preah Vihear 44
Preah Vihear Temple 33, 354–55
Preak Ket Mealea Hospital 197
Prey Veng 15, 44, 53, 113, 116, 238, 241, 247, 264
PRK *see* People's Republic of Kampuchea
Pursat 44, 266
Pyongyang 154, 156, 222, 231

Rao, Narasimha 142
Ratanakiri 44, 114, 116, 238
Red Khmers 74 *see* Khmer Rouge
Reng Thach 157
Revolutionary Armed Forces 123
Rogachev, Igor 174
Rokarkhnau 64
Royal Cambodian Air Force 213
Royal Cambodian Armed Forces 231, 245, 256–57, 336, 354
royal family 24, 210–11, 213, 307–8, 347
Royal Government of Cambodia 348
Royal Palace 66, 124, 188, 210, 214, 225, 232–33, 305
Rumrith 302

Saang 349
Sai Chhum 149
Saigon 56–57, 114, 163
Saint-Germain-en-Laye 158–60
Saloth Sar *see* Pol Pot
Sam Promonea 186
Sam Rainsy 32, 38, 148, 225–27, 230, 234, 252, 282, 284, 286–92, 297, 299, 311, 313, 352
Sam Rainsy Party 20, 285, 288, 292, 311, 314
Sam Sary 148
Samdech Chunnat 62
Samdech Euv Autonomous Zone (SEAZ) 38, 238–44
Samlaut 121
San Sanh 100, 276–77
Sanderson, John 39, 186
Sangkum Reastr Niyum 37, 56, 69, 74, 91
Sanskrit 49, 158
Sar Kheng 149, 152, 245, 358
Sar Not 117
Sar Sokha 358
Say Chhum 358
Say Phuthang 119, 147–49, 151
Say Sam El 358
Scowcroft, Brent 176
SEAZ *see* Samdech Euv Autonomous Zone
Second World War 54, 72
Senate 31, 35, 292–93, 304
Serey Kosal 253, 258
Shanghai 328
Shevardnadze, Eduard 133, 172, 178
Siazon, Domingo 288

Siem Reap 12–13, 44, 53, 122, 136, 183, 195, 197, 261, 290, 318

Sieng Lapresse 157

Sieng Ly 334

Sihanouk Trail 56

Sihanoukville 44, 57, 193, 195, 253, 266, 282

Sim Var 53

Sin Sen 244

Sin Song 117, 237, 240–46

Sina Than 230

Singapore 52, 128, 145, 167, 175–76, 181, 184, 192, 196, 200–201, 205–6, 249, 271, 279, 293, 315, 327, 335

Sisophon 206

Sisowath 53, 300–301

Sisowath Chivanmonirak 304

Sisowath Kossamak 233, 305

Sisowath Monikessan 211

Sisowath Monivong 54

Sisowath Pongsanmoni 211

Sisowath Sirik Matak 57

SNC *see* Supreme National Council

Snoul 91–92

So Phim 112

SOC *see* State of Cambodia

Sok An 225, 258, 333, 358

Solarz, Stephen 178, 202–3

Solomon, Richard 173–75

Son Ngoc Thanh 53

Son Sann 17, 37, 40, 42, 128, 130, 145, 157, 159, 174, 215, 219, 284, 354

Son Sen 165

Son Soubert 354

Song Be 28, 44–45, 96, 100, 105, 119, 276

South Korea 284, 326

South Vietnam 27–28, 56–57, 74, 91

Soviet Union: arms contributions to PRK/ SOC regime, 135, 160, 178, 180, 213; arms support for Vietcong, 57; China and, 164, 168–69, 175; Cold War and, 163, 169, 172; disintegration of, 24, 191, 206–7, 348; Hun Sen in, 140, 147; similarity to Cambodia, 183; support for PRK/SOC, 143, 163–64, 169, 172, 178, 180–82, 185, 187 190–91, 206–7, 350; United States and, 168–69, 172–73, 175, 178; withdrawal from Afghanistan, 133, 164, 169

SPK (Sarapordamean Kampuchea) 43, 123, 140

Sri Lanka 140

Sry Thamarong 21

State of Cambodia (SOC; formerly known as People's Republic of Kampuchea PRK, *q.v.*) 30, 35, 41–43, 131, 142–43, 159, 170, 182, 211–13, 225–26, 266, 349

Strongman 321–23

Stung Trang 26, 45, 61, 274

Stung Treng 44, 116, 195, 238

Suharto 60, 170

Supreme National Council (SNC) 43, 150, 177–78, 189, 210, 229, 248

Svay Rieng 37, 44, 113–14, 116, 122, 238, 264, 274, 279, 315, 358

Ta Hil 87

Ta Mok 35, 97, 117, 297

Ta Nou 87

Ta Prohm 51

Ta Sanh 121

Ta Tern 254

Taiwan 260

Takeo 44, 148, 193, 274

Takhmau 60, 257, 267, 278

Takhmau residence 14, 16–17, 21, 60, 127, 180, 255, 267–69, 272, 282, 320–21, 333–34

Tambu, Kamaralzaman 201

Tang Krasang military base 256–58

Tay Ninh 44, 96–97, 112–113

Tbong Khmum 45, 81, 87

Tea Banh 119, 149, 333, 353–54

Tep Ngorn 312

Tep Thida 315, 321, 326, 332–34

Thailand: ASEAN and, 167, 293; border conflict with, 33, 354–55; Cambodian civil war and, 74, 165, 198, 236, 278; financial aid from, 181, 206; historical relationship with, 48–50, 52–53; PRK/ SOC and, 164, 166–67; support for Khmer Rouge, 154; trade with, 186, 193

Than Shwe 294

Thayer, Carlyle 133

Thayer, Nate 282

Thommo Soccorach 51

Thu Dau Mot 105

Tioulong Saumura 189–90

Tiv Ol 64

Tokyo 150, 160, 167, 348

Tonle Bassac 196

Tonle Sap 12, 44, 52, 191–92, 196, 206, 265
Tran Van Tra 34, 114
trial of Khmer Rouge leaders 31–32, 204,
    297–98, 327, 352
Tum Teav 64, 316
Tunloung 100
Tuol Krosang 60
Tuol Sleng 352
Twining, Charles 178, 210

Uch Kiman 11, 203, 217, 238
Unalong Pagoda 62
Ung Huot 260, 264, 266, 313
Ung Phan 277–80
United Front *see* Kampuchean United Front
    for National Salvation
United Nations: as interim government,
    172–79; opposition to PRK, 43,
    143–44; seat occupied by Hun Sen
    representatives, 293; seat occupied by
    Khmer Rouge, 29, 130, 143–44, 161, 283;
    seat occupied by SNC, 43; supervision of
    1993 elections by, 181, 189, 215, 248
United Nations Transitional Authority in
    Cambodia *see* UNTAC
United States: bombing of Cambodia, 27,
    57, 70, 91, 93, 297; in Cambodian civil
    war, 27, 129; Cold War attitudes towards
    Hun Sen, 23–24, 163–79; endorsement of
    1998 elections, 286–87; ground invasion
    of Cambodia, 91, 93, 129, 164; loans to
    Cambodia, 357; NCR and, 166; perceived
    imperialism of, 72, 91, 236, 350; relations
    with PRK/SOC, 160–61, 163, 166–67, 172,
    175, 178–79, 203; Sihanouk's opposition
    towards, 56; Soviet Union and, 168–69,
    172–73, 175, 178; trade embargo *see*
    embargo against Cambodia; war against
    North Vietnam and the Vietcong, 56
United Nations Transitional Authority in
    Cambodia (UNTAC) 30, 39, 186, 190–91,
    202, 204, 206, 215, 218–23, 226, 228, 230,
    236, 238, 241, 247–48, 278, 284
University of Bristol 341
UNTAC *see* United Nations Transitional
    Authority in Cambodia

Van Tien Dung 34, 111, 114
Viet Cong 27, 56, 57, 104

Viet Minh 56
Vietnam: attacks against Khmer Rouge,
    112–14, 117, 120, 165; early history of,
    48–49, 50, 52; effects of Cambodian
    intervention on, 133, 136–37; as exporter
    of communist revolution, 164; food
    aid to Cambodia, 127; in liberation war
    against Khmer Rouge, 28, 34, 115–16,
    118, 121–22, 129, 163; military withdrawal
    from Cambodia, 30, 132–36, 142, 154,
    157–58, 160, 166, 168–69, 170, 175, 181, 191,
    207; partition of, 26; peace talks and, 167;
    PRK/SOC and, 128, 130–38, 143, 155, 164,
    182, 207, 349–50; resentment against, 137,
    165, 288; reunification of, 28; severing of
    diplomatic relations with Cambodia, 114,
    117–18; support for Cambodia's entry to
    ASEAN, 293
Vietnam People's Air Force 124
Vietnam Workers' Party 29
Vietnamese Communist Party 134
Vu Xuan Vinh 135
Vung Tau (Cap Saint Jacques) 254–56
Vyadhapura 49

Ward, Michael 190, 222
Wat Phniet 256
Wen Jiabao 355
West Point Military Academy 271, 336,
    341–43, 354
White Hotel 200
White Khmers 74
Wiedemann, Kent 311
World Bank 21, 143, 153, 190, 222, 336
World Trade Organisation 32, 351
World War II *see* Second World War

Yang Shangkun 168
Yim San 254
Yim Sokan 183

Zhou Enlai 307

ABOUT THE AUTHORS

HARISH C. MEHTA is a historian with a PhD from McMaster University. He specialises in the history of U.S. foreign relations, Southeast Asian history, the Vietnam Wars, world history, and human rights in history, and teaches at McMaster University, the University of Toronto, and Trent University. He is the author of *Cambodia Silenced: The Press Under Six Regimes*, and *Warrior Prince*, and he is working on a book on North Vietnam's people's diplomacy. He has published articles in the journals *Peace and Change*, *Diplomatic History*, and *The Historian*.

JULIE B. MEHTA has a PhD from the University of Toronto in English literature and South Asian studies, and teaches at its Canadian studies programme. She is the author of *Dance of Life: The Mythology, History, and Politics of Cambodian Culture*. Her award-winning translation of Rabindranath Tagore's play *Dak Ghar* was performed in Toronto in 2011. She has published widely in academic books and journals on food history, culture and global literatures. She is married to the co-author of this book and they live in Mississauga, Canada.